*I would like to dedicate this book to you, the reader. It takes a special kind of person to find the time and energy to broaden one's horizons and to explore the unknown, especially in the fast-paced and demanding world we live in. I applaud your tenacity and courage. We need more people like you, who are willing to take on challenges and to make the extra effort to expand your horizons and creative potential.*

*When I was growing up, my teachers always rewarded me for my curiosity and creativity. I hope this book rewards yours.*
—Shane Hunt
❧

# CorelDRAW®
# for Linux®
# f/x & Design

**Shane Hunt**

President, CEO
Keith Weiskamp

Publisher
Steve Sayre

Acquisitions Editor
Beth Kohler

Product Marketing
Manager
Patricia Davenport

Project Editor
Sally M. Scott

Technical Reviewer
Nancy Wood

Production Coordinator
Laura Wellander

Cover Designer
Jody Winkler

Layout Designer
April Nielsen

CD-ROM Developer
Chris Nusbaum

## CorelDRAW® for Linux® f/x and Design

### Limits of Liability and Disclaimer of Warranty

The author and publisher of this book have used their best efforts in preparing the book and the programs contained in it. These efforts include the development, research, and testing of the theories and programs to determine their effectiveness. The author and publisher make no warranty of any kind, expressed or implied, with regard to these programs or the documentation contained in this book.

The author and publisher shall not be liable in the event of incidental or consequential damages in connection with, or arising out of, the furnishing, performance, or use of the programs, associated instructions, and/or claims of productivity gains.

### Trademarks

Trademarked names appear throughout this book. Rather than list the names and entities that own the trademarks or insert a trademark symbol with each mention of the trademarked name, the publisher states that it is using the names for editorial purposes only and to the benefit of the trademark owner, with no intention of infringing upon that trademark.

The Coriolis Group, LLC
14455 N. Hayden Road
Suite 220
Scottsdale, Arizona 85260

(480)483-0192
FAX (480)483-0193
www.coriolis.com

Library of Congress Cataloging-in-Publication Data
Hunt, Shane.
   CorelDRAW for Linux / by Shane Hunt.
     p.  cm  (f/x and design)
   ISBN 1-57610-686-1
   1. Computer graphics.  2. CorelDRAW! 3. Linux.  I. Title.  II. Series.
T385 .H853  2000
006.6'869--dc21

      00-047430
      CIP

Printed in the United States of America
10 9 8 7 6 5 4 3 2 1

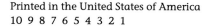

## Other Titles for the Creative Professional

# About the Author

**Shane Hunt** is a writer, artist, and interface design consultant with 18 years of experience in business computing, the last 11 as principal of a multimedia development company in Southern California. He has written several books on computer design techniques, including *CorelDRAW 9 f/x and Design* (The Coriolis Group, 1999), and he coauthored the *CorelDRAW Wow! Book* (1999). In addition, he is a regular contributor to CorelDRAW periodicals, including **www.designer.com**, Corel's Web site. When not basking in the glow of the computer screen, Shane can be found in his art studio working with traditional media, or building strange and dangerous-looking contraptions.

Shane can be reached at **slimydog@aol.com**.

# Acknowledgments

I would like to thank my friends and family for their support. I would also like to thank the brilliant people at The Coriolis Group, who were instrumental in focusing and directing my often meandering energies and keeping me on track. In particular, I would like to thank Beth Kohler, acquisitions editor; Sally M. Scott, project editor; Laura Wellander, production coordinator; and April Nielsen, designer of the color section.

Finally, I would like to thank Corel Corporation, and my friends and contacts there, such as Michael Bellefeuille, Kristin Divinski, and Susan Connerty. Thanks for your help, and thanks also for putting up with my ranting and raving!

—*Shane Hunt*

# Contents at a Glance

# Table of Contents

# Chapter 1

# Overview of CorelDRAW 9 for Linux

*This chapter introduces the user to the universe of*
*CorelDRAW and Photo-Paint.*

# An Introduction

CorelDRAW is the world's most popular design package. It also has the largest percentage of users who have little or no formal art background or computer graphics training. CorelDRAW artists are computer professionals working in a variety of applications for which they need some kind of computer-generated graphics. They also need speed and flexibility. So for simple business graphics, high-end advertising—and everything in between—CorelDRAW has become an integral part of their workday.

CorelDRAW's speed and flexibility, not to mention its use by professional artists, make it stand out from the other computer art programs on the market. We are not here just to make pretty pictures, but to put those images to work for us. You might have some art background or experience using traditional design tools, or no experience at all. I am assuming you are like me—that you want to get as much accomplished as you can with the least amount of effort and in the shortest amount of time. I have been working as a designer for more than a decade and as a computer professional for more than half my life. I love art, I love pretty pictures, I love computers, and I even love my job. But, I am guessing that, like me, you would prefer to finish your work as quickly as possible and get the heck out of the office!

# Getting to Know CorelDRAW 9

This book is about working smart. I have tried to use real-world examples and ideas you can use in your everyday work environment. My tips are from years of real-world experiences dealing with CorelDRAW on a daily basis and crunching out artwork for a living. Even if you are not a commercial artist and creating art is not the focus of your job (and that is many of you), I think you will appreciate the nature of this book. I have tried to make this a CorelDRAW book by and for Corel artisans!

In my experience, the CorelDRAW community, much like the open-source Linux crowd, has been a very close and friendly one. I hope to continue this tradition and will endeavor to make myself available for any questions or comments that might arise along the way. I will also endeavor to update the CorelDRAW Linux f/x & design Web site (**www.slimydog.com/corelfx**) in the coming year with any news or related info. Feel free to log in now and then to check up on things, and email me with any new tips or discoveries. Hey, this is all a big adventure for me too!

## Object-Oriented Package

CorelDRAW is an object-oriented illustration package. This means everything breaks down into individual elements that have their own attributes (such as outline width and fill color). The computer sees these elements as a set of mathematical coordinates and settings. A CorelDRAW image file is essentially a set of computer instructions that the program uses to build your objects and in turn to create your design. Object-oriented illustration with CorelDRAW objects is very efficient, and, more important, versatile.

The object-oriented nature of CorelDRAW brings with it a level of flexibility unique to the medium. You can select an object and change it any time within the life cycle of your design, something you can't do when you are working with a bitmap program (such as GIMP or Photo-Paint) or traditional paint brush or pen and ink. What this means is that when a client says, "I love it, except instead of a fire theme, let's try ice," or even odd requests like "Can we make the happy faces blue instead of black?" you don't have to start over—you only have to change the attributes of the objects already in place. Or, before the client even asks, you can save multiple copies of the same artwork, recolor or tweak each uniquely, and present them with a variety of options. Vector artwork is also infinitely resizable, without any additional file-size overhead. Since the information is basically math, a file set up to create a postcard-sized project can be enlarged to become a giant highway billboard without increasing the size of the file or losing image resolution. You just can't do that with a bitmap! CorelDRAW artwork is flexible, and flexibility is synonymous with *power*.

In today's competitive design climate, the advantages of working with an object-oriented application are many. Throughout this book, you will see many effects and examples used for a specific application, but the nature of the program is such that you can use the artwork in almost any imaginable way. Artwork designed for the Web can become—with virtually no additional effort—high-end color printed material, oversized banners, coffee mugs, almost anything you can imagine. CorelDRAW images are ready to be ported to printing presses, on-screen applications, slides for presentations, even other design programs. Its flexibility is unrivaled by any other application. You won't find any hidden cost, file sizes are not huge or unmanageable, and output is not difficult. CorelDRAW is a commercial artist's best friend—and closest ally.

What this also means is that you never have to be satisfied with a design. You can go back and fine-tune an image and tweak a design until it is exactly what you want. Or you can take an image and refine it for another application. You can customize an ad campaign to hit multiple demographics smack between the eyes. Whatever your needs, the power is yours, limited only by your imagination and your energy.

## Custom Fit

In addition to creating flexible artwork, CorelDRAW itself is very flexible, with customizable tools and commands. This newest Linux version of the software fully embraces Corel's concept of the free-flowing interactive interface to maximize your productivity. Both the interface and toolset offer an unprecedented amount of flexibility to make realizing your visions easier than ever. The full implementation of the Interactive Tool set means nearly every feature from previous versions is now available as an easy-to-use, powerful instrument, rather than a series of menus, dialog boxes, and cursor movements. You do not need to open a separate dialog box or interface to access the special effects available to you—you need only choose the appropriate "interactive" tool and use the on-screen features and context-sensitive options unique to that tool to accomplish what you want.

The increased workflow is facilitated by marrying the features of the Interactive Tool set with the context-sensitive Property Bar. The Property Bar is an ever-present toolbar that constantly changes and allows you to access options and features of the current task at hand. For example, if you use the Interactive Drop Shadow tool to add depth and dimension to an object, you can control the Opacity, Feathering, and even the Color options of the shadow element with the Property Bar (see Figure 1.1). With this interface paradigm, you are not faced with a constant need to open and close specialized dialog boxes, which only clutter up the workspace and hamper your workflow.

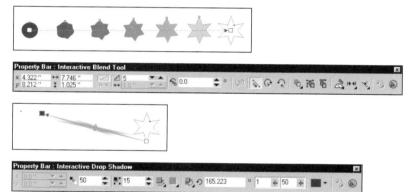

**Figure 1.1**
The Property Bar is a context-sensitive toolbar that offers ways to customize features and options of the currently selected tool, such as the Interactive Blend tool (top) and the Interactive Drop Shadow tool (bottom).

For features that still require the use of a specialized dialog box or options screen, CorelDRAW uses a *docker*. The docker is a dialog box that "docks" to the right-hand column of your screen. This is the common docker workspace; when you open and close dockers as you need them, they will appear in this space. Other features to help you control and organize your design—such as the Object Manager, View Manager, what have you—all "dock" in the dockers area. This means you can choose a handful of your most commonly used features and dock them on the right. Tabs make switching between your favorite dockers a snap (see Figure 1.2).

The theme here is "customizable." If you like the docker concept, run with it and stash your favorite features and functions boxes there on the right-hand side of the screen. If not, open and close the dockers as you need them. (Click the small x in the top-right corner of the docker to close.) Or open a docker,

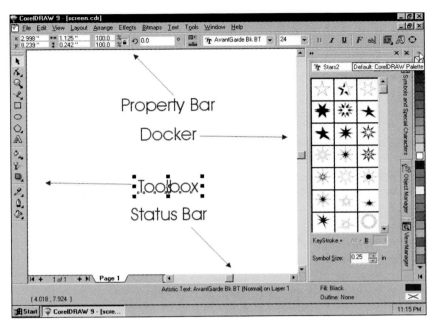

**Figure 1.2**
The CorelDRAW 9 workspace, with various elements labeled. Each element label is a Corel-DRAW text "object," in the drawing page area with "Tool-box" selected, indicated by the appearance of the sizing handles.

"tear" it off the right column (just drag on the docker with the cursor), and position and resize it anywhere you want. This feature holds true for basically every toolbar, docker, status bar, or palette in CorelDRAW, and the interface and features work essentially the same in Photo-Paint. You can tear off, reposition, resize, and even remove any and all of the interface components to customize the interface to your exact needs (see Figure 1.3). With the creative and quirky personalities artists generally possess, what a great feature!

**Figure 1.3**
CorelDRAW allows you to customize your workspace to fit your needs and preferences.

---

**Custom Key Clicks**

It is easy to change a keyboard shortcut in CorelDRAW 9 or Photo-Paint. Simply open the Options dialog box (Ctrl+J), then click Customize. Click the Shortcut Keys option, then find your target in the Commands hierarchy chart. For example, under the Edit folder, locate and click Nudge. Here you can change the Super Nudge series of commands. Click Super Nudge Left, and then click in the Press New Shortcut Key box. Now the system is in "record" mode, and you can press any keys that you want to assign to Super Nudge Left. I pressed Ctrl and the Left Arrow key simultaneously (this was the Super Nudge Left command in CorelDRAW version 7, which I was accustomed to using). Now click the Assign button to make this the new keyboard shortcut. Easy! Reprogram any shortcuts you want, then click OK to close the Options dialog box and activate the new shortcut keys.

---

In addition to being able to customize how the workspace looks, you can reprogram any of the keyboard shortcuts if you want. This is very useful if you are upgrading to CorelDRAW 9 from a previous version and are used to certain keyboard shortcuts or have a particularly fond "finger-dance" you like to do to perform special functions. (See the sidebar "Custom Key Clicks" for more information.)

# Working in CorelDRAW

CorelDRAW allows you to follow your creative impulses. You create curves, objects, and text within your Drawing Page (the boxed area in the middle of the screen). You can work anywhere on the screen, even outside the Drawing Page, just as an artist might have photos and cutout elements scattered on his or her desk. Anything you create in your workspace will save and load to disk just fine, but anything outside the Drawing Page will not appear in your print jobs.

You work in CorelDRAW and Photo-Paint by choosing a tool from the left-hand toolbar and then dragging on the screen. For example, select the Rectangle tool and drag on the screen to make a rectangle or square. No mystery here!

Some of the tools on the toolbar have a small down arrow next to them. Click this arrow to open a "flyout," which is like opening a drawer to reveal more tools. Click the tool you want to use it.

If you have never used CorelDRAW or Photo-Paint before, I suggest you consider working through the on-screen tutorials that ship with the program to get you up to speed quickly. Start CorelDRAW (or Photo-Paint), and then choose Help|CorelTUTOR. This will launch the CorelTUTOR program, with a unique

---

**Super Size, Please**

Bigger is better, at least when it comes to monitors. While you can get plenty of work done at 800x600 (such as the Figure 1.3 screen size), a larger monitor and screen resolution are worth their weight in gold. With technology prices falling, a 17-inch or even 21-inch monitor is not unobtainable, and the extra "breathing room" they afford is priceless. With so many features, functions, status bars, and toolbars on the screen, your actual image area continues to shrink. Use a big monitor and a screen resolution of 1024 x 768 (or higher) to maximize your CorelDRAW design potential, by offering you more work room and the ability to keep more tools and dialog boxes open and at your service.

---

**Gimme Some Help**

---

If you don't know what a tool or option in CorelDRAW 9 or Photo-Paint is, just hover the mouse pointer over it. Typically, a pop-up label will display a description of the tool's purpose. This means that even if you have just a beginning knowledge of the program, you should be able to follow along in these step-by-step tutorials just fine, because each tool or feature is labeled for you as you go.

If you need more assistance with a tool or feature, use the online help. Press the Shift and F1 keys simultaneously to switch the on-screen cursor to the What's This? cursor (an arrow with a question mark). Now click the tool that you want more information about, and a larger help balloon will offer an explanation.

For even more help, turn to the Help Topics feature under the Help menu. Selecting this feature will open the Corel-DRAW Help window, which offers a comprehensive table of contents, an index, and search capabilities to help you locate more information on a sticky topic.

---

set of lessons for both CorelDRAW and Photo-Paint. Follow the instructions in the Introduction, then work through the lessons to acclimate yourself quickly to the tools and features of the programs. But you really only need the "find a tool and drag it on the screen" level of ability to use this book!

## Vector Art vs. Bitmaps

For the most part, CorelDRAW objects are *vector* artwork. They are a series of mathematical coordinates connected with a line, like an electronic dot to dot. This keeps the objects infinitely scaleable and also relatively small in size. A bitmap, on the other hand, is made up of a collection of colored pixels, the size and density of which determine the physical size and resolution of the image. A bitmap might have too much or too little image information, depending on its size and the needs of the current project. You can always generate a bitmap from vector artwork, but the reverse is not always true. That's why CorelDRAW is a superior starting point even for projects that will eventually become bitmaps/painting tasks.

Vector artwork is much more flexible than bitmaps because it is, like I said earlier, basically a collection of coordinates. You can enlarge or reduce a CorelDRAW vector-based image without degrading the resolution or changing the file size because the computer needs to reset only a single mathematical scale attribute for the new size. A bitmap, which is a fixed-resolution entity, does not have this flexibility.

On the left side of Figure 1.4, a happy dancing puppy character off the CorelDRAW clip-art CD-ROM (\clipart\animals\pets) is duplicated and enlarged to create a second one in the foreground. If you try to do the same with a bitmap (on the right side of Figure 1.4), the resolution is fixed and becomes pixelated upon enlargement. On the other end of the spectrum, if you have a large bitmap and then duplicate it and reduce it, your image will look fine but your file size will be large. Even though you made the bitmap smaller on the screen, it still contains all the image information of the original and, therefore, you end up working with redundant information that just increases your file size.

**Figure 1.4**
Unlike a bitmap (on right),
CorelDRAW vector artwork (left)
can be enlarged or reduced
without affecting file size
or resolution.

The focus of CorelDRAW has always been creating and manipulating vector objects. Even from the beginning, though, you could also perform limited actions on imported bitmaps within all versions of the program. Corel has always bundled Photo-Paint, its powerful bitmap manipulation package, along with CorelDRAW for advanced bitmap massaging. The ability to modify bitmaps was introduced in version 7 of CorelDRAW Windows and is even better in version 9. Now you can create and modify bitmaps within the CorelDRAW environment itself. In CorelDRAW 9, the integration is so seamless you might forget the "vector" roots of the application!

In fact, CorelDRAW 9 blurs the line between "bitmaps" and "vector art" more than ever before. Now some of the effects in the program, while they act like "objects," are in fact "bitmaps." The Interactive Drop Shadow tool, for example, actually is an interactive bitmap generator within CorelDRAW. The program takes user input and a set of parameters (color, size, location, opacity, edge-blur, and so forth) to render this bitmap on the fly as you work. It remembers these settings for you, so you can work with the bitmap elements just like any other vector-based CorelDRAW entity (like an Interactive Extrude element, which is vector based, but you can select and modify at any time by changing its parameters). The Pattern and Texture fill options, available from the Fill flyout, also use "pixel-based" bitmap technology. So sometimes you work with vector pieces, sometimes bitmaps, sometimes CorelDRAW-controlled and -rendered bitmaps, and sometimes you will convert your vector elements into bitmaps manually using the Convert To Bitmaps feature.

Why would you want to convert your nice vector artwork into a less-flexible bitmap? Well, sometimes you just can't get the look you are after if your artwork is a crisp CorelDRAW vector object. Because of the hard-edged nature of object-oriented vector artwork, occasionally you will want to convert to a bitmap to create a soft, anti-aliased edge or to use a filter or built-in bitmap effect that simply will not work on vector artwork at all (which is why drop shadows, for example, must use bitmap technology, because you can't get a fuzzy-edge effect using vector objects).

For example, our hero Albert Einstein (\clipart\caricatre\historic) in Figure 1.5 (on left) is in the CorelDRAW native vector format. On the right, a shape placed

**Figure 1.5**
The Fish Eye lens will not
distort some bitmap information,
such as bitmap pattern fills or
texture fills.

in front of this artwork is given a Fish Eye lens from the Lens docker (Alt+F3). Notice how only the vector artwork in the face is distorted and not the checkerboard pattern (this checkerboard is a two-color pattern fill set from the Pattern Fill dialog box, accessed from the Fill flyout). Despite being native CorelDRAW entities, drop shadows, pattern fills, and texture fills are not vector information; they are bitmaps. The Fish Eye lens effect will not distort the bitmap information in a two-color pattern fill correctly.

We could redraw the checkers as individual vector box objects, and then the Fish Eye lens would work fine. However, the easier solution is to use the Convert To Bitmap feature from the Bitmaps menu and then use a filter effect to distort the image. After using the Convert To Bitmap dialog box to "rasterize" your objects (convert them to pixels), you can then choose from one of many filter effects to enhance it. For example, the Bitmaps|3Deffects|Shere command creates the rounded look in Figure 1.6 (left). The same bitmap can have a totally different look, using the Bitmaps|Art Strokes|Pen & Ink command (on right). And of course Photo-Paint (like its Linux pal GIMP) is an entire program dedicated to creating and tweaking bitmaps, so you can take your pixel tweaking even further. It all adds up to increased flexibility, power, and creative potential, right out of the box. Three cheers for the CorelDRAW Linux graphics suite!

**Figure 1.6**
You can use the Convert To
Bitmap dialog box to change
vector art to a pixel-based image
within the CorelDRAW workspace. This allows for more
image manipulation within the
program than ever before using
filter effects.

The bottom line is getting the results you want, regardless of whether the image is vector or bitmap. (I preach the philosophy of *ruthless creativity*, which is getting what you want no matter what it takes or how potentially unconventional the means.) CorelDRAW has always provided a great way to generate bitmaps, only now you can do it more easily and directly within the program. This functionality blurs the line a bit between CorelDRAW and bitmap manipulation programs such as Photo-Paint and GIMP, but, as you will see, the focus of each program is still pretty clear. Since I feel that CorelDRAW is generally more practical than Photo-Paint, the discussion will focus on CorelDRAW's bitmap features first. However, because Photo-Paint is bundled with CorelDRAW (and also the Deluxe version of Corel LINUX OS Version 2), and because Photo-Paint runs circles around CorelDRAW when it comes to bitmaps manipulation, I will not hesitate to turn to that program for help.

This is a book about working smart, so you don't have to force yourself to work entirely in CorelDRAW when Photo-Paint might be the better solution. Or you might find you need an additional utility or GIMP to bridge a gap or to solve a problem (such as working with Linux-specific file formats, creating screen captures, or scanning images with other third-party programs, etc.). Whatever it takes. Stay "ruthless" and "smart," using the tools available to you to get the best possible results in the least amount of time, using vector or bitmap technology.

The main thing to remember with bitmaps is to create images at a high enough resolution and appropriate color depth for their intended purpose. You can't use Web graphics in print or print graphics on your Web site! But what you need to know about bitmaps could be summarized in a single page. (See the sidebar "Essential Bitmap Information.") Don't worry—this is just a little technical information speed bump on our way to the graphics superhighway!

## How to Use this Book

This book was written so that you can either read it straight through or just flip to a section that interests you. Some of the later chapters, however, do assume that you have learned techniques from previous chapters. Where this is the case, you will find a chapter reference so you can just jump back and review

---

### Bitmaps on Parade

All images in the color section in the center of this book are CMYK TIFF bitmaps, printed using traditional CMYK offset printing techniques. The bitmaps used to generate these pages were created using the CorelDRAW Export feature (Ctrl+E). The CorelDRAW source files used for this process are the exact ones that can be found on the CorelDRAW 9 f/x & design companion CD-ROM. Transforming your CorelDRAW artwork into pixel-based bitmaps is often the easiest solution, especially for a cross-country, cross-application, and cross-platform project such as this book. In addition to facilitating the color section, the same bitmaps were simply downsized and converted for use on the CorelDRAW Linux f/x & design Web site.

---

### Essential Bitmap Information

Bitmaps are just collections of tiny colored dots, which come together to create a picture. The problem is that you need the right number of dots, with the correct number of colors in them for the application at hand. You can read volumes on this topic alone, but it really just boils down to these essentials:

Use 72 dots per inch (dpi) RGB color for on-screen applications (such as Web sites, multimedia, and PowerPoint presentations). Use the JPEG or GIF file formats. (GIF will reduce your colors down to 256, but is essential for Web-based animation graphics, as outlined in Chapter 18. Use JPEG with compression set to "high" when you can.)

Use 300 dots per inch (dpi) CMYK color for on-paper applications (such as magazines, full-color brochures, etc.). Use the TIFF or PSD file formats for problem-free image transfer to other applications or other computer users (on Macs or PCs).

Use the Export feature to convert your CorelDRAW images into bitmaps on disk, or use the Bitmaps|Convert To Bitmap dialog box to keep the transformation within your CorelDRAW workspace.

Bitmaps are just too powerful to ignore—and so easy to generate!

---

the material as needed. For the most part, though, you should be able to drop in wherever you want and follow along, step by step.

## The Book

As I wrote this book, I tried to keep in mind how a person like me would use it. I'd buy a "techniques" book like this one because I could always find something of specific interest in the color section that would make me think, "Cool. I want to do that!" I'd buy the book, take it home, flip to that section, and work through the tutorial. Yippee! Instant gratification!

Then I'd typically flip through the book some more, looking at the pictures and the step-by-step instructions until curiosity got the better of me and I found myself checking out another chapter. I'd then peruse the CD-ROM and check out all its goodies. Hey, I know the drill!

So I have tried to tailor this book to both the "jumpers" and the truly dedicated, who will plow through all of the material sequentially, unable to sleep until they have milked the pages dry of every secret and tip. It's up to you how you use this book. It's all here, with no expiration date! Use and enjoy at your own pace.

To entice you to read through the whole book and work through the projects, I was able to sneak in little funny stories and silly life experiences here and there. Trust me, I know how dull computer books can be to read (I've written enough to feel your pain!). Much of the real "juicy" material gets the axe from the censors and the editors, who just can't believe that anyone might scream and spout lengthy strings of expletives while using computers and graphics software (you and I of course know better!). Nonetheless, I have tried to keep the mood and tone informal and fun, because I couldn't stand to write another boring technical manual. I hope you will find this book both entertaining and educational.

## The Companion CD-ROM

One thing that has always bothered me about computer design books in general is that the artwork in print is not always available digitally. I hate that. Sometimes, no matter how good a set of instructions are, nothing beats loading the file and digging around in it firsthand. With an object-oriented program like CorelDRAW, this is especially true.

The reason most books don't include all of the artwork on the CD-ROM is simple. Most books use a collection of artwork from other artists who, although excited to have their images in print, are not at all excited about letting people dig through their precious art files, learn all their secrets, and steal the images for their own use. This is perfectly understandable.

However, I have tossed sanity and convention to the wind and have used only my own original artwork in this book. I have drawn from more than a decade of material to mix and match images to provide a variety of artwork. I've also provided each and every example on the companion CD-ROM. The files are there primarily so you can fully understand the techniques we are discussing, but feel free to pilfer the images and use them as you like. Consider it the "Crazy Uncle Shane" clip-art collection, a double bonus for buying this book!

Each chapter in the book has a matching directory on the companion CD-ROM that contains the finished art and sometimes other support pieces (scans of illustrations, stock photography, third-party utilities, etc.). I will point out in the text the name and location of the files in question so you can load them and see what is going on. Many files coincide with a page in the color section as well, so you can flip there and see what we are going to work on before you load the file or read the chapter (be sure to also check the bonus "digital" color section on the CD, which has the color images of projects that are not in the printed section). For chapters dealing with animation or on-screen artwork (Web pages, multimedia applications, etc.), I have also included the HTML code to view with your Web browser and self-running movies or animations to demonstrate a technique. A few extra files contain art I thought fit a chapter or technique, and I will point them out to you as we go along.

Also on the companion CD-ROM are the bonus fonts, utilities, and images that all computer books have these days. I tried to make it a CD that I would want if I were buying a computer book, so I think you will be really happy with what you find there. In my opinion, the CD-ROM alone is worth the price of this book. So don't miss out. Load it up—I guarantee the CD will offer something that will bring a smile to your face or add something useful to your design day.

## Newbie to Necromancer

CorelDRAW has evolved over the years from an entry-level package to a full-scale professional design suite. Along the way, with the never-ending addition of tools and functions, it has become a bit more intimidating to new users. With so much potential, the perceived learning curve seems pretty steep.

Fear not, CorelDRAW 9 is as accessible to the seasoned pro as it is to the new kid on the block. The tutorials are great, the Template Wizards are awesome, and the documentation is very complete. It should take no time at all to get up to speed and feel comfortable working in the program.

If you are new to the program, I suggest that you go through the tutorial and work through a few projects to get used to everything before you try the examples outlined in this book. Everyone has to crawl a bit before they can walk.

Users of all levels should be able to follow along in the CorelDRAW Linux f/x & Design tutorials. I have used keyboard shortcuts throughout to make it easy simply to punch up the desired command or feature. You can, of course, orient yourself with the pull-down menus and use their commands instead of the shortcuts. (I almost never use keyboard shortcuts. I am definitely a mouser by nature!) In CorelDRAW, you can customize your workspace and modify your work habits to suit your exact needs, and I encourage you to do so. I know I have my own quirky work habits that will haunt me until I go to my grave (I *refuse* to use anything but the traditional zoom flyout, for example). If you think the way I create something can be achieved in some other and perhaps easier way, try it. CorelDRAW is a universe full of wonder and magic, and even I have yet to uncover it all. With practically yearly upgrades and constantly added features, I don't think I will ever end this journey of discovery. So let's get to it.

## Moving On

Okay, enough of the basic introduction, bring on the f/x and design tricks! In the next chapter, we start off slowly working with simple shapes to create colorful comic characters, including the Linux mascot penguin. But don't fret, the pace picks up rapidly and we will move on from simple to complex characters and even create fast and furious scenes and scenarios. Burn the Sunday comics—it's time to break out on our own and get busy with the Corel for Linux graphics suite!

# Chapter 2

# Comic Book Heroes

*This chapter shows you how to start with the basic drawing tools to create comic characters and backgrounds entirely within CorelDRAW. You'll also learn how to use scanned images of hand-drawn illustrations to create bright and dynamic artwork that has a hand-drawn look and feel.*

# Learning to Draw with Comic Characters

Nothing is more American than the Sunday comic strip. These colorful and fun images have made their way out of the comic strips and into virtually every other type of media. From Roy Lichtenstein's fine art renderings of comic-style images to television commercials featuring animated cartoon characters, this style of art continues to grow in popularity.

CorelDRAW offers a flexible digital workspace that will appeal to both computer-based and pen-and-ink artists for creating stunning comic-book-style artwork. In fact, more and more commercially successful comic strip artists are using the computer as their media of choice because of both the design flexibility and, of course, those thousands of nifty fonts for the thought balloons.

For computer artists, CorelDRAW allows for easy creation of characters with the ability to use common shapes augmented by the flexibility of fill options. For traditional pen-and-ink artists, CorelDRAW and Photo-Paint offer tools for coloring scanned illustrations and for creating complex scenes for characters ranging from impressionistic to high tech. The modern virtual studio of CorelDRAW offers more flexibility than the traditional tools, allowing an artist to change and experiment with different scenes, colors, and poses quickly and easily. Art boards are out, my friend. Grab an accelerated, high-res video board with gobs of RAM instead!

This chapter will show you how to get started drawing in CorelDRAW, by creating comic-book-type characters and scenes using simple shapes and basic drawing techniques. We'll start by re-creating the Linux penguin, and then we'll demonstrate how easy it is to create and color simple cartoon characters in CorelDRAW. Next, we'll explore how to use CorelDRAW and Photo-Paint to color hand-drawn and scanned artwork, and we even create computer-generated scenes that look hand-drawn using bitmap effects filters. Finally, we'll look at a more complex example of coloring hand-drawn artwork and creating a dynamic high-tech scene around it. This example will make use of several techniques covered in the book, most notably blends and repeating images. CorelDRAW and Photo-Paint work really well for cartooning and this style of artwork, so this will be a fun chapter!

## PROJECT Our Hero, the Penguin

Anyone familiar with Linux has seen the penguin. Heck, he even comes as an inflatable toy in the CorelDRAW Linux retail box! So why not start off learning how to use the basic CorelDRAW drawing tools by rendering our hero out of a few simple shapes. To create the penguin, follow these steps:

1.  First, open a new CorelDRAW document by choosing File|New from the menu or using the shortcut keys (Ctrl+N). Next, select the Ellipse tool and drag in your image area to draw a circle (hold down the Control key to constrain the ellipse to a perfect circle if you want). Release the mouse to finish. Now, drag again to create another circle.

2.  Use the Pick tool (tap the Spacebar with nothing selected to toggle to the Pick tool from the current tool) to arrange and size your circles so that you have a large one beneath a smaller one. Click on an object to select it (click on nothing or press ESC if you wish to deselect). With the Pick tool, drag the "x" that appears in the center of an object when you click on it to move the object. Drag a corner sizing handle inward or outward to reduce or enlarge your circle.

3.  Once you have your two circles in place, select the top one, then choose Shaping|Weld from the Arrange menu. This will open the Shaping docker on the right-hand side of your screen. (This is where dockers appear and arrange themselves for handy use. If several dockers are open, you can toggle between them by clicking on the tabs.)

4.  Disable all of the Leave Original options. (Make sure no check mark appears in the box; if the box does contain a check mark, click the box to make it go away.) Now click the Weld button in the Shaping docker, and click on the bottom circle. This will "weld" (merge) them into a single shape (see Figure 2.1).

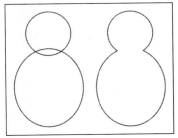 

**Figure 2.1**
Two circles drawn with the Ellipse tool are merged into a single shape using CorelDRAW's Weld feature.

5.  Now use the Shape tool to modify the nodes in your object. Objects in CorelDRAW consist of curves along a path, controlled by "nodes." The Shape tool allows you to modify the nodes, or add and delete nodes. Double-click on the pointy node that was created where the two circles meet (one on each side). When you double-click on a node, it is deleted. When you double-click on a place on the curve that has no node, a node is created. Double-click on the other pointy node to yield the rounded penguin body (see Figure 2.2).

6.  With the perfect penguin torso in place, we need a slightly smaller shape for the tummy. To create additional larger or smaller outlines of your object, use the Interactive Contour tool (located on the Interactive Tool flyout). Select that tool, then click on the edge of the torso object and drag inward. The more you drag inward, the greater the number of steps in your contour shape. Release when your guideline has the size of tummy you want.

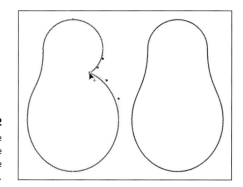

**Figure 2.2**
Deleting nodes with the Shape tool modifies the welded circle shapes into a fat bowling-pin–like penguin torso.

7. Use the Property Bar to manipulate your contour group. In this case, we need only one final shape, so change the value of Contour Steps to 1. Then manipulate the Contour Offset value until the end result is a slightly smaller version of the original torso shape (see Figure 2.3). Use the Arrange|Separate command to "freeze" the contour, allowing us to further manipulate the generated curve (deselect the group and select only the curve to make changes to it).

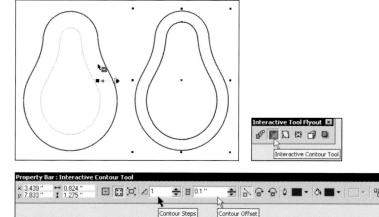

**Figure 2.3**
Use the Interactive Contour tool to create shapes based on an original. Use the Property Bar to modify the number and size of the Contour Steps.

8. The Shaping Docker once again will come to our aid to shave away the top of the inner contour to give us the desired shape. Draw another circle with the Ellipse tool, positioning it over the top center of the inner-torso shape. Now open the Shaping docker again with the Arrange|Shaping| Trim command. With the new top circle selected, click the Trim button in the Shaping docker, then click on the inner torso shape. This should "trim" (cut away) the top area where the circle shape overlapped the torso object (see Figure 2.4).

9. To give the new shape a color, simply left-click over the desired swatch on the on-screen color palette. In this case, click on the white swatch.

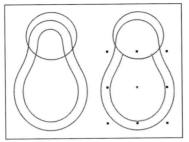

**Figure 2.4**
The Trim option in the Shaping docker cuts away areas where one object overlaps another.

10. Another way to give an object a solid color is to drag off the on-screen color palette and then drop the color over the shape you want to color (see Figure 2.5). This method is great for recoloring objects, especially since you don't have to select them first and you can individually re-color objects in a group without ungrouping them.

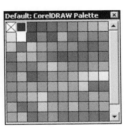

**Figure 2.5**
Drag and drop colors off the on-screen color palette to color objects.

11. Now let's draw the beak. From the Curve tool flyout, choose the Bezier tool. This tool is great for drawing shapes quickly; you simply click from one point to the next. Click to start at the top center of your would-be beak, move down and to your left, and then click-drag. Notice how the tool builds a line from your starting point to the next. Also notice how, as you drag, you're changing the curve of the line. Release the mouse, then click again at the bottom center of the "beak" to create a point (don't drag this time—just click). Now move up and to the right, and again click-drag to create the right curve of the beak. Release when you like what you see. Finally, move to the starting point and click again to create a solid beak object (see Figure 2.6).

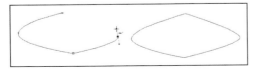

**Figure 2.6**
Use the Bezier tool to create objects with both rounded and pointed corners.

12. Right-click the mouse on the "x" in the on-screen color palette to remove the outline from your "beak." Then, click and hold the pointer over the yellow swatch on the on-screen color palette, which will open another mini-color palette, with colors similar to the current color swatch. Choose an orange color by clicking on it (see Figure 2.7).

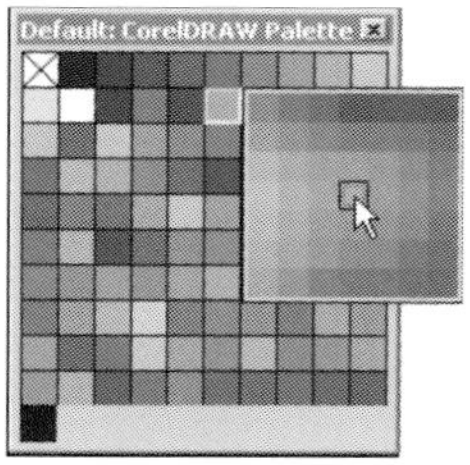

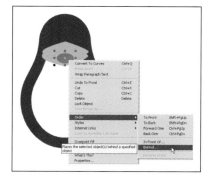

**Figure 2.7**
Holding the Pick tool over a color swatch reveals a pop-up palette of even more colors to choose from.

13. Duplicate the beak object (tap the + key) and move the duplicate up. This will become the top of the beak when you give it a light yellow color. Notice how the duplicate is on top of the original. Objects "stack" in the order of creation, with the newest shapes on top of the older ones. Use the options under the Arrange|Order menu (To Front, To Back, In Front Of, Behind, etc.) to change where in the "stack" your objects are.

14. Use the Ellipse tool to create a red ball for the "tongue." Then, with the ball selected, choose Arrange|Order|Behind from the menu, then click on the top beak object. This will arrange the tongue object behind the top beak shape, so it is in the correct order in the image "stack." You also have access to these Order options from the right-click menu, which makes for an easy shortcut to arrange your objects (see Figure 2.8). Draw more circles for the eyes and again make use of the Order options to place them behind the beak shapes.

**Figure 2.8**
Use the Order options from the right-click shortcut menu to arrange your objects on the screen in relation to one another.

15. With the Bezier tool, click from point to point to create one of the penguin "wings." Don't worry about getting things perfect on the first try—

just create a shape that is close. Now use the Shape tool to modify the control nodes to get the exact wing shape you want. Drag on the little black handles on the ends of the blue dotted control lines to change how a curve looks, or simply drag on the curve itself to reshape the object (see Figure 2.9).

16. Duplicate the wing shape (+ key); then, with the Pick tool, drag the left-center control handle to the right while holding down the Ctrl key. This will flip-flop your object horizontally, while maintaining its original size (if you don't hold the Ctrl key, you can flip-flop and resize the object at the same time). Now drag the bottom-center control handle up while again holding down the Ctrl key to flip the object vertically. Position the object to make it the right wing (see Figure 2.10).

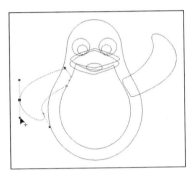 

**Figure 2.9**
(Left) Use the Shape tool to modify a curve to get the exact look you want.

**Figure 2.10**
(Right) Duplicating and flipping objects is a fast and easy way to create pieces of your CorelDRAW characters.

17. For the final touch, we need some penguin "feet." Again start with circles drawn with the Ellipse tool, and use the Arrange|Shaping|Weld feature to merge them into one object. Then use the Shape tool to modify the nodes and create a nice "gooey" foot! Duplicate and arrange the feet for each side of the penguin. If you double-click on an object with the Pick tool, the sizing handles change into rotation and skewing arrows. Drag on a corner arrow to rotate your object, or drag one of the center arrows to skew (angle) it (see Figure 2.11).

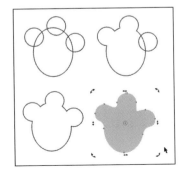

**Figure 2.11**
Welding circle shapes together forms the feet. Double-clicking on an object reveals the rotation and skewing arrows.

That's it! A few simple shapes becomes our pal the penguin! It is really easy to create almost any kind of basic comic character in CorelDRAW, as we will see in the next project as well. The more you work in the program, the more natural the shortcut key strokes and mouse clicks will become to you. Practice makes perfect! The final image can be found in the color section in the center of this book, and in the file in the \Chapt02\ subdirectory on the companion CD-ROM; it's called penguin.cdr. If you open the file, you can see the results of this project, as well as another version of the penguin that was made to look more "real," simply with the addition of some shading tricks (using the Interactive Fill tool and the Interactive Contour tool). Chapter 6 details how a little more time spent on coloring and shading can transform even the simplest of cartoon characters into a 3D-looking action hero!

## PROJECT Game Over

I am amazed at how people always claim to have no artistic skills. "I can only draw stick figures," people tell me when I show them some art piece I am working on, like it's an excuse as to why they don't draw or paint. I don't buy this. You don't have to be dripping with talent to be a good artist; you just have to learn how to use the tools that you have and be patient enough to work out any design problems that arise.

Take me, for example. Personally, I think I am a lousy artist when compared to my gifted associates. What my artist friends can render in one simple step takes me hours to sketch out in pencil and then ink up as line art. This is where CorelDRAW becomes the perfect creative medium for me. What I lack in talent I make up for in creativity and tenacity. I don't have to be able to draw a straight line or perfect circle—CorelDRAW does it for me. If I am not happy with the way a design is laid out, I can easily resize, rearrange, re-everything in CorelDRAW. It might take me a little longer, but with a little effort I can get the results I want. I am guessing you can too.

With very simple shapes, you can create very fun comic characters (see Figure 2.12). Even the most gifted artists start with simple shapes and move on from there. The same techniques apply to creating comic characters, where your work can be as simple or complex as you want. In any case, even if you just stick with the simplest of shapes, you can get fun and animated characters with just a little effort. To make fun comic characters using only CorelDRAW objects, follow these steps:

**Figure 2.12**

Simple shapes can create animated fun comic characters and scenes, with no illustration talent necessary.

1. With the Ellipse tool, draw a circle for the head. Then use the tool again to draw an oval for an eye. You can freehand draw the other eye, but I like to keep things symmetrical by duplicating objects (+ key) and then moving the duplicates into place using the Pick tool. Remember, you can always toggle between the Pick tool and the Active tool by tapping the Spacebar. Switch to the Bezier tool and click to create a pyramid-

like object for the torso. If you don't start and stop in the same place, the object will be an open curve. Click Auto-Close Curve on the Property Bar to convert an open path into a solid object.

2. Continue to use the Bezier tool to click around and make a skirt shape. Then create some pointy triangles for the legs. It's easy, huh? Now create the left and right arms, which require a little more attention. Finally, use the Ellipse tool to draw in other details, such as ear pieces (see Figure 2.13).

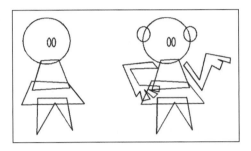

**Figure 2.13**
The Ellipse tool draws great circles, while the Bezier tool draws straight-lined objects with single clicks from point to point.

3. Draw more circles to fill in details like the shoulders and big, poofy hair. To speed things up and keep everything symmetrical, duplicate like object shapes (such as ears and hair) and flip-flop the duplicate horizontally by dragging a left-center sizing handle to the right while holding down the Ctrl key. You should now start to see the character emerge from the simple shapes (see Figure 2.14).

**Figure 2.14**
Duplicate and flip-flop objects to speed things along and keep the similar object pairs symmetrical.

4. Now our figure looks very much like a stick person, or robot, which is fine, but I like my cartoons more "gooey." With the Shape tool, select an object such as an arm or leg, drag-select all of the nodes, and locate the node-edit features found on the Property Bar. Click Convert Line To Curve and then click Make Node Smooth. This will convert the straight and pointy objects into mooshy sausages (see Figure 2.15).

5. Fine-tune the objects with the Shape tool. Some pieces, like the feet, need to have the nodes changed back to Cusp so you can make them

**Figure 2.15**
Use the node edit features on the Property Bar to convert the lines to curves and smooth out the nodes.

pointy again. You can get carried away, as I do, massaging the pieces until you get them just right. Now you can start to fill the pieces with colors and arrange them in front and behind each other to make the girl character come to life (see Figure 2.16).

**Figure 2.16**
The Shape tool makes it easy to fine-tune the objects to get the exact lines and curves. Assign outline and fill colors to change the wireframe objects into solid objects.

6. To add pieces such as the hair and the socks, don't try to draw objects that fit together—that takes too long. Draw a simple object with the Freehand tool and then use the Arrange|Shaping|Intersect command to create a new object where the two overlap. This way, you can quickly create custom-fit pieces for many details (see Figure 2.17). Add small details such as circles for gleam shapes and fingernails.

**Figure 2.17**
Use the Arrange|Shaping|Intersect feature to create new shapes where objects overlap for such elements as socks and hair.

7. For the boy character, first I used the Freehand tool to draw the pieces freehand and then I cleaned things up using the Shape tool and node-

edit options on the Property Bar. The tool you are more comfortable working with will depend on how adept you are at using the mouse or whether you have a graphics tablet. My Freehand mouse shapes look darned pathetic until I clean them up with the Shape tool! Once again, big simple shapes, such as the circles, will trim down nicely to become hair and other objects using the Arrange|Shaping|Intersect feature (see Figure 2.18).

**Figure 2.18**
Instead of the straight-line shapes created with the Bezier tool, try drawing objects with the Freehand tool. The Shape tool can clean up even the most clumsy shapes into what you want.

8. Color and stack the pieces as you did with the girl character. For the pants, open the Pattern Fill dialog box from the Fill flyout. Click the down arrow next to the current pattern to open the gallery and select the 2-Color checker pattern. Click the Front color chip and change it to red, and then click OK to fill (see Figure 2.19).

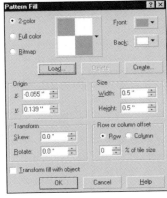

**Figure 2.19**
The 2-Color checker pattern fill provides some fun, cartoony fill options.

## A Place to Call Home

Characters alone are not always very interesting; they benefit from some sort of scenery. For these simple characters, I thought a video-game-type scenario would work well. To create an abstract high-tech scene for simple comic characters, follow these steps:

1. Use the Rectangle tool to draw a horizontal rectangle, and then use the Shape tool to round the corners.

   Now duplicate this object many times and arrange the duplicates randomly, varying the height and width of each copy. Fill some of the

**Note:** You don't need to switch from the Rectangle to the Shape tool—just hover the Rectangle tool over a node, and it switches to the Shape tool.

objects and leave others with no fill and a heavy .4-inch outline. For an interesting look, I used three shades of blue for all of the outline and fill attributes. When you use the same color for a fill in one object and the outline in another, the point where they overlap disappears. Mix and match your background to taste using three similar tones right off the on-screen palette to make things easy. If the colors are too strong, as I decided my blues were, you can adjust the color. Select all your background objects, then choose Effects|Color Adjustment|Brightness-Contrast-Intensity. Drag the sliders to modify the colors in your objects. Increasing the Brightness and decreasing the Contrast is a good way to mute the tones in your image (see Figure 2.20).

The Color Adjustment features (Brightness-Contrast-Intensity, Color Balance, etc.) work on both bitmaps and vector objects in CorelDRAW. They are also available and work the same way in Photo-Paint.

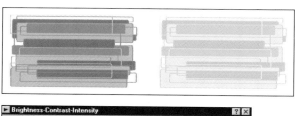

**Figure 2.20**
A hodgepodge of rectangle shapes becomes the background elements. Use the Brightness-Contrast-Intensity dialog box to soften the colors to taste without the hassle of recoloring each object manually.

2. Draw another curved-corner rectangle to serve as a stage for your characters and place them in the scene. For other action elements, I used star shapes from the Symbols And Special Characters docker. Open the docker (Ctrl+F11), locate in the drop-down list the Stars1 library, and drag stars to your liking onto the scene. Color the stars with the same colors used in the background shapes (see Figure 2.21). Or use the Polygon tool, located on the Object flyout, to create your own custom stars.

3. Throw in a smattering of text and other little tidbits to finish off the design. The Interactive Blend tool was used to blend a white circle to a black one for the collection of shapes to the left of the main text. The main text is a font called BauHaus, with a black fill and heavy .111 outline and the Behind fill option enabled in the Outline Pen dialog box (F12). The digital readout is a font called LCD, which is one of my favorites.

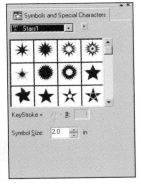

**Figure 2.21**

Use the Symbols And Special Characters docker to add other design elements to your scene.

See? I told you that anyone who can draw stick figures possesses the talent necessary to create interesting computer art. Look through popular gaming and techie publications, and you will see all kinds of artwork done in much the same way. My spin on the style can be seen in the digital color section, and if you are really hurting and can't draw these guys for yourself, the file is called gameover.cdr and is in the \Chapt02\ subdirectory on the companion CD-ROM.

## PROJECT Silly Putty

With your virtual comic strip coming to life, what could be more appropriate than to tweak it with some virtual Silly Putty? (See Figure 2.22.) Silly Putty is that toy from way back (still available, now in other colors and even with glitter!) that not only bounces around but also has the unique ability to capture the printed images from the Sunday comics.

Once the image is stuck in reverse to your Silly Putty blob, you can twist and distort the image to create funny images. (Silly Putty is the low-tech answer to today's MetaTools' Goo program!) Since it is my job to create strange things, I decided a computerized Silly Putty experience was in order. To capture an image and distort it in the computer, follow these steps:

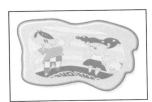

**Figure 2.22**

Using the Freeze option on the Lens docker lets you capture an image like Silly Putty, and, just like the real thing, you can twist and distort the picture using the Envelope tool.

1. First, open an image on which you want to use your virtual Silly Putty. I should point out that you can freeze any image, including bitmaps, using the Frozen option on the Lens docker. Only vector objects will distort correctly during the enveloping steps, however. I used the comic characters from the previous exercise, but you can use any image, including clip art. Draw an oval over your artwork; for the Silly Putty look, color it faded pink—Magenta-20, Yellow-20—set from the Uniform Fill dialog box (Shift+F11). Now open the Lens docker with the Effects| Lens menu option or keyboard shortcut (Alt+F3), set the Lens type to Transparency and the Rate to 50%, then click Apply (see Figure 2.23).

**Figure 2.23**
An oval with a Transparency Lens
creates the pinkish image.

## Freeze the Problems

If you are experiencing difficulty outputting a file, it might be because it has many active lenses. Lenses and other CorelDRAW functions are not PostScript based, and therefore they might crash the processor when you try to use too many of them (CorelDRAW has to convert lenses into things PostScript will understand). The Frozen feature will avoid this problem—the active lens is removed and replaced by ordinary CorelDRAW objects (albeit many of them!). Keep in mind that, just like converting text to curves, freezing a lens kills the flexibility (like replacing what you see through a pink glass lens with a photo of the image made with the pink glass lens). So if you're considering freezing the lenses, you might want to make a backup copy of the affected file. If you still have problems outputting a file after you have frozen the lenses, you can always resort to exporting the image as a CMYK bitmap, which virtually anyone anywhere can output for you.

2. Now enable the Frozen option on the Lens docker and click Apply. Instead of just changing the way the artwork below the lens looks, CorelDRAW will create new objects to look like the Lens effect. This process is complex (in this example, the Frozen Lens Group contains 970 objects), so it might take a while to compute. When finished, you will have a group of objects in addition to the originals, with the new group shaded like the Lens effect (see Figure 2.24).

3. To distort the object, use the Interactive Envelope tool to twist and tweak, similar to stretching the putty. Or use the Property Bar to adjust the Envelope settings to switch to Envelope Unconstrained Mode and the Putty setting, which allows for some serious tweaking (see Figure 2.25).

4. Use the Freehand tool to draw a blob around the distorted image, and color it dark brown. Duplicate the blob, and downsize by dragging in the corner sizing handles while holding down the Shift key. Color the duplicate the same faded pink as before, and use the Interactive Blend tool to drag between the two blob shapes. This will create a rounded-edge and finish up the Silly Putty look. You can also create highlight and shadow objects (the same way as the rivets in Chapter 11) (see Figure 2.26).

That finishes up the Silly Putty image, which you'll find in the digital color section and also in a file called sillyput.cdr in the \Chapt02\ subdirectory on

**Figure 2.24**
The Frozen feature of the Lens docker creates new objects to mimic the way the objects below the Lens effect appeared. You then can move and manipulate these objects.

the CD-ROM. If you look, I flip-flopped the final image so that, like real Silly Putty, the image captured would be the mirrored image of the original. Also, if you look closely, you will notice that the checkerboard pattern in the boy's pants does not distort. This is because it is a 2-Color pattern fill, which is essentially a bitmap. I told you that bitmaps won't distort! If you want a pattern like this to distort along with everything else, you need to use vector art (such as hand-drawn squares) instead of the bitmap pattern fill; then you can go through the enveloping process again, and the pattern will distort as well.

## PROJECT  Hydrant Hound

The little hound dog and hydrant in Figure 2.27 just popped into existence one day, and even became part of my novelty T-shirt line. I am not rich and famous, so I guess I was the only one who thought that a graphic of a dog who pees on a hydrant was a great way to adorn your body. Oh, well, I got to recycle the artwork a few times anyway, so it all worked out in the end.

The great thing about computers is that you can create artwork that doesn't look so computer generated. With today's design landscape suffering from a glut of computer-generated artwork, the hand-drawn/hand-painted look is getting mighty popular and very marketable. In this scene, I drew the comic characters by hand in pen and ink, then scanned them using a flatbed scanner. With the cartoon characters having a hand-drawn look, I used the Watercolor bitmap filter to change the CorelDRAW background elements into a matching hand-colored-looking element. To work with both actual hand-

drawn images and to convert vector pieces into hand-drawn looking artwork, follow these steps:

1. You will need to get your scanner hooked up and working in Linux to digitize hand-drawn pieces. You have several ways to do this, with detailed instructions available on the Internet (search keywords "scanner linux"). In a nutshell, you need a program that acts as an interface between your scanner and computer, such as the Xvscan or SANE (Scanner Access Now Easy) utility (see Figure 2.28) to digitize your illustrations. In this example, the dog and hydrant are scanned in as one-bit (black and white) bitmaps, which can be easily colored with CorelDRAW shapes (see the jester character in Chapter 9 for another example of this technique). With every scanner/computer having its own peccadilloes, especially in Linux, I'll leave it up to you to get your graphic digitized and in a black-and-white file format importable by CorelDRAW. (In these cases, I find the GIMP utility a valuable tool for manipulating bitmaps within Linux. It ships with Corel Linux, so don't hesitate to use this powerful image-manipulation program. For more on GIMP, check out *Gimp: The Official Handbook* by Olof S. and Karin Kylander, also available from The Coriolis Group. [1999; ISBN, 1-57610-520-2]) Also, SANE is available on the companion CD-ROM, in the \scan subdirectory, but the Web is a more up-to-date resource, especially in the ever-evolving world of Linux!

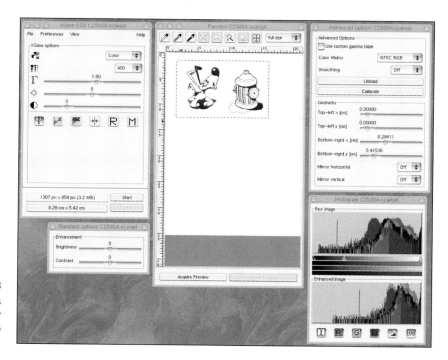

**Figure 2.28**
A utility such as SANE is necessary to operate a scanner and digitize hand-drawn images in Linux.

## Paint Buckets

You might prefer to use Photo-Paint to color your hand-drawn illustrations. Once you have scanned your image, open it in Photo-Paint (File|Open). Then, change the mode from Black And White to something full-color (Image|Mode|RGB Color). Finally, use the Magic Wand Mask tool to select the area you want to fill with color, then click the Fill tool in the selection area to fill with the current color (see figure). The downside to this approach is that it is not easy to change the fill colors, since they are not shapes you can select and modify in CorelDRAW; this is why in general I prefer the CorelDRAW coloring approach.

**Photo-Paint is a quick and easy, if not as flexible, way to color your hand-drawn illustrations.**

2.  Issue the File|Import command to import the black-and-white scan of your illustration into CorelDRAW. The great thing about black-and-white bitmaps in CorelDRAW is that you can change the colors for "black" and "white" by changing the outline and fill values. For example, if you right-click on an on-screen color chip with your bitmap selected, it will change the "black" ink to that color. The same is true for the "white" area, except you control it with the left mouse button. But even more interesting, in my opinion, is that the white area of a black-and-white bitmap can be rendered "clear" by right-clicking on the "x" in the on-screen color palette. Then your hand-drawn lines "float" on a clear background, and you can manipulate them as you please.

3.  Once your bitmap has a "clear" background, you can quickly draw shapes with the Bezier tool to add color to them. First, select your bitmap and right-click to open the pop-up menu, then choose Lock Object. This will keep you from accidentally selecting or moving your bitmap. Then, with the Bezier tool, click from point to point along the edge of your illustration to create a shape, which you can fill with any color (or another Fill option, such as Fountain Fill or Pattern) to color your illustration. Don't worry about creating the shape perfectly to the outline of the illustration—the imperfections add to the hand-drawn feel (see Figure 2.29). Issue the To Back command to move the colored

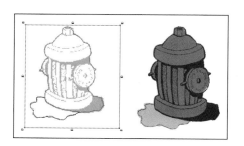

**Figure 2.29**
Locking a bitmap (left) prevents its accidental selection and movement when drawing shapes to give it color (right).

objects behind the bitmap (Shift+PgDn), so the black hand-drawn lines are on top of the colored shapes.

4.  Once your characters are colored (which in this case also means drawing a shape where you want white to appear, such as in the body of the dog), you are ready to create a scene to put them in. First, draw a rectangle for the page limit of your design. Place your characters where you want them on the page, and use the Bezier tool to quickly rough out some shapes and map out the dynamics of the scene. I created a vanishing point above and behind the comic characters on the horizon line. Using this point as a reference, draw lines to aid in drawing a fence, sidewalk, street, and building (see Figure 2.30). Remember you can always delete pieces later, or you can use guidelines. (See the sidebar, "Get Guided.")

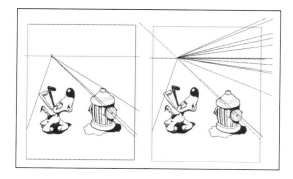

**Figure 2.30**
Use quick shapes to map out your comic scene.

5.  With the lines as a guide, use the Bezier tool to draw a triangle shape for the sidewalk. Use the Interactive Fill tool to create a white-to-dark fill to create the illusion of distance. Now duplicate the triangle (+ key) and grab the bottom-left node with the Shape tool. Drag the node up and to the right until it aligns with another one of the guidelines you drew. Because this shape is a duplicate of the sidewalk, the shared-edge is exactly aligned. Neat trick, huh? Use this duplicate and node-drag flip-flop trick to create three pieces: the main sidewalk, the street, and the far-off sidewalk. Shade the pieces using Linear Fountain fills to get an illusion of distance (see Figure 2.31).

## Get Guided

Instead of mapping out your illustration using guide shapes—which unless you delete them will print or export with your objects—try using guidelines instead. First, use the View|Rulers option to make sure that your rulers are viewable. Then, with the Pick tool, simply drag from a ruler out toward your image area to create a guideline. Now you can click on the guide again to reveal rotation handles, so you can create a series of guides to aid in your work. For even more "help" from the View menu, enable Snap To Guidelines. This will make your guidelines "magnetic," and tools like the Bezier will be drawn to the guides, creating nodes along those lines if you want (see figure).

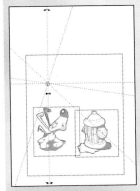

**As a design aid, guidelines offer "snap-to" options and don't have to be deleted when you've finished working.**

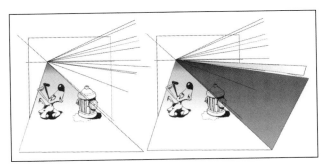

**Figure 2.31**
Create a triangle shape using the Bezier tool. Dragging the nodes of a duplicate of this shape creates the other filled areas, while ensuring that shared lines are perfectly aligned.

6. Continue to work on the scene to add details for the background. The sky is a Texture fill; you can access the fill in the Texture Fill dialog box, which you open from the Fill flyout. With the Texture dialog box open, change the Texture Library to Samples, then choose Clouds, Midday from the Texture List. You can change how the selected pattern looks by choosing new colors for the current color chips or by clicking the Preview button. Clicking the Preview button randomizes the settings for the current selected texture for an infinite number of texture combinations. Use the Bezier tool to draw rectangles for the building and window shapes. The windows also have the same cloud texture fill.

7. For the fence on the left, draw a rectangle using the Bezier tool and following the reference lines for what would be the large board closest

to you. Now duplicate the board, downsize it using the sizing handles, and position the tiny duplicate way off in the distance. Use the Interactive Blend tool to drag between the two boards to create a fence. If the blend does not look right, experiment with different numbers of steps, and also try using the acceleration options on the Property Bar (see Figure 2.32).

**Figure 2.32**
Use the Bezier tool to draw straight-line objects, such as the building and windows, using the lines drawn earlier for reference. Blending two boards becomes a fence image.

8. Select and delete all the hand-drawn guidelines and any other objects you don't want in your scene. Select the two comic characters and group them (Ctrl+G). Select all the background elements, and use the Effects|PowerClip|Place Inside Container command to stuff the pieces into a rectangle the size of your final page. You should have a complete, albeit computer-generated looking scene.

9. With the PowerClip Rectangle selected, open the Convert To Bitmap dialog box from the Bitmaps menu. (First, be sure to save a backup copy of this file to disk.) Set the Color option to RGB, and enable the Anti-aliasing and Use Color Profile options. You can use a high-resolution value; to speed things along and also make the image look more chunky and hand-drawn, however, try a lower setting, such as 100 dpi (see Figure 2.33).

10. Select the bitmap, and choose Bitmaps|Art Strokes|Watercolor. This is a neat filter set that makes your artwork look like it was done with watercolors. You can spend time dabbling with the settings, using the Preview button to see how your changes affect the outcome (see Figure 2.34). Or try one of the other Art Strokes filters. To save time, log on to the CorelDRAW f/x & design Web site at **www.slimydog.com/corelfx**, where you will find a complete visual catalog of all the available bit-

**Figure 2.33**
Constrain all of the objects to the page size with the PowerClip feature. Use the Convert To Bitmap function to create a malleable, pixel-based graphic.

**Figure 2.34**
The Watercolor bitmap filter creates effects that look hand-painted.

map effects filters. This makes choosing one simple and saves a lot of "experimentation" time.

11. If you are not satisfied with the results of the bitmap effects filter, try another. You can mix and match as many effects as you like, continuing to tweak your bitmap until you get the exact look you want. The Creative|Frame filter, for example, gets you away from the hard-rectangular look of computer generation for a very cool feathered-edge look (see Figure 2.35). Or use a Gaussian blur technique to make the background seem far away, with your characters "popping" out in the

**Figure 2.35**
The Frame bitmap effects filter creates the look of a feathered edge for a less rigid feel.

foreground (more on this technique in Chapter 6). Experiment and have fun until your background complements your characters to your satisfaction.

12. Text elements, using highlight and thick multiple outline effects covered in the next chapter, finish off the poster. I used a font called MarkerFeltWide.

You can see my finished poster in the digital color section, or you can load it from the \Chapt02\ subdirectory on the companion CD-ROM (it's called festival.cdr). Don't forget to experiment with the other Art Strokes filter effects to add a hand-drawn look to your computer-generated artwork. It's quick and easy, and it really gets away from the same-old geometric look that vector artwork alone creates.

## PROJECT Sword of Beauty

For a long time now (yes, even before it became trendy!), I have been a fan of Japanese animation. This choppy style does not appeal to everyone, but for me it hits home. Even as a kid, as much as I loved the classic Warner Brothers cartoons, my allegiance was for Japanese animated classics like *Speed Racer* and *Kimba the White Lion.*

The image in Figure 2.36 is a mix-match combination of my many favorite Japanese animated female characters. I love this image, and I have placed this poor girl in many chaotic scenes, including a series of paintings in my living room. In this comic scene, she seems to be under surveillance, as if she is invading the secret lair of the evil dark lord, Dr. Von ClickenDrag, who our heroine must stop from taking over the world!

Okay, so my imagination runs a bit wild at times! The point is, even a wild design concept can come to life much more easily in CorelDRAW than by using traditional techniques alone. In fact, the computer expands the design horizons further, and the artist is able to exploit the technology itself. For example, using screen captures and other computer-specific design elements creates new design potential that simply does not exist elsewhere. To create a fun comic scene combining hand-drawn and computer-generated elements, follow these steps:

**Figure 2.36**
Combining hand-drawn images with computer-aided design techniques results in images impossible to create using manual or digital techniques alone.

1. This project started as an ink illustration that I scanned and converted to Corel objects using the Corel Trace program on the Windows platform. Sadly, CorelDRAW Linux does not ship with the same utility. However, Linux utilities are available that do essentially the same thing, which is to convert bitmap information into vector objects that you can manipulate in CorelDRAW. The Linux AutoTrace program (included on the companion CD-ROM in the \scan\autotrace directory) is one such utility. AutoTrace will convert black-and-white images in

the PNM or PBM formats (use GIMP to save your scans in this format) and export them as PostScript, which you can import into CorelDRAW using the File|Import command. To trace a picture, a sample command would be **./autotrace test.pbm >test.ps**, where your black-and-white bitmap **test.pbm** would be converted to a vector line art PostScript file called **test.ps**. Import the file into CorelDRAW (File|Import), changing the Files Of Type setting to PostScript Interpreted, to get a set of shapes that you can then modify in CorelDRAW. You might have to issue the Arrange|Break Apart command to separate the pieces or the Arrange| Ungroup command to ungroup them in order to work with the converted shapes.

2. To color your pieces, use the on-screen color palette to drag and drop colors to your object shapes below. To speed things along during the coloring process, move the on-screen palette right to where you are coloring. That way, you don't have to move the cursor so far to drag colors off the palette and drop them onto your shapes to color them. To move the palette, click next to a color well and drag onto the desktop. Now you can size and position the palette to make drag-and-drop coloring a cinch! (See Figure 2.37.)

3. Because a Trace result typically is a collection of small shapes on a big black filled object, you can select it and give it a thick outline, with the Behind Fill option enabled in the Outline Pen dialog box (F12) to help isolate our heroine from a busy background. When you have finished coloring the character, drag-select all the pieces and group (Ctrl+G) them so you can easily position and size the character in the scene.

Default: CorelDRAW Palette

### Low Tech Meets High Tech

Photocopy your ink illustrations before you scan them. I sketch out an image first in pencil (which looks terrible, full of smudges and eraser marks!), then place a sheet of Duralene (a semi-opaque plastic illustration material) on top and trace the pencil image with an ink pen. This results in a nice crisp image, but Duralene does not scan well (at least not on my scanner) because it is only semi-opaque. Your results might vary, but I find making a photocopy of hand-drawn images, then scanning the paper copy results in crisper images and consequently better scans. The better the scan, the better Corel Trace or AutoTrace will work.

### No Need to Select

Drag-and-drop coloring works even on objects already within a group. Unlike clicking a color well with a group of objects selected, when you drag and drop color, only the object directly beneath it will receive the color, not all the objects in the group. Remember, too, that you can always hold down the Ctrl key and select a single object within a group.

**Figure 2.37**
Use the drag-and-drop coloring feature to add color quickly to the trace objects. Move the palette closer to speed things up even more.

### Quick and Easy Custom Palettes

If you have a collection of colors you like to use more than others, you can create your own custom palette. This feature is a pain in any other version, but CorelDRAW 9 finally makes this happen! From the Windows menu, you can choose Color Palettes|Create Palette From Selection or Create Palette From Document. Select All (Ctrl+A), then from the Windows menu, choose Color Palettes|Create Palette From Selection. Name the custom palette, and click Save to generate it. This only creates the palette to disk, so to use it, from the View menu, choose Color Palette|Load Palette. This will display and dock the available palettes on the right of the screen, adding easily accessible colors for drag-and-drop coloring. A custom palette makes it easy to color a series of cartoon panels all alike. Or if you have several people working on the same project and want them all to use the same colors, you can create and include a custom color palette along with any other template files and guidelines.

4. For the computer-monitor graphics within the scene I imagined, I needed a screen capture of our heroine. So to take a snapshot of the current image, use the File|Export feature. Choose File|Export, then change the Files Of Type setting to TIFF; give the file a meaningful name; and click the Export button. In the next dialog box, choose the color depth for the snapshot you want, and select the resolution. Click OK to export the current image to disk. Now issue the File|Import command to import this image to put your screen shot back into play in your design. Use the Selection tool to scale the bitmap back down to size.

5. Within CorelDRAW, you can crop down the screen capture using the Shape tool. Drag-select two nodes on any side and then drag the side to crop the image, holding down the Ctrl key to constrain movement to one plane (you can create odd-shaped crops as well if you want). Crop away all of the extra bits, leaving only the character. Now duplicate the bitmap (+ key) and crop down the character to zoom in on her face. Downsize the bitmap for the full-body shot to be the same size as the head shot by dragging the sizing handles with the Pick tool. When all bitmaps are at the desired size, use the Convert To Bitmap command from the Bitmaps menu to adjust to the correct size and to convert to grayscale. If you skip this step, CorelDRAW retains all the information in the bitmaps, including what was hidden during the cropping process. When you convert the image to bitmap, the object is frozen, with only the visible image converted to pixels; this makes for smaller files. Converting the objects to bitmap keeps you from carrying around excess image baggage that you don't need (see Figure 2.38).

6. To create a frame, draw two rectangles, round the corners by dragging the Shape tool on a corner node on the outside shape, and combine (Ctrl+L) the two together. Now arrange the bitmaps from the screen captures inside the frames and add detail elements, such as text. I used the font called LCD to add on-screen notations. For a third monitor,

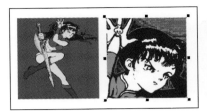 

**Figure 2.38**
Crop, downsize, and adjust the screen capture to fit in a square. Use the Convert To Bitmap function to make it grayscale.

duplicate the full-body shot, and alter it with the Edge Detect filter from the Bitmaps|Contour flyout. Arrange the three monitors vertically (see Figure 2.39).

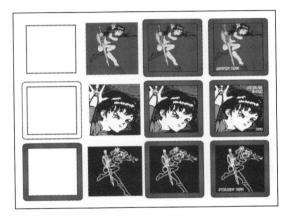

**Figure 2.39**
Create a frame with the rectangle shape and arrange the screen captures to make our heroine look like she is under surveillance.

7. For the target shapes in the background, first draw a circle and down-size/duplicate it three times to create a series of four rings. Draw lines for crosshairs, and add text to designate values for the rings. Drag-select the entire bunch, and then combine them (Ctrl+L). Now use the skew arrows (double-click on the object with the Pick tool to toggle to the skew arrows) to distort the target (see Figure 2.40).

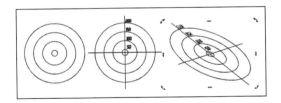

**Figure 2.40**
Circles become a target object with the addition of crosshairs and text.

8. Select the target curve and give it a magenta outline with no fill. Dupli-cate it (+ key), move the duplicate down, and give it a unique outline color. Repeat the process to get a tower of targets, like some high-tech, 3D map (see Figure 2.41).

9. The little crosshair grid is simply an "x" blended to a duplicate across the page. When you freeze this blend (Arrange|Separate), you can

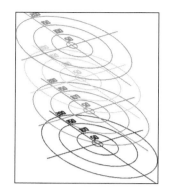

**Figure 2.41**
Duplicates of the target shape stack to suggest 3D space.

blend it again to a duplicate on the other side of the page. I used this method to create the grid of squares. You can also use the Graph Paper tool, located in the Polygon tool flyout, to make grids on the page. (See Chapter 14 for more.) Right-click to open the Properties dialog box for the Graph Paper tool and key in the number of cells for how wide and high you want the grid to be. Then click-drag to create a Graph Paper object (see Figure 2.42).

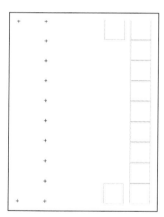

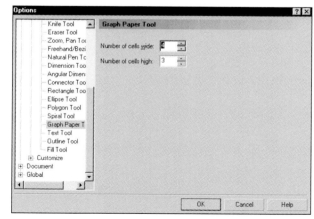

**Figure 2.42**
Blending objects creates even-spaced patterns for the x and square grid elements. You can also use the Graph Paper tool to create grids.

10. While working on this project, I wanted some sort of Japanese writing on it. I called my friend in San Francisco, and she faxed me the characters, which I digitized directly using a fax modem. I used the Corel Trace utility to trace the objects (which spell out "Sword of Beauty") but was unhappy with how thin they were. By using a thick .055-inch outline, I got the width I wanted. To get a black outline effect, simply stack a thinner red outline copy on a thicker black one (see Figure 2.43).

**Figure 2.43**
Corel Trace can convert bitmaps from any source, including fax modems, into vector artwork. I beefed up the thin characters with a heavy line weight. Stack multiple images to get a black outline effect.

11. Arrange the character and other design elements to create a busy image that creates a mood of urgency and excitement. Layer objects, such as pieces of the grid, in front of and behind the main character shape to add more depth. Draw a rectangle for the page limit, send it to the back, and open the Texture Fill dialog box from the Fill tool flyout. In the Samples 9 Texture library, locate Wood Grain in the Texture list. Change the mineral colors from the default greens to dark blue, pink, and blue again. This creates interesting visual noise in the background (see Figure 2.44).

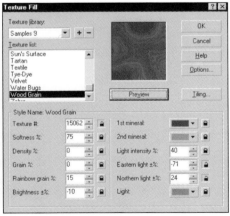

**Figure 2.44**
Use the Texture Fill dialog box to create a customized pattern by changing the color chips.

12. Depending on the amount of chaos desired, you can also add more elements to the scene. I added straight dotted lines. You can make any outline a dotted line by changing the Style option in the Outline Pen dialog box (F12).

You can see the finished poster in the color section, or you can load it from a file called swood.cdr in the \Chapt02\ subdirectory on the companion CD-ROM. So much is going on in this image that drawing everything by hand would have just been too tedious. Yet, because the main character started as an ink illustration, the image still retains a real cartoony feel. Increasingly, I find myself mixing and matching mediums to create the images in my mind. The computer just affords many design opportunities that would be far too tedious to do by hand. For example, choose Bitmaps|Plug-Ins|Fancy|Terrazzo to open a dialog box to convert a bitmap into a dizzying pattern design, which makes for a cool background variant (see Figure 2.45).

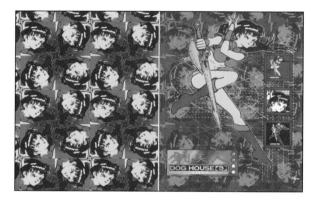

**Figure 2.45**
The Terrazzo bitmap filter creates patterns from your images.

# Beyond f/x

The potential is endless for a computer-based comic strip. You can color a black-and-white strip (or vice versa) and convert the text into different type styles, or even other languages. The same images for print can migrate into animations and Web sites, or pop up on merchandise—you name it. Beyond comic strips, the techniques for coloring hand-drawn illustrations lend themselves to many applications. You can use a hand-drawn illustration as the basis of an advertisement, using the same kind of coloring techniques from this chapter to avoid a cookie-cutter, computer-generated look. Using screen captures to create additional artwork for a design is also a great way to milk more out of your design day without adding much effort (such as the "double-vision" techniques in Chapter 9). A background pattern based on a screen capture, or a piece of a screen capture, adds a unique look to your design without adding much effort.

# Moving On

In this chapter, we looked at mixing traditional ink illustrations with CorelDRAW objects. For all you non-illustrators, we looked at creating creatures and characters entirely within CorelDRAW, using simple shapes and geometric objects.

The great thing about assembling comic scenes in CorelDRAW is that you are then able to go beyond the static printed page right into action-media. Because you can move and manipulate the characters within the scenes, you are only a heartbeat away from animating them. If you took the time to create multiple poses for the same character, you could then go right into the animation mode. In fact, this new kind of computer animation is gaining in popularity, with a handful of children's cartoons now embracing the technology.

In Chapter 3, we will explore some cool ways to take boring text elements and make them come alive in your designs. You will discover how to capture current design trends with virtual graffiti, transparency, and glowing effects, and even make your text float freely in midair. All these options and more, none of which are available on grandpa's typewriter.

# Chapter 3
# Cool Type Effects

*This chapter works with the Interactive Contour tool, the
Interactive Transparency feature, and the Interactive Drop
Shadow tool. In addition, it will show you how to convert
text to bitmaps for blurring effects, and how to use the
PowerClip command to create a mask.*

# Using Eye-Catching Effects to Make Your Headlines Pop

This chapter introduces popular and contemporary themes, and, because this is my book, we will also take a look at designs from the fringe element. I find I can learn much from artists far from the mainstream and even from the underground design scene, although these disciplines, if you will, are often scoffed at by traditionalists.

In this chapter, we will touch on several interesting type effects from the edge and the underground. First, we will use the Contour function to achieve a flashy, graffiti look that you might find applied to a local urban surface, complete with a spray of random bullet holes. Then, we will explore type effects created with the Interactive Transparency, Drop Shadow, and PowerClip tools, and we will also look at the blur effects from the Bitmap menu. Finally, we will create flashy, metallic-looking words with shading and beveling. All these examples will help get you out of any humdrum art slump and add some danger to your designs.

## PROJECT You Write?

While promoting my own line of apparel, I became acquainted with many interesting (and often frightening) characters. Hardcore, ex-con, gang-banger graffiti and tattoo artists were getting into clothing, and designs from the street were evolving into street wear. One company was promoting its apparel with a small bottle on a necklace. Inside the bottle were all kinds of different spray tips for aerosol paint cans. I thought that was pretty cool and tried to score myself a set! Don't get me wrong. I am not condoning tagging or graffiti; I hate to see anything vandalized. I find that the techniques are noteworthy, however, and I even support designated graffiti areas (such as organized murals or The Pit in Venice Beach, California). Personally, I love to grab a handful of spray cans and go nuts! I set up big sheets of plywood and have graffiti parties. Once I had a house with an empty, nonfunctioning swimming pool that we converted into a basketball court/skateboard park, and we covered it in graffiti. I guess I am just a controlled vandal.

Although I have not personally heard of anyone designing a tag or graffiti mural in CorelDRAW, anything is possible! You could easily design an entire

---

### Art on the Street

*Tagging* is a practice in which graffiti artists mark their territory with a special icon, their nickname, or a combination of both. More often than not, a tagger is not affiliated with a gang but is just a frustrated inner-city youth seeking attention or recognition. Taggers greet one another with "You write?" to announce their status and to verify that they are speaking to fellow taggers. They then compare techniques and styles as well as ambitious or dangerous *tags*. It is a subculture all its own.

wall at full size (choose Layout|Page Setup, set the Paper option to Custom, and key in the dimensions) and then use the Tiling feature (Print|Layout|Print Tiled Pages) to output the image at actual size to create stencils, masks, or any full-sized reference. Many sign companies will use a CorelDRAW file to generate masks using a computer-controlled plotter that cuts out an image from giant sheets of masking material. You can lay down the sheets and then spray-paint to get a crisp image. Usually this high-end process is reserved for expensive custom car paint jobs, but hey, who knows?

Since I imagine it is more valuable for you to re-create the look of graffiti and not actually design spray-paint graffiti projects, I will focus on the former. In this section, we will create type that has the flashy look of painted graffiti, including the texture of the wall it is on (see Figure 3.1). To vandalize a virtual wall, follow these steps:

1. Use the Artistic Text tool to set your headline. For my *CorelDRAW* text, I used a font called Dancin LET, but you can use this technique on anything. Locate and select the Interactive Contour tool, located on the same toolbar flyout as the Interactive Drop Shadow and Interactive Blend. Drag on your text from the center outward while watching the Property Bar. The Property Bar will show you how many steps are in the contour as you go along. Stop dragging when the number of steps equals two. You can control a Contour group directly with the Interactive Contour tool, or by working with the Contour docker, which you open with the Ctrl+F9 shortcut. In the docker, set the Offset value to .05 inches, set the Steps value to 2, and then click Apply. This will create the shapes needed for the multiple outline effect (see Figure 3.2).

**Figure 3.1**

You can use the Contour feature to add multiple outlines to a shape and, with the addition of a bright color scheme, create a graffiti look. You can use the pieces as is or use the Interactive Transparency tool to let the texture of the surface below show through.

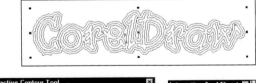

**Figure 3.2**

The Interactive Contour tool creates additional shapes with Offset and Steps variables, which you can control interactively or key in manually on the Property Bar or docker.

2. With the contour group selected, choose Arrange|Separate, then select Arrange|Ungroup from the menu. This will give you three separate curve shapes, which you can color white, black, and red (from the outside in) to create a cool look. To simplify and fine-tune each contour shape, select the curve, break it apart (Ctrl+K), and then delete all the objects except the main outline. Now when these images are stacked, they have a bold but simple look (see Figure 3.3).

**Figure 3.3**
You can use the shapes that result from the Contour command or eliminate any counters for just a thick outline.

3. To add a gleam to the text, select the smallest inside curve and duplicate it. Nudge the duplicate up and to the right using the arrow keys, and give it a white fill and white hairline. Now send it back one (Ctrl+PgDn) so that the original covers all but a sliver, resulting in a gleam. Draw a rectangular wall behind the text and use the Texture Fill option to give it the look of stucco. From the Texture Fill dialog box (which you open from the Fill tool flyout), change the Texture Library setting to Samples 7, select Concrete from the Texture list, and then click OK (see Figure 3.4).

**Figure 3.4**
Offset a duplicate to create a gleam highlight. Use the Texture Fill dialog box to give a rectangle a concrete fill.

### Nudge and Super Nudge

You can double the productivity value of the arrow keys by using the Nudge and Super Nudge options. Open the Options dialog box (Ctrl+J), and, on the Edit page, you can key in whatever values you want for Nudge and Super Nudge. I use a small value for Nudge (.005") for tiny, precise movement. Then I use a large multiplier (like 20) for the Super Nudge value. This way, I can make tiny or big leaps as I need them, with the arrow key alone or the arrow+Shift keys.

4. Use the Artistic Text tool to set more type. For the 9, I used a font called MarkerFeltWide, which has a thick, hand-drawn look. Give the text a thick, black .111-inch outline and select the Behind Fill option in the Outline Pen dialog box (F12). Give this text a radial fountain fill from white to blue using the Fountain Fill dialog box (F11) or the Interactive Fill tool. Use the Freehand tool to draw shapes that will become abstract reflections of the surrounding landscape, making the object look chromy. After you draw the abstract shapes, use the Intersection feature to trim down the blobs so they are within the main text shape. To do this, select one of the abstract shapes; then, from the Arrange|Shaping menu, choose Intersect. In the Shaping docker, change the Leave Original options to just Target Objects, click the Intersect With button, and then click on the number 9 object. This will create a new object, just where the two overlap, which is what we want (see Figure 3.5). Remember that this is supposed to be graffiti, so don't worry about being too detailed.

5. Move the cursor over the Polygon tool on the toolbar, right-click, and choose the Properties option. Enable the Polygon As Star option, change

## Texture Fill Image Resolution

For crisper images in your high-end projects that contain texture fills, be sure to up the Bitmap Resolution and Texture Size Limit values in the Texture Options dialog box. In the Texture Fill dialog box, click the Options button to open the Texture Options dialog box and then increase both options to the maximum values. This will make the texture fill usable for printed applications (the default setting of 120 dpi is just too low). Remember that these values act as multipliers when calculating the bitmap that makes up a texture fill, so your file size will also increase dramatically when you increase these values. To help save disk space with this now huge file, use the advanced settings in the Save Drawing dialog box (File|Save As). Click the Advanced button to open the Advanced Settings dialog box and then select the Rebuild Textures When Opening The File option. Now CorelDRAW will just save the settings associated with texture fills and recalculate them when you open the file rather than save the entire huge bitmap to disk.

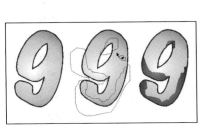

**Figure 3.5**
A plain text element is transformed into a chrome one with a radial fountain fill and objects meant to look like a reflected landscape.

the Number Of Points/Sides value to 4, and up the Sharpness slider to 65. This makes for a nice cartoony sparkle. Click OK and drag the Polygon tool to create the sparkle shape. Then use the Pick tool to position the sparkles on the top-left edges of the chromed letter (see Figure 3.6).

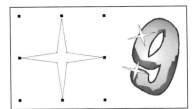

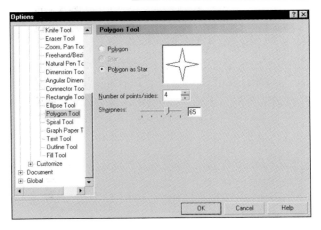

**Figure 3.6**
The Polygon tool creates all kinds of stars; they can have from 3 to 500 points.

6. For the *FX* text, I used the Bezier tool to hand-draw my own type. Select the Bezier tool and click from point to point to draw a big funky *F* and then a fresh *X*. Now select both objects and group them (Ctrl+G). Give the group a thick, black .222-inch outline, and in the Outline Pen dialog box (F12), select the Round Corners option. Use the Interactive Fill tool to create a yellow-to-magenta linear fountain fill, only with a harsh transition in the center (make the start and end points close together). Finally, duplicate the group and assign no-fill and a thinner .092 white outline. This thin-on-thick outline technique is an alternative to the Contour effect, with similar results (see Figure 3.7).

**Figure 3.7**

A thick, black outline underneath a thinner white one creates a multiple outline look similar to what the Contour docker can create, only in fewer steps. The Interactive Fill tool sets up a linear fountain fill and, by moving the points close together, creates a fast color transition (the same as adjusting the edge pad value in the Fountain Fill dialog box).

7. Arrange your pieces on the rectangular wall to complete the graffiti. The next step is to riddle it with bullet holes! First, draw a rough circle with the Freehand tool. Next, switch to the Interactive Fill tool and drag from the top right to the bottom left. Then, click the Conical button on the Property Bar. This will give the shading of an indentation. Now, use the Ellipse tool to draw a circle in the center and give it a medium-gray fill. Duplicate the circle (+ key), offset the duplicate to the top and right, give it a solid black fill, and send it back one (Ctrl+PgDn). This is the hole shadow (an indentation is shaded in reverse compared to how extruded objects are shaded). Now select the original circle, duplicate again, and move the duplicate to the bottom and left. Shade it white, and send it back one to create a gleam. Select all of the bullet-hole objects and group them (Ctrl+G), as shown in Figure 3.8.

**Figure 3.8**

The Interactive Fill tool creates a fountain fill across the bullet-hole shape. Clicking the Conical button changes the fill type, which provides convincing shading when teamed with a circle group.

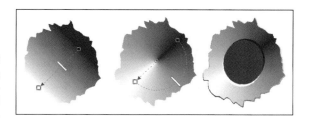

8.  Arrange your bullet-hole group on one end of the mural, duplicate it, and place the duplicate on the other end. Now Shift-select both and open the Blend dialog box (Ctrl+B), or use the Interactive Blend tool to create a blend between the objects by dragging. Reduce the Number Of Steps setting to 5, and click the Acceleration button to open that page. Here you can change the scatter of your bullets by dragging the Object Acceleration slider to the right or left. Click Apply to let loose a spray of bullets (see Figure 3.9).

**Figure 3.9**
The Object Acceleration option gives a staggered look to the bullet-hole blend.

9.  That finishes off the main graphic, but I wanted to add texture to make the image look more like graffiti. Select the rectangle with the texture fill and duplicate it (+ key). Now send it to the front (Shift+PgUp). On the toolbar, select the Interactive Transparency tool (it looks like a wineglass) and change the transparency type from None to Texture on the Property Bar. Drag the Starting Transparency and Ending Transparency sliders to adjust how much texture you want in your letters (see Figure 3.10).

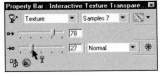

**Figure 3.10**
Use the Interactive Transparency tool and the Property Bar to adjust the opacity of the texture-filled box in front of the artwork to make it look like the art is painted on a wall.

10. For even more creative options, we can convert parts of the image into a bitmap to facilitate the use of special bitmap filters. (First save a copy of your file to disk before you convert anything to a bitmap, so you have a backup later.)

11. Select all of your text objects, but not the wall or the bullet-hole group. The easiest way to do this is to Select All (Ctrl+A) and then, holding down the Shift key, click on the wall and bullet objects to deselect them. From the Bitmaps menu, choose Convert To Bitmap. Change the

Color setting to RGB and Resolution to 300 dpi, and then enable the Anti-aliasing, Transparent Background, and Use Color Profile radio buttons. Click OK to "rasterize" (convert vector information into pixels) your artwork.

12. With your individual objects now a single bitmap, you can make use of the many filter effects on the Bitmaps menu. CorelDRAW 9 adds many "Creative" filters, but this example calls for Wet Paint, located on the Distort flyout. With this filter, you can make your artwork look freshly painted, complete with runny drips (see Figure 3.11). You can control how "runny" the paint is with the Wetness and Percent sliders in the Wet Paint dialog box.

**Figure 3.11**
Converting your vector artwork into a bitmap allows you to use special Bitmap effects filters, such as Wet Paint.

You will need to move the bullet-hole blend to the front (Shift+PgUp) on top of the transparent texture and keep them crisp. That's it! The results of this exercise can be seen in the digital color section as well as in the file called bulhole.cdr in the \Chapt03\ subdirectory on the companion CD-ROM. Load the file and fiddle with the Acceleration settings on the bullet-hole blend. Also, it is important to note the difference in how the Interactive Transparency tool Property Bar sliders work on a texture fill compared to the other types (such as Uniform and Fountain Fill). Open the file, select the semi-opaque texture object, and then select the Interactive Transparency tool. Now move the Starting and Ending Transparency sliders on the Property Bar to see how each affects the image. Have fun, you cyber-vandal!

**Figure 3.12**
If you convert text to bitmaps with the Transparent Background option, you can use filter effects while retaining a see-through look. You can stuff a copy of the background into a text object using the PowerClip feature, creating a "ghost" object, as with the big number 9.

## PROJECT Blurry Type

In a strange trend, many artists are creating images that are actually difficult to read and purposely out of focus. As more and more design is computer generated, you'll notice a backlash with images that attempt to look anything but. Artists strive for a non-computer-generated feel with images that are purposely out of focus and designed to look out of registration, poorly photocopied, or scratchy. The irony, of course, is that computers just make these images easier to create!

Using the functions available on the Bitmap menu, we will reverse traditional logic and create objects in the foreground that are out of focus, with faraway images crystal clear. This reverse-logic brings emphasis to a background image, manipulating and directing your reader's eye at your will (see Figure 3.12).

---

### Images on the Go

Corel has literally hundreds of useful photo collections to choose from on CD format. You can purchase these images as whole collections, or even one by one on an as-needed basis. On the Corel Web site (**www.corel.com**), you can gain access to the company's online image and clip-art library (Corel "studio"). While the CD collections are a great bargain, the real lifesaver is the immediate ability to locate and download images as you need them. This is particularly handy when you need an image to finish a project with an impending deadline. Nothing satisfies like instant gratification! The time you save using the powerful search functions on the Web site to locate images is also a value-added feature. If you budget your project wisely, you can locate, download, and exploit images as needed—and save yourself a lot of time and hassle in the long run.

---

It is a popular design look, made easy with CorelDRAW. To fuzz your type, follow these steps:

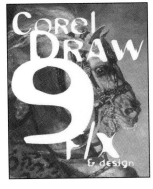

**Figure 3.13**

Import your background image and arrange your type pieces. Once the type is converted into bitmaps, you will not be able to enlarge them without losing resolution, so take some time on the layout.

1. Use the Artistic Text tool to set your type. This technique will work on any font (I used a freaky one called MonkeyCaughtStealing from Garage fonts). Arrange your type on the page in the size and position you desire. This technique involves converting the type into bitmaps, so you need to spend some time working out the layout; after the pieces are converted, resizing them can result in low-resolution images (which are bad, bad, bad). Import an interesting background image to help you lay out everything to your liking before you proceed. I used an image off the Masters 1 CorelDRAW photo CD. Import the image and arrange the text in a way that balances the image, keeping the area of focus open for later emphasis (see Figure 3.13).

2. Draw a rectangle, with no outline or fill, around each individual text object. This becomes a logical bounding box for the bitmap conversion step. If you do not provide a boundary, CorelDRAW will use the object size to calculate the bitmap size. This is fine, except that we need some breathing room beyond the edges of the text so we can use the Blur filter. If you don't provide a bounding box and use the Blur filter, the effect will end abruptly at the edges and look strange. (In CorelDRAW 9, you could use the Inflate Bitmap option to create this breathing room instead of drawing a bounding box, but in that case you could not easily control the size of the bounding box.) See Figure 3.14.

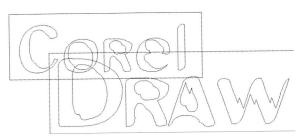

**Figure 3.14**

Draw a bounding box around each text element to define the limits of the bitmap. This extra area lets you use the effects filters with room to spare. (Overlapping boxes are not a problem, as you select only the text and its associated bounding box before converting to a bitmap.)

3. Select a text element and Shift select its bounding box, and from the Bitmap menu, choose Convert To Bitmap. In the Convert To Bitmap dialog box, change the Color option to Grayscale (8-bit), or one of the color options if your text is in color; enable Anti-aliasing; and select Transparent Background. Set the Resolution value to one appropriate for your project (the resolution should be set to 300 for print and 72 for screen output), and click OK. After a few seconds, your image will be transformed into a bitmap (see Figure 3.15).

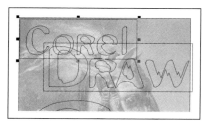

**Figure 3.15**
Use the Convert To Bitmap feature with the Transparent Background feature enabled to rasterize the vector art.

4. With the bitmap selected, select Gaussian from the Bitmap|Blur submenu. In the Gaussian Blur dialog box, drag the Radius slider to the right. The farther you drag, the more out of focus the type will be (see Figure 3.16). Click the Preview button so you can see how your text looks using different Radius settings. Click OK when you are happy with the blur effect.

**Figure 3.16**
Use the Gaussian Blur dialog box to make your type seem fuzzy and out of focus. The more blur, the less in focus it will seem.

5. Repeat this process for each text element (except the 9), varying the degree of fuzziness for each word to create the illusion of words scattered near and far. Images up close should have more blur than those far away. The concept of near and far is a bit blurry itself, however, as the background that is the farthest will also be the clearest! Experiment with the technique to get words at varied levels of focus (see Figure 3.17).

6. To give the image a darker feel, add a solid black rectangle over everything and give it a radial fountain fill transparency. Draw the rectangle and fill it black by clicking on the black on-screen color well. Then, select the Interactive Transparency tool and drag from the center out toward the edge. Now change from Linear Fountain to Radial on the Property Bar. Drag the outside control node to create the mood and shading to your liking (see Figure 3.18).

**Figure 3.17**
Scatter the words dimensionally by using different levels of the Gaussian Blur function.

7. To create the "ghost" effect in the number 9, we will use the PowerClip feature. First, in the Options dialog box (Ctrl+J), click Edit, disable Auto-Center New PowerClip Contents, and then click OK. The default Auto-Center setting will automatically align the contents of a PowerClip to its parent container, which isn't always what you want. With this feature disabled, you can control exactly where the contents of your PowerClip will be, a much more powerful option in my opinion. With the option changed, now select your big bitmap background. (In Normal View mode, hold down the Alt key and click on the background bitmap. If you don't hold down the Alt key, you will select the black rectangle with the transparency. The Alt key lets you select the object below the front object.) Duplicate it with the + key on the keyboard. Switch to Wireframe view, and then, from the Effects menu, choose PowerClip|Place Inside Container. Then, click on the number 9. Since the duplicate bitmap is in the same location, when you stuff it into the 9 object, you won't see anything. Use the Shift+PgUp shortcut to bring this PowerClip object to the front (see Figure 3.19).

**Figure 3.18**
A solid black rectangle becomes mood lighting when the Interactive Transparency tool transforms it into a radial fountain.

8. To make the ghosted text stand out a little better, use the Interactive Drop shadow tool. Drag across and down to reveal a shadow, then fine-tune it by changing the settings on the Property Bar. I changed the Opacity setting to 90 and the Feathering to 3 (see Figure 3.20).

**Figure 3.19**
(Left) A duplicate of the background bitmap, placed into the number 9 with the PowerClip feature, creates a "ghosted" character.

**Figure 3.20**
(Right) The Interactive Drop Shadow creates a feathered outline effect.

9. Arrange the text elements in front of or behind the transparent black block to highlight or shade the text. I ended up moving all the text elements in front of the transparency block so they would "pop" off the page better.

You can see the final result in this book's color section and also on the companion CD-ROM in the \Chapt03\ subdirectory—the file is called blurry.cdr. The Interactive Shadow Shape and Transparency should still be "live" if you want to select and manipulate the settings, but the text is already converted to bitmaps. You can still select the bitmaps and add more "blur" if you want, or start over with your own text.

**Figure 3.21**

Using the Interactive Transparency tool, you can de-emphasize text and make it more subtle. The Interactive Drop Shadow tool can be manipulated to create "glowing" text effects.

**Figure 3.22**

Arrange your text elements over a background image.

## PROJECT Subdued and Glowing Type

This style again falls in the category of reverse design psychology, where text elements are de-emphasized. Instead of making them blurry and out of focus, this time you make them more subtle using the Interactive Transparency tool. The secondary shapes are again created with the Contour tool; however, you must take additional steps to prepare the pieces because of their transparent nature. You can also use the Interactive Drop Shadow tool to create "glowing" text (see Figure 3.21). To make your text transparent or glowing, follow these steps:

1. This time, the text elements will remain vector objects throughout the life of the project so you can continue to fine-tune the layout forever. Import (Ctrl+I) a background image and resize it to fit your page. I once again used an image from the Corel Masters 1 photo CD. The image was too small, so I drew a black rectangle behind it at my desired page size to create a black border my text could fall off. I filled this border shape with 100K and 35Y because I was working in CMYK color mode and preparing this piece for professional offset print output (Web page designers will not be concerned with ink or overlap, and will choose their colors from the RGB or the indexed color palette). The yellow acts as a "kicker," which helps large areas of black ink look darker. I chose yellow because the "transparent" text color is 20% yellow, so the areas where the two overlap will have the same colors (instead of, say, a cyan kicker, which would make a green tint where my text overlaps the frame). Set the type with the Artistic Text tool (I used a font called Serb on the top and Modern on the bottom), fill it with a neutral color such as pale yellow, and assign it no outline (see Figure 3.22).

2. Drag-select the top text pieces and copy (Ctrl+C) them (you'll need a copy later on). Select one of the top text elements and open the Contour docker (Ctrl+F9). Enable the Outside option, change the Offset setting to .03 inches, decrease Steps to 1, and then click Apply. Repeat this process with the same settings on the other two text elements (see Figure 3.23).

**Figure 3.23**

Use the Interactive Contour tool to generate a set of outline shapes.

3. Now drag-select all of these text elements and choose Arrange|Separate to "freeze" the live contour groups. Drag-select the two curves that make

---

**Is it Live?**

When you work within CorelDRAW, many effects stay "live" and recalculate often during the life of your design. Blend groups, for example, will redraw themselves should you change the size, location, or any other attribute of one of the parent shapes. The same live characteristics can be observed with extrude groups, lens effects, contour groups, and even polygons, ellipses, and rectangles. If you attempt to node-edit a "live" rectangle with the Shape tool, you will only be able to round the corners until you convert it to curves (Ctrl+Q). When you resize a live contour group, it will recalculate the image using the original settings, which will result in a new image with effects out of proportion compared to the parent shapes. If you can, it is a good idea to freeze live Corel effects. Not only will this avoid resizing problems, but it will also speed up screen refresh. Frozen effects are simple objects, where "live" effects are dynamic, recalculating, rebuilding, reshading groups of complex objects. Use the Arrange|Separate command to freeze blends, extrudes, or contours. Use the Frozen option on the Lens docker to freeze those effects, and use the Convert To Curves command to freeze envelopes, perspectives, deformations, polygons, rectangles, and ellipses.

---

up each word and combine them (Ctrl+L). This will punch out the inner curve from the outer, resulting in a solid outline shape. Repeat this on the other text objects. Paste (Ctrl+V) the original text objects and send them to the back (Shift+PgDn). Now you have two sets of shapes, the inside originals and the outside contour (see Figure 3.24).

**Figure 3.24**
Combine the contour shape with the original to get an outline object with a hollow center (shown in black). The original objects (in gray) can then shine through.

4. Now give all the pieces the same pale yellow fill (20% yellow) and no outline (right-click the "x" on screen to remove any outline). Select one of the outside contours and, with the Interactive Transparency tool, drag from the top of the shape down. This will create a fade from solid yellow on top to transparent on the bottom. Repeat this process on all three outline pieces (see Figure 3.25).

5. The inside shapes will get the exact opposite fill. Select an inside shape, and, with the Interactive Transparency tool, drag from the bottom up. Repeat for the other pieces (see Figure 3.26).

6. To get the bottom text to "glow," we will basically repeat the same process we used to get the ghosted number 9 in the previous tutorial, only with a few twists. First, duplicate the background bitmap (+ key), and once again stuff it into the text with the PowerClip|Place Inside Con-

**Figure 3.25**
Use the Interactive Transparency tool to fade the fill color in the outside pieces from solid yellow on top to transparent at the bottom.

**Figure 3.26**
Use the Interactive Transparency tool again, only this time reverse the fade-out logic to fade from transparent to solid in the inside pieces to finish the effect.

tainer feature from the Effects menu. Then, use the Interactive Drop Shadow to create a shadow effect that we can modify to become a "glow." Drag on your text with the Interactive Drop Shadow tool, just to the edge of your text. Don't worry what kind of shadow you create with the interactive tool—we are going to change the options on the Property Bar. For starters, make sure the shadow position is at x=0.0 and y=0.0. Next, change the Opacity setting to 85 and the Feathering to 10. Set the Feathering Direction option to Outside and the Feathering Edges option to Linear, using the pop-up menus on the Property Bar. Most important, click the down arrow next to the current color chip on the Property Bar and specify the color you want for your "glow." I clicked the Other button, then specified a 20% Yellow to match the other colors in the design (see Figure 3.27). That's it!

**Figure 3.27**
Modifying the Interactive Drop Shadow tool options on the Property Bar can give you a "glow" effect.

You can view the end results in the digital color section and also in the trans.cdr file in the \Chapt03\ subdirectory on the companion CD-ROM. You might want to load the file and experiment with the Interactive Transparency fills and Interactive Drop Shadow in realtime by moving the control points and watching everything rebuild. If you have a problem with the Interactive Transparency tool (especially during printing), select the fill and click the Freeze button on the Property Bar. That should fix any strange rendering anomalies.

## PROJECT Chrome Headlines

Chrome and metallic shading effects are by far my favorite. I love things that look like cold hard steel or shiny chrome. The enigmatic nature of these textures is that they don't really have any color but rather reflect the color of the world around them. So to get a convincing look of shiny metal, you need to create a "landscape" fill (see Figure 3.28).

**Figure 3.28**
The Interactive Fill tool allows you to create the look of a reflected landscape for a metallic shading effect.

While this effect is dazzling, it is really a snap to create. To create a metallic look using the Interactive Fill tool, follow these steps:

1.  First, set your type in a font that is "fat" enough to benefit from the metallic shading look. "Skinny" fonts don't have enough surface area to be interesting. The font I used is called Tiger Rag. Give it a 100% Cyan fill or a shade of sky blue that's to your liking.

2.  With the Interactive Fill tool, drag from the top down. This will create the default color blend from your original fill color to white (see Figure 3.29).

**Figure 3.29**
The Interactive Fill tool fades your fill color to white as the default.

3. Now drag from the black on-screen color chip to the center of your Interactive Fill tool control line and release the mouse to create a new color point. Repeat the process with the white on-screen color chip, dropping it above the black point. Drag the two points together to create the look of a "horizon" (see Figure 3.30).

**Figure 3.30**
A white point directly next to a black one on the Interactive Fill tool control line creates the look of a reflected horizon.

4. Now with the horizon in place, you can tune what kind of environment is being reflected. For a "hot" desert look, drop magenta and yellow in place of the top two color points to color the "sky" and brown on the bottom for the "dirt." Or choose your own color scheme (for examples, load the reflect.cdr file from the \Chapt03\ subdirectory on the companion CD-ROM).

5. Once you have your horizon reflection in place, it is easy to further play on the theme using the Interactive Extrude tool. First remove any outline by right-clicking the "x" on the on-screen color well.

6. With the Interactive Extrude tool, drag across your "chrome" text piece. You don't need to drag much—just enough to create an "active" extrude group—because then you can alter the parameters on the Property Bar.

7. On the Property Bar, click the Bevels button to open the Bevels dialog box. Then, select the Use Bevel and Show Bevel Only options. Adjust the Bevel Depth setting to your liking to create the look of cut reflective facets in your text (see Figure 3.31).

**Figure 3.31**
The Bevels option of the Interactive Extrude tool creates shapes that share the fill of the original object, creating the look of cut reflective facets.

8. For more depth and dimension, click the Lighting button and then click Light #1. This will add shading to your object and the facets (see Figure 3.32).

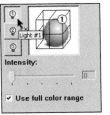

**Figure 3.32**
The Lighting option of the Interactive Extrude tool creates shading effects to suggest highlights and shadow.

9. If the effect of each bevel object having the same "horizon" color fill as the main text object doesn't appeal to you, you can control the colors of the bevels manually. Click the Color button on the Property Bar, then enable a different option than the first Use Object Fill default. For example, clicking the Use Color Shading button allows you to then select a highlight and shadow color manually for total control over how your text "shines" (see Figure 3.33).

**Figure 3.33**
The Use Color Shading button also creates effects that suggest highlights and shadow.

That's really all there is to it! With the Interactive Fill tool, you can create shading to simulate all kinds of reflected environments. Open the pierceme.cdr file from the \Chapt03\ subdirectory on the companion CD-ROM to see how you can modify the parameters of the Interactive Fill tool to create shading effects for tubular and round objects. Using the Radial Fountain Fill option in the Interactive Fill tool Property Bar lets you "curve" the horizon to match the spherical nature of a ball, while the Linear Fountain Fill is perfect for tubes and squares.

# Beyond f/x

The graffiti and type effects in this chapter are a great way to modernize your designs. Okay, admittedly not every project is screaming for a graffiti look, but multiple outlines and added texture are useful effects for many applications, such as logo design or interesting product layouts (a catalog with the products painted on a stucco wall instead of lying on a page, for example). The blurry, faded, and glowing examples are also fairly easy to create in CorelDRAW, making these new design ideas accessible without all the tedium that other programs require.

Using blurry type is a neat way to get a message across subtly without losing focus in the design. People are attracted to the extraordinary, and this kind of reverse-logic image—with the foreground blurry and background in focus—catches the eye in an almost subconscious way. It's like when you print the mirror image of a photo. Things look right at first, but somehow you know something isn't right, so you keep staring at the image until you consciously figure out the visual trick. You can combine this technique with another blurry concept, the speed blur (outlined in Chapter 18), for even more focus-changing tricks. For a more sophisticated audience, use subtle tricks that gain attention with a whisper, not a scream!

## Moving On

In this chapter, we used the Contour effect several times to create additional outlines for our text elements. We also used the Transparency functions to add texture or remove emphasis from our text. In addition, the blur effect came to our aid to fuzz out our text. The PowerClip feature made our text invisible by stuffing a copy of the background image inside it, then the Interactive Drop Shadow made this text visible with subtle shadow or glow effects. We also explored typographic metallurgy, making our text look like shiny chrome. All these techniques are useful to call attention to your headlines and certainly are not limited to the previous examples.

In Chapter 4, we put a few of these techniques to use, and then some. We'll see how the simplicity of computer-aided design is resulting in a new type of techno imagery. Using the automation features in CorelDRAW and borrowing images from 3D rendering software, this new style is seemingly haphazard and busy, but in the end becomes a balanced, workable design. Fire up the laser gun, watch a copy of *Blade Runner*, and get ready for some digital entropy!

# Chapter 4

# Digital Entropy and Media Madness

*This chapter explores the design possibilities of mixing all kinds of artwork (3D, geometric, computer-generated, hand-drawn) into your designs. "Floating" bitmaps, the Contour tool, Welding and Trimming, as well as the Interactive Distortion tool are examined.*

# Technology Collages

I am always fascinated by how new inventions can dramatically change our lives. Snowboards, a seemingly low-tech invention, have changed the entire ski industry, and imagine trying to live without a microwave (how did previous generations make popcorn, anyway?).

The same kind of dramatic mutation can be seen in the world of design. Computers and design power that was once limited to an elite few is now resting comfortably in the hands of millions. Design techniques that used to be slow and laborious now happen with a few mouse clicks. Even more frightening, the invention of virtual reality has artists producing objects and landscapes out of thin air, manufacturing realities as though they were gods creating universes.

Out of this evolving mass of techno-hysteria comes new kinds of designs that mix all types of media. Traditional cultural art is being incorporated into digital canvases with very cool results. On the other end of the spectrum, new designs mixing in text, vector, bitmap, and 3D information are popping up, with a unique sense of balance mixed into the mayhem. What was once alternative is now mainstream, opening up new doors and breaking down barriers for designers. "No rules" is the new rule, and this is an exciting time for artists.

In this chapter, we will look at new kinds of technology collages—combining text, vector, bitmap, and 3D information into one. In the first example, we play off a popular "gen-x" theme to create bright packaging art, exploiting the ease of use and power of the Interactive Fill tool, and we also introduce Artistic Text. Then we combine flat vector art with 3D objects, for a contemporary mixed-computer-media piece that is sure to catch your eye. Then, for you traditionalists, we mix hand-drawn illustrations with a hellish background made with the help of the new Twister option on the Interactive Distortion tool. After that, we use many new CorelDRAW 9 features and filters (such as the Object Sprayer and Convert Outlines Into Objects) for a fun color-barrage montage. Finally, we wrap up the chapter with a tour of the bitmap effects filters—available in both CorelDRAW and Photo-Paint—including a handy visual reference gallery. It's a chaotic hodgepodge of media mayhem that is just part of another day in the world of the contemporary computer artist.

## PROJECT Funky Fresh

A recent trend has been to incorporate images from the past into a high-tech feel of the present. The logo in Figure 4.1, which looks like a Tide detergent box, has found its way into many contemporary applications, including my own.

It is one of those graphics that you can see from across the room, and it always gets noticed. It is also incredibly easy to create, using the Interactive Fill tool in CorelDRAW on a series of duplicated and downsized circles. Follow these steps to incorporate that triple-exploding look into your own design:

**Figure 4.1**
Bouncing hard and loud, this image borrows from a popular detergent box for a bright, happy logo using the Interactive Fill tool.

1. Select the Ellipse tool and drag on the page while holding down the Ctrl key to draw a perfect circle, and left-click on the red on-screen color well to color it. Now select the Interactive Fill tool and drag in the circle to start a fountain fill, which defaults to white as the second color. Click the Radial button on the Property Bar to change the type of fountain fill from the default (see Figure 4.2). With the cursor, drag (click and hold the left mouse button) from the yellow on-screen color well, and drop (release the mouse button) on the center color point of the Interactive Fill control line (the little slider in the middle controls the midpoint setting). This makes a nice smooth color blend. Remove any outline by right-clicking the "x" box (no color) on the on-screen color palette (the "x" box on the on-screen color palette removes the fill color if left-clicking, and it removes the outline if right-clicking).

**Figure 4.2**
The Property Bar allows you to specify different options for the selected tool. For the Interactive Fill tool, you can change the type of fountain fill from linear to radial (shown), conical, or square.

2. To get a "harsh" color transition, drag and drop more color points onto the Interactive Fill control line. Drag and drop another yellow point along the line, and then drag and drop another red one. Now by sliding the points along the line, you change the way the blend works and looks. It takes a bit of finesse to move the points around and get the desired results (see Figure 4.3).

3. Select the circle with the Pick tool (tap the spacebar to select the Pick tool) and downsize it about 79 percent (watch the status bar as you drag) by dragging a corner-sizing handle inward while holding down the Shift key. Before you release the mouse button, tap the spacebar. This will create a duplicate circle and downsize it in one step. Because it is one step, you now can use the Repeat function (Ctrl+R) to create yet

**Draw or Paint**

While the power of object-oriented design in CorelDRAW allows for more flexibility, you don't need to learn a whole new tool set if you need to work with bitmaps in Photo-Paint. The programs share many tools (such as Interactive Fill and Image Sprayer), and they work essentially the same way in both programs.

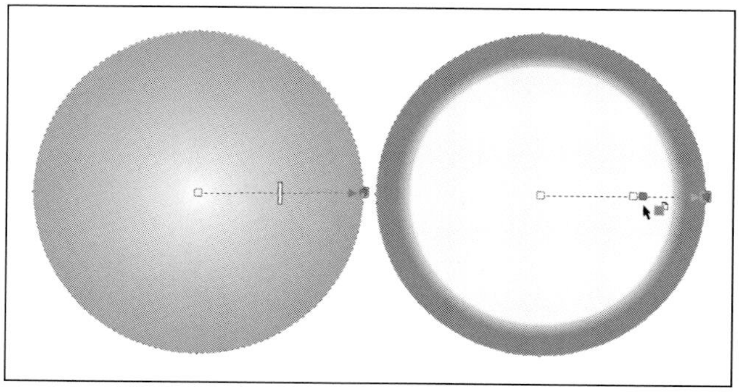

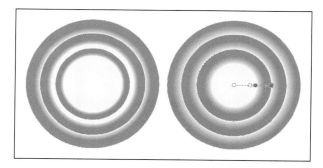

**Figure 4.3**

Drag and drop color spots from the on-screen palette to create and control a fountain fill using the Interactive Fill tool.

another downsized duplicate. You will create a downsized duplicate each time you press Ctrl+R, but for this project we need only a total of three circles. Use the Interactive Fill tool to move the points along each custom color blend to fine-tune the fill for each downsized circle shape (see Figure 4.4).

**Figure 4.4**

Duplicating and downsizing the circle creates the other color rings. To make things look right, tune each color blend with the Interactive Fill tool.

4. With the Rectangle tool, drag and draw a rectangle the size of the page, fill it with the same red as the circle blends, and send it to the back (Shift+PgDn).

5. Use the Text tool to set create some fat verbiage. Select the Text tool, click on the page to set a starting point, and then type your text. To change the font, drag to highlight the word you want to change, then you can choose any font you like from the Property Bar (I used a font called Swis721 Blk BT). Get new fonts from the Font list, or select your text with the Pick tool and open the Format Text dialog box (Ctrl+T), where you can control all aspects of your text (see Figure 4.5).

6. Double-click on your text with the Pick tool to reveal the rotation and skew handles. Click on the center-right skew handle and drag upward, to tweak the text from its standard layout into something interesting. Open the Outline Pen dialog box (first option from the Outline Tool flyout or F12) and enter a thick .153-inch black outline value in the Width box. Then click OK.

**To Pick or Not to Pick**

The process of changing fonts can be streamlined by first choosing the Pick tool—rather than highlighting your text with the Text tool—then choosing a font on the Property Bar. To switch from the Text tool to the Pick tool, press Ctrl+Space. Once you have the Pick tool selected, it is easier to choose from the Property Bar's Font list or the Format Text dialog box. If you don't first highlight your text or choose the Pick tool, you can access the Font list and select a new font, but you will not actually change the font.

**Figure 4.5**
Use either the Font list from the Property Bar or the Format Text dialog box to change the typestyle (font) of your text.

7. Duplicate the text (+ key) and give the duplicate a thinner .111-inch white outline. This will make for a thin black outline around the heavy white one, which will make the main text stand out more (see Figure 4.6).

**Figure 4.6**
Stack a thinner white-outlined copy of the text on a thicker black-outlined version to achieve a multiple-outline look.

8. Use the Text tool again to set the smaller copy. I used the same font I used for the title, only smaller. Instead of long sentences, set the text as smaller chunks. Click on the desktop, type your word, then click somewhere else and type another. Do this so you can more easily manipulate each word independently of the others.

9. With the Pick tool, select one of your text elements and set it up with the correct typestyle, fill, and outline attributes. Give the text a white fill, and from the Outline Pen dialog box (F12), give it a thick .111-inch black outline. Select the Behind Fill checkbox and change to the squared corner option (see Figure 4.7).

10. When one of your text elements is set up correctly, simply select all of the text bits, then choose Edit|Copy Properties From (Ctrl+Shift+A). Now you can enable the Outline Pen, Outline Color, Fill, and even Text Properties options in the Copy Properties dialog box. When you've selected the options, click OK. Now click on the text that you went to the trouble to format. In a single click, all of the attributes of that one text object will transfer to the rest. Bonus!

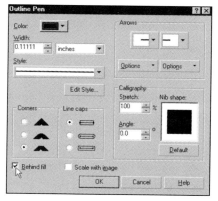

**Figure 4.7**
Use the Behind Fill and squared corner options from the Outline Pen dialog box to make other text stand out.

11. With the Shape tool, you can select an individual letter within a text string. Simply click the control node below the letter (see Figure 4.8) to modify that letter independent of the others in that text string. (You can also Shift-select multiple control nodes to select more than one letter, such as both the "C" and "D" in Figure 4.8.) Now you can drag the node to move just the selected letter without moving the rest of the word.

**Figure 4.8**
Use the Shape tool to select and change the font attributes of a single letter or letters within a text string.

12. With one or more letters selected in your text string with the Shape tool, you can also change the size, color, and even font choice for those letters. For size, style, and font, simply make new choices on the Property Bar. If you want a new outline or fill color for your selected letters, just right- or left-click on the on-screen color well. It's easy!

13. Arrange the text elements in a scattered yet readable layout over the triple blend.

Funky fresh, my friends! Once again, a bright and colorful image without even the hint of an aneurysm. The other elements in the design exploit techniques we already know about, like the "glowing" text from Chapter 3. The eye-poppin' goodness is goin' off in the color section, located at the center of this book. The file, called fresh.cdr, is located in the \Chapt04\ subdirectory of the companion CD-ROM, should there be anything you want to look at more closely.

# PROJECT Ducky

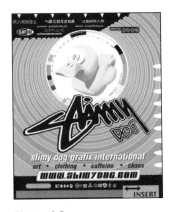

**Figure 4.9**

Mixing text, vector, and even 3D artwork into one design creates a contemporary barrage of visual information.

As cultural influences mix in the new world order, new styles continually evolve and emerge. The image in Figure 4.9, which seemingly has no purpose or direction, is heavily influenced by artwork I have seen from Japan in computer and gaming publications. The rich art history and quirky graphic style of Japan serve as a great source of inspiration. What I find so amusing about Japanese design is the insistence of using English names and phrases, which are often out of context or in an odd usage (Dew Dew and Chocolate Colon candy bars, for example!). With that in mind, this style looks right at home for promoting my own quirky graphics company.

This image mixes text and symbols into an interesting, albeit bizarre, image. International ads usually have text in many languages, including Arabic and Chinese symbols. I just used pieces from the corresponding Arabic and Chinese Symbol libraries, and I hope I didn't build words or phrases that are offensive in my random assembled symbol collections. (If so, I apologize profusely.) In any case, this is a fun graphic that incorporates vector art, text placed along curves,

## No 3D? No Problem!

While I like to mix and match images that include flat and 3D computer-generated graphics, as in Figure 4.9, you don't have to have a 3D modeling package to take advantage of this design style. You can get the same effect using real-world images instead of computer-generated models. For example, some images on the CorelDRAW clip-art companion CD work great. Locate the \Objects\ folder on your CorelDRAW distribution clip-art CD for some nifty "free-floating" photos. These "objects" are Photo-Paint bitmaps that are on transparent backgrounds, so, as with the 3D metafiles from CorelDream, you easily incorporate them into your designs. You'll find two rubber-duck photos on the objects\home\folder, for example, but something like the teddy-bear or toy car—or the propeller-head beanie that I found in the \objects\fashion folder, called Prophat.cpt—works well. Or you can scan your own photos, manipulate them in Photo-Paint, and copy and paste them into your CorelDRAW image. The point is to juxtapose a dimensional, "popping" 3D piece of artwork, either real or rendered, to contrast to the other flat design elements. I have had equal success with using photos instead of computer-generated artwork, so the preference is yours.

If you do not own 3D modeling software, you can get great results using real-world images instead of computer-generated objects.

**Note:** If you are not upgrading to CorelDRAW 9 Linux from CorelDRAW 8 Windows, or if you do not have Corel-Dream, skip to Step 6 and also check out the sidebar, "No 3D? No Problem!"

and 3D objects linked "live" via the use of metafiles. This 3D feature adds tremendous power and flexibility when incorporating 3D files into your CorelDRAW designs. Next, I'll describe how to mix vector and 3D images into one design.

First, you must convert a CorelDream file into a file format that is more flexible. On the CorelDRAW clip-art CD you'll find a directory called 3Dmodels, which has tons of objects from which to choose. I found the rubber ducky in the \3dmodels\home subdirectory on the CorelDRAW 7 clip-art CD. (You'll find "premade" files in the \3dmodels\3dmf\ folder on the CorelDRAW 8 CD; these files do not require this conversion process, and you can import them directly into CorelDRAW.) To convert a CorelDream file into the necessary 3DMF format for use in CorelDRAW, follow these steps:

1. In CorelDream, open the 3D model file, which will appear in a box on the screen. You don't have to know CorelDream to pull this off (I am a Dream novice, for sure). With your ducky on the screen, choose File| Export. Change the Save As type to 3DMF file (means 3D Metafile), enter the filename, and click Save. That's it. Exit the complex and intimidating world of CorelDream and return to the comfy confines of CorelDRAW!

2. In CorelDRAW, import (Ctrl+I) the 3DMF file, changing the file type to 3D Model to display it. You will see our pal in the default view—in this case, from the top right. You'll also see the 3D Toolbox and Property Bar set to 3D model options (see Figure 4.10).

**Figure 4.10**
You can manipulate a 3D metafile in CorelDRAW with the 3D Toolbox and the Property Bar.

3. Use the magnifying glass to zoom in on the ducky by dragging to the left or up (dragging down or to the right zooms out). Click on the 3D Rotate tool, which will surround the object with a ring in each axis. Dragging a ring will spin the object around in that plane. This interface lets you easily spin the ducky around to face you (see Figure 4.11).

4. In addition to the position and size of the 3D object, you can also control light and shadow effects if the default Ambient lighting doesn't appeal to you. Click the Distant/Ambient button on the Property Bar with the ducky selected. Change the type to Spot, and then click on

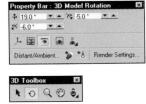

**Figure 4.11**
Use the 3D Rotate interface to spin the ducky around.

the + button to add a spotlight. Now you can enable shading and even change the color of the light. Illuminate the figure to your tastes and click OK when finished. You can then manipulate the spotlight within the mini-3D scene by using the movement and rotation tools in the 3D Toolbox window. Figure 4.12 shows how the ducky ended up after my manipulation of the 3D interface within CorelDRAW.

**Figure 4.12**
Use the Property Bar's many 3D features—including lighting, shading, and rendering options—to get the highlights and shadows just the way you want them on your 3DMF object.

5. When finished, click on a blank area of the desktop with the Pick tool to exit the 3D editing mode. 3D objects like this act like bitmaps with clear backgrounds (like the "objects" mentioned in the sidebar), so you can add CorelDRAW objects on top of or underneath them with no sweat. When we are ready to print out this image, CorelDRAW will render the 3D information as a bitmap automatically.

6. With your ducky in place, draw a perfect circle around him with the Ellipse tool. Duplicate (+ key) and enlarge the circle with the sizing handles and move it down off-center. Use the Interactive Blend tool (from the Interactive tool flyout) to drag between the two circles and create an active blend. Use the Property Bar to modify the blend. Change the Number of Steps setting to 20. Then, click Object and Color Acceleration and adjust the Object Acceleration sliders to make the circles closer together at the center (see Figure 4.13).

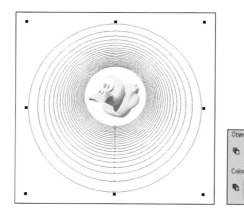

7. Select the ring-blend group and choose Arrange|Separate, then select Arrange|Ungroup All. Now, combine the objects (Ctrl+L) to create solid ring shapes. Use the Rectangle tool to draw a rectangle for the page limit.

8. For some strange reason, I wanted to hack off the top-left sections of the rings. If you feel the same way, begin by drawing a shape using the Bezier tool. With your newly drawn trim-shape selected, choose Arrange|Shaping|Trim. In the Shaping docker, disable the Leave Original options, click Trim, and then click on the rings (see Figure 4.14). This hacks off the corner.

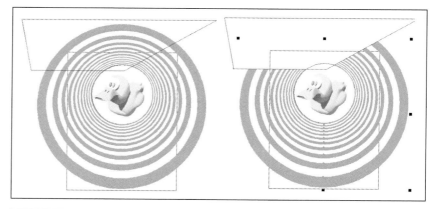

**Figure 4.14**
"Freezing" the blend lets you
combine the circles into a
multiring shape. The odd shape
across the top (on the left) is
used to cut away a section of the
rings using the Trim option of the
Shaping docker (on the right).

9.  Give the ring objects an orange fill and no outline. With the Interactive Extrude tool (also from the Interactive tool flyout), drag on the ring shape, but not far (dragging with the Interactive Extrude tool controls the direction and the depth of the created "extrusion"). Use the Property Bar to fine-tune your extrude group. Change both the x and y Vanishing Point coordinates to zero, so the extrude shapes point toward the center of the page. Click Color (looks like a color wheel), then click Use Solid Color (the center top button in the pop-up). Now click on the drop-down arrow next to the color chip and select a burnt orange color (see Figure 4.15).

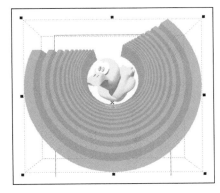

**Figure 4.15**
The Interactive Extrude tool adds depth by creating new 3D-looking shapes, with the solid fill color assigned using the Color option on the Property Bar.

10. Choose Arrange|Separate to allow independent control over your extrude shapes. Give the front rings a pink .023-inch outline. (Part of this look is created by using many colors from a very similar palette—in this case, light and dark tones of orange.)

11. Fill the page rectangle with black and bring the ducky to the front (Shift+PgUp). Now draw some more circles behind the ducky, and you have finished the basic page layout (see Figure 4.16).

12. The shapes around the ducky are pizza slices with a white circle on top to hide a large portion of them and to make the objects look like arced rectangles. Draw a circle with the Ellipse tool, then use the Shape tool to drag the control node to the right, on the *inside* of the circle, to create

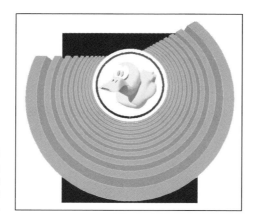

**Figure 4.16**
Arrange the elements on the page and separate the extrude elements so you can give only the front objects an outline.

a pizza slice. Duplicate and color the pizza slices in the same orange tones, throwing in a black one here and there for contrast. To create the solid and dotted arcs, use the Shape tool to drag a circle node on the *outside*, which creates an arc line (see Figure 4.17).

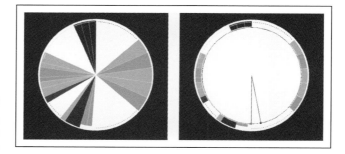

**Figure 4.17**
Create circle slices and arcs by dragging the control node on an ellipse with the Shape tool.

13. Some text in the circle area looks interesting. Draw a circle and then switch to the Text tool. Drag the pointer over the circle, and it will change from crosshairs into a bracket shape. When the pointer is over the circle and a bracket, click; when you type, the letters will be centered on and follow along the top arc of the circle. Cool! Or you can type the text first, then Shift-select both the text and the circle, and from the Text menu, select the Fit Text To Path option. Now you can change the placement of the text with the options on the Property Bar, so you can place the text on the bottom, on the inside, or on the outside, and even choose different letter orientation (see Figure 4.18).

14. To add the busy array of images, open the Symbols docker (Ctrl+F11). Drag and arrange a mixed jumble of pieces to create that international-communication look. Use characters from Japanese, Korean, and Arabic alphabets to get a real global village feel.

The rest of the design is pretty straightforward. I arranged all kinds of symbols and text around the page to make for a busy but interesting ad design. The

**No Symbols?**

If you can't locate a symbol set in your Symbols docker (Ctrl+F11), you can use the Custom option of the visual installer to add selected symbols. Use the printed clip-art reference manual to pick and choose which symbol sets to install. Don't install too many, or your system performance can suffer.

**Figure 4.18**
After you select the Fit Text To Path option, the Property Bar gives you many options for arranging text along a curve, or in this case, a circle.

even-spaced cutouts along the edge and top of the card are just two white shapes blended together using the Interactive Blend tool. The big logo in the center is a scanned image of a marker-drawn word, converted to vector artwork using Corel Trace, then skewed with the Perspective tool. When finished, all of the pieces were constrained into the page rectangle using the PowerClip function. (There are many references and tutorials throughout this book that will give you more information on Corel Trace and PowerClip; please see the index.)

You can see this image in this book's color section or in the ducky.cdr file nestled in the \Chapt04\ subdirectory on the companion CD-ROM. Due to technical and legal hassles (I cannot redistribute unaltered Corel clip art, which is what a 3DMF file essentially is), the ducky image in this file is just a bitmap. You can open your own copy of CorelDream and create a new 3DMF file on which to experiment in CorelDRAW using the 3D functions. Or you can find another 3D object source or use any other real-world photo to get the effect. You can load the file to pick apart the design, but first you will have to select the object and then use the PowerClip|Extract Contents function to manipulate anything.

## PROJECT 4th Dimension

I think it is safe to say that Norman Rockwell wasn't exactly a big influence on my artistic style. If you guessed Salvador Dali, Robert Williams, Hans Rudi Giger, Edvard Munch, Albrecht Dürer, or Hieronymus Bosch, you would be much more on the mark. I draw inspiration from all kinds of artwork, sometimes as a spoof, often just as a starting point.

The nightmarish vision in Figure 4.19 is another example of mixing classic Gothic gargoyle-type images with computer-generated effects. It is also a mixture of low-tech, hand-drawn images brought to life within CorelDRAW's high-tech, automated, digital canvas.

The background is the result of mixing the Twister effect and a texture fill, while a lens effect alters the image within the chain portal. It is the kind of art that would be too tedious to render by hand; by mixing in scanned ink images, however, you can maintain a traditional cartoonish feel while still

**Figure 4.19**

Mixing hand-drawn ink images with a plethora of CorelDRAW effects— including texture fills, a lens, and the new Interactive Distortion tool with the Twister option—creates a nightmarish vortex into the unknown.

exploiting high-tech computer effects (like we started with in Chapter 2). Let's look at mixing technologies to create whirling vortex scenes.

The centerpiece is a mixture of techniques we have already covered and artwork from my archives (which, with the purchase of this book, are essentially now *your* archives as well). The chain portal can be created with the techniques outlined in Chapter 8—blending link objects around a circle—or you can find an existing piece of art in the clip-art galleries. You will notice that the gargoyle guards are the same ones found in the Skull Angel image coming up in Chapter 9. I like to repurpose existing artwork whenever I can, because it can increase your profits. You've got to love CorelDRAW for this kind of simplicity.

1. The gargoyle is a group of objects containing a bitmap with Corel-DRAW shapes behind it to give it color (like the hydrant hound cartoon in Chapter 2). To manipulate an object within a group, you first need to select it independent of the others. While holding down the Ctrl key, click the main fill object within the group to select just that object (to verify that you have selected a single object within a group, the sizing handles will change from boxes to circles). Now open the Fountain Fill dialog box (F11) and assign a new body color scheme to the gargoyle (see Figure 4.20).

2. Press the Esc key to deselect the subgroup object and then select the gargoyle group. Duplicate it (+ key) and create a mirrored-image by

**Behind the Limits**

If you are having trouble selecting CorelDRAW objects behind a bitmap (even in Wireframe view), you need to disable the Treat Objects As Filled option. Right-click the Pick tool, then choose Properties. From the Pick Tool area in the Options dialog box, deselect the Treat All Objects As Filled option. The Pick tool defaults to Treat All Objects As Filled, which is really annoying! Disable this option to get more functionality out of the Wireframe view.

**Figure 4.20**

The Ctrl key lets you select a single object within a group so that you can manipulate it without first ungrouping or otherwise affecting the other objects.

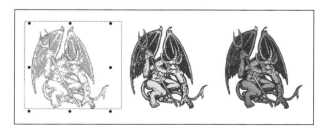

dragging the left-center control node right while holding down the Ctrl key. Arrange the gargoyles on either side of the chain gate. (I am the king of image swiping! I grabbed the f/x logo from Chapter 3 and plunked it into the center of the chains.) Use the "chrome headlines" technique from Chapter 3 to recolor the *CorelDRAW* and *9* using a red and yellow color scheme to match the future background (see Figure 4.21).

**Figure 4.21**
Bits and pieces come together to create a new image.

3. With the CorelDRAW clip-art book open to the "Crests" section, I spotted a file with some nifty design nuggets waiting to be mined. Import a file (File|Import) with cool knife objects from the \clipart\crests\misc directory off the CorelDRAW clip-art CD. Ungroup the objects and delete all but the pointy pieces. (If you want any pieces from these tutorials for your own designs, remember that you can also load this finished file off the companion CD and copy the bits you want.)

4. Now arrange these objects like rays of the sun around the chain circle, duplicating any objects that you need to finish the pattern. Use a white-to-cyan fountain fill (F11) to create a random reflection in the pieces. Create one side and then duplicate and flip for the other (see Figure 4.22).

**Figure 4.22**
Pieces from a clip-art crest are recolored and arranged to use in the new image.

5. The bat is an illustration I created just for this image, so it isn't all borrowed or stolen. This image was scanned and colored just like every other black-and-white bitmap in this book (by now you must notice a

trend in my design style). You'll notice one difference: Because the wings need to be behind the chains and the head in front, the image actually includes two bitmaps. The second bitmap had the areas behind the chains painted away in Photo-Paint using a white brush. (If you need to change a bitmap while in CorelDRAW, simply choose Bitmap|Edit Bitmap, which will launch Photo-Paint for you and let you edit the bitmap. Or you can copy and paste the bitmap into Photo-Paint and back into CorelDRAW when you've finished.) The bat is made up of a CorelDRAW shape filled with color and the black and white bitmap, which are grouped and behind the chain. On top of the chain are the pieces to colorize the face and then the bitmap with the areas painted away, resulting in the back/front illusion (see Figure 4.23).

**Figure 4.23**
A duplicate of the bat bitmap, with areas painted away, is in front of the chain objects, while the original is behind.

6. Now it is time to create the spinning vortex shape. First, draw a perfect circle with the Ellipse tool. Now, with the Shape tool, create a thin pizza slice by dragging the control nodes on the circle to the inside of the circle. With the Pick tool, first convert the object to curves (Ctrl+Q), and then change the axis of rotation to the top-center of the object (double-click the object, then move the little axis of the rotation target to the top-center of the object). Now spin the pizza slice to the right, then tap the spacebar to create a duplicate. Since this once again is considered a single action, pressing Repeat (Ctrl+R) over and over will create the "wheel spoke" design (see Figure 4.24).

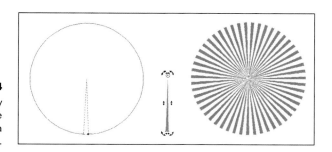

**Figure 4.24**
Create a spinning wheel by duplicating and spinning ellipse slivers made by dragging on a circle with the Shape tool.

7. Randomly delete every fourth spoke or so to create open areas in the "vortex." Drag-select all of the remaining spinning wheel objects and combine them (Ctrl+L).

8. Now select the Interactive Distortion tool from the Interactive tool flyout. On the Property Bar, click the Twister Distortion button, type "350" in Additional Degrees, press Enter, and stand back. Unleash the beast and watch it swirl! Finally, convert the vortex to curves (Ctrl +Q) (see Figure 4.25).

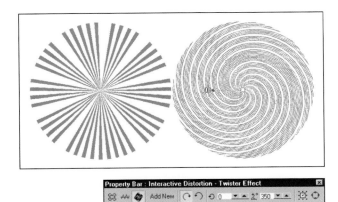

**Figure 4.25**
The Twister option on the Interactive Distortion tool Property Bar spins the object into a vortex illusion.

9. Fill the vortex shape with a custom color blend using the Interactive Fill tool; use an alternating yellow-red pattern. With the vortex shape selected, choose Arrange|Shaping|Intersect. Select only the Target Objects Leave Original option. Then, click the Intersect With button and click your rectangular page border object. This will limit the vortex shape to within the desired page size (see Figure 4.26).

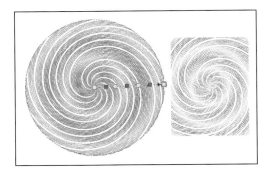 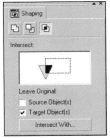

**Figure 4.26**
Color and trim down the vortex shape to fit within the page.

10. Arrange the new vortex shape and page frame behind the ghoul gate. Use a yellow outline on the vortex object to make it stand out more, and fill the page frame with a texture fill.

---

**Big as All Get Out**

When you export (Ctrl+E) a CorelDRAW file as a bitmap, the page size is determined by the largest object. For this reason, if you create a very large circle shape (as a guide for text or what have you), even if that object has no outline or fill attribute, CorelDRAW will create your bitmap as big as this huge overhanging object. To make an object "invisible" during the printing or export process, stick it on its own layer, then turn off the print attribute for that layer. Choose Window|Docker|Object Manager to open the Object Manager docker, where you manage layers. Then from the Object Manager Options flyout, choose New Layer. Then, select your object and drag and drop it onto the new layer name in the Object Manager. Now click the little printer icon to toggle off the Printable option, so any objects on this layer will not print or export. Other options for each layer that you can toggle on and off are Visible, Editable, and Master. If you set a layer as "Master," its contents will appear on all layers, so be careful with that one!

---

11. From the Fill Tool flyout, open the Texture Fill dialog box and change the Texture Library setting to Styles. Browse the list until you find Mineral, Cloudy 2 Colors. Select it, change the mineral colors from brown and cream to purple and yellow, and click OK. (For abstract backgrounds, you can leave the default Texture Fill values; to avoid chunky images, however, increase the values found in the Texture Options dialog box, which you access by clicking the Options button.)

12. To change the mood in the area inside the chain, draw a circle behind the gate and in front of the background and open the Lens docker (Alt+F3). I used a Transparency lens, filled purple and given a 50 percent transparency rate. You could make things even crazier with another lens choice, such as Invert or Heat Map.

This image, in its dizzying brilliance, can be seen in this book's digital color section and can also be found in the \Chapt04\ subdirectory on the companion CD-ROM; the file is called 4thdimen.cdr. Load the file and practice selecting an object in a group and recoloring the gargoyles. Try changing the lens shape to make the area inside the chains more or less wild. Also, you can dramatically change the mood by recoloring the vortex shape and the background rectangle. Go nuts and use the pieces to realize your own twisted visions. That's the advantage of mixing old art in a new computerized environment: unlimited potential.

## PROJECT Digital Daisies

CorelDRAW 9 has quite a few new features. The image in Figure 4.27 uses new bitmap effects filters, in addition to the new Object Sprayer, the new Interactive Mesh Fill tool, and the new Convert Outline To Object feature.

Some of these new features are very valuable additions to the already powerful tool set, while others may not immediately seem as useful (Chapter 8 has more on the Object Sprayer). Here are a few quick ideas on how to use these new features in your own designs:

**Figure 4.27**
CorelDRAW 9 offers a plethora of new features and effects to make creating eye-popping images in a snap.

1. Start with a bitmap image that you wish to make "artsy" using the new bitmap filters (I used a daisy image, but these effects filters work equally well on scans of family members). Work in Wireframe view to keep things speedy and easy to see.

2. Using the Rectangle tool, draw a perfect square (hold down the Ctrl key while dragging). Duplicate and arrange the square so that it divides your photo into as many areas as you wish, such as the four quadrants in this example (see Figure 4.28).

3. Now select your bitmap and duplicate it (+ key). Choose Effects|Power-Clip|Place Inside Container, then click on one of your squares. This should stuff the image into the square.

4. Select the PowerClip Rectangle, remove any outline (right-click on the on-screen "x" at the top of the palette) and convert it into a bitmap. Choose Bitmap|Convert to Bitmap to open the Convert to Bitmap dialog box. Here, set the Color option to RGB, as some filter effects simply will not work on CMYK (this holds true for most third-party filters). Specify the Resolution option for the minimum that is appropriate for what you are doing (massaging bitmaps takes plenty of memory and processor time, so the smaller the bitmap, the better). Select the Anti-aliasing and Use Color Profile options, and then click OK.

5. Now that your original bitmap has been isolated into a smaller section, changing it with an effects filter will create a dramatic contrast compared to the original. Select your isolated section, and choose a filter that you like from the Bitmaps menu (use the gallery in the digital color section to speed up the selection process; for a complete visual reference to all of the filters, log on to the CorelDRAW f/x Web site at **www.slimydog.com/corelfx9**). The selections under the Art Strokes flyout, for example, are a great way to get a "hand-drawn" look. I chose Color Transform|Halftone for this example (see Figure 4.29).

**Figure 4.28**
Import a photo and prepare to divide it up by drawing four squares.

**Note:** If your bitmap is not in perfect alignment after the PowerClip|Place Inside Container process, you need to disable the Auto-center New PowerClip Contents option. Open the Options dialog box (Ctrl +J), then click the Edit option. On the Edit page of the Options dialog box, locate and deselect the Auto-center New PowerClip Contents checkbox.

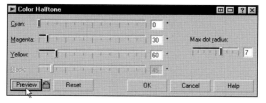

**Figure 4.29**
The Color Halftone Bitmap effects filter transforms the area of the bitmap isolated in the smaller duplicate.

6. That's really the whole process! Repeat Steps 3 through 5 two more times, for a total of three artistic interpretations using the bitmap effects filters. For added contrast, I like to juxtapose the artistic versions next to the "real" original.

## Phat Outlines

The wild text in Figure 4.27 takes advantage of the new Convert Outline To Object feature, located under the Arrange menu. This feature is a great addition, as anyone who ever wanted something other than a solid-colored outline will attest to. Here is how it works:

1. Create your object to which you want to give the "wild" outline effect. In my example, I use a text block, already tweaked with the Interactive Envelope tool.

2. In the Outline Pen dialog box (F12), specify a thick Width value of .111 inches, and also select the Behind Fill option (so the outline does not rest on top of and obscure the text object). Click OK to close the dialog box.

3. Now choose Arrange|Convert Outline to Object (Ctrl+Shift+Q). That's it! It will not look like anything has happened to your artwork in Normal view, so switch to Wireframe view to see exactly what is up. Your original object now has no outline attribute, and a second set of objects has been created to simulate the thick outline look (see Figure 4.30).

4. With the "outline" now a group of objects, you are free to fill them with any color or effect you want. I used the new Disco Nightmare option found in the Samples 9 Library in the Texture Fill dialog box to get a

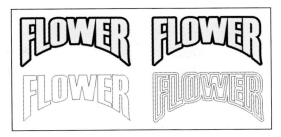

**Figure 4.30**
The results of issuing the Convert Outline to Object command are not obvious in Normal view (left) but dramatic in Wireframe view (right).

wild color scheme in my "outline." You can use such tricks as fountain fills, bitmap patterns—you name it—in these new outline shapes.

## Griddle Me This

To get the interesting multiple-color background shading in my design, I made use of the new Interactive Mesh Fill tool. This feature works much like the Interactive Fill tool, except that it is based on a rectangular grid of color points rather than a line. It works this way:

1. With the Rectangle tool, draw a rectangle the size of your page for your background object.

2. Locate the Interactive Mesh Fill tool on the Interactive Fill tool flyout. When you select this tool, a grid will appear, with control nodes at each intersection point (see Figure 4.31).

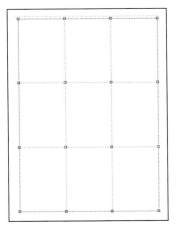

**Figure 4.31**
The Interactive Mesh Fill tool creates a grid of control points over your object.

3. Now simply drag and drop colors off the on-screen color palette to these control points to create a unique multicolor fill pattern. You can use as many colors as you wish, using as few or as many grid points to designate your colors. Cool, huh? (See Figure 4.32.)

4. For added control, you can double-click any of the grids to create a new color point. Or you can double-click an existing point to delete it. As

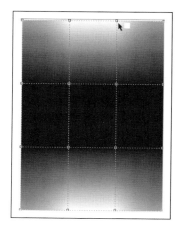

**Figure 4.32**
Create unique fill patterns by dragging and dropping colors onto the control points of the Interactive Mesh Fill tool grid.

with any other control node, you can move them around and modify the node type (smooth, cusp, symmetrical) on the Property Bar. It's a strange and wonderful way to create custom color blends that offers a staggering amount of control (see Figure 4.33).

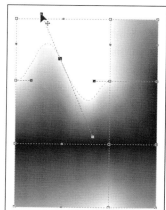

**Figure 4.33**
You can control the nodes with the Interactive Mesh Fill tool to create strange custom color blends.

## Splatter Paint

The last new CorelDRAW feature I used in the "flower power" image is the Object Sprayer, one of the modes available for the Artistic Media tool. When in Sprayer mode, you don't wield a brush or a pen, and you do not create a stroke or line. Instead, you scatter a series of objects across the page. These objects are from a Spraylist, which is a kind of mini-database filled with a collection of images. Each Spraylist has a theme (say, "bubbles" or "flowers"), so the collection of objects in that Spraylist has a similar theme. For example, if you choose the "leaves" Spraylist, you will create a scattering of the variety of leaf shapes contained in that Spraylist (see Chapter 8 on how to make your own Spraylist).

This tool has essentially two modes in CorelDRAW: assigning a Spraylist to a previously drawn curve or object, or using the brush to "paint" freehand, scattering images as you drag the cursor. I like the first option, which affords more control than my caffeine-induced, shaky-hand syndrome freehand drawing allows—and which is why I prefer to use the tool here in CorelDRAW and not Photo-Paint. (Photo-Paint, however, has better-looking images in the Spraylists, so be sure to experiment with the tool there as well.) Follow these steps to assign a Spraylist to an object:

1. Draw a shape, such as a circle, using the Ellipse tool.

2. Select the Artistic Media tool from the Curve tool flyout, then click Sprayer in the Property Bar.

3. Using the Artistic Media tool, click on the outline of the target object. Now click the drop-down arrow next to the currently selected Spraylist on the Property Bar and pick one from the drop-down gallery. That's it! (See Figure 4.34.) Modify the parameters of the current Spraylist (spray order, spacing, etc.) on the Property Bar.

### Freehand Object Flinging

To use the Object Sprayer in freehand mode (the same way it works in Photo-Paint), just select the Artistic Media tool from the Curve tool flyout, click Sprayer in the Property Bar, and go to town! Drag on the screen to scatter the images in the currently selected Spraylist. To choose another Spraylist, click the drop-down arrow next to the currently selected Spraylist on the Property Bar and choose another from the drop-down gallery.

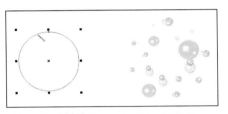

**Figure 4.34**

You can assign a Spraylist to any existing object (such as the circle on the left) by using the Artistic Media tool in Sprayer mode.

# Beyond f/x

Mixing media is hardly a new concept. Photos juxtaposed to computer-generated images and other design tidbits make up the majority of desktop publishing projects. The ability to mix up the mood a bit using the bitmap effects filters opens the doors to more "artistic interpretations" of otherwise ordinary photos. Instead of actual product shots, make things look a little more artistic by applying one of the Art Strokes filters (Watercolor, Sketch Pad, etc.). Or you can mix the "double-vision" concept of using the same image twice, but use a muted, "artistic" rendition of the main image as a background, with the original photo lying crisp and clear in the foreground. The potential is staggering!

Mixing real-world images with high-tech computer-generated artwork makes it more approachable. Without anything from the "real" world to use as a reference, a fully computerized design lacks scale or "approachability." Designs with only computer pieces might be perfect for some markets, but in general they seem "cold" or "mechanical" and may alienate a larger audience. Use real-world images to gain instant accessibility and to contrast the hard-edged, geometric feel of the computer and create a nice balance. You don't have to look far for real-world images to use in your designs. Scan textures and photos from around the house, such as leaves, fabric, your face, whatever, for use as interesting bitmap pattern fills or abstract backgrounds. In today's design climate, there are no rules, and mixing technologies just makes you look more skilled and your art more contemporary.

# Moving On

In this chapter, we explored the ever-evolving world of contemporary design. We looked at completely computer-generated artwork, which used text, vector, and even 3D images crammed into one canvas. We saw again how to work hand-drawn images into awesome CorelDRAW scenes, how to create unique background coloring, and how to take advantage of new features in the CorelDRAW 9 tool set to create artistically enhanced images.

Working in today's fast-paced world means managing the chaos of clashing technologies. Don't fight it—work with it! Traditional art and design philosophies, techniques, and tools should be a natural part of your modern art studio. Even if you were never skilled with "traditional" media, you can exploit the look using the new tools. Whenever you have to mix media, CorelDRAW will let you pull it off brilliantly.

In Chapter 5, we look at an even more common design task: creating photo collages. From merging images with subtle transparency effects to stuffing photos into hard-edged geometric shapes, we will cover a broad range of techniques. And the best part is there are no paper photos to cut out and no glue to spill. On to the montage!

# Chapter 5

# Photo Collages

*In this chapter, you'll learn creative ways to merge multiple images and photos into a single eye-catching and appealing graphic.*

# Mixing the Old and the New

Mixing scanned photos into computer designs is a staple of the contemporary art diet. It is an amazingly popular method of creating interesting images. This is because you need little illustration talent to mix photos together, and you can get great-looking graphics without too much effort. In addition, a much larger image base exists for photos than for vector-based clip art, with stock photo companies digitizing their inventory and even Corel Corporation offering literally thousands of photos for sale in its photo CD collections.

In a bit of an oxymoronic twist, you've probably noticed a trend to "antique" images, making them look old and weathered, and then using oh-so-high-tech and modern computer image-manipulation techniques to merge these photos together. What an enigmatic age we live in...

In this chapter, we endeavor to mix the old and new, creating collages of "old" bitmaps in modern ways. In the first example, we use the Interactive Transparency tool to smoothly mix photos and hard-edged elements in a catalog cover example. Then, we "antique" images with two-color (duotone) effects and merge the images together using transparency effects. In the third example, we use the PowerClip feature and lens effects to create a photo montage with a strong geometric feel. We then mix and match the lessons learned in this chapter in a pastel-colored Web home-page design. Finally, we use PhotoPaint and clip masks to get cool photo collage effects. It's fast and fun working with photos, offering "quick wins" in your design day.

## PROJECT Waves and Grids

Commercial artwork, while the bread and butter of most desktop designers, usually lacks the opportunity for introducing much pizzazz. Typical projects—such as product catalogs, brochures, Web pages, and the like—tend to suffer from small budgets and overbearing clients who limit your creative control. Top that off with "client math" (like when they supply 12 pages of information for an 8-page catalog), and it's all you can do not to flip out and squat in a tree humming show tunes.

Using the Interactive Transparency tool offers a way to help combine the less-exciting pieces of a design (such as graphs and charts) with other elements for a more appealing image as a whole. The image in Figure 5.1 uses this trick to make the data chart a part of the graphic. It also uses transparency tricks to merge the wave and graph elements. The result is an image that retains the pleasing aesthetics of the curling wave while also literally and figuratively communicating high-tech engineering.

This graphic is for the cover of a brochure. The fold is down the center, so the back half is on the left and the front on the right. The image uses only two colors (black and cyan), an effort to keep down the cost of printing. Establishing your project parameters initially keeps you from backtracking later. While

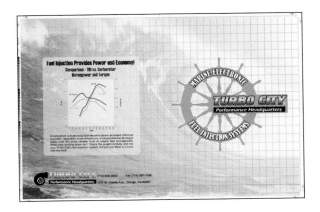

**Figure 5.1**
The Interactive Transparency tool helps merge individual elements—such as the graph, grid, and wave—into a uniform design.

you can "stack" images and adjust their relative opacity in Photo-Paint, it is easier to create and scale other elements in CorelDRAW as well as build the page as a whole. It's a matter of personal preference, and I don't like switching back and forth from Photo-Paint to CorelDRAW if I don't have to. Just keep in mind that essentially all of the bitmap features (such as Color Adjustment) in these tutorials are also available in Photo-Paint. Follow these steps to use the Interactive Transparency tool to merge elements into a single image in CorelDRAW:

1. Start by locating a graphic that is appropriate for your background. I like secondary images that are interesting but not overbearing. The wave is a photo from Corel's image library, available online or on the *Sampler II* Photo CD-ROM.

2. To make the wave a brighter blue, and to be in line with my project parameters, I removed all of the yellow and magenta from the photo. First, choose Bitmaps|Mode|CMYK to convert the image. CMYK offers more control than RGB, because you can reduce or increase the amount of each color ink independently of the others.

3. With your bitmap now CMYK, choose Effects|Color Adjustment|Level Equalization. In the resulting dialog box, you can specify the amount of each color in the image by using the Channel option. First, deselect the Auto Adjust option in the Channels area. Then, change to the Magenta Channel and remove all of this color by dragging the bottom-right slider to the left to reduce the Output Range Compression setting to almost 0 (see Figure 5.2).

4. Change the Channel option from the Magenta Channel to the Yellow Channel. Repeat the process of reducing the yellow ink, again by dragging the bottom-right Output Range Compression slider to the left. Click OK to remove the magenta and yellow from your wave graphic.

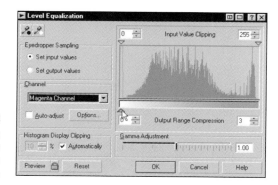

**Figure 5.2**
Use the Level Equalization dialog box to remove all of the magenta and yellow ink from your wave photo.

5. Now let's draw some objects on top of this bitmap. From the Object flyout, choose the Graph Paper tool. Right-click the tool and choose Properties to open the Options dialog box on the Graph Paper Tool page. Change the Number Of Cells Wide setting to 40 and the Number Of Cells High setting to 20. Click OK to close the dialog box.

6. Drag the Graph Paper tool across your desktop to create a 40×20 grid. In the Outline Pen dialog box (F12), give the grid a .013-inch cyan outline. Click OK to close the dialog box. Now you should have a nice grid on top of your wave image (see Figure 5.3).

**Figure 5.3**
The Graph Paper tool makes it easy to create a blue grid across your wave photo.

7. With the graph group selected, choose Arrange|Order|To Back (Shift+PgDn) to put it behind the bitmap. You can't use the Interactive Transparency tool on a group containing this many objects (800), so instead we will use the tool on the single wave photo bitmap object.

8. Click on your wave photo and select the Interactive Transparency tool from the toolbar. Now drag from the bottom-left corner to the top-right corner. This will fade the photo gradually from the bottom-left corner toward the top right, where it will fade out entirely to reveal the grid below. You can control how much or how little of the grid you see by moving the control points on the Interactive Transparency tool (see Figure 5.4).

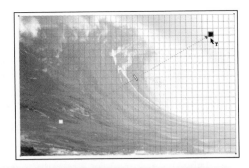

**Figure 5.4**

The Interactive Transparency tool fades out the wave photo to reveal the grid of boxes below.

9. Use the Rectangle tool to draw a square to designate an area for the comparison chart. Hover the Rectangle tool over a corner node and drag to round out the corners. Duplicate this rectangle (+ key) and downsize it by dragging a corner sizing handle inward while holding down the Shift key.

10. To get the uniform transparency for the product comparison chart area, instead of dragging the Interactive Transparency tool, modify the options on the Property Bar. Shift-select both squares, then click the Interactive Transparency tool. In the Property Bar, change the Transparency Type setting to Uniform, with a Starting Transparency Rate setting of 50. That's all there is to it. With one square on top of the other, the center area is almost pure white to display the comparison chart, but wispy enough to show the wave and other graphic below (see Figure 5.5).

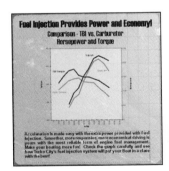

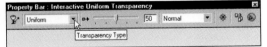

**Figure 5.5**

The Interactive Transparency tool with the Uniform Transparency Type option enabled creates a semi-opaque area for the comparison chart to sit.

The addition of some text and logos, which isn't worth walking through step by step, finished off this piece. It is the subtle effects created with the Interactive Transparency tool that make these otherwise standalone pieces merge into a more continuous graphic element. The finished result can be seen in the color section in the center of this book (hold the book sideways to see the image correctly) and can also be found in the \Chapt05\ folder on the companion

CD-ROM, in a file called marine.cdr. This is the actual file I used for the catalog project, at full size, so it is really big. I had to scale it down quite a bit to fit into the color section.

## PROJECT Historic Duotones

Using the Interactive Transparency tool is one way to help multiple images come together in a single pleasing composite. Another way to get the images to "match" even more is to convert each element to a uniform color scheme. The graphic in Figure 5.6 uses the same duotone settings for each element, then marries this coloring technique with seamless image transitions using the Interactive Transparency tool to create a solid composite. (Take a look at the image in the digital color section to see how everything looks in the same complementary bronze tones.)

To really hammer home the idea of an image composite, you can also physically merge all of the elements into a single bitmap. Once combined into a single physical image, you can add an artistic frame effect to the whole thing with a bitmap filter. Follow these steps to give multiple graphics the same duotone coloring and merge them into a single physical bitmap in CorelDRAW:

**Figure 5.6**
Giving each element the same duotone settings creates a like color scheme, which, along with the Interactive Transparency tool, makes for a seamless image collage.

1. Once again, start by collecting images for your photo collage. Scan your own photos. (This project presents some techniques that are perfect for making contemporary color photos match the look of antique photos. You can use these techniques to create cool photo collages for family reunions, Mother's Day cards, and so forth.) I turned to the online Corel image collection for an eagle and Statue of Liberty image, and I found a flag graphic in the CorelDRAW clip-art collection. You can mix and match vector clip art and photos using this technique, and all will merge together perfectly by the time we are through.

2. Use the Rectangle tool to draw a box to serve as a guide for your final image size. You will often work with elements that are bigger or hang beyond the edge of your page, but that is fine at this stage. Just use the boundary box to help you work out the layout of your design and to get a sense of balance and overall look and feel (see Figure 5.7).

3. With your elements basically in place, it is time to convert them all to the same color scheme. Select one of the photos and choose Bitmap|Mode|Duotone. This will open the Duotone dialog box, where you can recolor your image using "low color" techniques for a very stylized look. The types available vary the number of colors in your new coloring scheme, ranging from 1 (Monotone) to 4 (Quadtone). For this example, change the Type setting to Duotone, then click OK to convert the image (see Figure 5.8).

**Note:** If you don't like the default colors, simply double-click the color chips in the Duotone dialog box to open a color selection dialog box. Here you can choose a new color and create any color scheme you want.

**Figure 5.7**
Draw a boundary box to help you visualize how the pieces will fit together for your overall design.

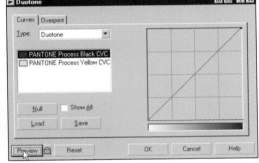

**Figure 5.8**
Use the Duotone dialog box to convert your full-color graphic to stylized "low color" images.

4. Repeat the process for all of your bitmaps, using the same duotone settings each time so that they share the same basic coloring scheme.

5. To get the vector artwork of the flag to match the recolored photos, you'll first need to convert it into a bitmap because the Duotone Filter works only on bitmaps. Select the vector group, and then choose Bitmaps|Convert To Bitmap to open the Convert To Bitmap dialog box. Change the Color setting to RGB and change Resolution to 300 dpi for print projects (or 72 for on-screen projects, such as for the Web). Finally, select the Anti-aliasing, Transparent Background, and Use Color Profile options. Click OK to convert your object into a bitmap.

6. With your vector flag now a bitmap, you can repeat the Bitmaps|Mode|Duotone process to recolor this image. You may see a warning dialog box telling you that the convert-to-duotone process will result in a loss of the transparent background, but ignore this warning and do it anyway. In my experience, the background has always remained transparent. Use the same colors in the Duotone dialog box as you did in Step 3 for your other images, so everything is colored the same.

**Recolor Vector Objects**

While you cannot transform a group of vector objects—such as the CorelDRAW clip-art flag—using the bitmap effects, you can recolor them as a whole using the Effects|Color Adjustment menu. For example, you can select a group of objects, then choose the Color Balance option from the Effects| Color Adjustment menu. Here you can use the RGB color channel sliders to bias the tint in your selected objects. Moving the Color channel sliders to the settings in Figure 5.9, for example, will give your vector objects a color scheme similar to the bronze-duotone bitmap effect discussed in this tutorial. Use this feature any time you want to slightly tweak the overall color of a group of objects, without having to recolor each piece individually. This feature will also work on a selected bitmap, making it a dang handy resource!

7. Use the Interactive Transparency tool to allow the smaller images to dissolve slowly into the background image. Drag the Interactive Transparency tool from the center of your photo outward. This will set up the default Linear Fountain transparency. Click Radial Fountain transparency on the Property Bar, then reverse the logic of the transparency by changing the color of the transparency control points on the object itself. Drag white from the on-screen color well and drop it on the black center of the Interactive Transparency control line on the object. Drag black from the on-screen color well and drop it on the outside white point of the Interactive Transparency control line on the object. This will reverse the default logic of the transparency, making the solid center fade out to clear (see Figure 5.10). Drag the control points around until you get the transition you like.

8. To get the same transparency effect on your flag object, choose Effects|Copy Effect|Lens From, then click on the bitmap you were working on in Step 7. After we have copied the effects to the bitmap, the Interactive Transparency tool control points will now be available on the bitmap, so you can easily fine-tune the settings with the Interactive Transparency tool by dragging the control points.

9. When you are satisfied with the layout and look of your photo collage, save a backup copy to disk (it's a good idea to save a project in stages so you can go back if needed, and, if you have clients like mine, you will always need to go back!). Now Shift-select all of the individual bitmap elements and also the background image, and then choose Effects|PowerClip|Place Inside Container. Click the resulting arrow on

**Figure 5.9**
Use the Color Balance dialog box to adjust the coloring of vector objects or even bitmaps. The settings shown here result in a bronze color scheme similar to the duotone settings used on the bitmaps in this project.

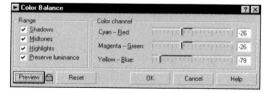

**Figure 5.10**
The Interactive Transparency tool, in Radial Fountain Transparency mode, can create a soft circular transition between your photo and the background.

## Battling Print Technologies

Both CorelDRAW and Photo-Paint can support many coloring schemes for whatever project you're working on. RGB is useful for on-screen applications, CMYK is good for full-color printing on paper, and Pantone is nice when you have specialty "spot" color print jobs. However, occasionally you will want to take advantage of a feature not available to your current coloring scheme. For example, the duotone coloring option supports only Pantone colors, so you will have to choose from this palette to use this feature. Lens and transparency effects typically are rendered using RGB technology, so this might conflict with other things you have going on in your design. Not to worry—you can mix and match all of the features and functions within CorelDRAW, within reason. For example, if you have anything destined for on-screen projects, you don't need to worry about palette conflicts, because CorelDRAW will take care of color conversions during the Export To Bitmap process (or you can always perform a screen capture). Also, if your design is headed for traditional CMYK printing on paper, you won't have a problem. CorelDRAW will translate any RGB or Pantone spot colors into the CMYK equivalents during the color-separation translation process for printing if you enable that option. However, if you have a specialized color need—such as creating a duotone to create specific color plates for printing—keep the color conflicts in mind, or you might have more color plates than you bargained for. The easiest way to keep the integrity of a duotone intact—and to limit the number of color plates produced—is simply to merge all of your elements in to a single RGB bitmap using the Convert To Bitmaps feature and then use the Bitmaps|Mode|Duotone command to convert that RGB image back into a true duotone. This approach will produce only the two color plates needed for offset printing. Or you can convert to other color spaces (duotone to RGB, or RGB to CMYK, etc.) as needed.

your boundary box to stuff all of the elements inside it. Right-click on the "x" in the on-screen color palette to remove any outline from the PowerClip rectangle.

10. Now, with the PowerClip rectangle selected, choose Bitmaps|Convert To Bitmap to open the Convert To Bitmap dialog box. Change the Color option to RGB, change Resolution to 300 dpi for print (72 for screen), and select only the Anti-aliasing and Use Color Profile options. Click OK to "merge" everything in your PowerClip rectangle into a single bitmap (see Figure 5.11).

**Figure 5.11**
The Convert To Bitmap feature converts all of the individual elements inside the PowerClip rectangle into a single bitmap object.

11. Now that all of your individual elements have been "homogenized" into a single bitmap, you can frame everything using a bitmap filter effect. With the bitmap selected, choose Bitmaps|Creative|Frame to open the Frame dialog box. This filter gives your bitmap an artistic frame effect, which you can choose from the Select Frame section of the dialog box. To change the options for the selected frame, click the Modify tab. Here, you can control the options for the selected frame. Change the Frame Color setting to white, and then modify the Horizontal Scale and Vertical Scale options until your image has the look you want. (You can click the Preview button to see how your changes affect the look.) When you are satisfied with the results, click OK (see Figure 5.12).

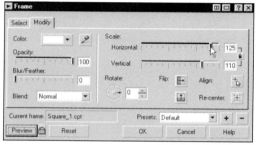

**Figure 5.12**
Use the Frame bitmap filter to get an artistic, ripped-edge look around your bitmap.

That's basically all there is to it. I slapped on some text to create the title, using white text with a drop shadow to make it stand out against the background. This image can be found on the companion CD-ROM in the \Chapt05\ folder, in the ushistory.cdr file, and in the digital color section. All of the individual bitmaps have already been merged into a single bitmap in that file, so you probably will want to try this technique on your own stack of digitized photos.

## Fat Frames

If you want to increase the size of your bitmap so that less of it is cut away with the Frame filter effect, use the Bitmaps|Inflate Bitmap|Manually Inflate Bitmap command. This will add an area around the bitmap, an effect similar to increasing the paper size in Photo-Paint. Or for a more visual approach to enlarging your bitmap, simply draw a larger rectangle around your image, with no outline or fill. Then Shift-select both rectangle and bitmap, and use the Convert To Bitmap command to merge the two into a larger bitmap with more image area on the edges. That way, you will have some breathing room when working with the frame filters.

## PROJECT Why Two Kay?

Boy, was 1999 miserable. I can't tell you how many people asked me "Is CorelDRAW Y2K compliant?" I would just grab these dolts by the neck and scream "Your graphics software doesn't care an inkling about the time of day or what year it is!" Why would it? There is nothing time sensitive about making pretty pictures that I can think of (unless you are working with acrylics and trying to finish before the paint dries).

The image in Figure 5.13 uses geometric shapes as a vehicle to organize, lay out, and even modify the photo elements into a single theme graphic. And, as you have noticed, the graphics community, as well as the rest of the world, has survived Y2K hysteria without incident!

I sometimes prefer strong geometric shapes to the wispy translucence that the Interactive Transparency tool offers when creating a photo collage, as in the previous two projects. You might prefer to stick to the soft transitions that the transparency effects provide. Or if you can't make up your mind (like me), skip to the next project, where both geometric framing and the transparency transition effects are used. My job is not to dictate your tastes and preferences, only to offer up different techniques and unique design options.

Now let's look at using a hard edge to define each photo by creating a unique custom-drawn shape in a photo-collage project:

1. Use the drawing tools to create custom geometric shapes. My design preferences are to use circles and pizza-slice type objects, but you can use any kind of shapes for your design. Drag the Interactive Blend tool between a large and small circle object to create a series of circles, as in the ducky example in Chapter 4. Choose Arrange|Separate, then select Arrange|Ungroup, so you can manipulate each circle independently of the others (see Figure 5.14).

**Figure 5.13**
Geometric shapes created in CorelDRAW offer a way to organize and modify your photos into a stylized layout.

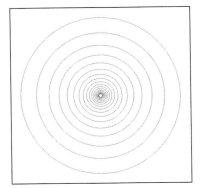

**Figure 5.14**
Use the Interactive Blend tool to create a row of concentric circles.

2. Select the outermost circle and duplicate it (+). With the Shape tool, drag a control node on the ellipse along the inside of the object to create a pizza slice. Make the slice as thick or as narrow as you like.

3. Double-click the pizza slice object to reveal the axis of rotation. While holding down the Ctrl key, drag the axis of rotation toward the pointy end of the pizza slice object, until it snaps into position at the end point. Now if you drag on one of the corner rotation handles, it will move in sync with the remaining whole circles, pivoting around on the axis of rotation point.

4. Duplicate (+) the pizza slice object nine times, and arrange the duplicates like rays of the sun shooting out of the center of the circle group (see Figure 5.15). Since you changed the axis of rotation on the first pizza slice object, all of the duplicates already have the axis of rotation in that same spot, making it easy to rotate the duplicates into position.

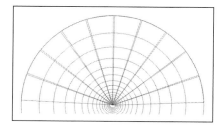

**Figure 5.15**
Duplicate and arrange the pizza slice objects to simulate rays from the sun.

5. Select all of the sun-ray objects and issue the Combine command (Ctrl+L). Now select the largest circle and Shift-select the next three smaller circles, for a total of four. Arrange|Combine these four circles (Ctrl+L), which will create two solid-ring shapes (see Figure 5.16).

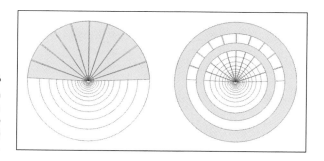

**Figure 5.16**
Combining the rays shapes (on the left in gray) creates a solid fan shape. Combining four of the circles (on the right in gray) creates two solid rings.

6. Select the combined sun-ray shape and choose Arrange|Shaping|Intersect. In the Shaping dialog box, deselect all of the Leave Original options, then click Intersect With. Now click on the two solid-ring shapes, which should result in the set of arched boxes (see Figure 5.17).

7. To enable you to place a unique photo in each of the arched boxes, choose Arrange|Break Apart (Ctrl+K). Draw a boundary box to help

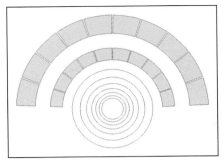 

**Figure 5.17**
Using the Intersection command on the sun-ray shapes and the solid-ring objects results in a set of arched boxes.

you visualize the page, and delete any of the arched boxes that are outside your image area.

8. Now you need a bunch of photos to stuff inside your arched boxes. Use the Import command (Ctrl+I) to load multiple images off the Corel-DRAW clip-art CD, or from another source (or use your scanner or digital camera to digitize your own personalized images). I found a bunch of images on the CorelDRAW clip-art CD-ROM, in the \business and the \com_tech folders. Hold down the Ctrl key to select multiple files, then click Import.

9. The screen will show the Import sizing cursor, which looks like the top-left corner of a square. Drag this cursor on the screen to designate the size that the selected file should import to in relation to your page. Release the mouse button to import, size, and position the first photo. Repeat the process for as many files as you selected to import, each time dragging to define the area you want the imported file to occupy. The multiple-file and size-as-you-import features save a lot of time when you're loading and positioning several images in your design.

**Note:** To import images at their original size, simply click the Import sizing cursor on the screen, rather than dragging. The image will appear at actual size in your CorelDRAW document, with the top-left corner at the position you clicked the Import sizing cursor.

10. One by one, arrange your photos around the arched boxes so you can begin to stuff them inside using the PowerClip feature. Use the sizing handles on the bitmaps to enlarge or reduce the photos so that they will fit within one of the arched boxes (work in Wireframe view so it is easy to see both the bitmaps and the frame shapes). When an image is in place, choose Effects|PowerClip|Place Inside Container, then click on the arched box. This will constrain the image to within that shape (see Figure 5.18).

11. Each one of these PowerClip curves was given the same "glowing" effect using the Interactive Drop Shadow tool, as outlined in Chapter 3.

12. Find an image of a computer circuit board to use as a background, or, if you have a scanner attached and installed, you can scan a real circuit board using the Acquire Image|Acquire command, which uses your

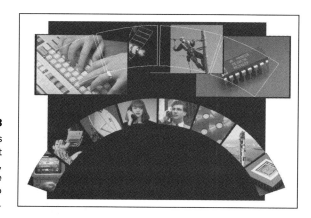

**Figure 5.18**
After the individual photos are sized and positioned to fit within an arched box (top row), they are "stuffed" inside the shape using the PowerClip feature (bottom row).

scanner's software to import the scanned image directly into Corel-DRAW. Modify this bitmap with an effects filter. Choose Bitmaps|Contour|Edge Detect to open the Edge Detect dialog box. Change the Background Color setting to Black, and click OK to get eerie, high-tech-looking white edges on a black field as the background graphic.

13. To create the light and dark ray patterns, repeat the process of creating, duplicating, and arranging pizza slice shapes from Steps 3 and 4. To get the light and dark shading in these ray shapes, use the Lens feature. Open the Lens docker (Alt+F3) and give every other ray shape the Tinted Grayscale lens, changing the Color option to Dark Blue. Then give the remaining rays the same dark blue color, using the Color Add Lens option.

The Y2K energy can be felt in the color section, or loaded from the \Chapt05\ folder on the companion CD-ROM in the y2k.cdr file. This image is a great example of the kinds of shortcuts that CorelDRAW offers. You can easily create image "masks" using the PowerClip feature and custom-made geometric shapes, or even text elements. The great thing is that you can then continue with your effects and, as we saw, modify a PowerClip object with the Interactive Drop Shadow tool. Or you can swap out the photos at any time with new ones. Use the Effects|PowerClip|Extract Contents command to remove a photo, then issue Effects|PowerClip|Place Inside Container to stuff a new one into an object. This would be a neat way to create an animation of swapping images, for a "live" Y2K chaos collage!

You can also modify the look of an image within a PowerClip using a lens effect. If you load the y2k.cdr file off the companion CD-ROM, you can send one of the Lens sun-ray objects To Front (Shift+PgUp) to see this happen first-hand. CorelDRAW is just a great, flexible workspace to design whatever comes to mind. No need to panic—CorelDRAW will perform these amazing feats just fine well into this new millennium!

# PROJECT E-People

So far in this chapter we have created photo collages using transparency effects, duotone coloring tricks, and geometric framing using the PowerClip feature. The image in Figure 5.19 uses all of these techniques to create a unique geometric logo that, at the same time, has a soft tone and unifying color scheme.

Once again, the power of CorelDRAW comes together to create a totally different-looking image, using essentially the same techniques we have already covered. Nothing like recycling a little knowledge to expand your design horizons! Let's look at using geometric framing, duotone coloring, and transparency effects in a photo collage project:

1. As in the previous example, use circle shapes to lay out the basic geometric framing elements. I took advantage of the circular "e" logo in the center of the page and continued the theme with ever-enlarging circles. Again, this reflects my tastes and preferences in design, and you might be big on triangles or hexagons (see Figure 5.20). Creating hexagons with the Polygon tool is easier than creating the arched boxes (see the previous project for step-by-step instructions for creating the arched boxes), but, again, it's your preference.

**Figure 5.19**
This logo design uses many tricks to create a unified image out of many different photos.

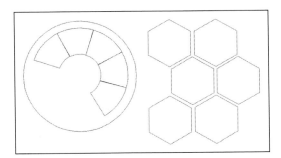

**Figure 5.20**
Basic geometric shapes work well to map out a design. I prefer circles (left), but polygons work just as well (right).

2. Once again, you need to find a collection of images for your photo collage. I turned to Corel's online image library and Photo-CD collection. (This isn't a product plug—I just happen to love the convenience of Corel's online service, and it is less expensive than other available online options. However, I also recommend Corbis images [**www.corbisimages.com**] as an online source of quality digital stock photos.)

3. As in the previous project, size and position the photos to fit inside the geometric shapes. With a photo selected, choose Effects|PowerClip|Place Inside Container, and click on one of the geometric framing shapes (see Figure 5.21).

4. Remove any outline on your PowerClip curve by right-clicking the on-screen "x."

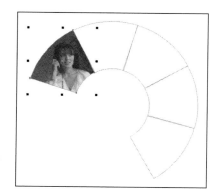

**Figure 5.21**
Use the PowerClip feature to place your photos within the geometric framing shapes.

5. With the PowerClip curve selected, choose Bitmaps|Convert To Bitmap to open the Convert To Bitmap dialog box. Change the Color setting to RGB, change Resolution to 300 dpi, and select the Anti-aliasing, Transparent Background, and Use Color Profile options. Finally, click OK to convert your image.

6. Now that your graphic is a malleable bitmap, you can modify it using bitmap filters as we did with the "flower power" example in Chapter 4. Or you can simply recolor the bitmap as I did using the Duotone feature. With your bitmap selected, choose Bitmaps|Mode|Duotone to open the Duotone dialog box. Now, you can keep the coloring scheme real simple, with the Type option set to the default Monotone setting. Simply double-click the current color (the default is Pantone Process Black) to open the Select Color dialog box. You must use Pantone colors for the duotone process, so locate a color that you like and click on it, then click OK. Click the Preview button in the Duotone dialog box to see how your current setting will modify your bitmap (see Figure 5.22). Click OK to recolor your bitmap. Repeat this process on all the photos that you want to recolor.

7. To create a less-hard edge on the bitmaps, use the Interactive Transparency tool. Drag the Interactive Transparency tool from the center of

**Figure 5.22**
Use the Duotone dialog box in Monotone mode to change the full-color scheme of the selected bitmap into a stylized one-color (and white background) version.

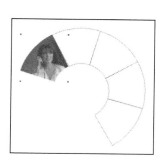

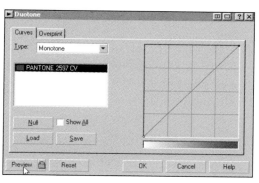

## Dialing-in Duotones

If you want more color in your image than the Monotone mode offers, try one of the other types. Change the Type setting in the Duotone dialog box to Duotone. Now you have two color choices to modify your photo. The top color in the color list controls what the darker tones will be. The color below that controls what the midtone colors will be. You can double-click on either of these colors to choose new ones. I chose colors from the same palette, such as dark blue and light blue, to create a nice duotone coloring scheme for each image in my photo collage.

The easiest of the duotone Type options is Monotone, where you have only a single color option. The most complex is Quadtone, where you have four color options to manipulate. Use as many or as few colors as you desire.

You can also load a Preset setting for the Duotone option. Click the Load button, then choose one of the duotone files that appear in the Load Duotone Files dialog box. These file names are a bit cryptic, but you can experiment with some of these files until you find some that you like. The file tcolor5.cpd, for example, creates a nice sepia tone, for an antique photo look.

your photo outward. This will set up the default Linear Fountain transparency. Click Radial Fountain Transparency on the Property Bar, then reverse the logic of the transparency by changing the color of the transparency control points, as we did in the first project. Drag white from the on-screen color well and drop it on the black center point. Then drag black from the on-screen color well and drop it on the outside white point of the Interactive Transparency control line. This will reverse the default logic of the transparency, making the solid center fade out to clear (see Figure 5.23). Move the control points around until you get the transition that you like.

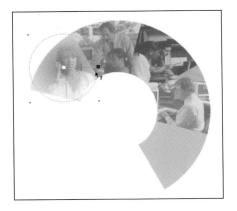

**Figure 5.23**
Use the Interactive Transparency tool to soften the edges of the geometric-shaped photos.

8. Shift-select all of the other design elements that you want to modify with the transparency effect, then choose Effects|Copy Effect|Lens From. Now click on the first element that you modified with the Interactive Transparency tool, which will give all of your objects the same settings. This way, everything has a similar look for a more unifying theme (see Figure 5.24).

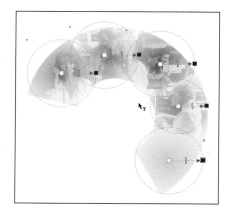

**Figure 5.24**
Use the Copy Effect feature to give all of your elements the same Interactive Transparency tool settings.

Once again, that's all there is to it! The process itself isn't hard at all. Using similar coloring schemes, the same transparency effects, and a unifying geometric pattern brings very different photos together in a single piece of artwork. You should by now be familiar with the rest of the design techniques (such as glowing text and fading graph), but, with the unique pastel color choices, the result is markedly different than the other examples in this book. The image can be found in the color section in the center of this book, and also in the epeople.cdr file found in the \Chapt05\ folder on the companion CD-ROM. I included this example because, while it retains many of my habitual techniques, it doesn't have the look of a typical "Shane" graphic. Sometimes you need to get away from even your signature look and feel to satiate a client or satisfy a unique design challenge. This might happen more than you like, as clients push you in directions you don't want to go or choose colors you don't care for. It is often the nature of the business, however, and many times personal taste and preferences can get in the way of a "successful" project. At least with a handful of design tricks, you can get the results you need, no matter how outside your personality they might be. Just remember that no matter how much you might not care for the colors your client picks, just smile and do as they wish—remember that the client also provides that magic color: "greenbacks."

## High-Speed Heroes

While I am typically drawn to work within CorelDRAW for the majority of my work, there are times when you simply can't do what you need in the program. One perfect example is creating a photo-collage where you want to cut-out the images in their own, unique jagged shapes. You could create a custom-curve in CorelDRAW, then use the PowerClip feature to place the image inside it; this again results in a hard-edged transition, however. To get the really cool photo-collage effects, you need to work in PhotoPaint, and you need to use clip masks.

A clip mask allows you to define the areas of your image that you want to hide, or show, in levels of black and white. You don't actually alter the image, rather like a Lens effect; it simply masks out areas where you paint. A mask allows you to "erase" areas of your image without actually erasing them; you just keep them from view with the mask. It sounds difficult, but it isn't, and once you learn how the magic works you will open a whole new dimension in your work. Here is how to create a mask in PhotoPaint, to merge images seamlessly:

1. In PhotoPaint, use File|Open or File|Acquire Image to get two photos into your workspace. One will be the background image, and the other the floating image we want to merge with the background. In my case, I created a background image in CorelDRAW, exported it as a bitmap, then opened it in Photo-Paint. Then I imported my floating image, a photograph of my friend Pete.

2. From the Window menu, select your floating image by clicking on the file name at the bottom of the menu. Then from the menu choose Mask|Select All (Ctrl+Shift+A), then Edit|Copy (Ctrl+C). This will place your image on the clipboard.

3. From the Window menu, now choose your background image by clicking on the file name at the bottom of the menu.

4. With the background image selected, choose Paste|As New Object (Ctrl+V) from the Edit menu. Your photo should now be on top of your background, as a unique floating object (see Figure 5.25).

**Figure 5.25**
Copy your image, then Paste|As New Object in your background file to create a floating object.

5. With the Object Picker tool, now position and size your floating object over the background. Use the Zoom tool to get a closer look at your target area.

6. Click and hold on the Rectangle Mask tool to reveal the other mask options, and select the option that allows you to draw an irregular mask (which looks like a rope blob). Now draw around your subject to create a shape that you want to remain visible, which will become our clip mask (see Figure 5.26).

**Figure 5.26**
Use the Freehand Mask Tool to create a mask around your subject.

7.  Now, to create our clip mask, choose Clip Mask|Create|From Mask from the Object menu. This will create a clip mask from your current selection, "hiding" everything outside of it, and revealing only your subject inside (see Figure 5.27).

**Figure 5.27**
The clip mask hides everything outside of it and reveals only your subject inside.

8.  "That looks like crap," you might think, and you are right! Now we need to use the power of the clip mask to soften the edges. First, make sure that the Objects Docker is open. From the Window menu, choose Dockers|Objects (Ctrl+F7). Here you can see your Background layer, and, on top of it, your floating object as well as its clip mask (shown after the + as a black rectangle with a little white spot). You need to remember to click on the clip mask, and not on the object itself, to edit it. If you don't have the clip mask enabled, you will spray paint all over Pete's face in the next step, and he'll hate that…

9.  Double-click the Paint Tool to open the Brush Settings docker, then choose a small brush clicking the down arrow next to the current brush. Since you are now painting on the clip mask, rather than on the actual photo, you don't have to worry about making any mistakes. Click white to paint areas that you want to reveal, or click black to paint areas that you want to hide. Paint away around the edges until you have just the floating subject over your background (see Figure 5.28).

**Figure 5.28**
Painting on the clip mask allows you to control what part of your image is hidden or revealed.

10. Modifying the clip mask changes how your image *appears*, but it does not actually corrupt or change the original image data. You can always go back to paint away or reveal new pieces of the image. You can also paint in shades of gray, to create transparency effects with your clip mask. Since black totally hides your image on the clip mask, and white reveals it, painting in dark or lighter shades of gray makes things less or more transparent. Or you can use Effects on the clip mask, such as Effects|Blur|Motion Blur, to modify how your image is revealed in a unique and artistic way (see Figure 5.29).

**Figure 5.29**
The clip mask can be modified with effects to create a unique look.

11. With your clip mask now active, you can get some cool effects with things such as the Interactive Drop Shadow tool. The shadow will build itself only to visible areas in the clip mask, and it will redraw itself should you reveal or hide more of your image by editing the clip mask (see Figure 5.30). This is where computer power really kicks in!

That's basically it! This file is called "peteback.cpt" and can be found in the \Chapt05\ folder on the companion CD-ROM and in the color section. This file does not yet have the clip mask, so it is a good one to load and practice with. The file "hero.cpt" in the same directory is how the final project ended up. It is a "hero card" project for my race-car driver friend Pete. "Hero cards" are brochures that drivers autograph and hand out to fans, kind of like very large baseball cards!

**Figure 5.30**

The Interactive Drop Shadow tool will automatically reference the clip mask to create a shadow only for areas that are visible.

Once you harness the power of the clip mask, you have infinite control over how and where you place your images. The coolest thing is to create a clip mask in Photo-Paint, then File|Import the image into CorelDRAW so you can create any and all "floating" objects that you want, not just the ones that come on the Corel clip-art CD! The clip mask is how all those amazing computer photo-collages are made, with the artists modifying the opacity of the blending images with clip masks. Now you know the secret, so go exploit the power!

# Beyond f/x

Finding creative ways to mix and match photos is the bread and butter of commercial designers. Catalogs, advertisements, brochures, flyers, and even Web sites often boil down to simple photo montages. Break things up with interesting geometric patterns or border effects, or use the power and flexibility of a CorelDRAW layout to stack the images right on top of each other using transparencies. With the addition of layers to Photo-Paint, this isn't as critical as it once was, but, with all of the other design elements coming together in CorelDRAW, and with so many design options available to you there, you might as well create the bitmap effects there.

---

### Choosing Between CorelDRAW and Photo-Paint

The addition of bitmap-editing features within CorelDRAW means that you do not have to use Photo-Paint as much as you used to. This is fine with me, because flip-flopping between applications always slows things down anyway. The problem with the bitmap effects in CorelDRAW, however, is that you are usually limited to filters that affect the bitmap as a whole (such as changing colors with the Duotone feature or using one of the Art Strokes effects). You cannot create a selection—as you can in Photo-Paint—to limit the area you want to change. For some effects, you have no choice but to modify the bitmap in Photo-Paint—such as the puzzle-piece examples in Chapter 7—because CorelDRAW offers no "magic wand" selection tool. Or if you want to first isolate a section of a bitmap, you will need to work in Photo-Paint. Photo-Paint comes with your CorelDRAW package, so go ahead and use it.

In addition to being primary design elements, bitmap collages also make interesting backgrounds, or even abstract patterns for other unique applications. Mix and match the new concepts from this chapter with some of the others (the adding depth idea from Chapter 6, double-vision from Chapter 9, and so forth) for your own take on the photo-collage concept. Or invent your own new ideas—the sky is the limit.

For a unique gift idea, instead of making one of those hideous hand-cut photo collages, create a digital montage instead. Scan and assemble the photos in the computer and then output the composite image at a service bureau on a high-end color printer. This will cost about the same as having duplicate photos made, it's easier than hand-cutting all of those pieces, and you can use incredible computer tricks to merge the images into one beautiful composite. With a little planning, you can create two unique 8 1/2-x-11 images on one landscape tabloid printout. Cut these out, frame 'em, and make your grandmas happy!

# Moving On

In this chapter, we looked at creating interesting photo montages mixing a variety of technologies and techniques. Using CorelDRAW, we created drop shadows, manipulated bitmaps, added captions, and even created neat collages with the PowerClip and Interactive Transparency features. With the Duotone option, you can recolor your photos to look alike or to become stylized individual elements. All in all, I think we looked at some very cool techniques, which should come in handy in your virtual studio to create all kinds of projects. You probably won't use these examples verbatim (unless you just happen to be designing a "U.S. History" book cover or assembling your own "Y2K global disaster" graphics), but the techniques will prove to be useful, I guarantee. Unless, of course, you happen to be the only computer artist in the world not using scanned photos!

Chapter 6 moves away from this world of personal augmentation and broadens the scope to include manipulating time and space itself. Am I suffering from a "god complex"? Maybe, but I speak of using CorelDRAW tools to create the illusions of depth and perspective. Let me demonstrate....

# Chapter 6

# Adding Depth and Dimension

*This chapter will look at using blur and transparency effects to manipulate the field of depth; simulating dimension by skewing your artwork; and using the Blend feature to build realistically shaded objects.*

# Creating the Illusion of Depth

For every task—be it building a house or creating a computer illustration—you need the right tool for the right job. Because CorelDRAW is an object-oriented illustration package, it offers a lot of built-in flexibility. This flexibility lets you change the look of your objects until you get a look you like, making CorelDRAW the tool of choice for computer illustration.

Within CorelDRAW, you can manipulate artwork to make it appear closer or further away from you. You can take flat art and create the illusion of depth by skewing it into a perspective orientation. Or you can use CorelDRAW tools to create 3D-looking artwork, either by using the Blend feature or, as we have already seen, manipulating the Extrude tool. In any case, it is always a challenge to simulate some sort of depth and dimension, given the flat nature of the computer screen and, of course, the printed page. However, no matter how sophisticated the ol' human eye is, it doesn't take much to fool it! Let us wield the smoke and mirrors...

## PROJECT Distant Horizons

While the Interactive Transparency tool continues to rank as one of my favorite CorelDRAW features, I get a bigger charge out of creating optical illusions. This technique pairs the Gaussian Blur bitmap effect with the Interactive Transparency tool to create landscapes where you can wield god-like power over space and time, as in Figure 6.1. Well, not really—but you can change the field of focus, making objects appear to be either close up or far away. This technique works equally well in CorelDRAW or Photo-Paint.

**Figure 6.1**
By blurring a bitmap, you take it out of focus. Stacking a blurred image on a clear original and then using the Transparency tool allows you to control what part of the image is in focus.

1. Start with a landscape photo that has some "depth" potential. You'll find this image in the \photos\thebeach folder on the third Corel-DRAW clip-art CD. It has a nice set of pillars that fades away in the distance. However—and this is important—both the objects up close and those far away are in focus, which means we are free to manipulate this image at will.

2. After you select File|Import to import your image, create a duplicate in the same position with a tap of the plus (+) key. Now you have two copies of this image, lying directly on top of each other. Select the top copy, and from the Bitmaps menu, choose Blur|Gaussian Blur. This filter will "fuzz" your image. Use the Radius slider to control the amount of blurring. Click on the Preview button to see the effect of your Radius setting, then click OK when you are satisfied (see Figure 6.2).

**Figure 6.2**
Use the Gaussian Blur bitmap effect to "fuzz" your artwork (original on left).

3. With the blurry image on top of the clear one, it is just a matter of manipulating the Interactive Transparency tool to achieve our illusion of "far" or "close." For example, drag the Interactive Transparency tool from the top down to fade out the bitmap slowly until it gets to the bottom. As the "blurry" bitmap fades away, it reveals the clear image below, creating the illusion of depth as things further away fade out of focus (see Figure 6.3). If you reverse the logic and drag from the bottom up, things in the foreground are blurry, shifting the viewer's focus to the distance.

**Figure 6.3**
The Interactive Transparency feature allows you to change the field of focus, revealing the crisp image below the fading blurry duplicate.

That is all there is to it! This is such a great trick, and it's so easy. By changing the area of focus, you subtly say "look here," directing where your viewer will look. Since you can manipulate the viewer's attention, you should take advantage of that and place something in the "focus area" that you want people to notice. The duplicate/transparency trick has a ton of potential, as we will see with more examples later in the book. To finish off the graphic for the digital color section, I imported "free-floating" images from the \objects\ directory of the Corel clip-art CD #3. These bitmap images don't have a background, so they float freely over your background. You can use the Bitmap color mask to create your own "floating" images, as discussed in Chapter 12.

## PROJECT Turbo-Charged Box Art

Prototypes are a huge hassle in design. Starting from scratch to create new packaging ideas—or any other project that does not already exist in one way or another—can be quite a challenge. More often than not, the biggest difficulty is not creating the necessary artwork, but creating images for the noncreative people involved so that they can share in your visions. Creating artwork to aid in the visualization process is also important to avoid mistakes by anyone in the production loop.

**Figure 6.4**

By skewing flat artwork, you can create 3D-like images, which are helpful for visualizing a finished 3D product.

The best way to work out problems with a packaging design is to create a physical mockup of the item (see the sidebar, "Wow 'Em"). Boxes have strange design parameters that depend on the project and the nature of the items to be packaged, so the more reference material for everyone involved, the fewer chances of communication errors and mistakes. In general, boxes are *die-cut* from a single piece of flat cardboard that has been imprinted with the appropriate artwork laid out in the correct orientation (or with a full-color sticker stuck onto the cardboard) for each panel. CorelDRAW is dimensionally stable, so you can design both the artwork and the *die guide* (the artwork used to create the actual cutting template) right on your desktop. The top half of the graphic in Figure 6.4 (which is also in the digital color section) shows the flat artwork for a box. The artwork is printed on card stock, cut out with a die, and then folded into a box (simulated in the image on the bottom).

In this example, we will take the panels from a box art project and use the skew feature to place them in a 3D orientation. You'll probably run across this kind of project often, where you take existing artwork—such as a client's logo—and place it in an angled 3D orientation. You can use the same kind of technique

### Wow 'Em

The best way to blow away your client—and to provide a clear reference for the production people—is to create an actual mockup of the box project. Output the box at actual size using a color printer. Most service bureaus offer a large-format (tabloid) printer at close to proofing quality. If you can't fit the box on a single sheet, output the panels separately and then glue them onto cardboard. Use a utility knife to cut along your guidelines, and then fold and assemble the box. It's easy to do, and the mockup will really impress your customer. This is an especially useful tool when you have clients who are insecure or dragging their feet on a project. With the box sitting on their desk, they usually lose any fears that you can't make it happen. And it is a handy trick when you need packaging for a photo shoot and the packages don't exist yet.

not only to fashion boxes, but also to mock up store displays, billboards, trac-
tor trailers—wherever you want to stick a piece of existing artwork. Keep in
mind that this technique works only for flat surfaces. If you want to stick artwork on a more complicated surface—say, a dimpled metal wall—you will
want to create a bitmap in CorelDRAW and then stick it to the "real" 3D surface rendered in a modeling package such as RayDream Designer, 3D Studio,
or Caligari TrueSpace. (Or you can try the Effects|Distort|Displace feature in
Photo-Paint, as described in the Displace This project later in this chapter.)
Follow these steps to get flat artwork to look 3D in CorelDRAW:

1. Start with the artwork needed to actually print and die-cut the box. This
   file—called turbobox.cdr in the \Chapt06\ subdirectory on the companion CD-ROM—is set up in the working mechanicals layout. You use
   this layout to generate the color-separated film that goes to the production people so they can create the box. It has the artwork and the
   outlines necessary to create the die for cutting. It isn't very interesting
   in Normal view (it is mostly black), but the Wireframe view will show
   you the die-lines, folds, and other details necessary for production. (The
   die-line is output separately as a guide for the die-maker.)

2. Isolate the artwork for the panels that will show in the 3D configuration. In this case, the front, top, and left sides are needed. Select the art
   for those sections and delete the rest (see Figure 6.5).

**Figure 6.5**
From the flat box artwork,
select the top, front, and left
side artwork.

3. Select the artwork for each section and group it. This will make it easier
   to select the three main panels. Select the front group and double-click
   to review the rotation and skew arrows. Select the left-center skew arrows and drag down while holding the Ctrl key to skew the objects 30
   degrees. Now select the right group and, using the right center skew
   arrows, skew the objects 30 degrees (see Figure 6.6).

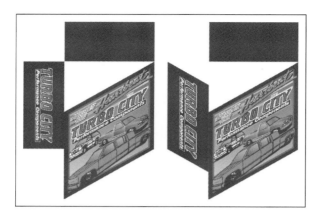

**Figure 6.6**
Use the rotation and skew arrows to give the sides a slanted orientation.

**Figure 6.7**
Drag the arrows to skew the top piece 45 degrees.

4. Align the front and side object groups to the bottom. Pull a guideline off the left vertical ruler so that it runs up the left side of the side panel. Now select the graphic for the top and use the top skew arrows to slant 45 degrees to the left (see Figure 6.7). Notice how this meets the guideline.

5. Select the top; now use the left-center skew handles and drag down 30 degrees. This just about fits things together, but not quite.

6. In Wireframe view, grab the left panel and use the left-center skew arrows to drop down the left side until it is perfectly aligned with the top angle (see Figure 6.8). Finito!

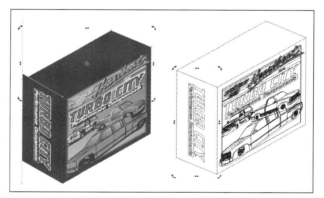

**Figure 6.8**
When you skew the top down, it almost fits, but not until the left front panel is skewed a little more.

This is what I call a quick-and-dirty solution. It looks good and is convincing enough for most applications. You can even use the Perspective function to place the sides in a perfect 3D orientation. I'm just a big fan of idealized reality and instant gratification, as you know!

Adding Depth and Dimension 117

## PROJECT Gorilla

Although the image of an enraged primate in Figure 6.9 is one of the first things I ever drew in CorelDRAW, I still like it. New features in CorelDRAW 9 can give even this old beast some new life. To emphasize the wet and shiny surfaces of the eyes and mouth, I purposely made the rest of the face kind of flat and dull by comparison in the original file. With the Convert To Bitmap feature available in CorelDRAW 9, it is also possible to "blur" the background and make the eyes and teeth pop out even more.

This image started as a quick ink illustration of just the main features of a gorilla's face, which I scanned and traced using the Centerline function. The hair and black outlines in the face are the results of that centerline trace, while the remaining objects were created in CorelDRAW.

Use multistage blends (as in the fangs) to get a round, realistically shaded object. Instead of blending just two objects, I blended three to broaden the color range of the blend and add more control. To achieve the shiny look, draw tiny solid-white circles, strategically placed to suggest reflection and texture. I won't walk you through this whole design, but I will show you some neat tricks in the eyes and teeth, which you can work into your own monstrosities. Follow these steps to draw shiny eyes and fangs:

1. Using the Freehand or Bezier tool (your preference), draw the main eye outline. The Bezier tool is great for this type of drawing, except that hard edges (as in the eye corners) are difficult to achieve. If you create a curve by dragging, the node you create is a smooth one. To get a cusped node, click (but don't drag) to get a straight line. It takes some practice to draw curved shapes with the Bezier tool, and I still prefer to draw simple straight lines and then modify the curves using the Shape tool and node editing. This approach also makes for very simple, low-node count shapes (see Figure 6.10).

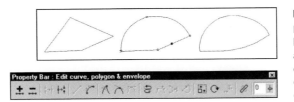

2. Draw the largest of the eye detail circles first using the Ellipse tool (hold down the Ctrl key while dragging to draw a perfect circle). If you make it a habit to draw the largest objects first and the smaller ones later, you will save time restacking the objects. Objects "stack" themselves in the order of creation. So if you draw a small circle and then draw a large one, the larger one will be on top of the smaller. The same is true for

**Figure 6.9**

Multistage blends can create the illusion of rounded objects, such as the teeth and eyes in this gorilla graphic. Converting some of the image to a bitmap, then blurring it, makes the hard-edged elements pop out even more.

**Figure 6.10**

It is often easier to draw straight lines and then use the Shape tool and the Property Bar to create a curved shape, especially one with cusped nodes (as in the corners of the eye).

duplicates. Select the circle, duplicate it (+ key), and reduce it by dragging a corner sizing handle inward. This duplicate is now on top of the original. Duplicate and downsize once more for the pupil shape.

3. Next, from the Arrange menu, open the Intersection docker and disable the Leave Original: Target Objects option. Now, one by one, select the eye pieces (largest to smallest again to maintain the correct order), click the Intersect With button, and then click on the main eye shape. This will place your iris and pupil shapes perfectly within the eye. Shade the eye with a black-to-white linear fountain fill from the Fountain Fill dialog box (F11), and give the two outside pieces a black fill and the middle piece a dark brown fill (see Figure 6.11).

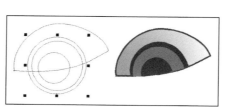

**Figure 6.11**

Use the Intersection docker to trim shapes to fit within a boundary object and then color the pieces for a realistic eye.

4. Select the largest black circle and Shift-select the brown one on top of it. Use the Interactive Blend tool to drag between the two shapes to create a blend. On the Property Bar, change the Number Of Steps setting to 5 (or use the default 20, for a smoother blend). Select only the top brown control curve, and then use the Interactive Blend tool to drag to the small black circle on top of it. The result is a compound element of three control curves and two blend groups (five total elements). If you change any of the control curves, all of the elements in the compound element group are affected. With this compound element selected, choose Arrange|Separate and then choose Arrange|Ungroup All. To make the retina more crisp, delete some of the resulting objects in the second blend. Use the Freehand tool to draw some vein lines, following a suggested curve of the eye, and give them a red outline. Use the Freehand tool to draw objects suggesting reflected light on a wet eyeball. These shapes can be very abstract; again, just follow a suggested curve of the eye to make things look more round. Color them solid white for a stark reflection (see Figure 6.12).

**Figure 6.12**

Three objects blended together form a compound element. The Freehand tool draws the jagged lines of the veins as well as the abstract reflection pieces.

5.  I used the same double-blend technique on some of the teeth to get a
    rounded look with a wider color range than a single blend can achieve.
    On some, I use a traditional blend on top of another object to accent
    the tooth. The trick to achieving smooth blends is to have the same
    number of nodes in each control curve. To guarantee that both objects
    have the same number of nodes, it is a good idea to generate the sec-
    ond control shape by duplicating (+ key) the first. Now use the Pick tool
    and sizing handles to drag, skew, and resize the duplicate. Also use the
    Shape tool to sculpt the duplicate shape into its final form manually
    rather than risk changing the node count (by using the Intersection
    feature, for example). To shade the big fang, I drew a smaller object
    inside the main tooth shape and gave it a darker orange fill. I then
    duplicated that object, shaded it gray, and used the Shape tool to form
    it. In this way, I kept the node count for both objects the same. When
    you blend these two objects with the Interactive Blend tool, the transi-
    tion is smooth because of the similar node orientation and number. Use
    the Freehand tool to draw shiny spots, which accent the illusion of
    wetness and roundness (see Figure 6.13).

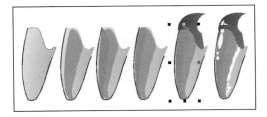

**Figure 6.13**

For smooth blends, both control
curves need to have the same
number of nodes. To ensure this,
create one control curve by
duplicating another. Use the
Shape tool to distort the second
control object; to keep the
blends smooth, however, do not
alter the number of nodes.

6.  Blending original objects to smaller duplicates always produces a nice,
    smooth blend. Accent the round look of these blends with solid-white
    gleam shapes drawn with the Freehand tool. It isn't difficult to achieve
    a convincing look; it just takes a little time to draw in all of the fine
    details (see Figure 6.14).

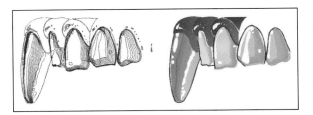

**Figure 6.14**

Blending a large object to a
smaller duplicate produces a
smooth and round look. Add
more steps for smoother blends,
fewer for a stepped look. Accent
with solid-white shapes to suggest wet sparkles and highlights.
The Wireframe view on the left
shows where the blends are.

7.  In order to take the image a step further, I needed to isolate the artwork
    that I wanted to keep as native CorelDRAW objects from the parts I
    wanted to convert to a bitmap. The easiest way to keep track of art-
    work—especially in a project like this where pieces are stacked on top of

## Make the Node "Count"

For smooth, predictable blends, both objects need to have the same number of nodes. The status bar displays the number of nodes in the selected object; you can use the Shape tool to add or delete nodes until the numbers are the same. Then, using the Map Nodes feature (found on the Miscellaneous Features tab on the Blend docker), you can tell CorelDRAW from which point to start the blend on each target object.

Click the Map Nodes button, then click the arrow on the starting node of the first object. Next, click the arrow on the corresponding node on the end object, and finally click Apply. This helps you control blends that seem to give oddball results otherwise. The easiest way to get predictable results with blends is to use the same shape for all control curves. Duplicate the parent object—which ensures the same node count and orientation—and then manipulate it for the blend. You can warp, twist, downsize, and recolor the duplicate; as long as you don't alter the node count, the blend should be smooth and predictable.

others—is to build and manage different "layers." CorelDRAW has the ability, like PhotoShop, Photo-Paint, or other design applications, to create multiple layers for your artwork. You can move art from layer to layer, make a layer "invisible," or "lock" it to prevent any changes. The ability to create layers is a nice feature. For this project, I created a second layer and moved the eyes and teeth objects there. To follow my example, open the Window menu and choose Dockers|Object Manager to open the Object Manager docker. You use this docker to manage your layers. Click the small arrow on the top right of the docker to open the flyout menu and select New Layer, which will create Layer 2 on top of your existing Layer 1. To move objects to a new layer, select them and then drag them to the layer name in the Object Manager docker, or use the Move To Layer command from the flyout. Once objects are on their own layer, you can toggle the visibility of that layer by clicking on the eye icon. I moved the eyes and teeth to their own layer, then clicked the eye on Layer 1 to make it invisible (see Figure 6.15).

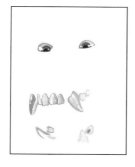

**Figure 6.15**
The Object Manager docker allows you to create and manage multiple layers, to stack and further control the objects in your image, or make them "invisible" by turning off the display attribute for a layer.

8. With my eyes and teeth isolated onto a single layer, I could lock and turn off that layer's visibility, and then concentrate on the objects making up the rest of the face, still on Layer 1. To continue with the example, click the eye and pencil icon next to Layer 2 (the eye/teeth layer) to disable visibility and editing on that layer. Now click Layer 1 in the

Object Manager docker to make sure you are back on that layer, and choose Select All (Ctrl+A). From the Bitmaps menu, select Convert To Bitmap, then change the Color option to CMYK, set Resolution to 300 dpi, select the Anti-aliasing option, click OK, and then go on a lunch break. It takes a few compute cycles to convert such a large area into a high-resolution bitmap—and it makes for a big file. These limitations are unavoidable if the file is destined for print, like this one. If you are doing on-screen artwork—for a Web site or presentation, for example— you can use the RGB, 72 dpi settings, which makes for a much smaller file and takes much less time to calculate (see Figure 6.16).

**Figure 6.16**

With the background objects isolated to their own layer, you can select them and use the Convert To Bitmap feature to rasterize the information.

9. Once everything but the eyes and teeth are converted to a bitmap, you can use the Gaussian Blur effect as in our first project. With all but the eye and teeth elements given the "fuzz" treatment, they seem to jump out even more at you. Sometimes you just have no choice but to convert objects to bitmaps to take advantage of the many effects available to "pixel-based" art, which is not an option for "vector-based" objects. Since we can do both in CorelDRAW, we can have it all!

In this example, both the original and converted versions of the artwork are available in the \Chapt06\ folder on the companion CD-ROM. The original file, gorilla.cdr, has just the vector objects, while gorilla3d.cdr has all but the eye and teeth elements converted to a bitmap and given the "fuzz" treatment. You can also examine the blends in the teeth, for example, to see how the multistage, compound blend elements work to get the 3D look. You can also see this image in all its glory in this book's color section.

## PROJECT Displace This

Another way to suggest depth and dimension is to distort a bitmap using the Displace feature, found in both CorelDRAW and Photo-Paint. This filter uses shades of gray in a source file (called a displacement map) to define areas of distortion in your target image. You can use one of the preset displacement maps, but the real power comes in defining your own. To distort a bitmap with a custom-made displacement map, follow these steps:

1. First decide what kind of effect you have in mind. I wanted to create an illusion of a sign on a corrugated panel, so the distortion needs to be a rounded series of light-to-dark "tubes." This effect is easy to create in CorelDRAW. First, draw a rectangle, then give it a Linear Two color, black to white fountain fill from the Fountain Fill dialog box (F11). Then drag the left-center control node to the right, while holding down the Ctrl key, remembering to hit the Spacebar before you release the mouse to create a perfect flip-flop mirror duplicate. Use the Repeat option (Ctrl+R) to create a bunch of flip-flopped duplicates, resulting in a group of objects resembling the light/dark color scheme of corrugated metal (see Figure 6.17).

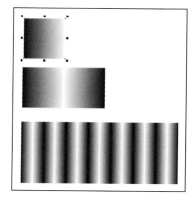

**Figure 6.17**
Repeating duplicates of a light-to-dark square take on the shading attributes of a piece of corrugated metal.

2. Drag-select all of the objects and issue the Group command (Ctrl+G). Now import the bitmap that you want to perform the effect on, so you can scale your "corrugated" group to match. Once your corrugated pieces match the scale of the imported bitmap, select the corrugated pieces to create the displacement map. With the corrugated group of objects selected, choose File|Export, then change the Files Of Type setting to CPT—Corel Photo-Paint Image. Also, choose the Selected Only option. Now name your file "corrugated" or something meaningful to you (so six months from now you won't stare at this file and wonder what it is) and click Export. Now you have a customized displacement map.

3. Select your corrugated pieces and use the To Back (Shift+PgDn) command to send them to the back. Now select your target bitmap and choose Bitmaps|Distort|Displace to open the Displace dialog box. Click on the little folder icon, locate the file you created in Step 2, and click Open. Change the Scale mode to Stretch To Fit so that your custom displacement map will cover the entire bitmap. Then, change the Scale options to taste (see Figure 6.18). I chose 10 for the Horizontal and 11 for the Vertical distortion values. Higher values make for more

**Figure 6.18**
Use the Displace dialog box to load your custom displacement map and to control the parameters of the distortion.

distortion, but if the settings are too high the distortion takes on an angular look. Click Preview to see how your changes affect the outcome, and click OK when you are satisfied.

4. Now your bitmap is distorted in exactly the manner you specified using your displacement map. The reason you want to scale the distortion to the bitmap is that you now can use the same corrugated pieces you used to create the displacement map to add some depth and substance with shading effects. This part is a snap. Select the bitmap you just distorted and click the Interactive Transparency tool. Now change the type to Uniform in the Property Bar and adjust the amount of transparency with the slider. This will allow the light and dark areas of the corrugated pieces below to show through; these areas match the distortion map perfectly, since they are essentially the same thing. So now your bitmap has the appearance of a corrugated piece of sheet metal (see Figure 6.19).

**Figure 6.19**
Use the Interactive Uniform Transparency tool to allow the corrugated pieces to show through your bitmap a little, adding light and shadow for the depth effect.

That's all there is to it! The displace feature has tons of uses beyond this simple illustration. (Search the Internet for keyword "displacement maps," and you can find many tutorials on the subject.) Always have fun and experiment with new features and functions as you find them. You may discover a technique you hadn't thought of before. Sometimes you learn more from your mistakes than from your triumphs.

# Beyond f/x

Although you may not find yourself rendering many saliva-covered teeth in your average workday, you never know what project will walk through your door. I had to create a "smiling, sunglass- and sombrero-wearing" iguana one day, and found myself drawing scales on the beast. So even "wet-fang" rendering knowledge may be useful one day. The multistage blending used to create the realistic, round-looking teeth is a great way to render other tubular objects, like coffee mugs or telephone poles.

Making flat artwork look dimensional is a common task for most of us. The techniques discussed in this chapter for modifying the field of focus are powerful ways to subtly manipulate your readers' attention and direct them to different areas of your artwork. Exaggerating depth with blur is a neat design vehicle to isolate other design elements or to de-emphasize other aspects of your design. Sometimes, for example, you are stuck with a bad photo, such as a product shot with a busy background. Using the blur tricks, you can "fuzz out" the bad stuff and direct the focus toward the good stuff. Remember that the Interactive Transparency tool has Radial as well as Linear options, so you can create a round illusion, where things get sharper toward the center. Trust me—you will find a great use one day for this effect.

## Moving On

In this chapter, we tweaked with the laws of nature, manipulating depth and distance with optical illusions. We twisted and slanted flat artwork into 3D-looking elements, and we created rounded objects with blending techniques. By using CorelDRAW objects, or converting elements to bitmaps, you can always find a way to realize even your wildest visions. Essentially, if you can imagine it, you can create it in CorelDRAW.

In Chapter 7, we will examine some interesting ways to explode your artwork into small pieces to create a puzzle-like effect. We will also examine how to manipulate CorelDRAW tools to add the extrude and bevel effects to photos that we have carved up into shapes. It's a very "puzzling" chapter, but one that blows the lid off some unique techniques available only to CorelDRAW users.

# Chapter 7

# Puzzling Pieces

*This chapter reveals tricks for creating puzzle pieces using the PowerClip feature and the Bitmap Pattern fill, and we will create illusions using import/export tricks.*

# Breaking Apart and Piecing Together

Breaking things isn't good—unless they deserve to be broken. My cell phone, for example, has a high probability of being smashed into tiny little pieces the next time it cuts out mid-conversation. In design, breaking up your image into smaller, more easily digestible chunks is also a good idea. Or, as we will explore in this chapter, you may want to "break apart" and then "piece together" images, as in a puzzle or optical illusion.

In this chapter, we look at several interesting techniques unique to CorelDRAW that allow you to break up and piece together images. The first example uses a PowerClip technique that automatically breaks apart a single image into many pieces. The second project also takes advantage of PowerClip, and makes use of the power and ease of Photo-Paint to help create a convincing puzzle effect. The final illusion is a very strange technique indeed, where multiple "snapshots" of the artwork in progress are pieced together to create the illusion of reflected surfaces. This chapter should give you that warm, fuzzy, happy-to-be-a-CorelDRAW-user feeling (if you don't have it already).

## PROJECT Picture Pieces

The PowerClip feature is a really powerful tool in CorelDRAW. It can stuff any image into any shape. You can even use the PowerClip feature on a curve that consists of multiple, unattached parts (such as a text headline). You can also put the tool to work to create puzzle pieces, as shown in Figure 7.1.

**Figure 7.1**

If you create a complex shape by combining small paths into a single shape, you can use PowerClip to place an image inside it. Then, when you break apart the PowerClip object, each little piece will have the corresponding image inside it.

This is one of those tricks I love—you enjoy a big payoff with relatively little effort. This technique has one drawback, however; the files can become large and unmanageable. As you will see, when you perform the Break Apart command on a PowerClip curve with sub-paths, CorelDRAW copies *all* of the image data to each and every resulting piece of the puzzle. So, if you have a 10-MB image and create a 10-piece puzzle, when you break apart all the pieces, then technically you create a 100-MB monster. So for your project, use an image that is as small as possible to start out with, or, better yet, use a CorelDRAW vector graphic as these tend to be really small anyway. Or, if your system resources are low, limit this technique to on-screen low-res applications that use small bitmaps like web graphics. Be brave and give it a shot. With memory prices as low as they are, quit your snivelin', slap in another 128 megs, and get serious! Follow these steps to make the puzzle pieces:

1. Import (Ctrl+I) a bitmap or any other design into a blank page (the PowerClip function works on vector and bitmap images, so you can use a CorelDRAW file instead of a photo if you want). Use as small a bitmap as possible and at actual size. (Use the Resample command from the Bitmaps menu to reduce the size of the bitmap. For the Web, use 72 dpi; for print, 225 dpi is about as low as you can go, and RGB uses less memory than CMYK.)

2. So you won't accidentally move the bitmap during the drawing steps, right-click your bitmap and select Lock Object from the pop-up menu (or choose Arrange|Lock Object). Switch to View|Wireframe to make it easier to see what you are doing. With the Freehand and Bezier tools, draw out areas of the image that would make good pieces (see Figure 7.2). You don't need to worry about perfection at this point; just make sure each object is solid (click Auto-Close Curve on the Property Bar to close up any open curves automatically). When you've finished drawing your puzzle pieces, draw a rectangle around the image to serve as a bounding box.

**Figure 7.2**

Draw shapes on top of a bitmap to create puzzle pieces. Use the image as a guide while drawing the shapes with the Bezier or Freehand tools.

3. Select one of the puzzle pieces and switch to the Shape tool (see Figure 7.3). Drag-select all of the nodes, and click Smooth on the Property Bar. This will remove any harsh angles.

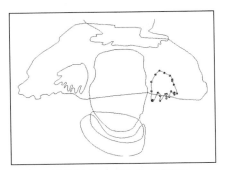

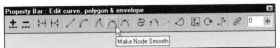

**Figure 7.3**

Use the Shape tool to edit the nodes and smooth out the puzzle shapes.

4. For this process, you need to create nonoverlapping pieces. This step isn't too hard, but it takes a little thinking and creative use of the Shaping docker. Select the top piece, for example, and choose Arrange| Shaping|Trim. In the docker, enable the Source Object option, click

Trim, and finally click the piece right below your selected object. This will knock away any place the two objects overlap ("trimming"). It takes a little practice to predict the results of the Trim function (I still mess things up!) and to get the order of selection right. Keep selecting and trimming until none of your objects overlap (see Figure 7.4).

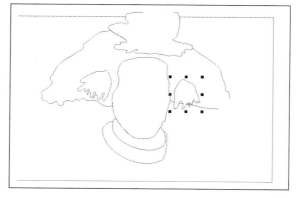

**Figure 7.4**
Use the Trim function to create nonoverlapping objects.

5. Once all of the smaller pieces have been trimmed away, you need to work out the problems of the bounding box, which also must not overlap. Drag-select all of the pieces inside the bounding box, click Trim in the Shaping docker, then click on the bounding box. This should punch a hole in the bounding box wherever a puzzle piece is lying on top, which is just what we need. I gave these a fountain fill so you could see each piece better (see Figure 7.5).

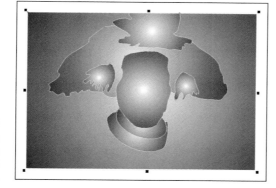

**Figure 7.5**
The Intersect and Trim functions within the Shaping docker help create each individual puzzle piece.

6. We are so close now, you can taste it! Select all of the pieces, including the bounding box, and combine them (Ctrl+L). Now select the bitmap, right-click, and select Unlock Object from the pop-up menu. With the bitmap selected, choose Effects|PowerClip|Place Inside Container, select Place Inside Container, and click on the puzzle curve. Zing! Almost there! Figure 7.6 shows where we are with this step completed.

**Figure 7.6**
Use the PowerClip command to place the bitmap within the puzzle shapes.

7. Now to get puzzle pieces that you can move and rotate individually, simply select the PowerClip object and break it apart (Ctrl+K). That's it! You now have a great cyberpuzzle, and you can do whatever you want with it (see Figure 7.7).

**Figure 7.7**
When you break apart the multi-part PowerClip object, each piece can be moved or rotated like pieces of a puzzle.

8. If you would like to give your puzzle pieces a drop shadow effect, as I did, simply click on a PowerClip curve with the Interactive Drop Shadow tool and drag (see Figure 7.8). The direction and distance that you drag defines the shadow. Use the Property Bar to adjust how dark you want your drop shadow (using the Drop Shadow Opacity option), how crisp you want it (using the Drop Shadow Feathering option), and other modifications.

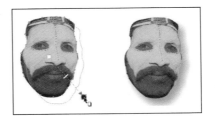

**Figure 7.8**
Use the Interactive Drop Shadow Tool to make your puzzle pieces look more realistic.

**Figure 7.9**
Use the Transparent Background option in the Convert To Bitmap dialog box to convert a Power-Clip curve into a floating bitmap.

9.  If you want your puzzle pieces to have an embossed look, like die-cut cardboard, you can use a bitmap filter. First, save a backup copy of your file to disk. Then, select a PowerClip curve that does not yet have any effects on it (such as the Interactive Drop Shadow object) and convert it to a bitmap. From the Bitmap menu, choose Convert To Bitmap. Now in the resulting dialog box, choose the appropriate resolution for your task at hand. Then specify RGB Color, select the Anti-aliasing option, and—here is the key—select the Transparent Background option (see Figure 7.9). This last option will create a "floating" bitmap and not a rectangular one on a white background.

10. Now that your bitmap is "floating," you can use the bitmap filters on it to give it an embossed look. With the bitmap selected, choose Bitmaps| 3D Effects|Emboss. This will create a "beveled" look, with highlights in the direction of the arrow, and at the Depth and Level settings you assign. Make sure the Original color option is selected, or you may end up with just a gray tile (see Figure 7.10). Try out different options, using the Preview button to view changes, until you are satisfied. Then click OK to apply.

**Figure 7.10**
Use the Emboss Bitmap effect to create a subtle bevel on your puzzle piece.

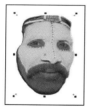

The Emboss filter unfortunately does some strange things to your images as a whole, not just to the edges. For "perfect" puzzle pieces, see the next project. This technique is quick and easy, and you can even add the Interactive Drop Shadow effect to the "floating" bitmaps after you "emboss" them, which makes for a quick solution to the puzzle challenge. Once you have your puzzle pieces, you can do a lot of things with them. You can, for example, animate the pieces, having them explode and reassemble themselves. Or you can create a cybergame or an actual puzzle to cut out and assemble. You'll find this file, in the exploded version, in the color section in the center of this book. You can also find the file, which is called indipuzl.cdr, in the \Chapt07\ directory on the companion CD-ROM. If you load the file, select one of the small pieces, and choose the Effects|PowerClip|Extract Contents command. You can see why these files are so big. Notice how the entire original bitmap then pops out of even the tiniest piece! Breaking apart a PowerClip object is a great trick, but it does eat up some memory.

# PROJECT Puzzle Parts

Puzzle analogies abound in the advertising world. I can't tell you how many times I have been asked to create images for "Bringing It All Together" or some other slogan that begs for a puzzle-like graphic. The image in Figure 7.11 was a design concept for a client that wanted to use puzzle pieces as navigation buttons in a Web site. On the Web site, as you move the mouse over a piece, it changes from black and white to color, and an identifier flashes to describe that part of the Web site you'll move to if you click. As you doubtless have noticed, creating interesting Web sites and intuitive site navigation is becoming increasingly challenging. I hope that the techniques in this book will help you make your own Web sites unique.

The complexity of this image belies the simplicity with which it was created. Using the PowerClip feature in CorelDRAW to stuff image shapes in the puzzle-piece curves is a no-brainer, and getting the 3D effect is a snap using a bitmap plug-in in Photo-Paint.

To harness the power of CorelDRAW and Photo-Paint to create a complex-looking puzzle graphic quickly, follow these steps:

1. First you need some puzzle pieces. Creating interlocking objects in CorelDRAW is really easy. Use the Bezier tool to create a puzzle piece. You will need to draw only this one piece, so don't fret. Now, draw a rectangle that overlaps the puzzle piece on one side. Choose Arrange| Shaping|Trim, and select only the Leave Object: Source Object radio button. With your drawn puzzle piece selected, click Trim, then click the rectangle. Now you have two perfectly interlocking pieces (see Figure 7.12).

**Figure 7.11**

The PowerClip feature places images inside curved puzzle shapes. Using plug-in filters in Photo-Paint, you make the puzzle pieces come to life with beveling and shadow effects.

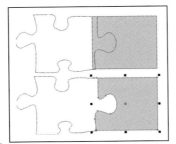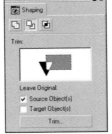

**Figure 7.12**

Use the Trim option in the Shaping docker to make puzzle pieces interlock.

2. Repeat the process until you have a collection of puzzle pieces in the shape you want. My example has the same proportions as the computer screen (wider than tall) because it was for a Web page, but your puzzle can be any shape or size.

3. Once you have your puzzle pieces in place, give each one a unique color, so they stand out boldly from one another. This step makes select-

ing the pieces much easier in Photo-Paint later. Select all of your pieces in their final position and duplicate them (+ key). Position the duplicate set directly below the original. Leave the top set of your puzzle pieces as solid-colored objects. Use the bottom set to "contain" your images.

> **Note:** CorelDRAW 9 allows you to import multiple files at once. Hold down the Ctrl key to select multiple files in the Import dialog box. When you click Import, you can then size and position each image one by one. This speeds up the process of populating your puzzle pieces, for example, because you can import, size, and position each bitmap in a single Import session.

4. Import a bitmap (Ctrl+I) or choose Acquire Image|Acquire to use an image from your scanner or digital camera. I used images off the Corel *Business* Photo CD. I purchased this CD as part of Corel's economical "Super Ten" *Business and Industry* Photo Packs (I used Corel's Web site, **www.corel.com**). I don't hesitate for a moment to purchase clip-art images, because they always come in handy, and in the "Ten Packs" they are obscenely cheap. I love "e-business."

5. Working in Wireframe view, size and position your bitmap over your puzzle piece. Then choose Effects|PowerClip|Place Inside Container, and click on the puzzle piece. This will stuff your image inside the curve (see Figure 7.13). If you don't like the position of the image inside the curve, use the Effects|PowerClip|Edit Contents command to move the image around inside the curve. Also remember to deselect the Auto-center New PowerClip Contents option on the Edit tab of the Options dialog box (Ctrl+J). When you've finished, choose Effects|PowerClip|Finish Editing This Level.

**Figure 7.13**
Use the PowerClip feature to constrain images within a puzzle curve.

6. Repeat the process for each of the puzzle pieces until you have a puzzle filled with the images you want. You could stop here, but I like to add a few steps to increase the realism. You should have two copies of your puzzle: one with just colored pieces, and one with image-filled pieces (see Figure 7.14). Export the entire graphic (to create both puzzles in one graphic file) (Ctrl+E), changing the Files Of Type setting to TIFF, and then change the Color setting to RGB. Select the Anti-aliasing and Use Color Profile radio buttons, and decide which Resolution setting is appropriate (I always work at 300 dpi—see the sidebar, "Work at High Res"). Click OK to create the bitmap, and then exit CorelDRAW.

**Figure 7.14**

The final steps in CorelDRAW result in two puzzles: one with colored pieces, and one with picture-filled pieces.

7. Launch Photo-Paint and open the puzzle bitmap you created in Step 6. Select the Magic Wand Mask tool, located on the Mask Tools flyout. Now click on one of the solid-colored puzzle pieces, which will "magically" create the desired selection (see Figure 7.15).

8. From the Object Picker flyout, choose the Mask Transform tool (it looks like four arrows pointing in all directions). Now you can drag your puzzle-shaped selection area over the same picture-filled puzzle piece in the duplicate set below. The solid-colored copy of the puzzle-piece pair makes creating this odd-shaped selection a snap (see Figure 7.16).

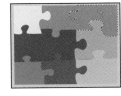

**Figure 7.15**

Use the Magic Wand Mask tool to quickly select the puzzle shape.

**Figure 7.16**

The Mask Transform tool lets you drag the selection area from the solid-colored puzzle over the bitmap-filled version.

9. With your selection now over the picture-filled puzzle piece, you are free to embellish it with a bevel. You can choose Effects|3D Effects|Emboss as in the previous project, or you can use a third-party plug-in for better

---

### Work at High Res

With images these days destined for both Web sites and print, you may often find yourself using the same graphic for both. If you design an image specifically for the Web using low-resolution bitmaps, however, it will look awful in print. Instead, design everything as if it is destined for print, then simply downsize the images as needed for any Web site needs. This way, you always have the right resolution parent file on hand. You can always downsize the high-resolution images and create perfect graphics for the Web, but you can't work the other way around. Use the Resample dialog box in either CorelDRAW or Photo-Paint to create smaller graphics for Web sites.

## Powerful Plug-Ins

Step 9 in this tutorial uses a plug-in not included with CorelDRAW 9—Alien Skin's Eye Candy. While Corel ships a lot of cool effects with its graphics suite, you may find that third-party plug-ins—from such vendors as Alien Skin, Auto f/x Corp., and others—offer a quick-and-easy way to enhance your images and your productivity. Corel Photo-Paint supports any third-party plug-in that is "PhotoShop" compatible.

When you install a plug-in, place it in the \ProgramFiles\Corel\Graphics9\Plugins folder. Or if you already have it on your disk, just tell CorelDRAW or Photo-Paint where to find it. Open the Options dialog box (Ctrl+J) and click Plug-ins. Then click Add and select the folder where you have plug-ins already on your system (so you don't have to install them twice on your system if, for example, you use another program—such as Adobe PhotoShop—that has plug-ins).

Most companies offer "free" demos of their plug-ins so that you can download and try them before you buy. Log into the **www.alienskin.com** Web site, for example, and download the demo for Eye Candy 3 (or Xenoflex, Alien Skin's other really cool filter set). I am betting that you, like me, will find the Eye Candy tool set a valuable addition to your design studio.

Another great online resource for information and links to plug-ins is the **www.i-us.com** Web site. This digital graphics community has several CorelDRAW/Photo-Paint specific forums, in addition to a content area dedicated to plug-ins. The site always has an ample collection of free plug-ins to download and use immediately to enhance your design day.

**Note:** You can perform other effects before you deselect your puzzle piece. For example, after you finish the Inner Bevel step, select Effects|Eye Candy 3.01|Drop Shadow to create the illusion that the puzzle piece is floating above the page. It is this simplicity that makes the plug-ins a worthy investment.

results, such as the Alien Skin Eye Candy filters. With the Eye Candy filter set installed, choose Effects|Eye Candy 3.01|Inner Bevel. This dialog box lets you create the illusion of a 3D bevel following along the contour of your selection. This is the perfect way to add depth and realism to our custom puzzle shapes. Change the Bevel Shape option to Button, and click the green checkmark to transform your puzzle piece (see Figure 7.17).

10. Before you can continue the process on the next puzzle piece, you must first remove the mask (Ctrl+Shift+R). Now repeat the process for all the puzzle pieces.

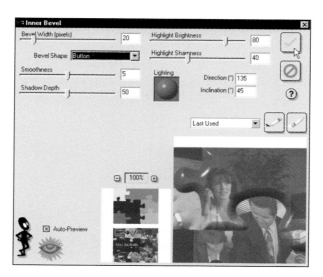

**Figure 7.17**
The Inner Bevel plug-in creates the illusion of a cut-out puzzle piece, adding highlights and shading along the selection contour.

## Workaround for Masochists and Skinflints

You can get similar results without the additional expense of a third-party plug-in, directly in CorelDRAW. With some effort, you can use the Lighting and Beveling options of the Interactive Extrude tool to create the 3D-looking puzzle piece. The problem is, the Interactive Extrude tool will not work on a PowerClip curve, so you lose the flexibility and ease-of-use of placing an image inside the shape using the PowerClip feature. You can, however, create shading and beveling on a curve by using a Bitmap Pattern fill. Follow these steps to create a beveled puzzle piece directly in CorelDRAW:

1. Select your object and open the Pattern Fill dialog box from the Fill tool flyout. Select the Bitmap radio button, then click Load. Now locate the bitmap that you want to place inside your puzzle piece (see Figure 7.18). Click OK to fill your object.

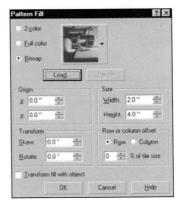

**Figure 7.18**
The Bitmap option on the Pattern Fill dialog box lets you select a bitmap to place inside your puzzle curve.

2. The problem with this technique is that it is hard to control the position of your image within the puzzle piece, requiring you to visit the Pattern Fill dialog box several times. Open the Pattern Fill dialog box and attempt to position the graphic correctly by modifying the Width and Height values, in addition to futzing with the x and y Origin numbers. Since no "preview" option exists, you have to repeat the process manually (see why I like the plug-ins solution?). With a little experimentation, you can get your picture in a satisfactory position within the puzzle curve (see Figure 7.19).

3. When you finally get your image in position, you can use the Interactive Extrude tool to create the 3D bevel look. Drag the Interactive Extrude tool from the center up to start the process. Then, click Lighting on the Property Bar and click the 1 light. Next, click Bevels and select the Use Bevel and Show Bevel Only options. This should give you results similar to the Inner Bevel bitmap plug-in (see Figure 7.20).

**Figure 7.19**
Modify the position of the image inside the puzzle curve by changing the Size and Origin variables in the Pattern Fill dialog box.

**Figure 7.20**
The Lighting and Bevel options on the Interactive Extrude Property Bar create a 3D puzzle-piece illusion.

In this case, the negatives outweigh the positives, which is why I always opt for the Photo-Paint/plug-in solution when building puzzle pieces. The few dollars' expense is hardly worth losing my sanity waiting for a page full of complex Interactive Extrude puzzle pieces to render.

The results of the plug-in version of this project can be seen in the companion CD-ROM. The CorelDRAW file is called puzzle.cdr, and you can find it in the \Chapt07\ subdirectory.

## PROJECT Puzzling Spheres

I showed a friend this technique—which involves stuffing a copy of the current file into a sphere, thus creating the illusion of a reflected environment. My friend watched the screen with wide-eyed amazement and finally said, "It's your job to invent weird stuff, isn't it? Well, you are doing a good job!" Take a look at Figure 7.21 and see if you agree.

Yes, it is indeed my job to invent weird stuff. This image within an image idea is a relatively new one for me, but it's already destined to be one of my favorites. It isn't really a "puzzle," but the technique is reminiscent of one of those "brain puzzle" games, so I decided to include it in this chapter. To create the illusion of a reflecting chrome ball, follow these steps:

**Figure 7.21**
Using the Export function to "capture" the current image, and also using a stack of distortion pieces, result in a reflection illusion.

1. Use the Rectangle tool to draw a box the size of your target image. From the Fill Tool flyout, select the Pattern Fill option. Select the Bitmap radio button, then click on the current pattern bitmap tile to reveal the gallery of available options. Choose a fairly geometric pattern that will help enhance the distortion techniques later. I chose the pattern of

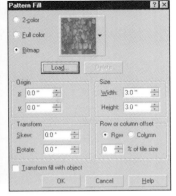

**Figure 7.22**

The Bitmap option from the Pattern Fill dialog box fills a rectangle with a stony-creek bottom texture.

stones, which could make our chrome spheres appear to be resting at the bottom of a creek bed (see Figure 7.22).

2.  Use the Ellipse tool to draw a perfect circle by holding down the Ctrl key as you drag. Give this circle a white fill and no outline, then duplicate it. Now, drag the top duplicate above the original, so you can see what you are doing in Normal view. Select the top circle, then choose the Interactive Transparency tool. You don't need to drag on your object to assign a transparency—you can just use the Property Bar. Change the Transparency Type option to Fountain, then click Radial Fountain Transparency. The logic of the default is the reverse of what we want, so drag 10% black from the on-screen color palette and drop it on the center control point of the Interactive Transparency object. Then drag black off the on-screen palette and drop it on the outside color point. Next, drag the center of the Interactive Transparency object to the top and right, which creates the illusion of a reflection on a glass sphere (see Figure 7.23).

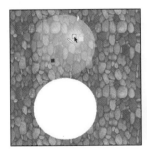

**Figure 7.23**

The Interactive Fountain Transparency tool transforms a solid-white circle into a "glass sphere" illusion.

3.  Now select the Interactive Drop Shadow tool from the Interactive Tool flyout. Click on the center of the solid-white object, and drag down and to the left to create the illusion that it is floating above the rocks and casting a shadow.

4. With the drop shadow group still selected, choose Arrange|Separate. This will "freeze" the shadow, so you are free to manipulate the white parent circle.

5. Select the white parent circle, and use the Edit|Copy Properties From command (Ctrl+Shift+A) to open the Copy Properties dialog box. Select the Fill radio button, click OK, and then click on the stone-filled background (see Figure 7.24). Duplicate the stone circle and set it aside. We will need a copy of this later.

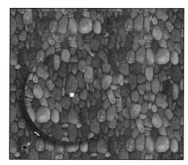

**Figure 7.24**
The Interactive Drop Shadow tool creates the illusion of an object hovering above the creek bed.

6. Now select the stone-circle object resting above the drop shadow. From the Bitmaps menu, choose Convert To Bitmap. Change the Color option to CMYK (this project is going to print) and select the Anti-aliasing, Transparent Background, and Use Color Profile radio buttons. Click OK to rasterize your object.

7. With the stone circle now a bitmap, we can distort it to look rounder. Choose Bitmaps|3D Effects|Sphere to open the Sphere dialog box. Here you can control the percentage of distortion. The default setting of 25 is fine, so click OK to "sphereize" the bitmap (see Figure 7.25).

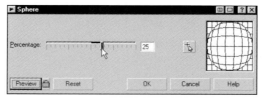

**Figure 7.25**
The Sphere bitmap effect filter distorts the image into a 3D-looking ball.

8. Now arrange your "glass sphere" circle over the "stone ball" bitmap, and you've got yourself a pretty darn convincing 3D-looking image (see Figure 7.26).

**Figure 7.26**
Stacking the transparent circle on top of the distorted bitmap creates a convincing 3D effect.

## Spheres Reflecting Spheres

This is a good stopping point, and perhaps I should have left well enough alone. But since it's physically impossible for me to leave "well enough alone," I decided to take the illusion a few steps further to facilitate the illusion of reflecting a second chrome sphere. Don't panic—it's not that hard, and the results are very cool. You can use the effect for other applications where you want to create the illusion of reflection. Here are the steps:

1. Drag-select everything in your image except the "extra" circle object that we made in Step 5 in the previous tutorial, and open the Export dialog box (Ctrl+E). Now create a CMYK bitmap of your scene, at 300 dpi.

2. Import the bitmap you just created in Step 1 at full size (instead of click-dragging the Import cursor to designate a custom import size, just click to import at actual size).

3. Arrange the circle duplicate from earlier so that it has a section of the sphere image passing through it on the bottom-left side (see Figure 7.27). Now select the bitmap, choose Effects|PowerClip|Place Inside Container, and click on the circle duplicate.

4. With the circle now containing a bit of a sphere "reflection," repeat the Convert To Bitmap and Sphere steps (refer to Steps 6 and 7 from the

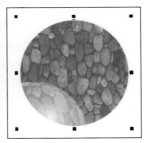

**Figure 7.27**
Use the PowerClip feature to place the screen-capture image into another circle shape.

previous tutorial) to create a new rounded sphere shape that happens to also have a bit of a "reflected" twin! Place the new distorted bitmap under the "glass sphere" shape (see Figure 7.28).

**Figure 7.28**
Using the screen-capture image in the sphere creates the illusion of reflecting another sphere.

5. Now select all of the elements that make up your chrome ball (including the drop shadow) and duplicate the object (+ key). Then move the duplicate above and to the right of the original.

**Figure 7.29**
Rotating the "reflection" bitmap toward the duplicate ball group finishes the illusion.

6. You need to rotate the fill bitmap on one of the balls so that the reflection is correct. This is easy. Simply hold the Alt key and click on the ball that you want to change the reflection in until you select the Color bitmap (watch the status bar as you click). Then click the center arrows again to reveal the corner rotation arrows, which you can then drag around until your reflection illusions line up correctly (see Figure 7.29). Shazam! You are a master of illusion.

This "eye-puzzle" can be found if you load the spheres.cdr file located in the \Chapt07 subdirectory on the companion CD-ROM, and it is also in the digital color section. It's an amazing—but really simple—illusion. You could flip-flop the image that you stuff into a sphere to make it "reflect" text or other objects.

# Beyond f/x

The puzzle metaphor is a natural for advertising, making for some very powerful imagery. Taking a group portrait, then pulling people out with the puzzle trick, can add visual impact to statistics ("One person in ten will be affected by violent crime...") or whatever you can think of. You can create images that build themselves using the puzzle pieces, or start as a whole and explode into oblivion, using the pieces to build an animation. Or you can follow my lead and use the puzzle pieces as Web-navigation buttons.

The optical illusion presented in the last project also has some interesting potential. You could create any number of images to stuff inside the balls, to create "trapped" people or products. Or you could use the technique instead to render "bubbles" to use in projects for beverages, diving equipment, or kids' toys.

A picture is worth a thousand words, they say, and I say a picture is worth even more if you work in some clever CorelDRAW effects!

# Moving On

In this chapter, we looked at how to make pieces, puzzles, and illusions with the PowerClip function. You'll find many uses for the PowerClip/break-apart trick, and remember that it is not limited to bitmaps. When you use CorelDRAW objects in your puzzle pieces, the files are not nearly as large. In addition, keep in mind that you can export a CorelDRAW image as a bitmap and then use a paint program to manipulate the pieces further. I like to do this because it makes it easier to use a bitmap filter effect to further enhance the images. Don't hesitate to mix and match technologies or techniques to get what you are after, or to invent your own wonderful variants. Just plan ahead when working with bitmaps so you don't end up doing the same work twice (see the "Working at High Res" sidebar in this chapter). Like everything in this book, my illustrations are just a starting point. Go forth and conquer, my wicked design minions!

In Chapter 8, we look at creating all kinds of "linked" artwork, using the Interactive Blend tool as well as the Image Sprayer. From barbed wire to chain links, we will create connected strands of all kinds of wonderful design elements. Let's hope that we won't create just enough rope to hang ourselves…

Chapter 8

# Barbed Wire, Rope, and Chains

*This chapter uses the Interactive Blend Tool and the Object Sprayer mode of the Artistic Media tool in CorelDRAW; it also includes an exercise using the Image Sprayer tool in Photo-Paint.*

# Creating Repeating Design Elements Using Spraylists

Barbed wire, chains, and spiky shapes are popular in the tattoo community, and they also make for interesting design elements. As the alternative becomes more and more mainstream, even the most conservative design studios might find themselves searching for appropriate art elements to suit a client looking for a more hardcore image. These kinds of design elements look great, and they are extremely flexible and easy to create.

**Note:** Since CorelDRAW creates vector "objects," the tool is called the "Object Sprayer." In Photo-Paint, since you are working with bitmaps, the tool works essentially the same but uses "images"; hence it is called the "Image Sprayer" there.

In this chapter, we will use both the Blend function and the Object Sprayer mode of the Artistic Media tool to create round wire and pointy tips as well as chain and rope. We will work again with metallic shading (like we saw in Chapter 3) to color some dangerous razor wire. All in all, we'll have a fine selection of linked and pointy things from which to choose!

The great thing about using the Object Sprayer mode of the Artistic Media tool in CorelDRAW for these techniques (rather than Photo-Paint) is that few limitations exist as to the shape of the curve that you can run the chain or rope links along, resulting in a variety of handy applications. You could easily create a signature or any other unique shape in chain or rope. And in CorelDRAW you can change your mind about how the curve looks, while in Photo-Paint you are limited to what you can "paint" in the first stroke.

Rope, chain, and wire make great border elements, but they aren't limited to that purpose. The CorelDRAW clip-art CD has plenty of pieces of rope and even chain in ordinary round or rectangular configurations, so it is our task to come up with a solution for any strange shape you can imagine. This is made possible with the Blend docker and the ability to blend along a curve, or applying a Spraylist of objects to a path using Object Sprayer. The computer-accurate spacing makes tasks like connecting chain links possible, but the same procedure could work with any shape or image (you could just as easily connect a series of plastic monkeys!). These kinds of designs are just too tedious to do by hand, but with a little computer assistance, heck, anything is possible! (See Figure 8.1.)

**Figure 8.1**
Blending objects along a path can result in chains, rope, or barbed wire in virtually any shape imaginable.

## PROJECT Barbed Wire

For some reason, barbed wire just really appeals to me. It suggests "danger" or "beware," and it works well in artwork for the more hardcore crowd. This market continues to grow, however, as cruiser bikes and gangster rap enter the mainstream. If nothing else, it makes for an interesting diversion from other, boring border elements. Let's lay some barbed wire:

1. Use the Bezier tool (located on the Curve tool flyout) to draw a sweeping horizontal line with soft waves in it by click-dragging points on the screen. Now draw another line in an opposite sweeping motion and on top of this one to create the wire shape (see Figure 8.2). Try to crisscross the lines at a distance that's close to uniform—this is how real barbed wire works. You can create barbed wire in virtually any shape or configuration, but this small piece of horizontal wire is a good place to start. Shift-select both lines and combine them (Ctrl+L).

**Figure 8.2**
Use the Bezier tool to create two overlapping lines in the shape of your choice.

2. Select the wire shape and give it a thick, black 8-point outline from the Outline flyout. Now duplicate it and give the duplicate a thin, white hairline outline. Drag-select both stacked pieces, then locate the Interactive Blend tool on the Interactive Tool flyout. Carefully drag from the thick line at the back to the thinner front copy to create a blend between them. This will result in a round-looking wire, as the thick black line bends to the thin white line. Notice that the objects do not look like two separate wires at the points where they cross—that is because we combined the lines into one shape. If you want individual wires, don't combine them (see Figure 8.3).

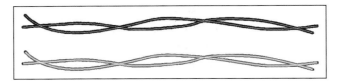

**Figure 8.3**
Blend a thick black line into a thin white one to create a rounded wire.

3. Draw a rectangle and round out the ends by dragging a corner node with the Shape tool. Duplicate (+ key) this shape and convert it to curves (Ctrl+Q). With the Shape tool, drag the bottom-center node down. Now, drag-select all the nodes in the lower half of the object; on the Property Bar, click Convert Curve To Line. This will make a spiky end on one of the twisted wire shapes. Duplicate the original object two

more times and the spike one more time. Arrange the objects to look like the twisted, spiked barbed wire hub.

4. Drag-select all the objects and open the Fountain Fill dialog box (F11). Create a linear custom color blend to suggest a shaded round cylinder. Enable the Custom option, then double-click along the preview ribbon to add a color point to the blend. Change the color of this point by clicking on a color swatch in the Fountain Fill dialog box. If you prefer, you can zoom in close with the Zoom tool (click the Zoom tool, then drag a box around your object to zoom in close). Now you can use the Interactive Fill tool to create the round shading by dragging color off the on-screen palette and dropping it onto points along the Interactive Fill tool control line (see Figure 8.4).

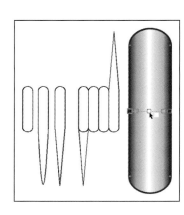 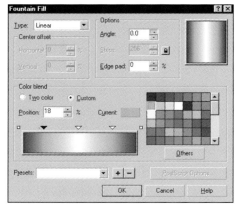

**Figure 8.4**
The Shape tool transforms a rectangle into a rounded wire object and then into a sharp barb. Finally, a custom color blend gives the shapes a round appearance.

5. Drag-select and group (Ctrl+G) the barb shapes. Duplicate the barb group and place the duplicates at each point where your wire blend crisscrosses. Double-click on the barb group to reveal the rotation arrows. Drag on a corner set to spin each barb slightly to orient it to the wires below (see Figure 8.5).

**Figure 8.5**
Place the barb groups at the points where the wires crisscross to finish the look.

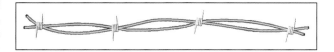

## PROJECT Prickly Pieces

You can create barbed wire in virtually any shape. To create a barbed spiral, follow these steps:

1. Select the Spiral tool, located on the Object flyout. Drag the Spiral tool on-screen to create a spiral (use the Property Bar to control the spiral options, such as Spiral Revolutions). Now place a barb group at each end of the spiral, Shift-select both, and drag between them with the

Interactive Blend tool. On the Property Bar, click Path Properties, select New Path, and then click on your spiral shape. This should blend the barbs along the path and space them out evenly (see Figure 8.6). On the Property Bar, you can control the number of steps, as well as the Object Acceleration, to get the even spacing you want.

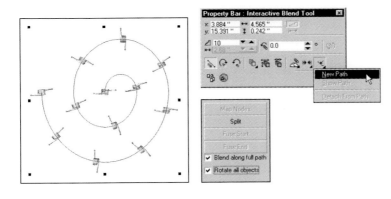

**Figure 8.6**

Use the Interactive Blend tool Property Bar to space out the barb shapes along any shape— in this case, a spiral.

2. Use the Freehand tool to draw in the wire shapes, crisscrossing at each barb point. Use the Shape tool to auto-reduce the nodes. Drag-select all the nodes in the line, then use the Curve Smoothness slider on the Property Bar to smooth out and clean up the lines (see Figure 8.7).

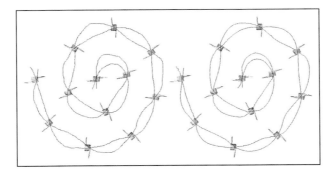

**Figure 8.7**

Use the Freehand tool to draw the wire shapes and then use the Shape tool to clean up the free-hand-drawn lines. The blend-spaced barbs act as guidelines for drawing the wire.

3. Now duplicate and blend the wire shapes as before. Send the wires to the back (Shift+PgDn) and you are done!

## PROJECT Pointed Painting

With the addition of the Object Sprayer option to the Artistic Media tool, you have an easy and flexible way to apply images such as the barbed wire to any path. The Object Sprayer option lets you use a "Spraylist," which is nothing more than a separate image file. You can select from a list of pre-installed Spraylists or, even better, create your own. To create a Spraylist and apply it to a path, follow these steps:

1. Starting with a single "barb" group from the previous project, we will create a custom Spraylist. For barbed wire, this single object alone could

become a "list," which would simply repeat the same barb over and over. For more visual variety, however, you can create a mirrored duplicate by dragging the left-center sizing handle to the right while holding down the Ctrl key, then pressing the Spacebar. This should create a mirrored duplicate (see Figure 8.8).

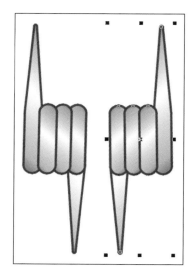

**Figure 8.8**
A mirrored duplicate of the barb shape will add to the visual variety of a Spraylist.

2. Make sure each unique barb is its own group (Ctrl+G). A Spraylist file uses each object grouping as a piece of the list. You can create any number of barbs—perhaps recoloring one to look "rusted"—for as complicated a Spraylist as you want. (The ability to add unique pieces to your Spraylists is why this feature is much more powerful than blending a single barb along a path.) Next, save the file (call it "barbs.cdr") in the \CustomMediaStrokes folder. This folder is located in the Corel folder (wherever you installed it, such as \ProgramFiles), in the \Graphics9\Draw\ subfolder). Once you have saved the file in this directory, it will appear as an option on your Object Sprayer Spraylist drop-down menu, but only after you quit and restart CorelDRAW. So quit and restart CorelDRAW now.

**No See-um Spraylist**

If you have disabled the Thumbnail option in the Save Drawing dialog box, you won't see a visual representation of any Spraylists you add to the \CustomMediaStrokes folder. So make sure that this option is enabled when you're creating your own custom Spraylists.

3. Now let's get to paintin'! Choose File|New (Ctrl+N) and select the Artistic Media tool from the Curve flyout. Now on the Property Bar, switch to the Sprayer mode, then click on the Spraylist File List and scroll down until you see a thumbnail of the barbs you created in Step 2 (see Figure 8.9).

**Figure 8.9**
The Property Bar is where you enable the Sprayer option of the Artistic Media tool, as well as choose which objects to "spray" from the File List.

4. Now simply drag the Object Sprayer cursor to spray a row of barbs. To make the barbs rotate along the path, use the Rotation option on the Property Bar. Click the Rotation button, then enable the Path Based Rotation option (see Figure 8.10).

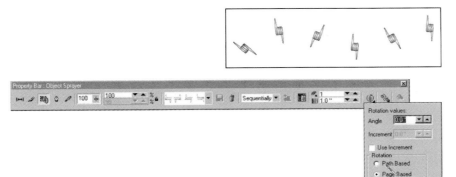

**Figure 8.10**
Use the Rotation option on the Property Bar to force the barb pieces to rotate correctly along the painted path.

## PROJECT Well-Mannered Pieces

"Painting" freehand with the Artistic Media tool using the Object Sprayer mode is fun and can give you cool results (especially in Photo-Paint, where painting freehand is the only option but the Spraylists are much more colorful and interesting), but the real power to this feature lies in the ability to apply a Spraylist to an existing path. This can't be done in Photo-Paint, so you must use the Spraylist tool in CorelDRAW. Here's how it works:

1. In CorelDRAW, create a path or object to which you want to apply a Spraylist. It can be any shape—even text, if you want.

2. With your object/path selected, click on the Artistic Media tool again, then select the Sprayer option. Now simply choose your desired Spraylist from the Spraylist File List, and voilà! The objects of your choice are now flowing across your path. Use the Property Bar to change the Size, Spacing, and Rotation settings to get the desired results with the active Spraylist—almost none of them in their default mode seem to produce useful results (see Figure 8.11).

That's all there really is to the Spraylist. It is loads of fun to play with, especially when you go the extra effort and create your own Spraylists. In the

**Figure 8.11**
Use the options on the Property Bar to get your Spraylist to build to your liking on your custom path.

\Chapt08\ folder on the companion CD-ROM, you will find a handful of my own Spraylist creations, such as rope.cdr, chain.cdr, barbed.cdr, and others. Copy these to your \CustomMediaStrokes folder or create your own Spraylists.

# PROJECT Razor Wire

As cool as Spraylists are, with some projects you can't find an automated "fix" and need to build the pieces by hand, such as in this razor wire example. Razor wire is usually a solid strand of metallic tape stamped with a razor shape every few inches. This effect is kind of bland, so I created a more spacey-looking razor wire with more defined individual blades attached to the tape, which took some tricks and the Blend feature to accomplish. To make my razor wire, follow these steps:

1. Draw a rectangle with the Rectangle tool, duplicate it (+), and downsize the duplicate by dragging one of the corner control handles inward. From the Interactive Tool flyout, select the Interactive Envelope tool. Click Envelope Straight Line Mode, then with the Shape tool, drag the top-center node of the envelope inward while holding down both the Ctrl and Shift keys. This will move all the center nodes inward simultaneously, creating a star shape (see Figure 8.12).

**Figure 8.12**
A rectangle becomes a razor blade with the help of a straight-line envelope.

2. Shift-select both objects and combine them (Ctrl+L). Now borrow the chrome custom color blend from the headline pieces in Chapter 3, or create a new one with a similar color scheme (using the Fountain Fill dialog box or the Interactive Fill tool). Or you can load the blade.cdr file, which you'll find in the \Chapt08\ folder on the companion CD-ROM, so you can copy the fill (see Figure 8.13).

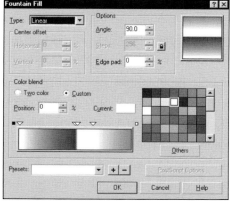

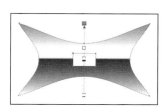

**Figure 8.13**
Use a custom color blend to give the razor piece a metallic look.

3. To give the razor a beveled edge, use the Interactive Extrude tool. Drag on the object to create an Extrude group. On the Property Bar, click Lighting and enable a light source at the top-right position by clicking the *1* light icon. Then, click Bevels and enable the Use Bevel and Show Bevel Only options. Change the Bevel depth to .05 inches, or modify it to be as wide or as narrow as you want. Because the default option on the Color page is Use Object Fill, the resulting pieces all have the custom color blend of the original, only shaded according to the light source setting. The result is a polished-looking razor (see Figure 8.14).

> **Quick Fill**
>
> To copy a fill from one object to another, click the object from which you want to copy the fill and, holding the right mouse button, drag and release over the object you want to copy to. When you release the right mouse button, a popup menu will give you options, including Copy Fill Here.

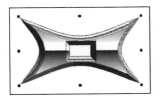

**Figure 8.14**
Use the Lighting and Bevel options on the Interactive Extrude Property Bar to create a polished razor object.

4. You cannot use a "live" object in a blend group without first "freezing" it with the Arrange|Separate command. Separate the razor Extrude group, then select and group the objects—which you can now duplicate and use in a blend. Draw a smooth *s* shape with the Bezier tool. Select and duplicate (+ key) the razor group and place a duplicate at each end of the *s* curve. Select both and drag the Interactive Blend tool between them. Then, click Path Properties on the Property Bar and make the *s* curve the New Path to blend the two objects along the curve (see Figure 8.15).

**Figure 8.15**
Use the Blend docker to spread razors along any curve—in this case, an *s* shape drawn with the Bezier tool.

5. Draw a small circle on top one of the parent razor groups. Duplicate it and move the duplicate to the razor shape at the far end of the blend. Shift-select both circle objects, and use the Interactive Blend tool again to create a blend along the same path as the razor shape (see Figure 8.16).

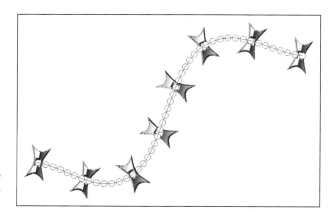

**Figure 8.16**
Blend some circles along the same path as the razor blend.

6. Select the circle blend, use the Arrange|Separate option to "freeze" the blend, and then use the Arrange|Ungroup All option to separate all the shapes. Zoom in; then, while holding down the Shift key, click on the blend path to deselect it, and combine (Ctrl+L) all the circle objects into one curve. Select the blend curve again and duplicate it (it is still the control curve for the razor shapes). With a free curve selected, use the Interactive Contour tool to create a single-step outside contour with an offset to be larger than the circle shapes, which will create the snaking "ribbon" metal band (see Figure 8.17).

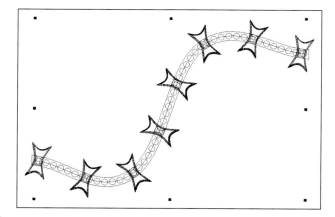

**Figure 8.17**
Use the Contour tool to create a long, snaking rectangle larger than the circle shapes (shown here in Wireframe view).

7. Select the contour and issue the Arrange|Separate command, and then select Arrange|Ungroup All to separate the objects. Next, select just the contour shape, Shift-select the circle shapes, and combine them (Ctrl+L). This will create the winding metal tape with hollow circles used to connect the prickly razor objects. Use the Copy Properties From

option (Ctrl+Shift+A) on the Edit menu to copy the fill from one of the razors to the connecting ribbon. To alternate the razors front/back, first select the blend and free each razor object from the blend with the Arrange|Separate and Ungroup (Ctrl+U) commands. Now Shift-select every other razor shape, then bring them to the front (Shift+PgUp), as shown in Figure 8.18.

**Figure 8.18**
Combine the Contour shape made from the control curve with the blend of circles on the same curve to create a winding metal tape to connect the razor objects.

These barbed wire examples can be seen in this book's digital color section or in the file called barbed.cdr, which you'll find in the \Chapt08\ subdirectory on the companion CD-ROM. Now all you have to do is create your own wire or metal tape shapes, steal one of the barbs or razors from the CD-ROM, and you are ready to run danger-wire around anything you desire.

## PROJECT Pretty in Pink

While not nearly as versatile as the Object Sprayer mode of the Artistic Media tool in CorelDRAW, the same tool in Photo-Paint does yield some incredible results. Since the Spraylists in Photo-Paint consist of bitmap objects, they tend to be more colorful and "realistic" looking than their CorelDRAW brethren. So what you lose in flexibility and power (you can't modify custom paths applied to Spraylists in Photo-Paint), you gain in "beauty." The tool works this way in Photo-Paint:

1. Once again, select File|New to start with a new image (Ctrl+N), and select the Object Sprayer tool from the Brush Tools flyout. Choose from the Spraylist to find a list of images useful for your project. (I have found that "Fire" is a really cool use of this tool, as is "Foliage" and "Rain Drops.")

2. Drag to paint a stream of images on your canvas. If you change the parameters on the Property Bar, your image will not rebuild dynamically as it does in CorelDRAW (why the Object Sprayer mode of the Artistic Media tool isn't as useful in Photo-Paint, in my opinion), but

rather will only set them for the next time you use the tool. So you might find yourself using the Edit|Undo (Ctrl+Z) feature a lot until you get the settings you want on the Property Bar.

3. To help control where you are painting—to create, for example, a rope spelling out a word—create a shape from CorelDRAW to use as a guide. For instance, use the Freehand tool in CorelDRAW to create your "signature." Now, fine-tune the path with the Shape tool until it looks the way you want. Then, select Edit|Copy (Ctrl+C) to copy the path in CorelDRAW, switch to Photo-Paint, and from the Clipboard menu choose File|New. This will give you an image with your path in it (see Figure 8.19).

**Figure 8.19**
Create a reference path in CorelDRAW and copy/paste it into Photo-Paint.

4. Now from the Object menu, choose Create|New Object. This will create a layer on top of the reference path, so you can paint on top of it without disturbing it.

5. Select the Object Sprayer tool, then choose the Brown Rope option. Now drag the tool along your reference path to spell out your word (see Figure 8.20). It isn't as easy as in CorelDRAW, but the Rope options in Photo-Paint look really cool!

**Figure 8.20**
While limited to the accuracy of your stroke, the results of Object Sprayer in Photo-Paint can be quite striking.

# Beyond f/x

Chains, ropes, and wire are great ways to lay out a page. Because you are not limited to any particular size or shape for your linked graphic, your links can wind around and through the page as you want. This serves not only to break up the page into smaller chunks, but also to direct the eye of the viewer to different parts of the design. Chains or rope also offer interesting associations—from Western motifs and nautical designs to creepier, darker subjects. Barbed wire can add a touch of danger to a logo, or reinforce a theme of war or persecution.

Since you can run the links along any path, you can use handwriting-style lettering to create words with a connected path, then run the links along it. This makes for cool thematic logos or promotional graphics ("Western days," "jailhouse rock," etc.). Blending along a path is always a great way to get proportionately spaced object duplicates, like saw-teeth, gears, or rivets. The Spraylist feature expands that capability to include multiple unique objects along a path, so there is no limit to what you can create. Just don't give your clients enough rope to hang themselves.

# Moving On

This was a fast-paced chapter, putting the Blend function to work linking objects like wire, rope, and chain. Many times, you will want a unique shape—in a chain or rope or wire—that you will need to build using the Blend feature. The Blend tool is a great way to space out objects evenly along a path, even if they are not part of a "linked" theme (like blending two different-colored shapes along a path for a rainbow pattern of geometric shapes around your artwork).

In Chapter 9, we will ignore the Blend function entirely and focus on how to circumvent a common design problem. Having limited resource material for a project (like a single product shot instead of a variety to choose from) presents a situation where you need to create "more" with "less." We will look at some simple solutions to this daunting problem, using creative duplication techniques. Rub your eyes and break out the eyedrops—it's time to get into double vision!

# Chapter 9

# Double Vision

*This chapter explores using multiple copies of the same image to enhance a design. We'll discuss converting images to bitmap duplicates and then manipulating the bitmaps with lens effects and filters. We'll cover other multiple-image design styles as well.*

# Using Multiple and Repeating Images in a Design

Multiple-image designs are pretty common these days; you see them in all sorts of media, including television, print ads, and Web sites. I have seen award shows where the host stands in front of a wall of TVs with a close-up live-feed image of the host's face on the monitors, and I've seen catalogs with a close-up of a product and its full-view image as a subdued background. Web sites use this strategy a lot to get an interesting image out of essentially one picture.

In this chapter, we look at ways to work multiple images into your artwork. This design style is a great way to add visual interest to an otherwise limited graphic. If you have ever had to try to make something from nothing, or you have had to stretch some customer-supplied artwork a little further than you wanted, then you will find these techniques of interest.

First, we take an illustration of a female jester and duplicate the image for both an engaging subdued background graphic and as the main focus of the design. Second, we use the powerful export features of CorelDRAW to create a bitmap background image, which you can make larger than the original and in different colors than the original foreground characters. Then, we create a flower-like pattern with duplicates of the same model photo and surround that with a chaotic pattern made from resized and recolored duplicates of the headline text. Finally, to enhance a product shot we use water as a means to reflect and distort an image. You'll see how even images and objects that are alike can be made to look very different, resulting in some very exciting design possibilities.

## PROJECT Jokers Wild

The jester image (see Figure 9.1) is from a T-shirt and other items commemorating the fifth anniversary of our design studio, nicknamed the "Dog House" because that is where Slimy Dog, our mascot, was whelped years before. I had scanned the ink illustration to work out some other design issues and ended up creating this double-vision layout by combining duplicates of the image in the foreground and background.

This example illustrates how you can milk a design for more than its original purpose. The image is really tall and thin—which made it perfect for the T-shirt design—but it has strange dimensions for standard print applications, and it's really unsuitable for a Web site (where images need to be wide rather than tall). By duplicating and using the objects in a background image, I fattened up the image; even though the original image is still tall and skinny, the overall page is more balanced. Often the pieces are lying right in front of you and all you need to do is assemble them creatively to get what you are looking for. To combine images into a foreground/background double-vision orientation, follow these steps:

**Figure 9.1**
Using one image in the foreground and a muted version of the same image in the background adds depth and interest—and you don't have to build entirely new pieces.

1. I had misplaced the original illustration of the jester image that I wanted
   to use, so I could not simply scan and use Corel Trace (or AutoTrace) to
   trace and convert the image (as in the examples from Chapter 2). All I
   could locate was a "chunky" 1-bit bitmap image, which did not provide
   suitable results when I tried to convert it to vector using Corel Scan (see
   the girlnbox.cmx file in the \Chapt09\ subdirectory on the companion
   CD to see my attempt at tracing the scan). I did not get totally discour-
   aged, however—I knew the bitmap still had some potential. Because
   you can set the "white" color of a 1-bit bitmap to "nothing" by clicking
   the "x" on the on-screen palette, you can get a black ink image on a
   transparent background. Then you can color the bitmap with shapes
   you draw by hand using the Freehand and Bezier tools. It sounds difficult, but it really isn't. First, import (Ctrl+I) the bitmap, called
   girlnbox.tif, from the \Chapt09\ subdirectory on the companion CD.
   Once you've imported the bitmap, right-click it and choose Lock Object
   from the pop-up menu (alternatively, you can choose Arrange|
   Lock Object). This will keep you from accidentally moving the bitmap
   while you are drawing shapes by hand to color it.

2. Switch to Wireframe view, which will make it easier to see what you are
   doing because it displays the black bitmap as gray. Now use the Bezier
   tool to draw shapes that you will place behind the bitmap to color it.
   You need to draw shapes that fill in the "clear" areas only (which display as white on your screen)—the "gray" areas are the black ink. It is
   not difficult to click along the contour of an area using the Bezier tool
   to create a solid shape (see Figure 9.2). Don't worry about perfection,
   because the black ink will cover anything behind it. Besides, you can
   always use the Shape tool to fine-tune these curves later, if you need to.

**Figure 9.2**
Use the Bezier tool to create
shapes to color the "clear" areas
of a 1-bit bitmap.

3. When you have finished drawing your shapes, you can fill each with
   color to bring the black-and-white image to life. Right-click the bitmap and select Unlock Object. Then, right-click and select To Front

(Shift+PgUp) to bring the bitmap to the front, on top of the coloring shapes you drew. This results in a colored bitmap (see Figure 9.3). Save this full-color version to disk so that you can work on the background duplicates.

**Figure 9.3**
Hand-drawn shapes (shown in Wireframe view on the left) add color to a black-and-white bitmap.

4. Once you have your primary image group assembled, it is easy to duplicate and recolor the objects to create the "double-vision" illusion. You could create a background image of jester duplicates in all colors of the rainbow just by changing the hue of the coloring shapes. Or you could use a mirror as a vehicle to exploit the double-vision trick. We'll leave these ideas for the next projects and use a trick more appropriate for this "jester" image, which is a playing card analogy. Your typical deck of cards uses a "double-vision" trick of duplicating and flipping the main image, which will work great here. Select your jester group (both the bitmap and all the shapes) and choose Arrange|Transform to open the Transformation docker. Click on the Scale And Mirror page to switch to that page of options, then click both the Horizontal and Vertical Mirror buttons. Next, move to the positioning grid and click in the right-center square (see Figure 9.4). When you click Apply To Duplicate, you will create a flip-flopped copy of your original image in the location

**Figure 9.4**
The Scale And Mirror page on the Transformation docker allows you to create duplicates of your original artwork quickly, and then rotate and position those duplicates.

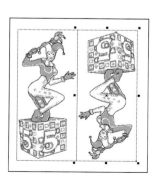

that you selected in the positioning grid. If you clicked Apply To Duplicate over and over, or used the Repeat command (Ctrl+R), you'd create a row of tumbling jesters.

5. With the duplicate jester images in place, the playing-card motif begins to emerge. Draw a rectangle about twice as wide and as tall as the jester. Remember that if you hover the Rectangle tool pointer over one of the corner nodes, it will turn into the Shape tool. You can then drag and round the corners to create a playing-card outline. Duplicate the card and divide the card duplicate in half by adding two nodes at the center of the top and bottom lines with the Shape tool and then deleting the rest on one side. (Or you can draw another rectangle and use the Intersection tool to get the other half—whatever works best for you.) Use the Artistic Text tool to name your playing card—in this case, the Joker. I used a traditional-looking serif font called PalmSprings. Change the coloring scheme so that everything that was white on the left is red on the right, and vice versa (see Figure 9.5). Choose the Select All command (Ctrl+A) and then the Group command (Ctrl+U) to place your finished playing-card pieces into one easy-to-handle group.

6. Double-click on your card group. Then, use the rotation handles to rotate the card so that you break up the vertical bias that these tall figures create. To add some depth, use the Interactive Drop Shadow tool. If you drag from the center of your group down and to the left, your card will appear to float above a flat surface behind it, as if you were looking down at the card from above (see the card on the left in Figure 9.6). If you drag from the bottom of your group across to the left, you create a shadow cast as if your card were standing on the edge of a flat surface, as viewed from the side (see the card on the right in Figure 9.6). Either shadow type will add a lot of depth and dimension with very little effort and you can use options on the Property Bar—such as

**Figure 9.5**

Transform the duplicate images into a playing card by adding a frame and reversing the color scheme for each side.

**Figure 9.6**

Use the Interactive Drop Shadow tool to cast either a traditional drop shadow or one in a horizontal perspective.

Drop Shadow Feathering and Opacity—to get a look you like. Another way to do this is with the Drop Shadow Perspective types drop-down list on the Properties bar.

7. This color image looks great on its own, but it will need to be subdued in order to be appropriate for the background (so save it to disk now in case you want to use the color version for another project). With its current bright color scheme, it would compete with our future foreground image. A quick and nondestructive solution to de-emphasize the artwork is to use a lens effect. I say "nondestructive" because a lens changes only the appearance of objects and does not actually modify the objects themselves. So, draw a big box over everything with the Rectangle tool and select Effects|Lens (or Alt+F3). From the Lens docker, choose the Tinted Grayscale option to transform the colors into shades of gray. Then, if you want to mute the colors even more, select a lighter shade of gray from the Color drop-down box. This creates a nice, muted tone, which you can fine-tune at any time by selecting and changing the lens value (see Figure 9.7). Remember, behind this lens object is our original, unchanged, full-color artwork.

**Figure 9.7**
Use the Tinted Grayscale lens effect to change the way the background image appears.

8. For the main image, import (Ctrl+I) the full-color version of the jester girl that you saved in Step 3. To make the object stand out even more, give the main outline around the object a thick yellow outline.

## More Lens Options

The other options in the Lens effect docker—the Frozen, Viewpoint, and Remove Face—change the way your lens works. *Frozen* transforms the objects behind your lens, to permanently take on the look of your lens effect (if you plan on changing your mind, don't use this option!). *Viewpoint* changes where the lens is "looking." Enable the Viewpoint option, click the Edit button, then drag the "X" to a new area that you want to display in your lens object. This is a useful way to enlarge a section of a map, for example, to show detail off to the side with a lens object. *Remove Face* allows you to ignore the blank image area behind your objects. For example, if you use the Invert Lens and want only your object to change color, and not the image area behind it, enable the Remove Face option.

**To Export or Not to Export**

To convert CorelDRAW objects to bitmaps, you can use either the Export (Ctrl+E) dialog box or the Convert To Bitmap command from the Bitmaps menu. I have tested both methods and found that it takes about the same amount of time for each conversion to take place.

The Export feature is nice because it creates a file that you can then load and massage in Photo-Paint if you want to perform many changes or do some fine-tuning while retaining the original CorelDRAW objects. The Convert To Bitmap option, however, is super convenient. Unless you then choose Edit Bitmap from the Bitmaps menu to launch Photo-Paint, however, or you export the image, it limits the tweaks to within CorelDRAW. In some cases, the Convert To Bitmap option is better, depending on the kinds and types of changes you want to make on the bitmap. You need to remember to save the original file before you use the Convert To Bitmap option, because once you convert your objects to a bitmap, you can't go back to the vector data unless you have a backup file. It is a matter of personal taste, but, like many things in CorelDRAW, there is more than one way to skin the proverbial cat.

9. All that's left is to arrange the crisp color image over the background image. Change the color value on the lens shape that's on top of the background images to mute or emphasize the background. If you want to create the illusion that the background is out of focus, use the Convert To Bitmap and Gaussian Blur technique outlined in Chapter 6. Whatever your wish, you can make it happen in CorelDRAW.

You can see the final image in this book's center color section; the jester playing card file, called jestrgal.cdr, is in the \Chapt09\ subdirectory on the companion CD-ROM. Load the file and view the various effects that the unique Interactive Drop Shadow options generate.

Using a little creativity, I got to milk this illustration one more time, despite its poor resolution and odd proportions. Much to my delight, I know you are thinking about which of your own designs could go another round using this technique. I'm so proud to make you a design-recycler weenie like myself.

## Skull Angels

I was on my way to creating an image similar to the jester girl, with the muted gray background, when curiosity got the best of me. Rather than muting the image with the Tinted Grayscale lens, it is just as easy to recolor it using other lens options. This can dramatically change the mood of the image—in this case, we made things more nightmarish and chaotic, which is, of course, perfect! (See Figure 9.8.)

Again, we are taking a single image and, through nothing more than creative duplication and manipulation, making it much more unique and absorbing than the original design alone. What was once limited subject matter now has an almost endless number of potential variants. What could be better than getting something for nothing? Follow these steps to use the double-vision technique to achieve dramatic, chaotic results:

**Figure 9.8**
Once you have a double-vision
file set up with the Corel objects
in front of a grayscale reproduc-
tion in the background, you can
subdue the background (left) or
get chaotic results with other
lenses, such as Invert (right).

1. This image started as a file I had created a while back. I had drawn ink illustrations of an angel, skulls, and little demons, and then I colored them. (I have sort of a clip-art library of things I have drawn, scanned, and then colored using CorelDRAW. I can mix and match my illustrations to create twisted images—ah, the power of CorelDRAW....) The angel illustration has a strange history; if you look in the hair and folds of cloth, you will find eerie faces and skulls looking back at you. Anyway, for this double-vision exercise, use the Export (Ctrl+E) dialog box to produce the grayscale background bitmap—which you can later import (Ctrl+I) back into the design. Open the Export dialog box (Ctrl+E), change the Save As Type option to TIFF Bitmap, assign a unique file name, and click the Export button. Now in the Bitmap Export dialog box, change the Color option to Grayscale, the Size option to 1 to 1, and the Resolution setting to 300 dpi. Select the Anti-aliasing and Use Color Profile radio buttons but deselect Transparent Background for this image. Click OK to write the bitmap to disk (see Figure 9.9).

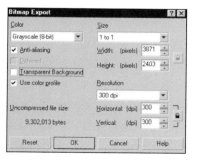

**Figure 9.9**
Use the Export function to create
a grayscale bitmap of the angel
image to use as a backdrop in
the same file later.

2. Import the image (Ctrl+I) back into your CorelDRAW drawing. Corel-DRAW 9 lets you assign the relative size of your bitmap when you import it, so drag a very big box over your page to designate the import area,

and then release the mouse. This will make the image very large compared to the original artwork, for a "zoom-in" effect. You can use the Shape tool to drag the nodes of the big bitmap if you want to cut it down to the size of your page. Or you can stuff it into a rectangle the size of your page using the PowerClip feature.

3.  Arrange the bitmap so that it is behind the original artwork, creating a powerful double-vision image (see Figure 9.10). To create a dramatic difference in size, downsize the original pieces and enlarge the bitmap in the background.

**Figure 9.10**
Import the bitmap you created by exporting the original artwork; the enlarged version will serve as a dramatic background image.

4.  Now, just as before, draw a white rectangle over the background bitmap but behind the other image pieces. Use the Arrange|Order|Behind command, then click on the foreground image to sandwich the rectangle behind the foreground objects but in front of the bitmap. Open the Lens docker (Alt+F3) and, for the muted look, choose the Transparency option. For a freaky, nightmarish look, instead choose Custom Color Map. Select the Forward Rainbow option, change the From and To colors to 100% magenta, and click Apply (see Figure 9.11). Ooh, freaky, dude!

**Figure 9.11**
Instead of using the Transparency lens to mute the background, use the Custom Color Map option to change the background bitmap into a strange, nightmarish backdrop.

5. For even more variety, with the lens object selected, change the fill value from white to magenta. The result is pretty wild. Now change the fill value to cyan. Now that is just sick! Try yellow. Wow! Fiery heat. Experiment until you find a look you like (see Figure 9.12).

**Figure 9.12**
Changing the fill color value of the shape containing the Custom Color Map lens dramatically changes the look of the background.

You can see a composite of images resulting from different Lens settings in the digital color section, while the angels.cdr file in the \Chapt09\ subdirectory on the companion CD-ROM contains the original pieces. Load the file and experiment with the Lens option to get an entirely different background look. Some of the settings I tried include Heat Map, Tinted Grayscale, and Color Limit. For really strange results, change the Palette rotation value with the Heat Map lens. It's a dramatic change in the look—because it takes so little effort, I almost feel guilty about it.

## PROJECT World of Weirdness

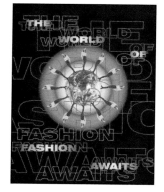

**Figure 9.13**
Multiple copies of text elements—enlarged and using outline-only shading—add a chaotic sense of energy to this image. The Bitmap Color Mask feature lets the model bitmaps float freely on a clear background.

While working on the Y2K image in Chapter 5, I imagined the models standing on the planet, surrounded by buzzing text elements (see Figure 9.13). Okay, so maybe I had too many double espressos that day, but that was the image that popped into my mind. When I look at the finished version of this art, I can see the text buzzing around like in a hyper television commercial. It is easy to animate these kinds of text elements, and we will in Chapter 18.

To free the models from their square bitmap prisons, you can use the magic of the Bitmap Color Mask option, which allows you to render areas of color "invisible." Again, this design technique takes a limited subject matter and uses duplicates to liven it up. To create the free-floating models and the noisy double-vision text elements, follow these steps:

1. Find an image with a solid background color, or use the File|Acquire command to scan a photo. You can use the Bitmap Color Mask option to "hide" any color in a bitmap, which is a great way to remove the background and allow the image to "float." The Bitmap Color Mask option makes a color transparent regardless of where it is. This means that if you designate a blue background as transparent and your subject's eyes are the same color blue, they will be transparent as well. So choose your subject photo wisely.

2. To make the background transparent, select Bitmaps|Bitmap Color
Mask to open the docker. Click the Color Selector on the docker, then
click on the color you want to "hide," such as the white background.
Click Apply to make the selected color transparent, and then use the
Tolerance slider to fine-tune the results. A greater Tolerance value will
help eliminate a background color "halo" around your subject (see
Figure 9.14).

**Figure 9.14**

The Bitmap Color Mask "hides"
selected colors in your bitmap
images, so that they appear to
float free of a background.

3. With the Freehand tool, draw a horizontal line by clicking and then
moving the pointer across the page while holding down the Ctrl key.
Now duplicate (+ key) and rotate this line 90 degrees to create a cross-
hair, which you will use as a reference point for creating the circle of
duplicates. Select the bitmap and place it at the top center of the vertical crosshair. With the bitmap still selected, click with the Pick tool to
reveal the rotation arrows and the axis of rotation. Drag the axis of
rotation down until the crosshairs of the target match the reference
crosshairs you just drew (see Figure 9.15).

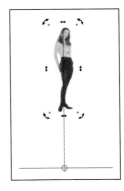

**Figure 9.15**

Draw two lines for reference and
then change the axis of rotation
of the bitmap to the point where
the two lines cross.

4. With the bitmap selected, open the Transformation docker (Alt+F9),
and then click Scale And Mirror. Select just the Horizontal option, click
the radio button in the middle of the positioning grid, and click Apply
To Duplicate. This will flip-flop and copy the bitmap in one step without moving it. Now with the Pick tool, grab and drag the top-left
rotation left arrow while holding down the Ctrl key to spin the duplicate around 30 degrees (see Figure 9.16).

5. Continue to duplicate and rotate the bitmap, alternating the left- and
right-facing models until you complete the circle (see Figure 9.17). Now
you have created an exciting pattern shape out of a single "boring"
image. Not a bad trick! You can now select and delete your guidelines.

6. Use the Ellipse tool to draw a circle shape, and select the To Back command (Shift+PgDn) to send it to the back. Use the Interactive Fill tool to

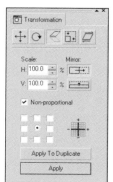

**Figure 9.16**
Use the Scale And Mirror docker to duplicate and flip the bitmap. Then rotate the duplicate 30 degrees by holding the Ctrl key while dragging a rotation arrow.

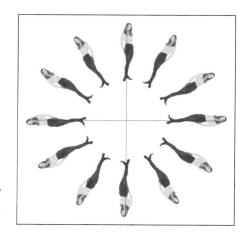

**Figure 9.17**
Repeat the duplicate-and-rotate process to create a ring.

create a custom color blend. Drag from the center of the circle outward, then select the radial fountain fill from the Property Bar. Next, click the yellow color chip on the on-screen color palette, then drag to the center point on the Interactive Fill control line and release. You can drag and drop colors anywhere along the Interactive Fill control line to create a cascade of different colors (see Figure 9.18). Create a fountain fill that goes from black to cyan, to magenta, to yellow. The redundant black points along the color blend control how and where the circle

**Figure 9.18**
Use the Interactive Fill tool to create a brilliant custom color blend.

fades to black. Since this object rests on a black background, without the extra points for the black, the transition is harsh and noticeable (see Figure 9.18).

7. To make the models appear to be standing on the earth, import (Ctrl+I) a bitmap of the earth from the \Objects\misc\ directory on the Corel-DRAW clip-art CD (or you can place them on a funky glass sphere like the one from Chapter 7). Arrange the globe behind the models, as shown in Figure 9.19.

**Figure 9.19**
Import a bitmap of the earth and arrange it behind the models to make them bigger than life.

8. Draw a black rectangle the size of the page and send it to the back (Shift+PgDn). Use the Text tool to set text elements around the background. I used a font called Swis721 BlkEx BT, with a gray-to-white radial fountain fill. Once all of the text is in place, Shift-select all the pieces, duplicate them (+ key), and use the Send Back One (Ctrl+PgDn) command. Now enlarge the duplicate text shapes by dragging a corner sizing handle outward while holding down the Shift key. Give the duplicates no fill and a .023 magenta outline. Now, one by one, arrange the word duplicates randomly around the originals (see Figure 9.20).

**Figure 9.20**
Set the main text elements on the screen and duplicate them; then enlarge, recolor, and scatter the duplicates.

9. Repeat the duplicate-and-scatter process two more times, each time choosing a different outline color. Scatter and enlarge these text objects even more for a totally random size and placement look. Don't worry if the text elements hang off the edge of the page boundary in your efforts to achieve the perfect balance of chaos (see Figure 9.21).

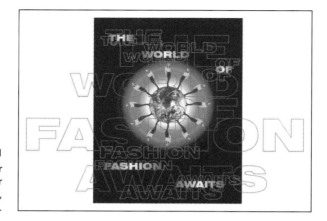

**Figure 9.21**
Duplicate, enlarge, and scatter the text objects a total of four times to create a really chaotic, energy-filled image.

10. Issue the Select All command (Ctrl+A), then hold down the Shift key and click on the black background box to select everything but the box. Then choose Effects|PowerClip|Place Inside Container and click on the black background box to stuff everything inside the page limits. We'll call that "controlled chaos."

You can see the results of this mayhem in the color section, and you can find the world.cdr file in the \Chapt09\ subdirectory on the companion CD-ROM. If you want to play with this image, you will first need to select Effects| PowerClip|Extract. Then you can see firsthand how the Bitmap Color Mask option works and the way the custom color blend in the background circle is controlled with the multiple same-color nodes.

## PROJECT 4×4×2

My taste in vehicles—much like my taste in art and music—has always been eclectic. I favor rugged-looking, "square" cars and trucks over the contemporary trend to make vehicles look like strange bulbous sea creatures. But that's just me (and why you will find me tooling around like a masochist in a 27-year-old Land Cruiser). The illustration of a contemporary Defender 90 (see Figure 9.22) has the classic look I like. To broaden my design horizons, I used Corel Trace to scan and convert the illustration to CorelDRAW objects. The results are crisp and detailed—and the perfect subject to illustrate several computer design tricks. First, now that it is not a photograph but instead is a CorelDRAW file, you can make the vehicle any color you choose and place it in any location that you want (or create a fleet of duplicates for a multiplicity effect). You can also duplicate the image with ease and flip-flop it to create the illusion of a reflection in water (as in Figure 9.22), or exploit any "double-vision" technique.

Taking the reflection a step further, converting the artwork in the water to a bitmap allows you to add a "rippling" effect. You can also use bitmap filters or other tools to achieve the artistic interpretation you envision. To get the reflecting-water effect, follow these steps:

**Figure 9.22**
Using a rasterized version of your original artwork, you can get a reflection-in-water look using bitmap filters.

1.  Start with the image that you want to "reflect." (It can be a collection of CorelDRAW objects, like my example, or you can start with a scan of a photograph or any other bitmap.) Select all of your objects and open the Transformation docker (Alt+F9). Click the Vertical option, select the bottom-center radio button in the positioning grid, and click Apply To Duplicate. This will create a flip-flopped duplicate aligned directly beneath the original (see Figure 9.23).

**Figure 9.23**
Use the Transformation docker to duplicate and flip-flop your artwork.

2.  With your duplicates still selected, choose Bitmaps|Convert To Bitmap (unless, of course, your original object was already a bitmap, in which case your duplicate is also a bitmap, so you can skip to Step 3). Set the Color option to RGB, because some filter effects (especially third-party filters like Kai's Power Tools, Alien Skin, etc.) do not work on CMYK color images. Set the Resolution option to what you need for your project (generally 300 dpi for print, 72 for on-screen applications), and select the Anti-aliasing and Use Color Profile radio buttons. Then, click OK.

3.  With your duplicate now a bitmap, you can take advantage of the filters on the Bitmaps menu. Select Bitmaps|Creative|Smoked Glass to modify the bitmap coloring to look more like a water reflection. In the Smoked Glass dialog box, click the Color option button, then select a turquoise color from the pop-up palette. Click Preview to see what the image will look like, and use the Tint and Blurring sliders to modify the results, checking the impact each time with Preview. When satisfied, click OK to transform your bitmap (see Figure 9.24).

**Figure 9.24**
The Smoked Glass bitmap filter shades the duplicate to look like a reflection in water.

4. To add a "ripple" to the water, select Bitmaps|Distort|Ripple (imagine that!). The default Ripple settings are a bit dramatic for our purposes, so modify the parameters in the Ripple dialog box. Select the Distort Ripple and Perpendicular Wave options, then increase the Period setting to 53 and all Amplitude settings to 2. Click Preview to test the settings, and if you like what you see, click OK—or continue to modify the settings until you do (see Figure 9.25). Arrange your bitmap behind the original (Shift+PgDn), and you have your reflection effect.

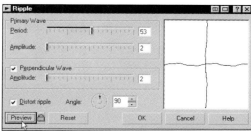

**Figure 9.25**
The Ripple bitmap filter creates the distorted look of moving water.

You can see the finished results in this book's color section, and in the rover.cdr file in the \Chapt09\ subdirectory on the companion CD-ROM. This is a quick and easy way to double the size of an original. I eventually placed some ad copy over the reflection image. Because the parent image is made up of CorelDRAW objects and the duplication/reflection technique is so simple, you can just smile and nod happily when the client asks, "Can we change the color of the car from yellow to red?"

# Beyond f/x

The double-vision technique is a great shortcut for making a little bit of artwork go a long way. Oftentimes you are faced with a situation where you have painfully little original source material but plenty of space to fill. The double-vision technique lets you get away with using the same image both in the background and as the primary image in the foreground. Even if you have other options, it is a great trick and the results always look nice. Using this technique also double-emphasizes the subject, but not in a harsh or even obvious way, which is a great sales and marketing tool. Product catalogs, brochures, and other support materials can benefit from the foreground/background treatment of the same subject. If you have the resources, the same subject—viewed from two different angles—is a great use of the double-vision technique.

Using multiple copies of the same text is also a very popular design trick. With a master set of text in place to get the message across, you are free to experiment with duplicates of the same words. Enlarging, fading, or blurring the duplicates adds visual interest and subtle emphasis, and you don't have to worry about legibility or content, because the original text is still in place. This is especially true with animation—you can have the duplicate text flying around to create a unique and attention-getting graphic. The possibilities are quite literally dizzying—you don't need bifocals to take advantage of double vision.

# Moving On

In this chapter, we explored ways to expand the uses of a single piece of art from a boring solo flight into a total visual barrage. With the use of duplicates, the original artwork becomes interesting background material as well as other design elements that help flesh out an otherwise dull or inappropriate graphic. You'll probably use this technique a lot, since most designers are often called upon to make something mundane look totally exciting. (Our studio has had some wonderful design challenges, such as making bronzed dog turds—no joke—look interesting!)

Using a lens object to change the way things behind it look is another technique that has a lot of potential and is almost exclusive to CorelDRAW. From the obvious and predictable use of the Transparency lens to lighten or darken objects, to the seemingly bright and random results of using the Custom Color Map, you have plenty of room for experimentation. For example, the antepenultimate image in the color section, of the flag and fireworks, gets its wild coloring via the Heat Map lens. These lenses also provide a great way to add color to a grayscale image. Of course, I love lenses because they let you do so much with so little work. How else could you take a low-quality, black-and-white image a client brings you and use it in a color brochure?

From double-vision techniques, we now move on to even more bizarre tricks to play with your eyeballs in Chapter 10. With the CorelDRAW rendering engines doing all the work, it is easy to create dizzying artwork reminiscent of the '60s psychedelic movement. So throw in a Hendrix CD, plug in the lava lamp, and grab those rose-colored glasses, 'cuz we're getting into the groove, baby!

# Chapter 10

# Psychedelic Mind Trips and Other Eye Candy

*In this chapter, you'll take advantage of the Blend feature to create multiple copies of an object, which are used to create bright pattern effects.*

# Creating Dazzling and Dizzying Patterns and Other Eye-Catching Designs

In today's chaotic climate, getting your audience's attention and pulling them into your design is harder than ever. With millions of bits of information bombarding a potential reader from other sources, your printed art—with nothing but visual tricks—must somehow stand up and scream "Read me!" It's no easy task, but not impossible, to create art that is interesting enough to accomplish this. We have already covered many great techniques that are anything but boring.

One great attention-getting device borrows from ideas that originated during the psychedelic '60s, techniques that use high-contrast coloring and dizzying patterns to create bright and, above all, interesting graphics that are impossible to ignore. The look isn't always appropriate, but when it is, it's as subtle as a car crash, with the same attention-grabbing effect.

In this chapter, we will look at different ways to create eye-catching graphics using a variety of dazzling techniques. In the first example, we'll use the Interactive Blend tool to create multiple-outline shapes that, when combined, create dizzying patterns of light and dark colors. We'll look at how this technique can be custom-tailored to any shape, making it an ideal base for an advertisement. Then, we'll finish things off with a laser light show, again using blends but taking advantage of the rotation options. I hope you are not prone to motion sickness.

## PROJECT Tripping Adtastic

It's the summer of love, man, with peace, happiness, joy, and the best deals in town on cellular phones. Come on down! Even something as blasé as a phone suddenly looks darn interesting when it is at the center of the eye-grabbing pattern in Figure 10.1.

Using the phone object as basis for a curve drawn by hand in CorelDRAW, you open the door to wild, eye-catching effects. Once you have the phone curve, you can create multiple copies with either the Interactive Contour or Blend tool, and from there you can get psychedelic using the Combine command. To create a custom shape—and from there create the dazzling high-contrast checkered illusion—follow these steps:

1. Start by importing the image you want to draw attention to. You can use a photo from your digital camera or scanner, if your system is set up for that, or find and Import (Ctrl+I) a piece of clip art, as I did. A bunch of phone images are on the CorelDRAW clip-art CD #3, in the \objects\communic (communications) directory. The nice thing about the images in the \objects directories is that they use clip masks and appear to be free floating with transparent backgrounds, so you can

**Figure 10.1**
You can use any shape—including those custom fit to a specific application—to generate the pieces for a dazzling psychedelic effect.

### On-the-Fly Tracing

If you have a bitmap selected (such as the phone object in this example) and then choose the Freehand tool, you can perform AutoTrace functions directly within CorelDRAW. With the bitmap selected, click the Freehand tool, then move it to the left of the object and click. CorelDRAW will now scan to the right and, following along the first dark pixels it comes across, attempt to create a shape. You can attempt to fine-tune the results by right-clicking the Freehand tool and modifying the properties. Decreasing the AutoTrace tracking and Corner Threshold values makes for "tighter" tracing. This feature works well only with high-contrast photos, but it can usually provide a shape that at the very least is a good starting point, which you can then clean up with the Shape tool.

stick them anywhere. (See Chapter 5 for more on Clip Masks and creating "floating" objects.)

2. Deselect the bitmap (Esc), then use the Bezier tool to click along the edge of the phone from point to point, creating a simple, straight-line outline of the phone. Start and stop at the same point to create a solid object (if you don't create a solid object, click Auto-Close Curve on the Property Bar). Then go back with the Shape tool and use the Property Bar options to convert lines to curves, so as to smooth out the edges for a smoother curve.

3. Shrink the phone outline until it is really small, then duplicate it and enlarge the duplicate to the edge of your page. Now select both outlines and drag the Interactive Blend tool between them, which will create the 20 new outline shapes (20 steps is the default). Use the Property Bar to reduce the steps to 10 (see Figure 10.2).

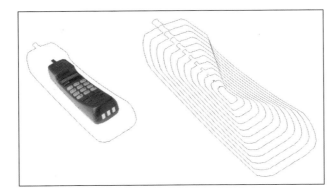

**Figure 10.2**
Use the Bezier tool to draw a simplified outline of the target image. A large and small duplicate of the outline are blended together.

4. Now "freeze" the blend by issuing Arrange|Separate, Arrange|Ungroup All, then combine (Ctrl+L) the pieces into a single curve, and give the shape a Yellow fill (see Figure 10.3). Things are already getting interesting!

5. For an even more exciting effect, add a sunburst to draw the eye to the center of the graphic. Draw a perfect circle by holding down the Ctrl key as you drag the Ellipse tool. Use the Shape tool to transform the circle into just a "pizza slice" sliver, by dragging the control node to the

---

**Freeze**

When you "freeze" a blend group, you stop it from being "live." A "live" blend will rebuild itself dynamically when you modify one of the control objects (such as recoloring or resizing a control object). To manipulate the objects within a "live" blend, you first must "freeze" them, with the Arrange|Separate command, then use Arrange|Ungroup All to make each piece a unique object that you can select and manipulate independently of the rest.

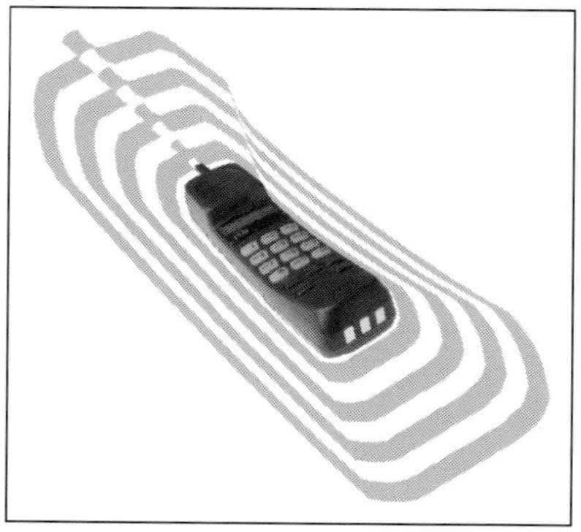

---

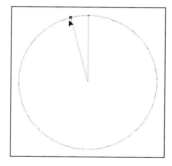

**Figure 10.3**

Separating the pieces in the blend and then combining them into one curve creates the fill/open pattern unique to this effect.

inside of the ellipse, again while holding the Ctrl key (see Figure 10.4). Holding the Ctrl key constrains the movement of the control nodes with the Shape tool to 15-degree increments, but you can just "eyeball" it without the Ctrl key for smaller sliver shapes.

**Figure 10.4**

Dragging the control node on an ellipse with the Shape tool can transform it into a "pizza slice" object.

6. Double-click this object to reveal the rotation handles and rotation axis (the small circle in the center of your object). Drag the rotation axis point, again while holding down the Ctrl key, down to the bottom-right point of your slice. Now drag a top-corner rotation handle to the right, while holding the Ctrl key. This will "snap" the rotation in 15-degree increments so you can easily rotate the object 30 degrees. Before you release the left mouse button, tap the Spacebar to duplicate the slice. This will leave you two copies of the slice (see Figure 10.5).

7. If the duplicate/rotate move was your last action, using the Repeat command (Ctrl+R) will create another "ray" of the starburst in the desired rotated position. Use the Repeat command a total of ten times to

## Can't Repeat?

Getting CorelDRAW Linux to acknowledge the spacebar tap and therefore create a duplicate is dependent on your system's speed. On slow systems, it will take some practice to get the rhythm down perfectly for the rotate/tap-spacebar/duplicate single step. Practice makes perfect; if you just can't get it to work, however, use the Arrange| Transformation dialog box on the Rotate page. There you can key in the rotation amount (such as the 30 degrees in this exercise) and use the Apply To Duplicate button, which will duplicate and rotate your object in a single step. Multiple taps of the Apply To Duplicate button should result in the same starburst shape as the "repeat" trick.

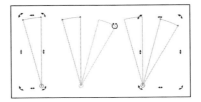

**Figure 10.5**
Changing the axis of rotation allows you to spin a slice around in a circular fashion, and right-clicking before you release duplicates the object in one step.

spin rays into a complete circle (if you are having difficulty with the "repeat" feature, see the "Can't Repeat?" sidebar). The more "rays," the busier your design will be (see Figure 10.6). Use smaller "slices" (don't hold down the Ctrl key) and more of them for a really dizzying sunburst, or use fewer—it's up to you. Being an extremist, I used many small slices for a dizzying effect.

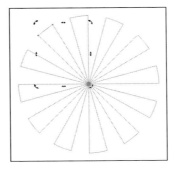

**Figure 10.6**
The Repeat command quickly creates a sunburst by duplicating/rotating the slice shape with a single keyboard shortcut (Ctrl+R).

8. Select all of the sunburst pieces and combine them (Ctrl+L). Place the sunburst so that its center is at the center of the phone, to ensure that all eyes are drawn there. Then select both the sunray and the phone curve graphic from Step 4 and combine them (see Figure 10.7). Bang, right between the eyes!

9. Use the Rectangle tool to draw a box the size of your page, and arrange it around your artwork. Now select all your objects (Ctrl+A), but then hold the Shift key and deselect the page-limit rectangle you just drew. Now, from the Effects menu, choose PowerClip, then select Place Inside Container. Click the arrow on your page-limit rectangle to stuff all the sunburst pieces into the rectangle. With all the pieces stuffed neatly into the page limit, add some text and call it a day.

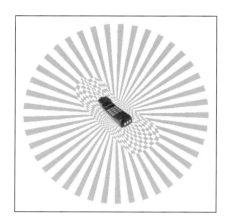

**Figure 10.7**
Combine the sunburst with the phone curve to create a dizzying pattern.

The image is exploding in the digital color section and also in the phone.cdr file found in the \Chapt10\ subdirectory on the companion CD-ROM. If you want to manipulate the pieces in this file, remember you first have to extract the contents from PowerClip (Effects|PowerClip|Extract Contents). You can select the sunburst curve, break it apart, delete the phone pieces, and steal the spokes for your own designs. Images like this that just suck your eye to the center are perfect for drawing attention to objects that fail to excite on their own. As another bonus, the high-contrast and effective attention-getting design is perfect for low- or no-color print applications. The graphic in the digital color section would be just as effective printed only in yellow and black (the phone does have some other colors in it, but they are not critical to the success of the design). You have to remember that back in the '60s when this kind of graphic was in its heyday, printing technology was low tech, so simple one- and two-color designs were very popular and also more cost effective. You can exploit these savings today as well. Frugality is not an anachronistic concept!

## PROJECT Laser Specialties

Often associated with space scenes, laser beams also make interesting design elements by themselves. A crisp single-colored line, blended with others, creates a dazzling light show (see Figure 10.8).

In this example, the busy colors of the background are a result of a blend of simple outlines, while the laser in the center uses the thick-to-thin-line blend technique. The center laser acts as a baseline for the text to rest on, and the blast offers a point of visual interest to draw attention to the text—no easy task in this busy sea of laser light! As they say in the laser industry, "Avoid looking into bright light with your remaining eye." To create a laser beam and sparkle effects, follow these steps:

**Figure 10.8**
The Blend function creates not only the round laser beam, but also the background pattern and even the exploding sparkle.

1. Draw a straight line with a quick click at the starting point and a click at the ending point with the Bezier tool. Give this line a thick .08-inch magenta outline from the Outline Pen dialog box (F12). Now duplicate

it (+ key) and make the duplicate a white .003-inch hairline, again from the Outline Pen dialog box. Drag-select both, and drag on them with the Interactive Blend tool to create the round-looking laser beam (see Figure 10.9). No sweat.

**Figure 10.9**
Blend a thick magenta line to a thin white one to create a rounded laser beam.

2. The sparkle is a series of blend steps, which can also be used to create an explosion effect. Open the Symbols And Special Characters docker, either from the Window menu or with the keyboard shortcut (Ctrl+F11). Change to the Stars1 symbol library, then scroll through the gallery to locate the four-pointed star and drag it onto the desktop. This little shape plays a big role in this design (see Figure 10.10).

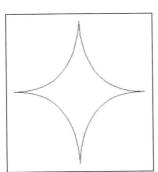
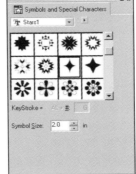

**Figure 10.10**
The Symbols And Special Characters docker is a valuable source of cool pre-drawn shapes.

3. With the Ellipse tool, draw a tiny little circle. Duplicate it (+), and drag the duplicate off to the right. With the Interactive Blend tool, drag between the two objects to create a blend group. Press Esc to deselect the blend, then Shift-select just the original control circles. Align these control curves on top of one another using the keyboard shortcuts (press C and E to align Center horizontally and Center vertically). Now the blend pieces appear as a single object, with all the elements stacked on top of one another.

4. Press Esc to select nothing (deselect any selected object), then drag-select the circle blend group (clicking on the stack will just select the control

## Gimme the Symbols

Not all of the symbols are installed during the typical installation of CorelDRAW. To add more symbols or fonts, use the Custom install option. From this option you can select which font families and symbol sets you would like to install. Pick and choose carefully. If you get carried away with installing fonts and symbols, it can hamper your system performance.

curve closest to you, which is not what you want). On the Interactive Blend Tool Property Bar, click Path Properties, then select New Path and click the star curve to run the circles along the edge of the shape. Click Miscellaneous Blend Options and enable the Blend Along Full Path option. Increase the number of steps to 50 to create a pattern of circles along the star shape (see Figure 10.11).

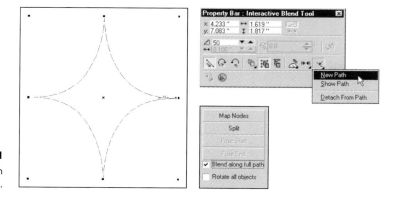

**Figure 10.11**

A star becomes the blend path for a series of little circles.

5. Select the blend and separate the pieces with the Arrange|Separate and Arrange|Ungroup All commands, hold the Shift key to deselect the star control curve, and then group the circles (Ctrl+G). Now duplicate the circles (+), ungroup them (Ctrl+U), and align them center to center (press the C and E keys). This will make them look like a small dot, which is actually a stack of 52 circles. Group these again (Ctrl+G), then click the white color chip in the on-screen color palette to color this group of circles. Align the center stack in the center of the star shape.

6. Drag between the outside and inside circle groups with the Interactive Blend tool to create a starburst. To give a tighter cluster of objects in the center of the blend, drag the Object Acceleration slider to the right. Pow! You have your starburst (see Figure 10.12).

**Figure 10.12**

The Interactive Blend tool creates a burst by blending the two circle groups together. The Object Acceleration slider changes the blend to cluster objects closer to the center.

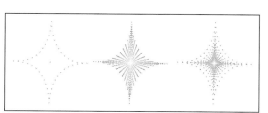

## Light Show

For the background image, you will need the same star shape that you used for the burst; this time it won't be a blend path, however, but the blend object itself. To create the laser light-show background, follow these steps:

1. Use the Star curve from the previous steps, or just grab it off the Symbols And Special Characters docker again. Double-click the star, and drag the corner rotation handles to spin the star 45 degrees. Then click the shape again to activate the sizing handles, and drag to enlarge the star way beyond the size of your page. Duplicate the star, and reduce the duplicate to just a small dot in the center of the page. Shift-select both star curves and give them a .022-inch cyan outline (or as thick or thin as you want) from the Outline Pen dialog box (F12).

2. Drag the Interactive Blend tool between the two star curves to create a blend group. On the Property Bar, increase the number of steps to 300. Now to get that great spinning effect, change the Blend Direction value to 360 degrees. To get the wonderful rainbow coloring, click Clockwise Blend on the Property Bar (see Figure 10.13). Better than a laser light show, and no parking hassles.

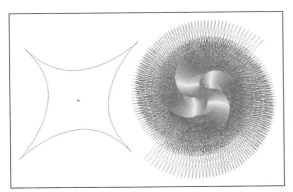

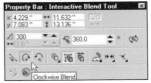

**Figure 10.13**
The Interactive Blend Property Bar, with 360-degrees rotation and the Rainbow functions enabled, creates a laser light show blend between the two star shapes.

That's the whole process! As with the previous project, add a page-limit rectangle, then select all (Ctrl+A) and PowerClip everything into it. Add your text, if any (I used a font called Serpentine), send your client a large bill, and call it a day. The light show starts in the color section in the center of this book and also in the lasers.cdr file found in the \Chapt10\ subdirectory on the companion CD-ROM. Open the file and play with the laser blend for your own personal light show. For even more rotation, select either the outside or inside control curve and spin it manually.

# Beyond f/x

Explosive, bright designs such as these help draw attention because of high contrast, both within the designs themselves and in a broader sense. Things naturally stand out when they're different; for a market that is normally sedate, therefore, a bright, fun graphic might work really well. However, these images might just look boring and ordinary in a demographic that is already suffering from a glut of visual noise. That's why it's wise to research your market so you know if the design is right for it or if it is inappropriate because of the shock value.

Almost anything can benefit from a bit of eye-blasting imagery now and then. A graphic using these techniques could draw attention to new products in an ad or new pages in a Web site. The techniques work equally well as primary design elements or as secondary pieces like borders or edge designs. Promotional materials—such as stickers, T-shirts, or buttons—can push the design limits and benefit greatly from a violently interesting graphic that won't go unnoticed. Perhaps you could take the idea too far, though. Is a dizzying billboard that literally stops traffic a bad design? Hmmm.

# Moving On

In this chapter, we looked at creating bright designs using CorelDRAW. We again saw how the Blend docker can be used to create all kinds of shapes, including the simple, the mechanical, and the downright dizzying!

The examples in this chapter were extreme and used many bright colors. You can use the same kinds of techniques to get much more subtle images for more conservative designs, with muted or a limited number of colors. Remember not to get carried away trying to make your artwork as loud or garish as possible. A portfolio full of loud, jarring images would probably appeal to recording companies, but won't get you an account with the Fortune 500, button-down crowd.

In Chapter 11, we will explore animated options and uses for CorelDRAW. In keeping with the low-tech/high-tech theme, we will endeavor to create designs and images reminiscent of the middle half of the twentieth century. Contemporary design tools like CorelDRAW make creating crisp and visually engaging designs a snap, even for anachronistic images. So, crawl into your bomb shelter, grab a TV dinner, and get ready for a '50s flashback!

# Chapter 11
# Fifties Flashback

*In this chapter, we borrow simplistic but sound design principles and images from the past, and then use modern computerized techniques to take them into the future.*

# Blasting Ideas and Images from the Past into the Present

Back when life was simpler, before computers, before multiple operating systems, before the Internet, before umpteen versions of CorelDRAW (eek, that is a long time!), designs were also simpler. Because everything was more difficult to do—often requiring physical cutting and pasting—art had a clean-cut look to it. Designs were thought out way in advance, and many more interim steps were involved to make sure the end result was perfect. The less-is-more lesson here is worth looking into, though; in our current digital age of visual noise and information overload, simplicity seems darn appealing.

Too much art these days is created with an artist's "see what I can do" ego rather than the artist intelligently trying to solve the specific design problems for the project at hand. You also have to take into account the question of appropriateness; not every piece of art needs to be dripping with technical complexity. Use your technical ability to create good designs faster, and use the extra time doing something else, like, uh—well, I can't remember, but something other than working on the computer!

In this chapter, we will create simple but visually engaging pieces with a retro look to them (and not just limited to the '50s, but I liked how that sounded). In the first example, we will see how a simple, two-color design using classic and clean page layout can produce an interesting and professional-looking design that's right at home in the modern world. Then, continuing with the theme, a simple layout is brought to life and given a retro look, with select shape, font, and color choices. After that, we switch on the idiot box to work the American pastime into another flashback image; we'll use the PowerClip function and other tricks to put an image on TV. Finally, we capture the spirit of a '40s pinup, launching scans of images from the past into the present in the form of digital stock photography. The technology of the present works well to create images from the past!

## PROJECT Contact

I am a huge fan of the history of art and graphic design. We can learn so much from the past, and, if nothing else, books on the subject serve as great sources of inspiration. Many times I have been stumped trying to come up with some new look or design twist only to find the art history archives were the catalyst I needed to ignite my creativity. If you have not already taken some time to browse through books on the topics of art and graphic design history, I recommend you do so.

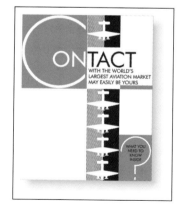

**Figure 11.1**
Modern artists can learn from the past and create simple, cost-efficient designs that are interesting and professional.

The image in Figure 11.1 has a simple and clean layout, which takes advantage of a commodity many people lose sight of: white space. In design, remember the adage: "It's not always what's there, but what isn't there that's important."

## What Isn't There

My favorite example of the importance of what *isn't* there is a story that involves airplane silhouettes. During World War II, the British were searching for ways to reduce their airplane losses and got mighty creative in the process. After each mission, an artist would come out and inspect a returning airplane for bullet holes and flak damage. The artists would mark the damaged areas of the plane on a sheet of cellophane that had a diagram of the plane on it. Then they would stack up sheets from many different damaged planes until a pattern began to emerge for that model of aircraft. Distinct areas of light and dark created a pattern of damage that was common to the returning aircraft. They took this graphic to the aircraft factories and added armor and reinforcement to the planes on the areas in the diagrams where the markings *weren't*. This is because the blank areas on the diagrams were where the planes that *didn't* make it back were hit. Pretty clever, eh? What's *not* there can be mighty important!

To keep costs down on a project, you are often limited to one or two ink colors. Use the white color of the paper as a third color option, creating interesting patterns and making use of the negative space in a positive way. The white creates nice areas of contrast and rest where the eye can linger away from visual noise. It is a natural tendency to try to cram as much as possible into a design, but you will find that less is more, and it's also very effective.

To use contemporary tools to create a clean two-color design, follow these steps:

1. Use the Rectangle tool to draw a box the size of your paper and then open the Transformation docker (Arrange|Transformation). Click Scale And Mirror to open that page of options. Set the H (Horizontal) Scale value to 50% and click Apply To Duplicate. This will create a rectangle that is half the width of the original. Click Apply To Duplicate again to create a shape one quarter as wide as the page.

2. Shift-select all of these shapes and use the Arrange|Align And Distribute command to open the dialog box, or just use the single keyboard short-cut R, to align the elements to the right. Now select just the full-sized rectangle, and on the Transformation/Scale And Mirror docker, change the Vertical value to 50%, set the Horizontal value back to 100%, and click Apply To Duplicate. With the new duplicate selected, change the Vertical value to 80% and again click Apply To Duplicate. Shift-select these objects and align them to the top (the keyboard shortcut is T). This will divide the page into neat and orderly sections (see Figure 11.2).

3. Select the one-quarter-page vertical block and fill it black. Now flip-flop it by dragging the right-center control handle left while holding down the Ctrl key. Next duplicate the shape (+ key), squeeze it horizontally until it is just a thin line, and fill it white (left-click on the white color chip). Shift-select the thin box and the one-quarter-page object and align them to the vertical Center (hit the C key). Now duplicate the thin white line, Shift-select the one-quarter-page object again, and align it

**Flip-Flop Non Stop**

To save time, you can dupli-cate, change the size, and also control the position of the duplicate, all within the Trans-formation docker. On the Scale And Mirror page of the Trans-formation docker, just above the Apply To Duplicate button, you can control the destination of your duplicate. Click in the box to change from the de-fault center to the desired new position (such as to the right and top of the original) before you click Apply To Duplicate. This will place the duplicate in the desired position relative to the original, saving you the steps of aligning things later.

**Figure 11.2**

The Scale And Mirror page of the Transformation docker divides the page object horizontally and vertically to create an orderly page layout design.

**Note:** If your Interactive Blend does not result in even-spaced objects, check the settings on the Property Bar. Click Object And Color Acceleration, and move the sliders to the middle, neutral position. This should result in even blend spacing.

to the Left (hit the L key). Finally, drag between both thin rectangles with the Interactive Blend tool to create a blend to produce a perfectly spaced pattern on half of the one-quarter-page black object (see Figure 11.3). Use the Property Bar to modify the number of steps in the active blend group if you want.

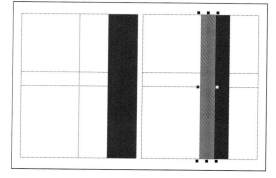

**Figure 11.3**

Use the new single-key shortcuts or the Align And Distribute dialog box to place white lines in the center of and on the left of the black shape, then blend them together.

4. Open the Symbols docker (Ctrl+F11), select the Transportation Symbols Library, scroll down until you find a plane to your liking, and drag it onto the desktop (or use the File|Import command to import a plane silhouette from the Corel clip-art library). Now flip the plane vertically, fill it white with no outline, and move the plane to the bottom of the page. Shift-select the one-quarter-page shape and align the plane to its vertical center. Duplicate the plane and drag the duplicate up the page while holding down the Ctrl key to keep it aligned with the original. Use the Interactive Blend tool to create an active blend between them, reducing the Steps setting to 5 on the Property Bar (see Figure 11.4).

5. Select and color the sections of the design in white and green. Green is a nice, neutral color that has universal appeal. (For a cooler look, you could substitute light blue; for a hotter look, use orange or red.) If this job were destined to go to press at your local print shop, you would

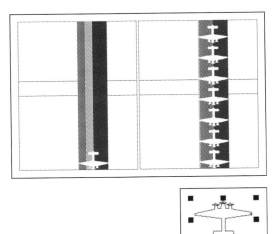

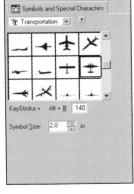

**Figure 11.4**

Use a plane from the Symbols And Special Characters docker as a white silhouette, and then create an evenly spaced row of planes using the Interactive Blend tool.

want to use a spot color for the green. From the Windows| Color Palettes menu, choose Pantone Matching System to switch to a spot color theme. Each spot color outputs as a single plate when you create color-separated film to give to your printer. Duplicate the shapes and reduce with the Transformation/Scale And Mirror docker to produce more proportional copies. You might need to change the order in which the objects are stacked. The Arrange|Order|In Front Of and Arrange|Order|Behind commands make stacking easy. Use the Align And Distribute dialog box or the keyboard shortcuts to keep all objects perfectly aligned.

6. Draw a perfect circle in the top-left box of the page (hold down the Ctrl key as you drag the Ellipse tool) and align it to the top and left in relation to the box. Duplicate the circle, and then downsize it by dragging a corner handle inward while holding down the Ctrl key, which will

## Color Tricks

Understand the parameters of a job before you begin to build the artwork. For a two-color job such as this example, it is illogical to use a CMYK color for a traditional offset printing project. CMYK colors will result in additional film and higher printing charges. Use a PMS spot color instead, which will create only one color plate on output. Because this book does not use spot color (it uses CMYK), I chose Grass Green, which is a CMYK color choice off the on-screen palette. In the real world, I would have chosen Pantone 3288 CV as the fill color and produced exactly the artwork that my printer needs—which is a separate color plate for each color (black and green). Alternatively, you can use CMYK colors to produce the color plates for "spot-color" jobs such as this. If I chose the green from Corel's on-screen palette—which is 100Y and 100C—I could still produce just two color plates by printing only the black and yellow. I wouldn't print the cyan plate, since I don't need it for printing. I just need to label the "yellow" film as "Pantone 3288 CV" so my printer will use that ink instead of yellow. The color separations are the same. Why do this? Well, if your artwork is already set up as CMYK but you really don't need all the color plates for printing, you can use this trick to save time and money.

move all sides in unison toward the center. Shift-select the original circle and combine (Ctrl+L) the two, creating a solid doughnut shape. To trim away the right side, draw a rectangle over the trim area and use the Arrange|Shaping|Trim command to create a big letter *C*. Set the rest of the letters using the Text tool. I used a classic-looking font called Futura Bk (see Figure 11.5).

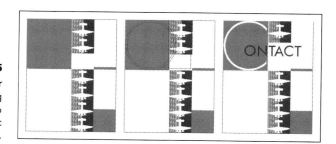

**Figure 11.5**
Divide up the page with color and shapes and then create a big letter *C* from a perfect circle to stay with the clean, geometric look of the design.

7. To make the letters *ON* in the word "CONTACT" white, simply Shift-select the two control nodes for those two letters using the Shape tool, and then click on the white on-screen color well. You can use the Shape tool to modify each letter in a text object independently of the others if you want. The question mark is made up of the same shape as the big *C*, just downsized and rotated with two white bars to create a *?* object.

8. Okay, I do admit to modernizing the look a bit with the addition of a drop shadow, but it's just so easy! Select the original full-sized rectangle and drag the Interactive Drop Shadow tool from down and to the right to create a traditional drop shadow. You can change the parameters, such as the Feathering and Opacity values (as well as the color of the shadow, perspective, angle, and fade), on the Property Bar (see Figure 11.6).

**Figure 11.6**
Use like shapes when possible to save time; the *C* can become a *?*. The Interactive Drop Shadow tool gives you a quick and easy way to add convincing depth to an object.

Well, this image is perhaps not as exciting as some we have walked through, but I think it is important to address simple design strategies as well in this book. You can see the finished piece in the \Chapt11\ subdirectory on the companion CD-ROM, in a file called contact.cdr. I like this graphic because it starts first with layout in which the page is divided into neat quadrants, and then adds pieces to enhance visual interest. By nature, humans like to divide and conquer, and subconsciously that is still how we digest visual information. Neat and tidy sections are appealing, and that is why you will find that most good design has pages that are divided into easy-to-digest chunks. Take a clue from the past and don't overdesign a project.

## PROJECT Avocados, Plums, and Carrots

Here in the new century, we're witnessing a strange mix of the decades of the previous century, especially in such areas as art and fashion. Today's trends borrow heavily from the past but simultaneously mix in pieces of the present. Nothing compares to seeing a kid in bell bottoms, wearing a "Charlie's Angels" T-shirt, playing with a Game Boy, listening to MP3s on his RIO! Or how about classic black-and-white movies on DVD? Enough of these technology oxymorons could stop time....

Getting a retro look means sticking to the formula of the times. Older graphics use lower tech printing and design methods, which help define the look. Simple geometric shapes, natural colors (avocado green, carrot orange, plum purple, banana yellow, etc.), and fonts from the same era all add up to a blast-from-the-past look (see Figure 11.7).

These designs are all the rage again. People appreciate not only the look, but the simplicity at all levels of production. To capture that groovelicious look:

1. Draw a rectangle and fill it with a lovely avocado green. You can expand the on-screen palette by holding down the left mouse button on a color chip until a larger palette of similar colors appears and choosing one of those. Or, to create colors that aren't on the on-screen palette, open the Uniform Fill dialog box (Shift+F11). Click on a green color in the rainbow slider to get started and then drag the selector in the mixing window to change the CMYK values. I use a color reference swatch book, which tells me the CMYK values I need in order to get certain colors in printing. This is a handy item, especially when trying to convert spot colors into CMYK. (CorelDRAW now does this automatically and fairly accurately, but I like to double-check.) For the green, the values are C-47, M-0, Y-88, and K-0, which you can key directly into the Uniform Fill dialog box when using the CMYK color model. Now draw an oval with the Ellipse tool and fill it with a what's-up-doc orange (C-0, M-60, Y-100, K-0).

**Figure 11.7**

In addition to kitschy design and funky fonts, the right choice of colors really screams retro-funky.

---

### Color Consistency

Matching on-screen colors to their printed counterparts has always been a problem. In CorelDRAW 9, a color-corrected display is the default, with the on-screen images very closely representing their printed values. The Corel Color Manager utility will help you fine-tune your equipment to provide the best on-screen color representation possible. I work with color correction enabled, so I see an image on my screen that is close to the CMYK printed equivalent. If you are working on Web graphics, however, you might be surprised if you work with CMYK color correction while creating RGB graphics! So set your screen for the task at hand. In CorelDRAW 9, open the Options menu (Ctrl+J), and on the Global|Color Management options page you can turn Calibrate Colors For Display on or off (the default setting is on).

If you are serious about calibrating color, forget the gadgets, gizmos, and companion software; just do the math. So many variables are involved (including heat, color of your clothing, time of day, etc.) that change the way on-screen colors look—the chances of ever calibrating your monitor are nil. What you can do is monitor the color mixes in your artwork and compare the mathematical values to a trustworthy printed reference. Use a printed swatch book to pick colors and then key in the CMYK values for that color as your fill value in the Uniform Fill dialog box (Shift+F11). Now it really doesn't matter how it looks on screen; the printed result should be what you keyed in—or close to it.

Make sure your printed reference is new, not faded, and from a reputable source. Compare the final printed version to the reference and take notes on how the color varies so you can adjust the colors the next time. Differences in output machines, film developing chemistry, printing presses, and so on all alter the outcome—you'll have to track what happens so you will know how to fix things. If the jobs you send to your local print shop always look blue, you need to adjust the levels of cyan in your artwork. If things look green, you might need to increase the magenta level (green is yellow and cyan, so what's left? Magenta!). Unfortunately, no plug-in or upgrade is available for good ol' real-world experience!

2. With the Text tool, set your ad copy on the page. I used a font called Balloon for the top text and AdLib for the lower text. Use the Shape tool to Shift-select the nodes of the first letters of the top text. Now double-click one of the nodes to open the Format Text dialog box and add 10 to the value in the Size box. Click OK to enlarge just these selected letters. With the Shape tool again, select the second text element and drag the bottom-left arrow up to change the line spacing. This will make less space between the words vertically. Now with the Shape tool, select and drag the letters one at a time so that they are not all aligned along the baseline, to make them seem more excited and happy to see you! Give these words a thick, white .333-inch outline and enable the Behind Fill option in the Outline Pen dialog box (F12) (see Figure 11.8).

**Figure 11.8**
You can change the letter and line spacing, in addition to manipulating each letter individually, using the Shape tool.

3. Open the Symbols And Special Characters docker (Ctrl+F11) and locate the Stars1 library. Now scroll down until you find the star that looks like a "jacks" child's toy (a little metal star with rounded ends on the points that your mom was always stepping on) and drag it onto the desktop. Give it a plum/pink fill (C-5, M-75, Y-0, K-0) and a .029-inch yellow outline, with the Behind Fill outline option enabled in the Outline Pen dialog box (F12). Duplicate and arrange a whole bunch of these guys, enlarging or reducing the duplicates as you go to create a random-looking barrage of those non-slip shower flowers (see Figure 11.9).

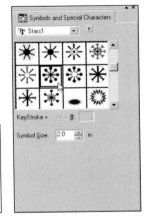

**Figure 11.9**
Use the Symbols docker to find the perfect star icon to duplicate and scatter around your page.

4. For the final element, we want a starburst kind of shape. You could use the Interactive Deformation tool's Zipper mode to distort an oval into this object or use the Polygon tool (as I did). Right-click over the Polygon tool, then click Properties to open the tool's Options dialog box. Select the Polygon As Star option, change the Number Of Points/Sides value to 44, and drag the Sharpness slider until you get the look you are after. Click OK, then drag the Polygon tool onto the desktop to draw the object. (Remember that the Shape tool is useful for fine-tuning a polygon object if necessary.) Fill this funky polygon with cyan and call it a day (see Figure 11.10).

The image can be viewed in this book's color section, or you can retrieve it from the \Chapt11\ subdirectory on the companion CD-ROM (the file is called 50sad.cdr). The burst in the file is a curve, so the Shape tool won't perform the same way as it would if the shape were still an active polygon. Open the Polygon tool settings, draw a star, and then see how the Shape tool changes things. Remember that you can drag the outside points as well as the inside points to modify an active Polygon or Polygon As Star object with the Shape tool.

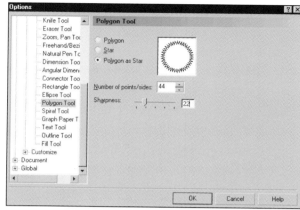

**Figure 11.10**
Use the Polygon tool to create a circular burst behind the text.

## PROJECT Classic TV

Part of putting any contemporary project together is working out the peripheral details. Corresponding Web sites, brochures, mailers, postcards, you name it—all this stuff will start to pop up on your job board. The fun thing is combining the past with the present. For example, a Web site design could benefit from the clean, quirky styling of a retro look incorporated with such modern twists as animation or interactive buttons. With the popularity of Macromedia's Flash Web-content creation program ever increasing, the demand for creative vector-based artwork is also on the rise. With a Flash plug-in available for CorelDRAW (search on the **www.corel.com** Web site to download the filter), your Web destiny is sealed! While the technology waits to catch up to bandwidth, clean and simple retro-styled Web graphics that render and download quickly rule the day.

This design is just such a project, where a printed image will work into an on-screen Web experience (see Figure 11.11). I decided a television is a good way to swap images for an animation—in a campy classic TV kind of spoof—to add motion and interest to a Web page. You can create a series of images for the screen and swap them to create animation cells to make your "television" change "channels." For the Web, you would want to slice the image into three separate GIFs so that just the center is animated; this cuts down on load time and file size.

We'll walk through the process of putting the first image into a screen shape and making that image look like it's appearing on an old 1950s vintage TV. We'll also create a background that combines retro coloring and modern objects. We'll even throw in some modernistic text effects:

**Figure 11.11**
Even a simple-looking design can benefit from high-end tricks. The TV image is a bitmap and static lines stuffed into a screen shape with the PowerClip feature; the design elements are Symbols; and the FX logo was created with the Combine function.

1.  Draw a TV screen by creating a rectangle and curving the corners with the Shape tool. Import an image for your screen. (I used a photo from the \photos\entertain directory on the CorelDRAW clip-art CD.) Select the photo and align it to your screen. Choose Effects|PowerClip|Place Inside Container and then click on the screen. Since you will be stuffing

this image into a different screen object later, again using the Power-Clip function, this step is just to help you visualize the screen and aid in the layout of the TV graphic (see Figure 11.12).

**Figure 11.12**
Put an image into the TV screen with the PowerClip function.

2.  To create scan lines or static, use the Interactive Blend tool to create a row of straight lines across the screen. For "snow" instead of static, increase the number of blend steps, and in the Outline Pen dialog box (F12), change the line style to dotted. Add any text or other tidbits to your screen to create the "program" you want to display. (Another great way to get the effect is with the "Television" filter, available from **www.alienskin.com** in the Xenofex filters collection.)

3.  Drag-select everything, and select Bitmaps|Convert To Bitmap. I used a grayscale setting for a "golden age of television" look, but you could also set it to RGB to get an old-fashioned color TV look. (If you go with RGB, use the Effects|Color Adjustment|Color Balance command to reveal sliders with which you can add yellow to your image, which makes the picture look just like my uncle's old TV set!) Convert the bitmap to either Grayscale or RGB, and then click OK (see Figure 11.13).

**Figure 11.13**
Use the Convert To Bitmap command to transform your pieces into a pixel-based image. Then use the Bitmap filters to add noise or change the colors of your image.

4.  Now we need a TV! I did a file search on the CorelDRAW clip-art CD for "tv*.*" to see what was out there. (I find this approach is faster than thumbing through the reference book, although I always have the book close at hand.) The search gave me 11 choices, and I picked one from the \clipart\home\electron directory on the CorelDRAW clip-art CD. At this point, Import (Ctrl+I) the TV and use the Ungroup (Ctrl+U) function

so you can select the individual objects. Now take the image that you want, click on your object again to reveal the Rotation and Skew arrows, and drag the left skew arrow up to tilt your image into position. Switch to Wireframe view and choose Effects|PowerClip|Place Inside Container, then click on the clip-art TV screen shape. Hey, look, your art is on TV!

5. For a final touch, add a white rectangle with curved corners to the top of the screen and use the Interactive Transparency tool to turn the solid box into a subtle gleam. Simply click the Interactive Transparency tool, then change the Transparency Type in the Property Bar from None to Uniform or Fountain (see Figure 11.14).

**Figure 11.14**
Your custom image is placed in the picture tube with the Power-Clip feature. You give the TV screen a highlight by applying an Interactive Transparency lens to a solid white box.

6. Position your TV in the center of the page. Now draw two kidney-shaped blobs, oh so typical of '50s designs (my buddy has an awesome kidney-shaped coffee table from the '50s that I covet!). You can use the Bezier tool, or start with a curved-corner rectangle and issue the Convert To Curves (Ctrl+Q) command. Use the Shape tool to delete all but two of the nodes for a relaxed, sweeping blob (see Figure 11.15).

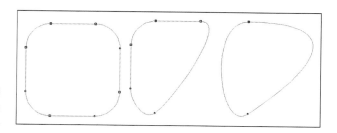

**Figure 11.15**
Node-edit a rectangle into a kidney shape.

7. Duplicate and flip-flop the blob and arrange the original and the duplicate behind the TV shape. Fill one with a light chalky yellow (Y-60) and the other with a pale green (C-47, Y-88).

8. To create a pattern of abstract objects, use shapes off the Symbols And Special Characters docker. Open the docker (Ctrl+F11) and drag shapes from the Electronics Symbols library (or import shapes off the clip-art CD) for a high-tech but interesting abstract pattern (see Figure 11.16). Drag off the symbols and color them ice blue (C-40).

 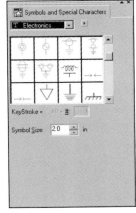

**Figure 11.16**
Use the Symbols And Special Characters docker to decorate the page with interesting objects.

9. The FX Channel logo, with its reversed-out areas, is actually easy to create using the CorelDRAW Combine command. First, draw a perfect square, then set the text "F" and "X" as separate text elements using the Text tool. Align the letters to the upper-left and lower-right corners inside the box. Now select the box and duplicate it twice. Move one duplicate up and to the left and use the Arrange|Shaping|Trim command to create a flopped-over *L* shape.

10. Select the other box duplicate and drag the top-left corner inward to downsize it so that the area of the box that passes through the *F* is about as thick as the flopped-over *L* shape passing through the *X*. Convert this box to curves (Ctrl+Q) and double-click on the bottom-right node with the Shape tool to delete it, resulting in a triangle. Now drag-select all three objects and combine them (Ctrl+L). This will create a solid black shape with open areas that appear white where the objects overlap. Keep in mind that these white areas are open and that anything below this image will show through the holes. To prevent this, draw a white box behind the *FX* curve that is large enough to accommodate the rotated *Channel* text (see Figure 11.17).

**Figure 11.17**
Create three objects that, when combined, create an interesting logo with an alternating black/white pattern.

You can view the image in this book's color section and in the classictv.cdr file in the \Chapt11\ subdirectory on the companion CD-ROM. I usually disable the Auto-Center PowerClip Contents option on the Edit page in the Options dialog box (Ctrl+J); to make a series of animation cells using the television, however, leave it enabled. Then you can select a bitmap and stuff it into the TV screen frame using the PowerClip function, and it will automatically center in the same step. You can then select the TV objects and export them as a single GIF for use in an animation that automatically "changes the channels" on a Web site graphic. Chapter 18 discusses animation more thoroughly.

## PROJECT   Pinup Posters

Because I have always studied and enjoyed airplane nose art, I naturally love the image in Figure 11.18. It has such a classic look, and, thanks to modern imaging tricks, it doesn't take nearly the effort or time that previous generations of artists had to spend to create the same look (heck, with just a few clicks an image can even be yellowed and weathered to look old and beaten, like some of the images from Chapter 5). Sometimes I mix so many modern tricks with classic art techniques that I feel guilty!

**Figure 11.18**
Adding rivets and other details changes a classic pinup image from a third-party clip-art collection into a convincing piece of aircraft nose art.

This image uses a derivative of the retro formula to achieve the desired effects. Instead of symbol shapes, a pinup illustration from the era provides the first piece of the puzzle. The pinup girl alone provides a date reference for the image, with a classic '40s-era pose, hairstyle, clothing, illustration style, and even a coloring scheme from the time. The font looks like the hand-lettered style used to personalize aircraft bombers during World War II; it's from a new collection of old-style fonts from House Industries (who, unfortunately, wouldn't give me the fonts for the companion CD-ROM because of licensing reasons; however, the pinup girl is from **www.timetunnel.com** and is on the CD). To create an old pinup graphic, follow these steps:

1. First, locate an appropriate pinup girl graphic. Time Tunnel (**www. timetunnel.com**), a unique supplier of digital images, was gracious enough to provide us with a sample collection of its images, including its brand-new Pinups collection. We need to prepare the bitmap in Photo-Paint for use in CorelDRAW. You should take control of your images and make sure they are the correct size and color depth in Photo-Paint before importing them into CorelDRAW. This will save you some headaches later. Start Photo-Paint and load the file called pinup1.jpg, located in the \timetunl\ directory on the companion CD-ROM. This is a great-looking image with the signature style of '40s pinups.

2. With the image loaded in Photo-Paint, make sure the size and resolution are correct, which you can monitor from the Resample dialog box. Using the Image menu, open the Resample dialog box and make sure

the resolution is 300 dpi and the dimensions are what you want. Click OK to close the dialog box. Then convert the image to CMYK for printing by selecting Image|Mode|CMYK Color.

3. Next, you need to remove the busy background to use the Bitmap Color Mask back in CorelDRAW. You could paint away the background using a neutral color like white—or "erase" the background to create a "floating" image like we will in the next chapter—but I thought of a different approach for this graphic. I discovered that the background is pure cyan (see the "What Color Is That??" tip); however, we don't really need cyan anywhere in this graphic (the orange tones in the model consist of yellow and magenta, with her hair and bathing suit in shades of black). By removing cyan from the image, you'll also clean up the background and solve your background problem. This doesn't work all the time, and you may have to come up with other solutions to remove your background (such as Clip Masks from Chapter 5). Choose Image| Adjust|Level Equalization. Change to the Cyan channel in the Equalize section and drag the right Output Range arrow all the way to the left. Click OK to modify the image. This will remove the cyan from the background, leaving only a faint yellow tint. You can get rid of this yellow by increasing the Brightness and Contrast settings in the Brightness-Contrast-Intensity dialog box (Ctrl+B). Save the bitmap and exit Photo-Paint (see Figure 11.19).

> **What Color Is That??**
>
> To determine what a background color (or any other color) is, use the Eyedropper tool. Simply select the Eyedropper tool, then click on the color in question. This will make the selected color the current Fill color (as indicated by the color chip in the bottom right-hand corner next to the word "Fill"). Double-click on the bottom-right-hand corner color chip to open the Uniform Fill dialog, which will display the information about this current color. Then you can see exactly what the CMYK or RGB values are.

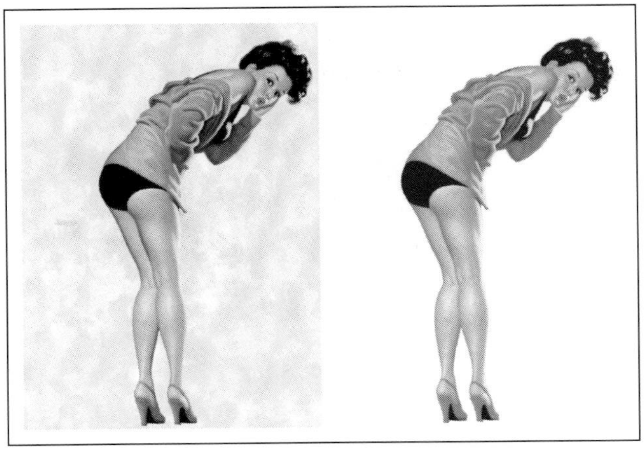

**Figure 11.19**
Use the Level Equalization dialog box in Photo-Paint to remove the cyan background pattern, and increase the brightness and contrast of the pinup girl image.

4. Start CorelDRAW and begin a new drawing. The pinup girl needed to be stuck on the side of an airplane, reminiscent of World War II nose art. To simulate a plane, create the look of riveted metal sheets. To start, draw a rectangle, and, from the Fountain Fill (F11) dialog box, use the Presets option to add a cool custom coloring scheme without any effort.

Click the down-arrow next to the Presets box on the Fountain Fill dialog box, and scroll down until you find the Cylinder-Grey 02 option (see Figure 11.20). This has a nice metallic look to it. Change the Angle value to –45 degrees and click OK.

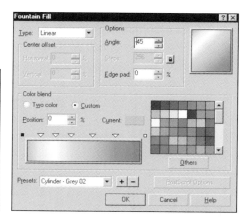

**Figure 11.20**

Use the Presets option in the Fountain Fill dialog box to assign a preprogrammed custom color blend to your object.

**Note:** A quick way to copy outline and fill attributes from one object to another is to right-click. Select the object that you want to borrow an outline or fill from, then right-click the object and drag over the object you want to copy to (the cursor will change to target crosshairs). When you release the right mouse button, a context menu will give you these options: Copy Fill Here, Copy Outline Here, or Copy All Properties.

5. Draw a circle in each corner of the rectangle and fill the circles with the same metallic custom color blend as the rectangle to make them look like rivets.

6. Drag the Interactive Blend tool between the two top circles, and then change the number of steps on the Property Bar to 15 to create an even-spaced row of rivets. Repeat the same blend for all the corner rivets to create a blend group of rivets all around the edge of the object (see Figure 11.21).

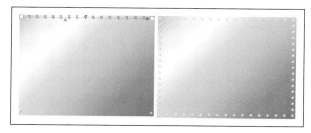

**Figure 11.21**

A rectangle with a preset fountain fill becomes a riveted metal sheet when four circles create rivet rows with the help of the Interactive Blend tool.

7. Duplicate and arrange the riveted panel to create a large wall of metal sheeting. To get away from the cloned look, select every alternate sheet and reverse the angle of the fountain fill from –45 to 135 degrees by adjusting the Angle value in the Fountain Fill dialog box (F11). This will create a more flowing coloring scheme. Then select all the shapes and rotate them 5 degrees to avoid a grid feel.

8.  Draw a rectangle over the sheets the size of your page. Then, open the Lens docker (Alt+F3) and apply a Fish Eye lens to distort the sheets so they look like an aircraft fuselage. Change the Rate setting to 50% to give a slight distortion that is perfect for this application. Select the Frozen option and click Apply. You will end up with a collection of pieces that are distorted and trimmed down to the desired page size (see Figure 11.22). You can then delete or save the original panels to disk. At this stage, things were looking busy, so I deleted a bunch of the rivets.

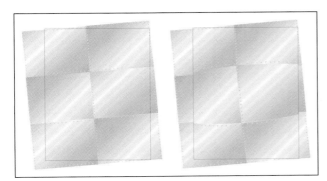 

**Figure 11.22**
Modify the fountain fills to create areas of light and dark. Use the Fish Eye lens to distort the objects slightly for the look of a rounded plane fuselage.

9.  Use the Import (Ctrl+I) feature to bring your color-corrected pinup image into this design. Size and position the bitmap on top of the metal-looking objects. Choose Bitmaps|Bitmap Color Mask, and use the Eye-dropper tool to select and "hide" the white background in the pinup bitmap. Bump the Tolerance value up to 24% and click Apply. This should leave just the image of the pinup on the side of the airplane.

10.  To get the look of raised rivets (an artistic leap, as airplane rivets are really flush and flat), add a highlight and gleam to each rivet. It isn't hard. First, select all the desired rivets in Wireframe view and combine them into one curve. Then, duplicate the curve, offset it down and to the right, and use the Arrange|Shaping|Trim function to get the shadow shapes. Repeat the process, moving the duplicate to the top and left, to get the highlight shapes. The shadow shapes are filled black, the highlights are filled white, and all are given a 50% Transparency Lens (see Figure 11.23).

11.  Set your text to name the plane. Pilots were very superstitious—and also sentimental—and would name their planes after sweethearts back home (ships and airplanes are almost always given *female* names, sticking to tradition and superstition). Modify the text with the Interactive Envelope tool to give it a curved look. I used a font called Fink from House Industries. Using the Behind Fill option from the Outline Pen

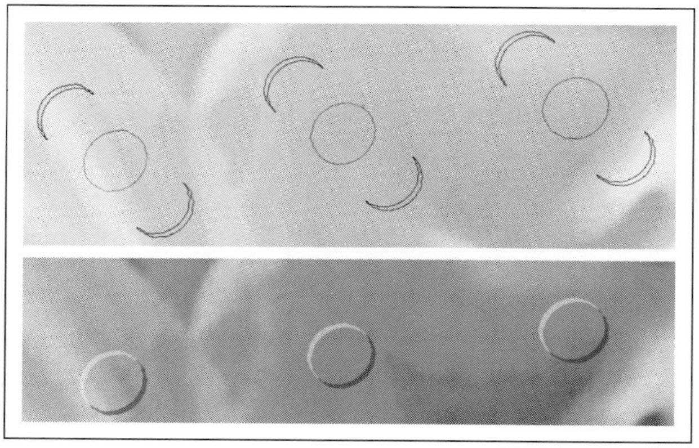

**Figure 11.23**

Use the Trim function to create highlight and shadow shapes from a duplicate of the rivets (top, in Wireframe view). When given a 50% Transparency Lens, the rivets look round and shiny (bottom).

dialog box (F12), give the text a really thick .133-inch black outline, duplicate it, and give the duplicate a thinner .083-inch white outline. This will give the text the double-outline look (see Figure 11.24).

**Figure 11.24**

Use a retro-looking font distorted with an envelope and given the double-outline effect to name the plane.

**Figure 11.25**

The Interactive Transparency tool transforms solid-white rectangles into effects-shaders that create a fade-away soft-edged look.

12. Swipe the bullet holes from Chapter 3 to add a sense of danger to the graphic. To get the image to fade away to white, use the Interactive Transparency tool on white rectangles. Draw white rectangles over each edge and use the Interactive Transparency tool to drag from the outside inward to get the fade-away look (see Figure 11.25). Or convert the entire graphic into a bitmap and use one of the edge-effects bitmap filters, as discussed in Chapter 5.

You can see the final image in this book's color section, or you can load it from the file called pinup.cdr found in the \Chapt11\ subdirectory on the companion CD-ROM.

# Beyond f/x

In what I am calling a reaction *against* the computer design revolution, more and more designs are embracing a retro or low-tech look. This is great news for everyone—old-school images are easy on the eyes, simple to build, and usually a breeze to output and print. Web programs such as Macromedia's Flash prefer the use of simple-to-render vector graphics such as those created by CorelDRAW, so now more than ever Web designs are taking on the clean, simple look of retro design.

Everything from annual reports to advertising campaigns can benefit from the eye-catching yet simple look of the past. Using existing stock images, like the pinup girl, you can add a sense of nostalgia to artwork with little effort. In fact, you can "stand on the shoulders of giants," as the saying goes, and "steal" amazing artwork from the ever-growing archives and use them as your own. What a cool deal, especially with trends the way they are. Why not use those images and start your own line of nostalgic silk ties, or promotional posters, or whatever you can dream up? I am a huge fan of the retro look and will be working it into every design opportunity I can. The beauty of using this kind of artwork is that it is really hard for things to go wrong. You'll run into very few color-correction hassles; if the colors do end up looking kind of funky, just call it an "effect" and pretend you did it on purpose!

# Moving On

In this chapter, we looked at ways to take advantage of the modern conveniences of CorelDRAW to create designs that look like they are from past decades. We also looked at how to achieve the modern retro look by combining old design ideas with more modern ones. And we proved that you can create artwork that is really fun and engaging without losing its simplicity.

In Chapter 12, we exploit more bitmap features in both CorelDRAW and Photo-Paint to help us get the campy, pulp feel of sci-fi publications from the first part of the twentieth century. Using original and stock images of antique magazine covers, you can produce very cool results with just a few image manipulation tricks. No need to read under the covers with a flashlight—this pulp fiction is okay out in the open! Leave your highbrow tastes behind as we take on the fun and frolic of trashy novels.

# Chapter 12

# Pulp Vision

*This chapter looks at exploiting classic sci-fi pulp images for use in modern designs. Tricks for merging old images with new; painting away headlines and adding your own; and creating a fun, campy style are all explored.*

# Using Sci-Fi Images for Retro-Cool Results

People placed a great emphasis on the future in what is now the past, and the combination makes for great contemporary artwork. People were just as wacky about alien invasions back in the '30s and '40s as they are today; and with Roswell, New Mexico, and "paranormal" activities appearing in daily headlines, why not bank on the trend and add a little sci-fi pulp to your daily design diet?

Not only is using a "pulp" comic-book style for commercial artwork unique, it can also be very easy. Working with the volumes of stock images available, you can quickly and easily create a piece of art that works great to draw attention. The bold, graphic nature of illustrations, coupled with the simplistic use of type, almost guarantees good results in any media.

In this chapter, we will look at exploiting the campy pulp fiction styles of yore in modern design applications. In the first project, we will take a sci-fi image from the first half of the twentieth century and make it feel right at home in a modern computer ad. Then, we will manipulate an old comic book magazine cover, painting away the existing copy using the Clone tool in Photo-Paint. Finally, we will generate that signature pulp look using an original ink illustration and other 3D extrusion tricks.

**Figure 12.1**
Old-time images can be worked into contemporary designs with great success, using Photo-Paint to clean up the images and CorelDRAW to merge all the design elements.

## PROJECT Computer Bugs Attack!

I have always been a fan of space and comics, and I have an eclectic collection that includes such great titles as *True Alien Stories* and the like. (What wonderful drivel to fill a kid's head with, to keep him looking into the skies in fear!) When I discovered that Time Tunnel (the same company that supplied the pinup girl from Chapter 11) had a "Sci-Fi Pulps" collection, I had to have it. (Samples from this collection are also included in the \timetunl\ directory on the companion CD-ROM, and be sure to check out the company's Web site at **www.timetunnel.com**.) This collection is a great source of the kind of campy, Buck Rogers art that I so love.

I especially enjoy my job when I get to mix business with pleasure, so to speak. I have some very cool clients who, on occasion, let me cut loose and do something different (as in Figure 12.1). This flexibility works to our mutual benefit—when I like what I am working on, I put more effort and time into the project without charging more, the client gets great eye-catching art that usually generates sales, and everyone is happy. This technique borrows heavily from the tried and true Wall Street ad formula: interesting photo + (bold text/ catchy slogan) = mass appeal + sales + repeat business. If you flip through any high-end publication, you won't find a lot of amazing CorelDRAW illustrations (unless it's a computer art mag, of course). What you will find is the ad formula at work, with interesting photos accompanied by catchy taglines. So why not make it work for you?

The beauty of the formula is that as a contemporary digital artist you can also draw from volumes of amazing images, such as the Sci-Fi Pulp collection, already digitized and royalty free. If you use "stock photography" rather than "royalty free" images, you have to pay a licensing fee every time it appears in print, and a hefty price tag up front (we once plunked down $10,000 for a one-year "limited use" contract on an image the client insisted it had to have!). Now for a measly $99 you can score an image CD with no usage limitations or additional fees. With a little image massaging in Photo-Paint, and text and layout in CorelDRAW, even the non-illustrator can make money in the ad game.

I like to keep the original look and feel of a period piece as much as I can when using it for a contemporary design. Something is lost if you get too flashy with modern design tricks or contemporary fonts. You don't have to be dead on, but if you shoot for close to the original—or incorporate popular techniques of the period (such as having characters block out part of the title, as in this example)—things look better. If you can nail the original spirit of the design in your makeover, the result is almost like an optical illusion, where your viewers at first think they are looking at an antique image. The surprise is that elements like Web addresses and fax numbers bring the image into the digital age. To use a classic stock image in a modern application, follow these steps:

1. Find an image from the archives that suits your application. Don't try to stretch the reader's imagination too much with images that don't match the ad copy in any way. This can be kind of hard, but I found a workable image in the Time Tunnel collection of a very mechanical-looking monster thing attacking the obligatory damsel, with our hero space-boy coming to the rescue. I've often imagined my computer as an unruly beast, so I decided the image would work. This image has the cryptic title fu-05_50.jpg and is in the \timetunl\ subdirectory on the CD-ROM.

2. Load the image at the largest size available into Photo-Paint for manipulation—the more image data, the better. (The Time Tunnel images are already at 300 dpi, but some PhotoCDs give you a size option when you load. Use the Poster option—the largest—when you are given an option.) You need to paint away the existing type so you can add in your own, and you need to address other issues in Photo-Paint to make the image right. First, most PhotoCD images are not set up for print applications. (Kodak developed PhotoCD technology originally for on-screen applications.) You need to convert the image from the on-screen version to something you can use for print (obviously the parameters are different if you are doing Web-only graphics). From the Image menu, select Resample. The Resample dialog box shows the current stats on the selected bitmap. Check out those dimensions (of the

bitmap, not the damsel!). Many times these PhotoCD images will have huge physical dimensions (Width: 22 inches, Height: 32 inches, and low 72 dpi resolution). Not exactly useful. To fix this, enable the Maintain Original Size option on the Resample dialog box, then key in the desired resolution—in this case, 300 dpi. Now, with the denser dots, the physical dimensions reflect the size that is appropriate for offset printing, down in the 7 × 10 areas. Change the physical settings of your bitmap to what you need, and click OK. (Get into the habit of taking control of these kinds of bitmap details and you will have fewer surprises. This dialog box is also available in CorelDRAW under the Bitmaps menu.) Now your image is the correct size.

3. Image collections are often in RGB format, which is again on-screen technology. For the kind of control you require to build this image correctly in CorelDRAW, you need CMYK. This is because, in order for the background objects to match up seamlessly, they all need the exact same fill colors. RGB will translate into CMYK automatically from CorelDRAW, but you have no way to guarantee that new objects will translate the same as the bitmap. Eliminate the guesswork and convert the image to CMYK now. From the Image menu, select Mode, then choose CMYK Color (32-bit) from the flyout. Now the image is at the correct size and color depth for offset printing. Save the image to disk and use only a nonlossy compression (JPEG will *lose* information in order to save space, so it is a "lossy" technology). I use the TIFF format, using LZW compression.

4. At this point, you can start manipulating the image for your application. You might want to adjust the contrast or brightness, or even one of the CMYK levels (like we did with the pinup in Chapter 11 to remove the cyan background). I bumped the brightness and contrast just a hair, because I like high-contrast images.

5. Now use the Eyedropper tool to sample the background color. Try several places to make sure you don't sample some strange color mix. I found my image to have a background color of 79% yellow. Left-click the Eyedropper to select the underlying color as your paint color. Now use the Paint tool (F5) to replace any of the text with just a blank yellow area by brushing over it. Try to get in close to the areas that you know you will crop later with a bitmap color mask, and paint the yellow color right up to the edge. A smooth yellow line around the characters' heads will allow for better results later in CorelDRAW. Use the Selection tool to crop the image down to just above the figure's heads, save the image to disk, and exit Photo-Paint (see Figure 12.2).

### Rule the Printer

If you work in a controlled environment, where you use the same service bureau and the same printer time after time, you can control your artwork to get better results. For example, if in the printing process your images become dark, you can brighten them up in Photo-Paint using the Brightness-Contrast-Intensity dialog box (Ctrl+B). If this doesn't fix the problem, you can modify the density of the dot patterns in your output. Anything that isn't a solid color is made up of a pattern of dots (called a "halftone"). You can open up the dot patterns in your halftones by using a looser line screen to compensate for bad paper or poor printing. A typical printing line screen is 133 lines per inch (lpi) (this book uses a tight 155 lpi in the color sections). Drop the line screen to, say, 100 lpi if printing on less than optimum paper or on a press that leaves a lot of ink. (Newspapers, for example, typically use a loose 85 lpi to compensate for their printing process and paper.) If tweaking dot density doesn't help, try tweaking one color independent of the others. For example, if your images consistently seem to turn yellow, or any other combination of colors, you can tweak the levels of each CMYK color individually in the Level Equalization dialog box (Ctrl+E). Select the desired color channel from the Equalize window, then drag the sliders to increase or decrease the value. Use the Preview window to check your progress. You can use the same process to color-correct before going to print. Generate a match-print or high-end color proof, and you can adjust the levels of the images to correct for almost anything. Take control of your printing projects, and you will be much happier with the results.

**Figure 12.2**

An image from Time Tunnel Sci-Fi Pulps (left) is the starting point for the design. The bitmap is manipulated in Photo-Paint so it is the right size and color depth. The Paint tool is used to color away any existing text.

6. Open CorelDRAW and Import the bitmap (Ctrl+I). Now draw a rectangle behind the bitmap at the desired ad size. With the new CorelDRAW 9 Eyedropper tool, it is a snap to give this new background color the exact fill value as the background in the bitmap. Select the Eyedropper tool from the toolbar, and click on the yellow background in the bitmap. The tool will "suck" in the color value of 79% yellow (like a turkey-baster). Now move the Eyedropper tool over the rectangle you just drew, and press the Shift key. The Shift key toggles between the Eyedropper and Paintbucket tools (and vice versa if you have the Paintbucket selected). With the tool now in Paintbucket mode, simply click to fill the background object with the 79% yellow from the background of the bitmap. This tool makes color-matching objects in both CorelDRAW and Photo-Paint a breeze. With identical background coloring, should you decide to stick with a solid-colored background, no one will ever know where the original bitmap ends and your CorelDRAW box begins (see Figure 12.3).

**Figure 12.3**
Drawing a box behind the bitmap (on the left in Wireframe
view) will create a seamless
background if you fill it with the
same CMYK value as the bitmap.

7. Now start to lay out your text elements. I imported a thumbnail of the original cover and placed it next to my artwork to refer to as I worked. This made it easier to match fonts on my system to those used in the original period piece. Back when CorelDRAW 3 shipped with exactly 256 fonts, I probably could have found the fonts used in the original artwork in two seconds, but in today's font-fat design environment I can never seem to locate what I want! (See the last project in this chapter for more on font phobias.) Use the Text tool to set your type on the page. I used a font called Faktos for the headlines, which is similar but not exactly a match for the original. The other font is called Futura, which has a clean, simple, and retro look to it despite its oxymoronic name. Use a simple, flat color scheme in line with the original (fountain fills are a no-no if you want a period look).

8. While I liked the solid yellow color, making the bitmap image "float" on a transparent background will allow more creative freedom. First select the bitmap and bring it to the front (Shift+PgUp). Then, from the Bitmaps menu, select the Bitmap Color Mask option to open the docker of the same name. Now click Color Selector, then click on the yellow neutral background of the bitmap. To avoid spots where you missed painting, or that are slightly deviant to the 79% yellow fill, up the Tolerance setting a tad to 17%. This will also soften the edges a bit where the characters meet the background by cutting into those anti-alias pixels that surround them. Click Apply and the background should disappear, leaving only the characters on top of the text. The extra effort during the painting stages back in Photo-Paint will pay off now with a clean cutaway of the characters from the background (see Figure 12.4).

The cyber-battle rages in the digital color section, as well as in the file called upgrade.cdr, lurking in the \Chapt12\ subdirectory on the CD-ROM. Load the file and see how tweaking the Tolerance value in the Bitmap Color Mask docker

**Figure 12.4**

The Bitmap Color Mask renders the background transparent, leaving the characters on top of other design elements.

affects the bitmap. At some point, too great a value will make other yellow areas also transparent, but too little and you might not get the clean cutout effect you are after. A uniform solid background in your color bitmap makes for much more flexibility than one that is busy or filled with other art, as we will see in the next example. You can use the Bitmap Color Mask option to make a solid background color transparent, and then you can change the background color to anything—or nothing at all (see Figure 12.5). Or, if you prefer, you can instead eliminate the background completely in Photo-Paint to create a free-floating object, as we did with the racecar in Chapter 5. Use the most practical and efficient technique for the project at hand.

**Figure 12.5**

For infinite variety, a bitmap with a transparent background can be given new backgrounds within CorelDRAW.

## Thrilling Invasions

Don't you just love how past predictions of how the future would appear in the new millennium were at times so silly? My favorite section at Disneyland has always been "Tomorrowland," with all those fantastical inventions that were supposed to revolutionize our lives. Two-way wrist radios, indeed! What wild imaginations they all—uh, hang on. My cell phone is ringing, and I've just received some email....

**Figure 12.6**
The Clone brush in Photo-Paint lets you erase existing text from a magazine cover and then add texture to text and other details in CorelDRAW.

Okay, so we are living in what 40 years ago would seem like a very bizarre age. Machines that talk, wireless computers that fit in your pocket, the whole technology-based society thing. For my money, though, I will take the more stylish aerodynamic art-deco vehicles of the '20s and '30s than this trend to make cars all look like amoebas!

To that end, I appreciate the more idealized reality that these old graphics offer of the future and technology, and I like to use them in designs (see Figure 12.6). Using these old images—which seem to range in quality from crisp to crappy—can be quite a challenge. Poor image quality, page texture, rips, tears, and other visual noise add to the problem. On top of everything else, images such as magazine covers are often cluttered with text or other design items you need to remove. With the original artwork often long since lost, you have no choice but to make do with what you have.

Fortunately, today's modern bitmap editing packages offer tools that are designed to help retouch photos and make bad art good again. To use Photo-Paint to touch up an old magazine cover so that you can add your own text, follow these steps:

1. Once again, a fine Time Tunnel image was the starting point for this project. Of course, as luck would have it, the image I wanted to use was in need of much touchup before I could use it for what I had in mind. (Sigh.) Well, it makes for a good tutorial, anyway. Start Photo-Paint, and from the \timetunl\ directory, open the file called tw_06-51.jpg, and you will see what I mean. The image is really dark, strange stains appear on the character's face, her skin is blue, and you see a bunch of text in the bottom-right corner where you want your headline to be. Well, we'll just have to fix that....

2. With the image loaded in Photo-Paint, once again check the size in the Resample menu, and then convert it to CMYK by choosing the Mode| CMYK command from the Image menu. You can adjust the Brightness/ Contrast setting to make the image a little more vibrant, but unfortunately that isn't going to fix everything. Zoom into the face, and you can see that some nasty things have happened to this poor woman over time. Use the lasso to select just the offending areas in her face, then open the Level Equalization dialog box from the Image|Adjust flyout. Change the Channel setting to Cyan, and then drag the bottom-right Output Range Compression slider to the left. This will reduce the cyan in the selected area, which is exactly what is needed to remove the blues from the character (see Figure 12.7).

3. Repeat the process to remove unwanted colors from different areas of the bitmap. Make your selections along existing lines—such as the edge

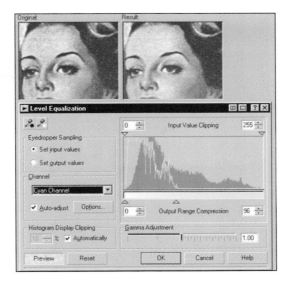

**Figure 12.7**
Adjust the levels to remove unwanted colors from sections of the bitmap to clean up the image.

of the elbow and the rocket—to help hide any color shifts. To remove the spot in the character's face, use the Levels trick and reduce the black in the stain. Poof. Gone. For some reason, a lot of unwanted cyan appears all over the character's left side. When you edit it out, she stops looking so Smurf-like. Also, her right shoulder has too much magenta in it— from some cosmic tanning salon accident, no doubt. Use the Levels trick to bring all her body parts back into her pasty-white skin-tone range, and suddenly things are looking much better (see Figure 12.8).

**Figure 12.8**
Select and adjust levels to remove spots and unwanted color from areas of the image, such as the skin tones. Removing all the extra blue from the character makes her stand out better.

4.  Now comes the lovely hassle of removing the existing text. Zoom in to the text, then, from the Brush flyout on the toolbar, select the Clone tool (it looks like two little cloned brushes). This tool lets you paint an area using another section of the image as the source material—in other words, you're "cloning" the pixels. Move the cursor to an uncluttered area on the red dress. Now set the reference point (a set of crosshairs) with a right-click. Move the brush over a similar area that contains offensive, unwanted text. Now drag to paint away the text, with the clone image designated by the crosshairs painting over where you drag your brush. With an image such as this—which contains so many random grains in the scan—you have no other way to paint away sections of the graphic with solid color without making the image look strangely smooth. It takes a little practice, but you can make almost anything disappear by painting over it with the Clone tool (see Figure 12.9).

5.  Keep painting over details with the Clone tool until all the old text is gone. Use existing details from other parts of the image; the left fold, for example, was cloned to replace the center fold, which had text over

**Figure 12.9**

Use the Clone tool to paint away existing details with similarly colored areas from other parts of the image.

it. You don't have to be perfect, and don't try to match the old image exactly. You only need something close—your own headlines will obscure the details and any imperfections you leave behind. It isn't really that difficult to end up with a workable image, and it is kind of mind-boggling when you finish to see just how believable it is (makes you think about a career with the tabloids!). When you've finished with the touchup, save the file and exit Photo-Paint (see Figure 12.10).

**Figure 12.10**

The Clone tool removes the unwanted text (inset) and lets you paint an abstract fold of drapes in its place.

6. With the original text gone, you are free to add your own headlines back in CorelDRAW. Import the file (Ctrl+I) into a fresh document so you can start to add custom text elements in CorelDRAW. Again, I tried to use a font and layout similar to the original, which turned out to be Futura Md BT (Bold). Back when these images were created, text was added in a very low-tech way to full-color images, using manually typeset words and photographic techniques. For this reason, the text is simple, bold, and often one color. Graphic art included additions like boxes or lines, which were literally cut into the film manually or scraped away with a blade. Feeling spoiled? You should! Art like this originally took hours to paint by hand, followed by quite a bit of additional effort to include text and other details, as well as prep time for the printing press. Give your computer a hug!

7. Use the Rectangle tool to draw a square, and duplicate and arrange it to become the Corel Corporation logo (work off to the side, away from your imported bitmap). To distort the logo as if it is on the globe, use the Fish Eye lens. Draw a box over the original logo, then open the Lens docker from the Effects menu (or press Alt+F3). Scroll down and locate the Fish Eye option, and set the rate at 75% to get the desired round-ness. To transform the pieces themselves—not just how they look— enable the Frozen option on the Lens docker and click Apply (see Figure 12.11). Now you can issue the Ungroup (Ctrl+U) command and have actual distorted pieces, instead of just the illusion of distortion created with the Lens object.

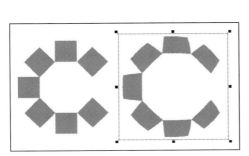

**Figure 12.11**
Use the Fish Eye lens, with the Frozen option enabled, to distort a Corel logo into a round configuration.

8. Drop the logo on the globe, and use the Color Add lens, with the color set to red, to get the see-through but vibrant logo in the globe. Trim away the shape in areas that should be obscured—by the glove, for example. Use the Shape tool to add and delete nodes to change the shape, or draw another shape with the Freehand tool and then use the shape with the Trim feature to chop away areas that should be hidden (see Figure 12.12).

---

**Freeze Frame**

Lens effects normally do not change your objects at all—only the way they appear. Just like a glass lens, when you look through it, it changes the way things behind it appear. This is exactly how an object with a lens effect works in CorelDRAW. The benefit is that you can move the lens (or change the lens effect) to select a different area below to view with the effect; the program will automatically calculate the changes and display a new image (like we saw with the double-vision examples in Chapter 9). The downside is that this is then a "live" entity that needs constant recalculation to generate the image below. Also, since you never actually change your objects, you just create an illusion— they are not modified objects that you can later select and manipulate. You can change all of this by selecting the Frozen option on the Lens docker. With this option enabled, the program will not only change the way the objects appear, but will also build an entirely new set of objects to create the illusion. This way, you don't have "live" elements, and in the end you will have objects that you can ungroup and manipulate. It can take a few compute cycles to get a Frozen lens group to calculate, but the end results can be very handy, as you saw in this project.

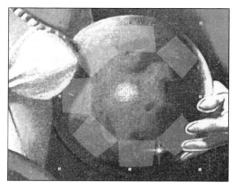

**Figure 12.12**
Use the Color Add lens to add
the logo to the globe.

9. To get the logos on the rocket ships, use the Interactive Transparency tool, modifying the parameters on the Property Bar. With the solid red logo in place, change the Type setting to Uniform, then change Rate to 15 and Transparency Operation to Add. Using these settings rather than the Normal setting produces a more realistic look. Again, you can fine-tune this look back in Photo-Paint.

10. To maintain the graininess of the bitmap, you can't just stick new CorelDRAW objects into place without them looking too "new" and out of place. It is hard to get a convincing look in CorelDRAW, but you can if you convert the objects into bitmaps. Select your text, for example, and, from the Bitmaps menu, choose Convert To Bitmap. Set the Color option to RGB—unless you are really trying to match some particular CMYK color, in which case you should choose CMYK (or if your project is destined for print rather than appearing on screen). (Unfortunately, many bitmap filters support only RGB, so you might be forced to use this Color setting. The upside is that RGB uses less memory.) Enable Anti-aliasing, select Transparent Background, and leave Use Color Profile enabled (this feature cross-references the conversion to whatever color profile you have set up, or uses a default setting—either way, you should be fine). Choose a suitable Resolution setting (300 dpi for print, 72 dpi for on-screen), and click OK to convert your objects into a uniform bitmap. (Remember that you might want to save a copy to disk first, because you can never modify the contents of the text once the image is converted.)

11. Once you have converted all the individual objects into a single bitmap, you can modify it with the bitmap filter effects. Choose the Add Noise option from the Bitmaps|Noise flyout, for example, to open a dialog box that lets you add random dot patterns to help make the text look weathered and not sparkly new. Or experiment with the Dust and Scratch filter—also available from the Bitmaps|Noise flyout—to get your new text to match the old, antique look of the original image (see Figure 12.13).

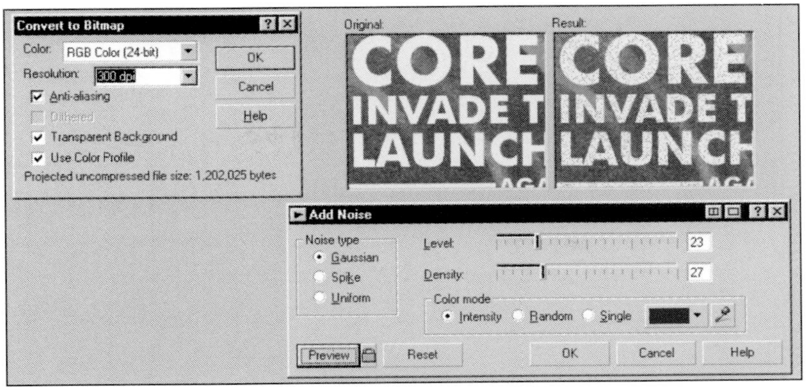

**Figure 12.13**
Use the Add Noise dialog box to make new additions to the old graphic seem weathered as well.

You can convert bits and pieces of your object to bitmaps in CorelDRAW, or export the image as a composite bitmap and manipulate things further in Photo-Paint or another bitmap manipulation program. The point is that you are not limited to the "hard-edged" results that CorelDRAW objects afford, but you can use them as a starting point and move on to other effects that bitmaps offer. Mix and match "objects" and "bitmaps" to get the exact look you are after.

This image can be seen in this book's color section, or in the spacegrl.cdr file in the \Chapt12\ subdirectory of the companion CD-ROM. I waffled back and forth with this image, at times laughing hysterically at the original *Thrilling Wonder Stories* magazine title, and then the next moment thinking I might come up with a different title. Well, I didn't come up with a title that made me laugh like the original, but I went ahead and painted out the headline anyway. It is called spacegrl.tif, and I stuck it back in the \timetunl\ directory on the CD-ROM. If you come up with a better title, let me know (see Figure 12.14).

**Figure 12.14**
Here's the original stock image with all remnants of the cover removed, waiting for your own custom application!

### PROJECT Fonts Ate My Brain

The image in Figure 12.15 was supposed to accompany an article I did ranting and raving about a big font fiasco in an earlier CorelDRAW version upgrade. When CorelDRAW first hit the market, it used copycat fonts, which looked similar to Adobe PostScript fonts, but without having to license them (like "Brooklyn" instead of "Bookman"). Well, somewhere along the line, the copycat fonts were replaced by the real ones, and I ended up with both versions on my poor choking computer, and I just went nuts. While *Corel* magazine didn't print my rant, I still love this artwork, and it fits in nicely with our pulp theme.

To get a campy graphic with electric sparks, a 3D Saturday afternoon matinee horror marquee headline, and exploding type balloons, follow these steps:

1. Duplicate the objects for which you want to create a fuzzy background, and drag them off to the side to make working on them easier. Now

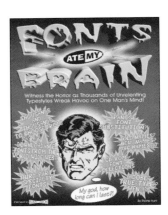

**Figure 12.15**
Electricity sparks can add an interesting glow behind objects to draw interest to them and to pull them away from the background.

---

### Font Hell

Back when all of this lunacy started, with CorelDRAW 1, you got a much, much smaller box. It had a handful of 5 1/4-inch floppy disks, a smattering of clip art, a VHS training tape, and a bunch of fonts. Well, it seemed like a bunch of fonts, but compared to today's giant box-o-draw goodies, with a handful of CDs, it doesn't seem like that many at all! Ah, those simple bygone days of CorelDRAW 1 and 2. (Even Corel 3 had only 256 fonts total, with a handy chart to stick on the wall to find them all!) Why is it that back then I had only a quarter of the fonts, but I always found exactly what I wanted, and yet now, with thousands and thousands to choose from, I am never satisfied? Power corrupts, I suppose. Fonts also eat up system resources big time. If you ever want to commit computer suicide, you might consider installing all the fonts that come on those shiny CorelDRAW CDs. Well, forget about it! You will never recover your system again! (The sad but true tale of a total Corel geek like myself who actually decided to try it one day…) Actually, as a rule of thumb, you should try to have fewer than 400 fonts actually installed on your machine at any given time. This number seems low, but anymore than that and your system chugs, taking longer to boot up and run any application that uses fonts. (Hmm. Reality check—that would be *all* the programs you use.) Just be realistic about any fonts you install and don't get carried away and install too many. Use an online resource (such as **www.1001freefonts.com**) and preview and install fonts on an "as-needed" basis. Remember also that fonts don't travel with a file unless you enable the Embed Fonts using the TrueDoc option in the Save Drawing dialog box. Therefore, unless you have the same fonts installed on another machine, be sure to use this option.

---

assign a black fill and outline for these objects. To control the area occupied by the sparks, use a thicker or thinner outline. A thicker outline will result in a more dramatic, wider spark area. Draw a box the size that you want your bitmap to be, with no outline or fill. Now select all the objects, and from the Bitmaps menu choose Convert To Bitmap. Set the Color option to Grayscale and Resolution to 300, and then click OK to convert (see Figure 12.16).

**Figure 12.16**
Color all objects black, draw a boundary box around them, and then convert to a grayscale bitmap.

2. Now fuzz the grayscale bitmap with the Gaussian blur effect, located on the Bitmaps|Blur flyout. The more blur, the larger the area of your sparks. It takes a little practice to predict the appropriate line weight and level of a Gaussian blur, but experimenting is easy.

3. To convert the soft gray "fuzz" into a harsh set of dots, use the Mode option on the Bitmaps menu. Choose Black And White from the Mode flyout to open the Convert To 1 Bit dialog box; 1 bit just means a pixel is either "on" (black) or "off" (white). The default Conversion method and options work fine for this technique, or you can experiment with this dialog box (see Figure 12.17). For bigger chunks, use a lower dpi setting when converting to grayscale, like 200 or 150 instead of 300.

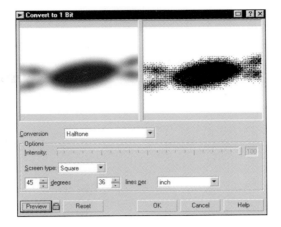

**Figure 12.17**
Use the Preview option of the Convert To 1 Bit dialog box to experiment with settings to get a "chunky" version of your original.

4. Give the black-and-white bitmap a yellow outline, no fill, and arrange it behind the original objects to create a glowing effect (see Figure 12.18). With a 1-bit bitmap, you can assign any color value for the "black" pixels the same way you would assign the outline color to an object, either from the Outline Pen dialog box (F12) or by right-clicking on an on-screen color chip. Color the "white" background of a 1-bit bitmap like you would assign any normal Fill value, either with the Uniform Fill dialog box (Shift+F11) or by left-clicking on an on-screen color chip.

**Figure 12.18**
You convert the grayscale to a black-and-white bitmap to make it chunky. You then color the bitmap yellow and arrange it behind the original objects to complete the effect.

5. You can use this effect on any group of objects, such as the colored comic face in this graphic. Select the objects that make up the face, duplicate, and move the objects off to the side. Now color the objects black, draw the boundary box, and repeat the convert to grayscale, Gaussian blur steps as before (see Figure 12.19).

**Figure 12.19**
Anything can be fuzzed—even object groups containing bitmaps.

6. Convert the bitmap to black and white to create the electricity as before, and assign a magenta outline, no fill. For a twist, enlarge the bitmap by 120%. Now duplicate the bitmap, reduce it 90%, and change the outline to yellow. Duplicate and reduce again, with the small center

having a white outline. This way, you can create electric bursts, much like the explosion blend techniques discussed in the previous chapter. You can't use the Interactive Blend tool on bitmaps, however, so you have to create the interim steps by hand (see Figure 12.20).

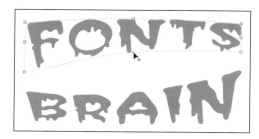

**Figure 12.20**
To create an electric blend, duplicate and downsize the bitmaps manually, changing the outline color each time (shown in Wireframe view on the left). This way, you can create a glow with color changes behind your original objects.

7.  The 3D headline text at the top of the page looks complex, but creating it is no sweat in CorelDRAW 9. First, use the Text tool to set the words "FONTS" and "BRAIN" on the page; use the font called Horror, in a green color. Make the single text object into two individual words by using the Break Apart (Ctrl+K) command. This way, you can manipulate each word independently of the other and tweak each slightly with the Interactive Envelope tool. In the Single Arc mode, distort your words into a creepy, twisted layout (see Figure 12.21).

**Figure 12.21**
The Interactive Envelope tool distorts the text.

8.  Once your individual text objects are distorted and arranged as you want, Shift-select them both and use the Convert To Curves (Ctrl+Q) command. With the text now a single object, you can get some cool depth with the Interactive Extrude tool.

9.  With the Interactive Extrude tool, drag on the text to create an Extrude Group, which you can then modify using the options on the Property Bar. Click Bevels, select the Use Bevel option, and set the width to .05 inches. Then click on the Lighting button, and click the *1* light-bulb button on the

**Figure 12.22**
Use the Interactive Extrude tool to transform flat text into a 3D-looking headline.

pop-up dialog box to enable a light source, which in turn enables 3D shading on your object. That's all there is to it! (see Figure 12.22).

Witness the cerebral carnage in the book's color section and in the fonts.cdr file nestled in the \Chapt12\ subdirectory of the companion CD-ROM. Open the file and create a blended electricity blur by duplicating and downsizing the black-and-white bitmap behind the comic face. It's not as automated as using the Interactive Blend on vector objects, but with a little effort you can get some unique exploding effects this way. Or if you prefer less "chunky" glowing effects, use the Drop Shadow trick from Chapter 3.

The star-looking objects around the words are symbols from a library called Balloons. Use the Shape tool to move around the spikes in each balloon duplicate to make it look unique.

Using the Bitmap menu to create low-res, chunky sparks is a quick and easy way to get a unique effect. Manually blending a bitmap can expand the concept into explosions or bursts. Don't hesitate to experiment by mixing and matching effects in this book or other CorelDRAW effects. For example, instead of using a Gaussian blur, create a white-to-black blend in CorelDRAW, then convert it to a black-and-white bitmap to get some nifty variants (see Figure 12.23).

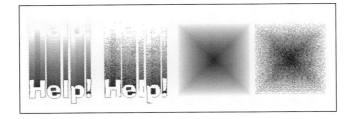

**Figure 12.23**
Start with CorelDRAW objects instead of a grayscale bitmap, and then convert to a dithered, black-and-white bitmap.

# Beyond f/x

Even if you don't see an immediate need for Buck Rogers graphics in your world, keep the magic ad formula in mind. The same technique of adding a catchy slogan to a unique image or enhanced photo can get you through almost any advertising challenge.

Other uses for the retro-pulp look are almost unlimited in today's graphic climate. You could create a whole spacey Web site, with heroes and heroines on every page, and perhaps even throw in the robots from Chapter 13. Specialty graphics—such as album covers or even alternative apparel—will gobble up images based on Time Tunnel graphics, I guarantee! You can add personalized headlines and make fun color birthday cards right off your own printer for your friends and family (use the New From Template option and let the Template Wizard find a card for you, then add your own graphics). Be a hit at the next Trekkie convention with your own line of retro place mats. The sky is the limit! Up, up, and away!

## Moving On

In this chapter, we looked at using images from the past in contemporary designs. We modified the available artwork so we could add our own text and tailor the designs for our own needs. We also saw how we could start from scratch to create a graphic in a similar vein.

With retro all the rage in everything from movies to music, once again you can ride the current trends using resources from the past to fatten your bank account in the future. It's nice if history repeats itself after the statue of limitations is up, with all those tasty image archives from the first half of the twentieth century just waiting to be plundered. The images are striking and unique, and—dare I say—pretty easy to use. It almost makes you feel guilty for charging so much. Nah!

In Chapter 13, we will examine some very exciting ways to create 3D-looking tubes and gears, and even robots that you could work into your "pulp vision" designs. If you haven't been amazed with what you can do within the "flat" confines of CorelDRAW yet, well, sit tight—you are about to see some really amazing things that you can do with this program! It's a strange but wonderful place, here on planet Corel...

# Chapter 13

# Robots, Gears, and Tentacles

*This chapter explores mechanical-looking designs such as toothed gears, belts, and pulleys, in addition to unique high-step blend techniques to render solid-appearing tubes and tentacles.*

# Using Gears, Machines, Belts, and Pulleys to Create a High-Tech Look

Before desktop publishing, computers were used more for their number-crunching abilities than for making pretty pictures. With the ability to perform such complex computations, architects and engineers were quick to exploit the power of computers. Computer-aided design (CAD) programs emerged and are still a powerful force in the engineering world. Back in the world of images, we can use the flexibility of a computer program like CorelDRAW to not only create the look of CAD and high-tech drawings, but to bring them to life as well.

In this chapter, we will use the design flexibility of CorelDRAW to create mechanical-looking illustrations. Gears and machines can work well as secondary design elements, or even as a layout strategy. In the first project, we take advantage of the computer's ability to recalculate blends in order to animate the limbs of a robot character. Then we use the Blend and Weld functions to create gears, which can be used as flat objects or can be given depth and shading with the Interactive Extrude tool. Next, we take these gears and use them in a design to add structure. Finally, we look at how to create belts and pulleys, which work in conjunction with or as a replacement for gears as unique design elements. You can achieve so many looks—only your needs and preferences will decide where CorelDRAW will take you. Grease the wheels and turn on your imagination machine!

## PROJECT  Brain vs. Hydra

I was attending a big CorelDRAW conference in Baltimore when I met a fascinating person by the name of Martin Boso (pronounced BOSS-oh). He is a medical illustrator who uses CorelDRAW to generate the images for medical training films and multimedia applications. He took great delight in showing me his unique techniques and, of course, plenty of raw, icky footage of the insides of people. Eew! Making me squirm became his favorite hobby.

Although I almost never need to illustrate the intricacies of human organ systems, I did walk away with some neat ideas of my own (in addition to an upset stomach!). Instead of using Martin's blending techniques for veins and intestines, I would use them for tubes and tentacles (see Figure 13.1).

I was looking for a robot avatar to use as a guide in an educational multimedia program for kids, which was a perfect use of the "tentacle" technique. By creating solid-looking tubes and tentacles using "live" blends, you can easily reposition these elements in your design for a comic-book type project or animation. When you're working on robots and other mechanical creations, you can take advantage of the computerized medium to cut corners and speed things along. For example, all of the objects on the left side of this robot are mirrored duplicates of the pieces on the right, which cuts your design time in half. With modular art objects like the limbs, you can easily reposition them

**Figure 13.1**
Using a high-step blend technique, you can create "movable" tube and tentacle objects.

to create different poses. You can also duplicate the whole robot—creating an army of invading beasts—and move arms or change other details to make each duplicate unique. With CAD (that's CorelDRAW-aided design!), you have many options. First, we will discuss the "tentacle" technique; then we'll see how to make Brian the BrainBot with movable limbs:

1. With the Ellipse tool, draw a circle. Now open the Fountain Fill dialog box and use the Cylinder-Green 03 (or similar) preset. The key to this technique is the custom color blend that has the dark edges and highlight in the middle (see Figure 13.2). You can create this color blend manually or use a Preset option that is similar. For the hydra octopus arm, my custom blend went from black to red to white to magenta. Change the Angle setting to get the gleam in one of the top corners, and then click OK. Remove any outline on the circle by right-clicking the on-screen "x."

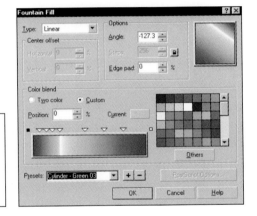

**Figure 13.2**

A custom color blend is critical to the success of this effect. The idea is to have shadow, highlight, and then shadow again in the color scheme.

2. Duplicate the circle (+ key) and reduce it by dragging a corner sizing handle inward with the Pick tool. Use the Bezier tool to draw an *s* curve—or any other shape—to eventually run the blend along. Now move the two circle objects to the start and finish of the curve and drag between them using the Interactive Blend tool. Change the Number Of Steps setting to 300 on the Property Bar (see Figure 13.3).

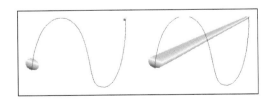

**Figure 13.3**

Although a curve is drawn for the blend to follow along, initially you must blend to objects directly using the Interactive Blend tool.

**Cut the Chatter**

To ensure that your blends are as smooth as possible, try not to use any outline attributes in your control curves. Blending objects with outlines creates a more perceptible stagger-step than those without.

3. On the Property Bar, click Path Properties, select New Path, and click on the curve you want your objects to blend along. Click Miscellaneous Blend Options and enable the Blend Along Full Path radio button, which will generate a twisty, curving tentacle (see Figure 13.4).

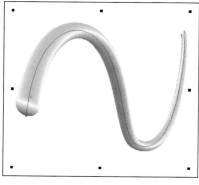

**Figure 13.4**
Blending along a path transforms the straight tube into a wiggly tentacle shape.

4. Select the control curve and right-click the on-screen "x" to remove the outline color. That completes your tentacle. To change the orientation of the tentacle, simply change the order of the parent shapes. For example, select the right control curve and send it to the front (Shift+PgUp). The blend will redraw, changing the way the tentacle looks; instead of looking like it is going away from you, it will look like it's coming toward you (see Figure 13.5). It is essentially all an optical illusion, but it works great!

**Figure 13.5**
Sending a control curve to the front or to the back changes how the blend redraws itself. This makes the tentacle seem to be either going away from you or coming toward you.

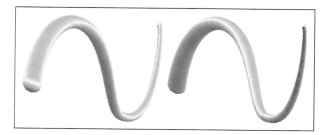

## Danger, Will Robinson, Danger

The tentacle process allows for flexible, movable limbs, either as gooey octopus arms or straight rigid tubes. Here's how I made the main robot character, with tube arms:

1. For the brains of this robot character, I used, er, brains. From the Corel-DRAW clip-art CD, import (Ctrl+I) a nice, squishy, pink brain from the

\medical\organs\ directory. Starting with this clip art, add details to get the look of a mechanical creation. (I tend to get carried away adding details. You might want to create a less-complicated robot and skip to Step 7, where the "tentacle" technique begins.) Draw a metal plate over half of the front exposed brain area using the Bezier tool and give it a shiny, metallic fill with the Cylinder-Grey 02 custom color blend preset found in the Fountain Fill dialog box (F11).

2. Duplicate the metal plate shape and downsize it. Now use the smaller duplicate (with fill and outline removed) as the reference path to blend rivets along and bolt the plate into the brain. (The rivets are simply circles with black-to-white radial fountain fills and the center offset to create a gleam.) Use the Interactive Blend tool to create an active blend group, then use the Property Bar. Click Path Properties, choose New Path, and then select the metal plate shape duplicate to place the rivet blend there. Click Miscellaneous Blend Options and enable the Blend Along Full Path radio button.

3. Duplicate and flip the plate and rivets shape for a symmetrical look. Now draw more fountain circles around the brain for sensors and use the Freehand tool to draw wires connecting them to the plates. If you draw a thick line and then blend it with a thin one on top, you can create rounded "wires," just like the lasers from Chapter 10 (see Figure 13.6).

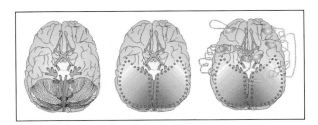

**Figure 13.6**
A clip-art brain is wired with sensors and metal plates.

4. Draw a base with the Rectangle tool to rest the brain on and use the Bezier tool to draw the pointy supports. Give the supports a black fill and duplicate them. Downsize the duplicate using the Shape tool and fill it with white. Blend it with the original to create a rounded, pointy brain support. Duplicate the support to create a total of four, downsizing two for the distant pair. For eyes, fill circles with custom color radial fountain fills. Draw rectangles connected with spheres for articulators, on which the eyes will rest.

5. Draw ovals with the Ellipse tool for the glass dome shape and the beehive ear electrodes. To make the bottom of the glass dome flat, draw a

rectangle and use the Trim function to cut away a uniform base quickly. With the rectangle selected, choose Arrange|Shaping|Trim, click the Trim button, then click on the dome shape. Place all the objects—except the eyes—behind the glass dome shape. Give the dome a semi-opaque look with the Interactive Transparency tool. If you click the tool and change the parameters in the Property Bar (instead of dragging on the object), you can assign a Uniform transparency. To heighten the glass look, draw a reflection shape with the Bezier tool and fill it white (see Figure 13.7).

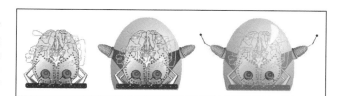

**Figure 13.7**
Place the brain on a stand, level it, and give it eyes. Then place everything under a glass dome, an egg-shaped object with a 50% Uniform transparency.

6. Create another rectangle to rest the head shape on and make it look cylindrical with the Cylinder-Green 03 fountain fill preset (presets are great shortcuts!). Then create another rectangle and finally, a third rectangle, which you make into a double parallelogram with the Interactive Envelope tool, using the Envelope Straight Line option on the Property Bar. (In this mode, when dragging a corner node while holding down the Shift key, the opposite corner node will also move in the opposite direction.) Give each of these objects the look of a cylinder with one of the cylinder fountain fill presets. Draw circles for the shoulder, elbow, and hand, and use a custom color radial fountain fill to make them look round. (Load the file brainvshydra.cdr from the \Chapt13\ subdirectory on the companion CD-ROM to see all the custom color blends.) Use the same technique to create round casters underneath the robot for him to roll around on.

7. Use the Graph Paper tool to create a grid for the speaker grill. Locate and select the Graph Paper tool on the Object flyout (where the Polygon and Spiral tools are). Right-click the tool to open the Properties dialog box, where you can change the Number Of Cells Wide and High values. Drag the Graph Paper tool to create a grid, and give it a white outline to become a speaker grill. Stuff the grill into an oval shape using the Effects|PowerClip|Place Inside Container command.

8. Now draw a circle on the left center of the shoulder shape, and give the tentacle a custom color blend from the Fountain Fill dialog box (F11), such as the Cylinder-Green 03 preset. Duplicate this shape and move it to the center of the elbow circle. Duplicate it again for another elbow

shape and then once more for the hand. These four shapes will connect with blends to create the arm. Duplicate and reduce the shape three more times for each finger (see Figure 13.8).

**Figure 13.8**
Simple geometric shapes, given life with fountain fills, stack up to become the body of the robot. Control curves are put into place to create the arms and fingers in the blend steps to come.

9. Now select the small circles in the shoulder and elbow and connect them with a 40-step blend, using the Interactive Blend tool. Repeat this process to create the other arm section and the fingers. Arrange the objects with the blend groups so that they start in front of a joint, such as the shoulder, and end behind the next joint, such as the elbow. This will create an arm group, which you can duplicate and flip-flop for the other side. To make all the gleams and shadows alike, right-click and select Copy Fill Here to copy the fill properties from the left arm pieces to the right (see Figure 13.9).

**Figure 13.9**
Use the Interactive Blend tool to connect the small circles into solid arm shapes. Arrange the blend groups and the joints to create a dimensional arm and then duplicate the blend groups for the other side.

10. Switch to Simple Wireframe view, where only the control objects in a blend are displayed. This makes it easier to select the end of a finger, for example, and move it. When you switch back to Normal view, you will see how the live blend rebuilds itself to reflect the new position of the control object. You can now easily place the limbs of your character in any position (see Figure 13.10).

11. Use the bitmap-fuzz technique (see Chapter 12) to create a row of ions connecting the ear electrodes and to create static behind these objects.

**Figure 13.10**
The control curves can be selected and moved in Simple Wireframe view (left), and the limbs will automatically rebuild themselves in the Normal view, thanks to the live blend groups (right).

For skip-around readers who have not yet read Chapter 12, draw a thick black line between the two electrodes and then convert this into a grayscale bitmap. Inflate the bitmap to enlarge the image area, then use the Gaussian Blur bitmap filter to fuzz the line. You can achieve the desired pixelation (chunky dots) by converting to a dithered black-and-white bitmap.

12. For additional bits of animation, add blends of circles for rows of lights. The great part about these blends is that you can drag and drop a new color on any of the control curves to change the interim light colors. These simple circles also help show emotion and mood for each frame. (If you were animating a multimedia character, this section could be its own film loop, with the circles advancing like lights for each cell.) The addition of a little screen to speak words—using a font called LCD—finishes off the robot companion.

This file is called brainvshydra.cdr in the \Chapt13\ subdirectory on the companion CD-ROM, and the images can be seen in the digital color section, also on the CD. Open the file to see how the custom color blends give the circles depth. Try moving the control curves around and watch the limbs rebuild for yourself.

## PROJECT Geared for Success

Everything I needed to know about mechanical engineering I learned from LEGOs! I still have quite an impressive collection of these plastic wonder-bits, from which I fashion all kinds of strange things in my spare time.

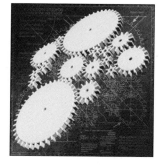

**Figure 13.11**
The Interactive Blend tool and the Weld command make gear shapes in any size. These objects can be used for the background blueprint image or made into 3D objects with the magic of the Interactive Extrude tool.

The LEGO parts that always won my favor were the gears. Even now, I tend to be fascinated with gears and find they make great design elements (see Figure 13.11). They are interesting geometric shapes; they are visually interesting and easy to render; and they have a great deal of connotative meaning in our society (precision, constancy, high technology, and so on). Gears are also easy to animate and pop up in places like my sample Web site (see Chapter 18). Gears serve as all kinds of visual vehicles in art—from primary to secondary design elements. In the next two tutorials, I'll show you how to create gears and how to use them in artwork.

## Gears, Gears Everywhere

CorelDRAW is an awesome tool for creating images that are geometric as well as mechanical in nature. The Interactive Blend tool creates such nice and even-spaced duplicates, it is a natural for such elements as rivets, bolts, and even the teeth in a gear. Once you create your basic gear shape, you can use it as a 2D design element or take things further with the Interactive Extrude tool. To create gears of any size and then make the shapes look 3D, follow these steps:

1. Start with a rectangle and round the edges with the Shape tool (hover the Rectangle tool over a corner node, which automatically swaps to the Shape tool, then drag to round the corner). Now use the Interactive Envelope tool with the Envelope Straight Line option enabled as before to squeeze the top closer together. (Duplicate this gear tooth and set it aside for later.)

2. Double-click the gear object to reveal the axis of rotation (it looks like a bulls-eye in the center of your object). Drag this center of rotation down while holding the Ctrl key to snap the axis of rotation down to the bottom center of your object (see Figure 13.12).

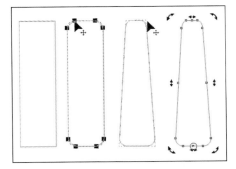

**Figure 13.12**
A rectangle becomes a gear tooth when you round the corners with the Shape tool and distort the object with the Interactive Envelope tool.

3. Now duplicate the object (+ key), and move that object off to the side. Use the Interactive Blend tool to drag between the two objects. The default number of steps is fine. Shift-select both control curves and align them to Horizontal and Vertical center, by pressing the C and E keys.

4. Once you have your blend group of gear teeth stacked neatly on top of each other, you are ready to spin them into a round gear. First, press the Esc key to deselect anything you might have highlighted, then drag-select around the blend group to select all the elements (if you click on the group, you select only the top Control Rectangle, which is no good). Now in the Property Bar, change the Blend Direction value from 0 to 360. Since we changed the axis of rotation on the Control Rectangles, the result is a perfect circle of spokes (see Figure 13.13). If

**Note:** With the removal of the Blend docker, it is impossible to create a blend group using two objects directly on top of each other using the Interactive Blend tool. You will have to move the objects apart, create the blend, and then align them, as we did here. Or reprogram your Shortcut keys to once again open the Blend docker, as discussed in Chapter 1.

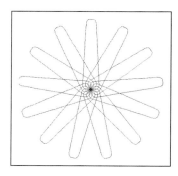

**Figure 13.13**

With the axis of rotation moved in the Control Rectangles, when you change the Blend Direction value in the Property Bar to 360, the objects spin around in a complete circle.

the spokes are not perfectly spaced, click Object And Color Acceleration in the Property Bar and move the sliders to dead center.

5. Choose Arrange|Separate, and then select Arrange|Ungroup All so you can manipulate the objects individually. Now, select and delete the one extra and redundant gear object at the top center of the once active blend group.

6. Issue the Select All (Ctrl+A) command to select all the gear objects, then choose Arrange|Shaping|Weld. Disable any of the Leave Original radio buttons, click Weld To, and then click on the selected group. Yippee! A giant asterisk! (See Figure 13.14.)

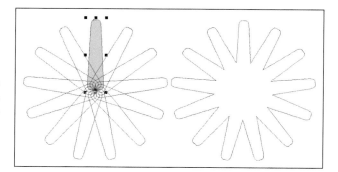

**Figure 13.14**

All of the blend objects are separated, and the extra gear shape (in gray) is deleted. At this point, all of the objects can be merged into one using the Arrange| Shaping|Weld command.

7. Draw a perfect circle and center it to the star shape using the Align And Distribute dialog box. Shift-select both the circle and the star shape, and choose Arrange|Align And Distribute. In the resulting dialog box, enable the top Center and the left Center radio buttons. (Take note of the underlined letters in this dialog box, as these are the single-key keyboard shortcuts to these commands.) Click OK to align your two objects.

8. Select your circle shape and choose Arrange|Shaping|Weld. Disable the radio buttons, click Weld To, and then click your star object. This should result in a nice, gear-like object (see Figure 13.15).

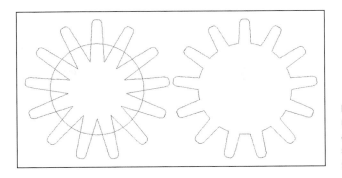

**Figure 13.15**
Using the Shaping|Weld command on the circle and star shapes results in the final gear object.

9. Duplicate the gear shape and arrange the duplicates so that they mesh nicely together. When you have the gears in the configuration you like, Shift-select them all and combine them into one curve (Ctrl+L).

10. With all the gears combined into one curve, it is easy to then use the Interactive Extrude tool to add depth, a bevel, shadows, and high-lights—and even to rotate them in 3D space! First give everything a neutral color, such as gray or gold. Then drag on the gear curve with the Interactive Extrude tool to create an active extrude group, then modify things to your liking using the Property Bar. Click Lighting to enable a light source, which results in the automatic highlight and shadow effects. Click Bevels, then enable that feature by clicking the Use Bevels radio button. To spin your gears in virtual space, simply double-click on the extrude group and then drag the 3D rotation arrows to spin your gears around (see Figure 13.16).

> **Rack 'Em Up**
>
> The Align And Distribute dialog box has many handy options not available as keyboard shortcuts. The Align To Center Of Page and Align To Edge Of Page options are very useful. Click the Distribute tab to reveal many heretofore unavailable ways to arrange your objects predictably. Occasionally you might want more perfection than "eye-balling" it affords to align and distribute your objects, and here is where you do it. I use the keyboard shortcuts so often that I almost forgot about showing off this amazing and practical feature.

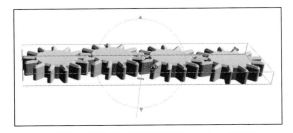

**Figure 13.16**
The Interactive Extrude tool converts a gear curve into a set of dimensional objects with shading and even a bevel.

That is essentially all you need to do to create any kind of gear shapes. I went a little nuts in my example in the color section in the middle of the book and also in the gears.cdr file located in the \Chapt13\ subdirectory on the companion CD-ROM. I made gears of all shapes and sizes, and used them in both their original "flat" state as a background design, then used the Interactive Extrude tool on a duplicate of those shapes for the 3D effect. I spent way more time on this image than any sane person would, but, like I said, I love gear shapes!

## The Imagination Machine

Ever find something you created a long time ago and say to yourself, "What was I thinking?" The image in Figure 13.17 (well, only pieces of it now) was something I submitted to the Corel International Design contest many moons ago, and gee whiz, it didn't win anything. When I first reopened the file, I was so aghast at some of the amateurish techniques that I immediately closed it again, too embarrassed to look. Many weeks later, I remembered that the image used gears, so I opened it again for potential inclusion in this chapter. I liked the layout, but I spent so much time fixing the artwork, I probably would have been better off starting from scratch!

Gears work well in advertising or other commercial artwork on both a visual and connotative level. Here the "grease the wheels" and the "imagination machine" concepts are reinforced by the gear image. This machine would, of course, produce nothing but noise and maybe some static if you could turn it on, but the laws of mechanical engineering don't apply to the art world. As an interesting visual vehicle, it rolls along just fine.

This project introduces a totally different way to create gear shapes. In addition, these gear objects look different than the ones in the previous tutorial because the objects have been given big cutout areas in the gear centers for a more stylized and less realistic look. The electric static is created using the exact process as outlined in Chapter 12, and the metallic fills resemble the metallic headlines in Chapter 3. (Pretty soon I won't even have to explain anything; I'll just point you back to chapters we have already covered!) Of course, some new techniques worth mentioning are available, so read on. To create gear shapes using the Polygon tool and make them stylized design elements, follow these steps:

1. Select the Polygon tool from the Object flyout. Before you use the tool, right-click over it and choose Properties. In the Options dialog box, enable the Polygon As Star radio button, increase the Number Of Points value to 8 or so, increase the Sharpness setting to a whopping 75, and then click OK.

2. Now, to create a perfect star, drag the Polygon tool on the desktop while holding down the Ctrl key. Remember that you can drag on the inside or outside nodes in a symmetrical polygon with the Shape tool to fine-tune it.

3. Use the Ellipse tool to draw a perfect circle by holding down the Ctrl key while dragging. Shift-select both the circle and the star, and use the C and E shortcut keys to align them perfectly both horizontally and vertically.

4. Select the star shape and choose Arrange|Shaping|Intersect. Disable the Leave Original radio buttons, and then click on the circle. The result is the beginning of a gear shape (see Figure 13.18).

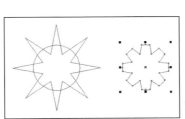
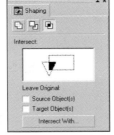

**Figure 13.18**

Use the Shaping|Intersect command to chop away the star points.

5. Draw another perfect circle, aligned with the gear shape, to get rid of the inside star points. Then, issue the Arrange|Shaping|Weld command. Once again, disable the radio buttons before you click Weld To, and then click your star object (see Figure 13.19).

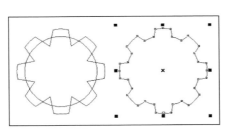

**Figure 13.19**

Use the Shaping|Weld command to remove the inside star points.

6. Draw two more perfect circles, aligned and inside the gear object. When you select all three objects and combine them (Ctrl+L), you create the stylized gear object. Use the Cylinder-Gold 07 fountain fill preset to give this a nice, metallic shading (see Figure 13.20).

7. The addition of the custom color blend to your gear shape will result in some very nice shading effects when you modify the shape with the Interactive Extrude tool. Just as before, drag the Interactive Extrude tool on the curve, then change the parameters in the Property Bar to include Bevel and Lighting options. The result is an interesting set of gears that share a common light source and vanishing point (see Figure 13.21).

However you choose to make your gears is fine with me. Heck, you could forget the whole "custom" gear idea altogether and find some very useful gear shapes in the Symbols And Special Characters dialog box (GeographicSymbols has a nice set, for example). The clip-art library that ships with CorelDRAW also has some fine gear shapes for you to use, so weigh your choices and do what you like. Me? I like making my own gears!

That's all of the real magic behind this piece. All of my secrets are basically now yours (and a huge portion of my personal artwork to boot!), so for the

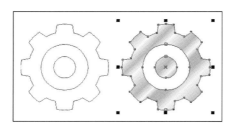

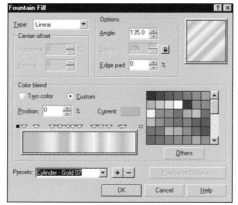

**Figure 13.20**
Combining two circles to the gear curve results in a stylized shape with a clear open ring through it. A custom color blend preset creates the look of metallic shading.

**Figure 13.21**
The Interactive Extrude tool works on the complex gear curve to create a dynamic 3D object with shared shading and a shared vanishing point.

**Note:** This file contains handy little screw heads, which you can load and steal for your own designs later on. Why build when you can pilfer?

remainder of the book, it will be mighty difficult to wow you, I'm sure. You can see this piece in the book's color section or load the imagine.cdr file in the \Chapt13\ subdirectory on the companion CD to look at things firsthand.

## PROJECT Belts and Pulleys

In the same way you create gears, you can create belts and pulleys. It is sometimes useful as a design element to connect objects with a belt or other visual vehicle to guide the reader's eyes around the page (see Figure 13.22). Belts and pulleys also share the same kind of high-tech and mechanical connotations that gears do, but they are not as obtrusive or harsh as all those toothy gears. It is also difficult to create a border with gears that isn't too busy, but a border is a perfect application for belts and pulleys.

**Figure 13.22**
Like gears, belts and pulleys make interesting mechanical additions to a design to add a sense of motion and high-tech edge. The pieces can also work to unify a logo or act as a border element.

The same type of graphic works for the printing industry as well. Large printing presses that print newspapers and other big publications print onto giant rolls of paper that weave through many rollers, just like belts and pulleys. For the printing-press look, add more depth to the rollers and pulleys, and decrease the thickness to look more like thin paper instead of a thick belt. To connect pulleys with a belt, follow these steps:

1. Use either the gear-tooth blend technique or the Polygon As Star option to create a multi-toothed pulley object. Or here is another option: Use the Interactive Blend tool and small circles, rather than gear teeth, to blend along a round path (see Figure 13.23). When you use the Arrange|Shaping|Weld command on all these objects, you get a nice, round-toothed pulley shape.

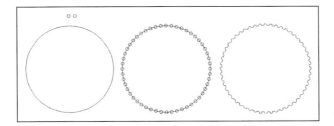

**Figure 13.23**
Use the Interactive Blend tool to scatter circles along a round path; then merge them into a pulley shape using the Shaping|Weld command.

2. Use the Polygon tool to create a six-sided shape and then center it with the outside circle. Now combine the two (Ctrl+L) to finish off the hollow-centered pulley. Give it a solid gray color fill, arrange any duplicates that you want; then once again add depth with the Interactive Extrude tool (see Figure 13.24).

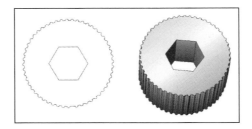

**Figure 13.24**
Use the Interactive Extrude tool to add depth and shading to the pulley wheel.

3. As you did with the gears, you can duplicate and arrange multiple pulley curves and then combine them into one curve (Ctrl+L). Use the Interactive Extrude tool again to add depth and shading to the curve. Draw a shape with the Bezier tool to connect the pulleys with a belt (see Figure 13.25).

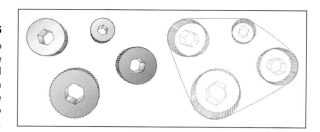

**Figure 13.25**
Combine all pulley circles into one curve and use the Interactive Extrude tool to give them all depth and shading and a shared vanishing point. Use the Bezier tool to draw a belt to connect the pieces.

4. With the belt curve selected, duplicate it (+ key), and hold the Shift key as you drag a corner sizing handle outward to enlarge it symmetrically. Then Shift-select both belt pieces and make them solid by using the Combine command (Ctrl+L). Click on 50% black to give the belt some color.

5. Now that you have a solid belt object, all you need to do is copy the Extrude settings from your pulleys and you're in business! Choose Effects|Copy Effect|Extrude From, then click on the pulley extrude group. Modify the extrude group for the belt on the Property Bar by increasing the Depth value if you want.

6. Use the To Back (Shift+PgDn) command to send the belt group to the back of the image stack—and make sure you don't get a finger stuck in the belt (see Figure 13.26).

There you have it. You can place gears and pulleys in, around, and through your next design!

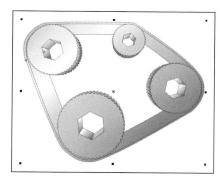

**Figure 13.26**
Use the Copy Effect command to assign the same Extrude values in the belt shape as in the pulley objects.

# Beyond f/x

Gears, mechanical elements, and modular designs have a ton of design potential. From logos to animations, these art elements can have many uses. In fact, we will be animating these gears in Chapter 18.

The pulleys can pull a belt through a design, guiding the reader and directing attention throughout a publication. Or you can connect parts of your page using the tubes and tentacle shapes, creating a pattern to direct the reader through your page like a roadmap.

Gears add that sense of action and mechanical feel that are right at home in the corporate logos of many industries. Animated gears also make interesting button elements, adding a sense of danger. It is against your better judgment to stick your fingers (or in this case, the cursor) into the intermeshing and rotating gears, so it is kind of a reverse psychology design trick. Since the virtual experience is safe, you can create all kinds of moving, dangerous, sharp machines for your viewers to interact with. Using modular design tricks, or the blending techniques we used with the robot arms, your Web machines can easily be animated and come to life when you click them.

In advertising, you can play off the mechanical nature of these graphics with tag lines such as "Put us to work" or "Working to bring you the best deals" or "Geared for success" or any of a gazillion phrases. Now get in gear and get to work!

# Moving On

In this chapter, you learned how to create robotics and mechanical-looking designs. The robot image used symmetry to cut design time in half, and it used tricks to make moving and animating the limbs easy. The gear sections showed how to create gears of any size and shape with the Interactive Blend or Polygon tool. You also saw how to add depth to the gears by using the Interactive Extrude tool and how gears and pulleys can be used as interesting design elements in their flat state, in three dimensions, and even as a frame element.

In Chapter 14, we will be using grids and lines, rather than the Interactive Extrude tool, to create dimension. The great thing about the human mind is how easily it is fooled, and we will endeavor to trick readers into seeing depth and dimension where none exists. So let's leave robots (except maybe Maximilian, the evil villain robot from the Disney *Black Hole* flick) and machines behind for now and head into the mysteries of grids and black holes.

# CorelDRAW for Linux
# Studio

*This color studio includes final images from all of the
step-by-step projects in this book, and it complements the
"electronic" color gallery on the included CD-ROM. The
CD also contains all of the tutorial files, in CorelDRAW
format, so you can "load and learn." Use this color section
for reference, inspiration, or as a quick guide to the cool
techniques outlined in this book. When you see something
you like, point your finger, exclaim "Cool! I wanna do that!"
and then flip to the chapter that explains the process.*
*Enjoy!*

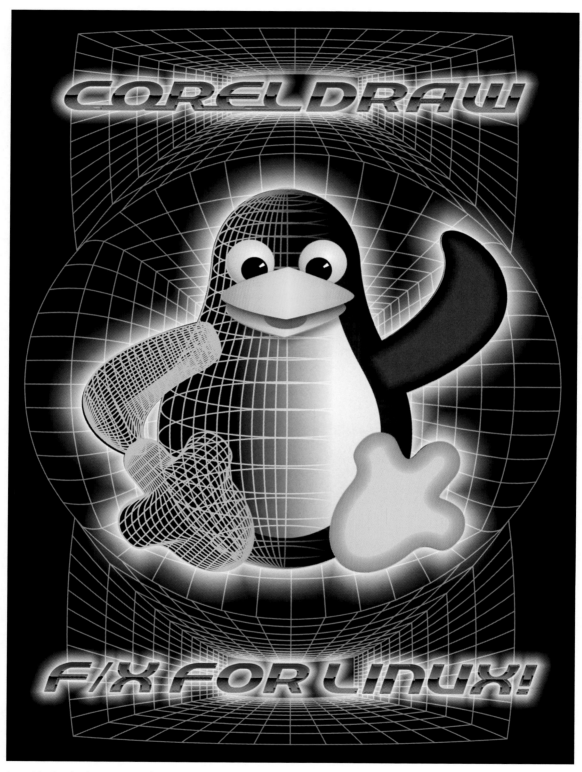

Starting with simple shapes, even the "artistically challenged" can create fresh and fun comic-book characters like our pal the Linux Penguin (Chapter 2). A few more tricks create the sparkling and glowing chrome headlines (Chapter 3), while "bending" and blending grids create the illusion of three dimensions (Chapter 14).

Converting scanned artwork into CorelDRAW vector objects makes it easy to colorize a comic character to populate a computer-generated scene (Chapter 2). Screen captures and bitmap effects broaden your design horizons (Chapter 9).

By converting vector objects into bitmaps directly within CorelDRAW, you can then exploit a new range of effects. The type was blurred to change the field of depth, while the PowerClip and Interactive Drop shadow features create the "ghosted" look (Chapter 3).

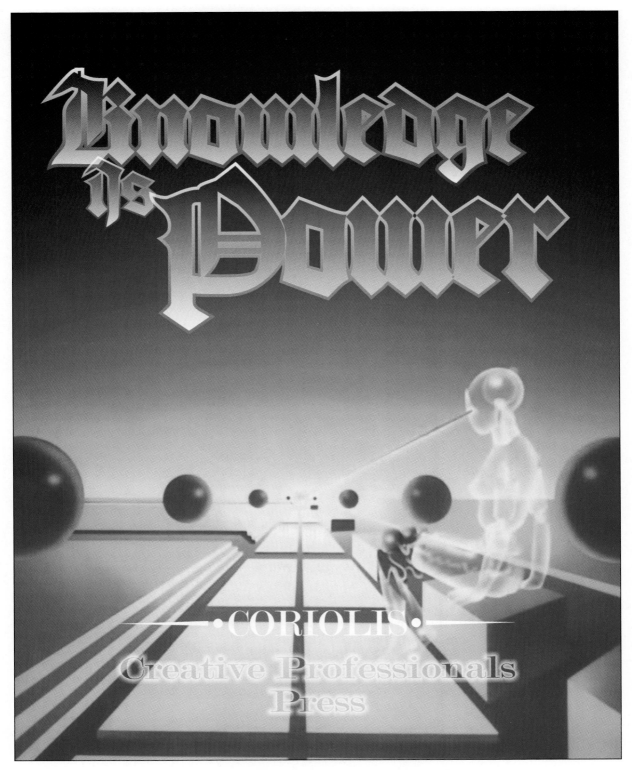

The Interactive Transparency tool allows you to control the opacity of objects, while manipulation of the Interactive Drop Shadow feature can create a "glow" effect (Chapter 3).

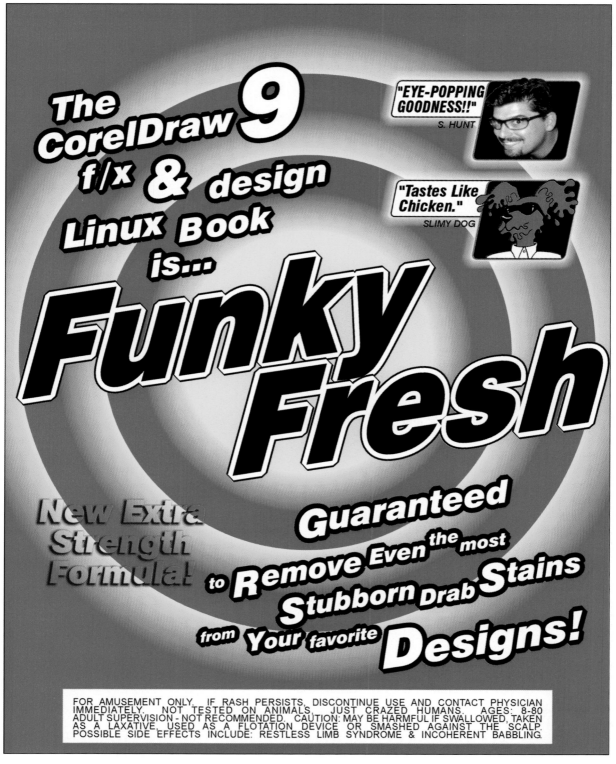

Using a motif made popular by 1970s household products, the Interactive Fill tool lets you create and control the bright fill effects with just a few mouse clicks (Chapter 4).

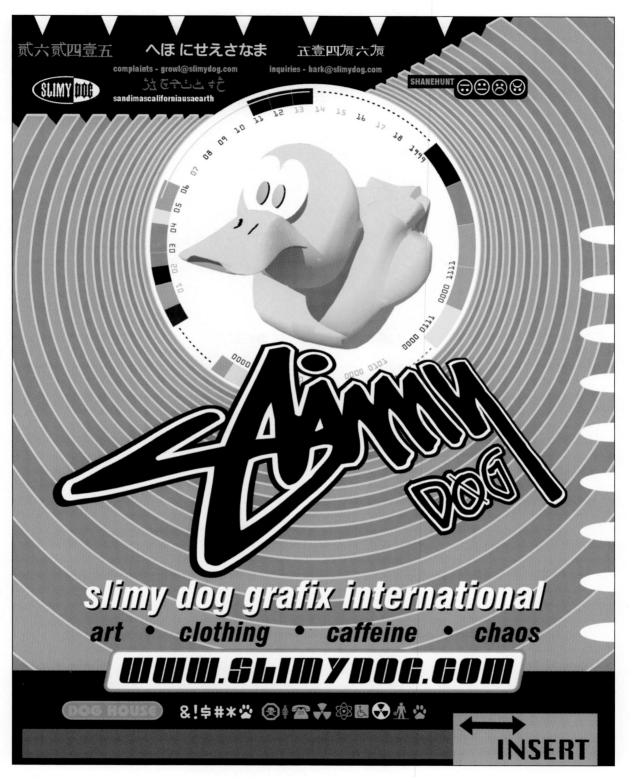

Combining contemporary design elements, including 3D rendered images along with strong geometric shapes, results in a contemporary image appealing to the video-game set (Chapter 4).

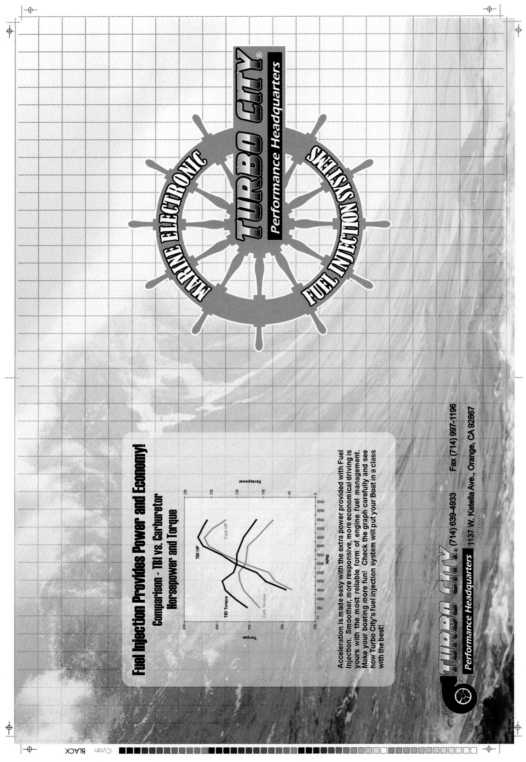

The Interactive Transparency tool allows you to combine multiple elements in a design in a subtle and more pleasing way than hard-edged stacking affords (Chapter 5).

Using the power of Corel Photo-Paint, you can create "free-floating" objects. Masking effects, layering, and background-erasing tricks allow you to merge multiple images into a single photo-collage (Chapter 5).

The Intersection, Weld, and Trim features allow you to generate new custom shapes from just a few originals. Here a single "ray" and circle object are used to generate the arched boxes, which serve to frame images placed inside them with the Power Clip feature (Chapter 5).

**e People**

**The Leader In On-Line Staffing**

**About Our Services** ●         ● **Legal Information**

**Get Connected** ●         ● **Our Members**

CorelDRAW allows you to convert a bitmap into a Duotone, and then stuff it inside any shape you wish with the PowerClip feature. This in turn can be further modified, with the Interactive Transparency tool, into a photo montage with soft edges (Chapter 5).

Multistage blend techniques create round and shiny-looking objects, while selective blurring makes some details appear to leap off the page. These and other tricks that add depth and dimension are discussed in Chapter 6.

Special Power Clip tricks automate the task of breaking an image into puzzle-like pieces. Adding shadows and even bevels creates realistic-looking puzzle pieces (Chapter 7).

The Artistic Media tool allows you to apply groups of images (Spraylists) to a path to create colorful designs. Chapter 8 shows you how to create your own Spraylists, or you can use the ones included on the companion CD.

When faced with limited resources for a project, duplication and other image-manipulation techniques allow you to create an interesting "double vision" design (Chapter 9).

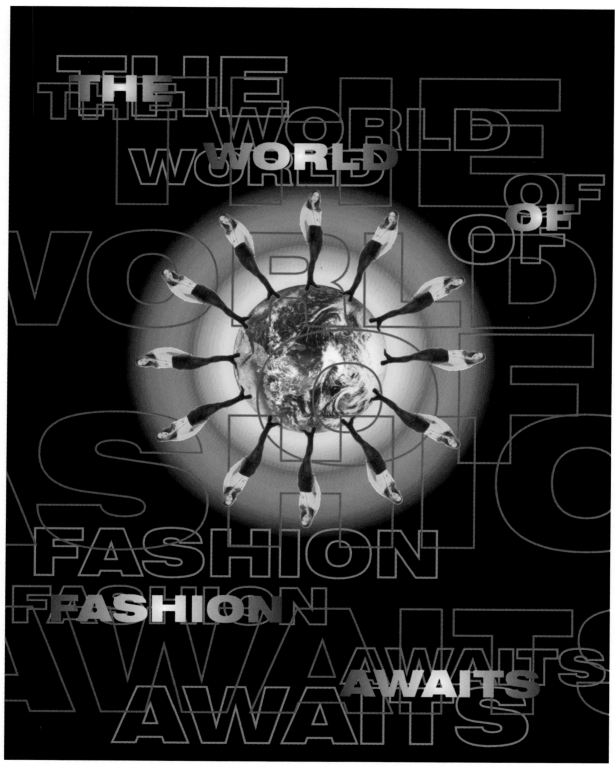

The Bitmap color mask feature allows photos to "float" free of the confines of a rectangular mask. Duplicating the main headline text makes for a dynamic, visually engaging image, using a popular design theme (Chapter 9).

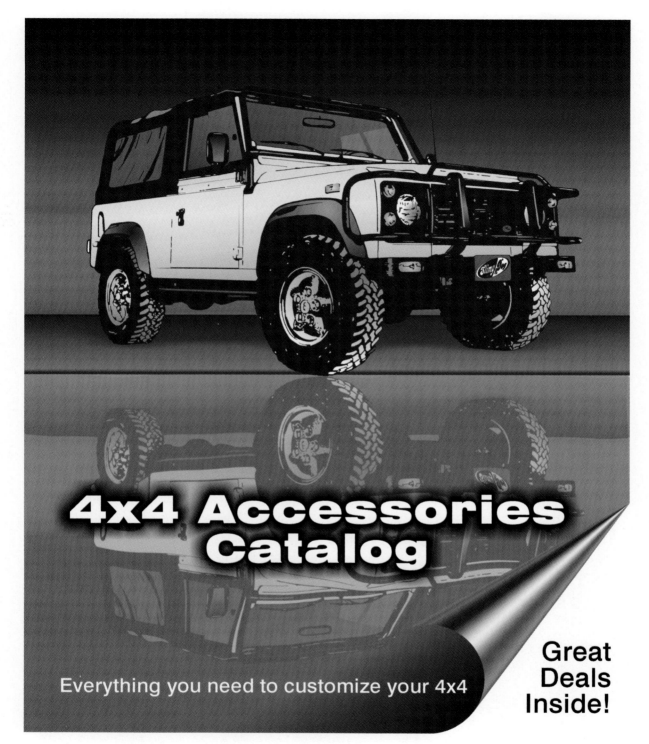

Water reflections are made possible with duplication, while bitmap manipulation changes the coloring of the images, adds the "waves" to the water, and can even "curl" the page (Chapter 9).

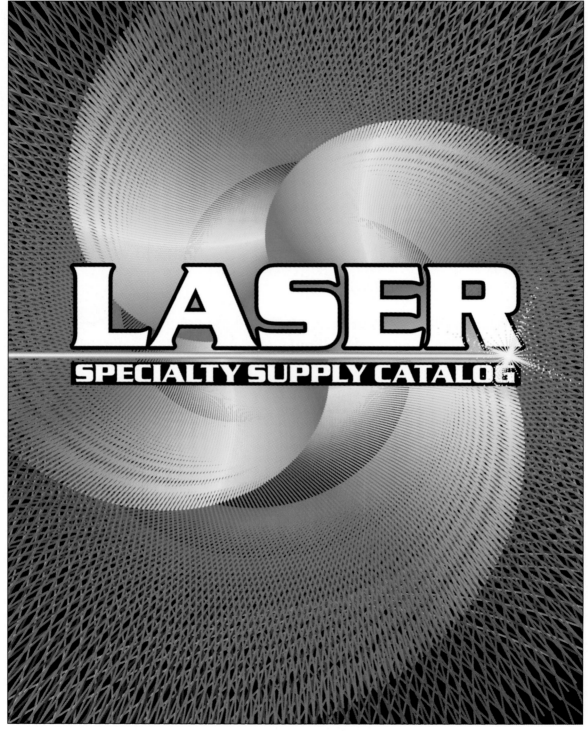

Modifying the parameters on the Interactive Blend property bar can create instant-wins with colorful, dynamic images that are a snap to produce (Chapter 10).

Computerized tricks such as Bitmap color masks, "frozen" lens effects, and the Interactive Transparency tool come together to create an image reminiscent of the late 1940s (Chapter 11).

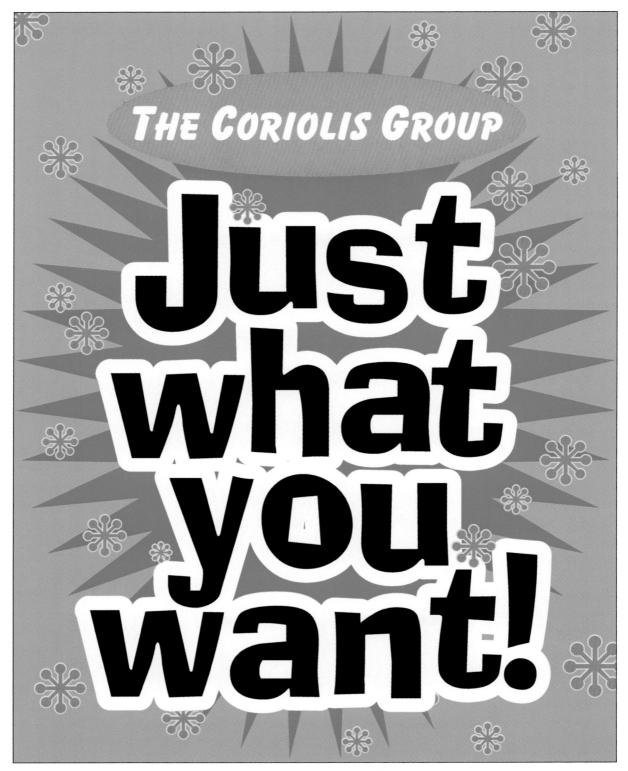

Simple geometric shapes, bold text, and a quirky color scheme create a "retro" design, perfect for clients wanting a "flashback" feel (Chapter 11).

CREATE MAGIC WITH CORELDRAW!

LINUX F/X CHANNEL

# Tune In!

CorelDraw 9 f/x & design.
On an idiot-box near you!

Power Clip tricks put your images on screen, while period-looking geometric shapes create an image perfect for the "TV-dinner" generation (Chapter 11).

Capture the spirit of Buck Rogers by using provided retro images from *Time Tunnel* in your own modern-day designs. Remove existing text and other details from a classic magazine cover to add your own timely headlines (Chapter 12).

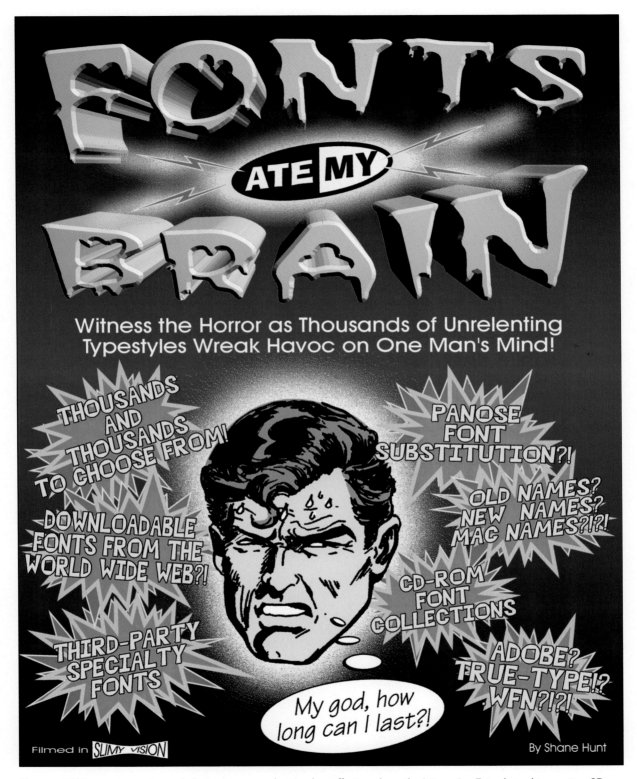

Use special bitmap conversion techniques to get an electric glow effect, and use the Interactive Extrude tool to create a 3D headline for a fun, campy feel (Chapter 12).

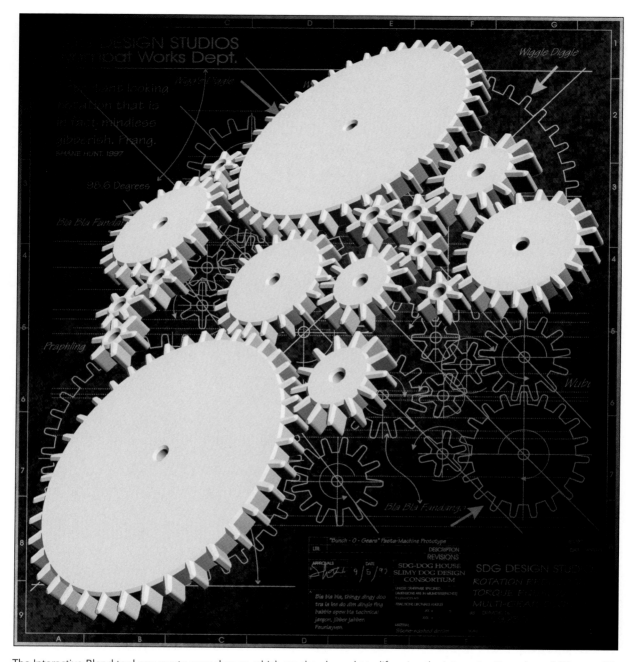

The Interactive Blend tool can create gear shapes, which are then brought to life using the Interactive Extrude tool (Chapter 13).

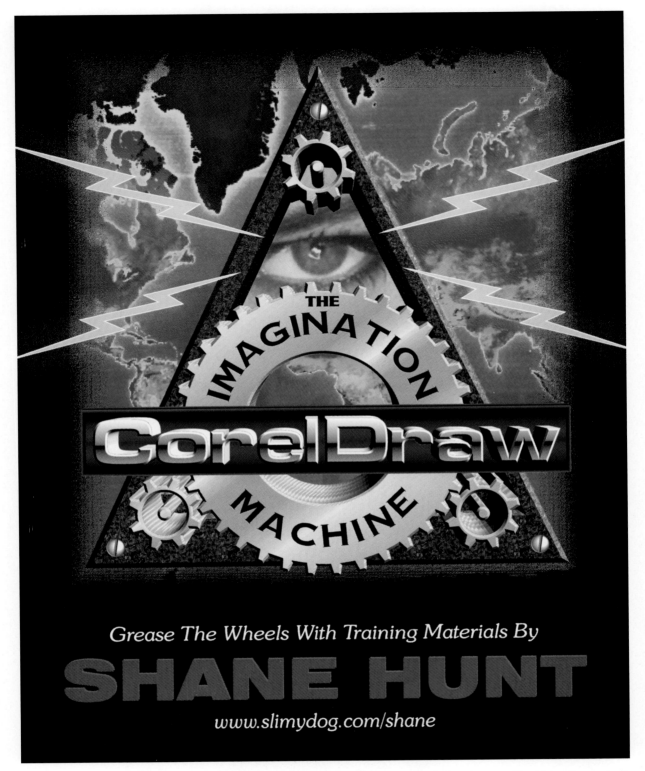

Gear shapes, with their multiple spokes and mechanical appearance, make interesting design elements. Combining "generated" objects with scanned photos creates a unique collage of real and surreal images (Chapter 13).

The Graph Paper tool can be used to create grids of all shapes and sizes. These can be given a 3D feel with the Perspective feature and distorted with the Interactive Envelope tool into all kinds of strange illusions. Grids and lines can work into many design projects, resulting in artwork with high visual interest and complexity, belying their simplistic nature (Chapter 14).

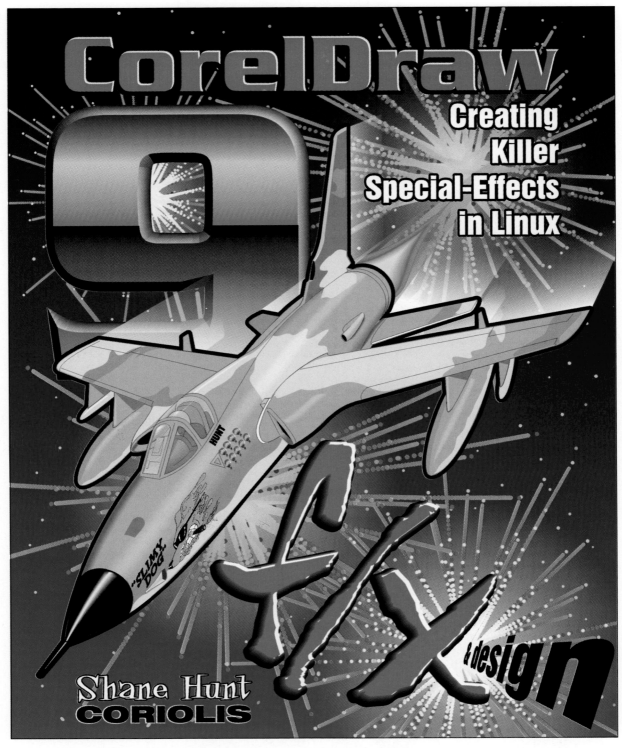

A few simple techniques can create the illusion of motion (Chapter 15), while the Interactive Blend tool can easily create dynamic "exploding" fireworks with a few mouse-clicks (Chapter 18).

Combining a blurred duplicate of your artwork with the crisp original can suggest speed and motion in your design (Chapter 15). Blur effects can add a sense of drama, as well as direct the reader's attention to where you wish (Chapter 6).

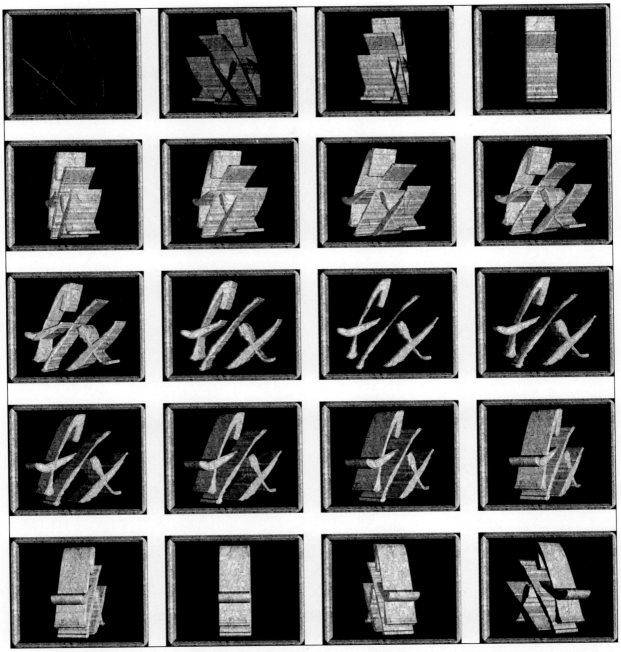

Modifying the rotation parameters on the Interactive Extrude property bar can make objects appear to spin in space, an effect that lends itself to animations for Web sites (Chapter 18). CorelDRAW also facilitates other Web effects, such as multiple-state buttons, animated GIFs, and even objects for use in Macromedia's Flash (Chapter 17).

Customizing clip-art and incorporating it into your own explosive designs is a time-saver. Using duplication/coloring tricks, an eye-catching graphic such as this can be created in just a few minutes by even the most novice CorelDRAW user.

From animated buttons, ad banners, and animated GIFs to background tiles and borders, you can create any and all elements for a Web page with CorelDRAW and Photo-Paint. CorelDRAW will also publish complete Web pages, facilitate the creation of image-maps, and is a perfect companion to Macromedia's Flash program (Chapter 17).

This image, along with the others from all the tutorials in this book, is available as a native Corel file on the companion CD-ROM. Load the files and see firsthand how the techniques work, or simply modify the images for your own use.

Use this book to harness the power of CorelDRAW and Photo-Paint for Linux and let your imagination run wild.

# Chapter 14

# Grids, Black Holes, and Bending Light

*In this chapter, you'll create the illusion of depth, dimension, and structure using lines, the Graph Paper tool, the Perspective feature, and Interactive Envelope effects.*

# Using Lines and Grids to Create Depth and Substance

In the vein of idealized reality, it is often advantageous to simplify your designs by using grids and lines to suggest depth and substance. Sometimes you have no option but to include a manufactured object to create a dimensional environment in a universe that has little definition, such as a grid to give the vast blackness of space tangible dimensions. Grids and lines are excellent visual vehicles to create a dimensional universe that the reader can comprehend and explore.

In this chapter, we will develop universes using the powerful illusions created with grids and lines. Using the mathematical accuracy afforded by CorelDRAW's functions, you can easily create perfectly spaced lines that suggest depth and substance. First, we will use the Graph Paper tool to create grids of all sizes and shapes. Then, we'll add depth with the Perspective function, and we'll add some special effects with a light-bending lens. Next, we will create a spinning light show with the Interactive Blend tool, using the rainbow-coloring options and object-acceleration features. We will then add the illusion of depth to create a multicolored black hole or tunnel into another dimension. We will combine the techniques of the grid and light show and work them into a practical design example. Then, we will create evenly spaced patterns with the Interactive Blend tool and use some low-tech design tricks to create a high-tech image of a black hole appearing to bend rays of light. Finally, we will explore how these techniques can make our happy Linux penguin look like a 3D wireframe. This chapter uses our powers of imagination to fill in the blanks, with images that trick the eyeballs and scream "Neat-o" at full volume.

## PROJECT Grids in Space

Believe it or not, Figure 14.1 was the first graphic I created for this book series. Before I signed any contracts or made any deals, I spent a few days brainstorming, trying to put my finger on the pulse of what a CorelDRAW for Linux f/x & design book would be about. This image went together so easily—and the results were so cool—I made it into an animation and sent it to the publisher. Within a week, not only did I get the go-ahead for the project, but we had hammered out the table of contents—which in turn became this book. It is just the kind of cool—but not insanely difficult—type of effect I was after. You also might recognize it as the background from the techno-penguin color image in the center of this book.

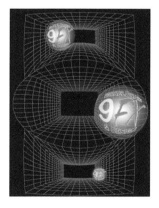

**Figure 14.1**
The Graph Paper tool easily manufactures grids, which are made to look 3D with the Add Perspective feature and distorted with the Interactive Envelope tool.

Grids provide a great way to tie images together in a design. They can add depth when placed in perspective and structure when left flat, and they can even suggest shapes when distorted. Grids can also bring about other designs, such as art that looks like video games or menacing target-acquisition-type displays for fictitious weaponry (as in the sword character from Chapter 2).

## Instant Invoices

If you are ever stumped on a design, start with a grid and go from there. At the ad agencywhere I used to work, we had a generic formula for generic clients, and it worked every time. Set a row of type in a brush font, set it on top of another row in a sans-serif font, and then float them both over a grid. Bang. Instant graphic, happy client, job done. Works every time.

123 Nowhere Lane, Somewhere, CA 91234          Phone: (909) 555-1212

Grids make for a universal design element to add interest to almost any design.

Grids and line art hark back to simpler times, when computer graphics were not as insane as they are today. My favorite video game from my misspent youth, Battlezone from Atari, uses simple vector graphics and grids to build a 3D world. The same kind of imagery—where you *suggest* objects and space— can be more dramatic than photos of the real thing.

To use the Graph Paper tool to create grids and then give them depth with the Perspective function, follow these steps:

1. Right-click over the Graph Paper tool icon on the toolbar to open its Properties dialog box (the Graph Paper tool is on the Object flyout with the Polygon and Spiral tools). Change both the Number Of Cells High and Number Of Cells Wide values to 12 and then click OK. Now drag the Graph Paper tool to create the grid, holding the Ctrl key down to create a perfect square (see Figure 14.2).

2. With the grid selected (by the way, the grid is nothing more than a group of identical rectangle duplicates, in case you want to ungroup and manipulate the objects), choose Effects|Add Perspective. Now with the Shape tool, drag the top-right node inward while holding down both the Shift and the Ctrl keys, which will bring the opposite node in as well. Drag until you like what you see, and then release the mouse button to place the grid in the distance. Then use the Pick tool to drag the top-center sizing node down while holding down the Shift key to squash the grid vertically (see Figure 14.3).

3. Duplicate the grid (+ key) and flip it vertically by grabbing the bottom-center sizing handle and dragging upward while holding down the Ctrl key. You will create two planes that disappear at the same horizon line— a quick and convincing way to add depth to a design (see Figure 14.4).

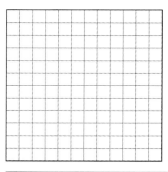

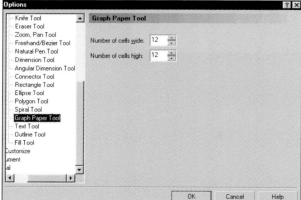

**Figure 14.2**

A setting of 12 across and 12 down creates a grid when you drag the Graph Paper tool on the desktop.

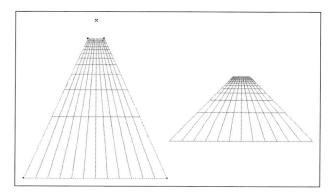

**Figure 14.3**

The Perspective tool places the grid in what appears to be a 3D orientation, and reducing its size vertically makes it look less stretched out.

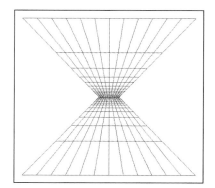

**Figure 14.4**

Simply duplicating and flipping a grid vertically instantly creates an illusion of depth.

4. It is a little tricky to get all the lines to match up to get a grid box, but it's not impossible. (First, delete the vertically flipped duplicate from Step 3. I just wanted to show you how easy it is to get 3D with a grid.) Start with the bottom grid element and duplicate it, but this time rotate it –90 degrees by dragging a corner rotation handle while holding the Ctrl key. Now, Shift-select both grids and choose Arrange|Align And Distribute. In the Align And Distribute dialog box, select the Bottom and Left checkboxes, then click Apply. Now select the left grid, and, using the Pick tool, align it perfectly to the original by resizing horizontally and vertically (see Figure 14.5).

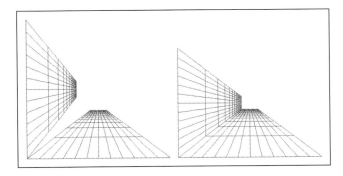

**Figure 14.5**
Duplicate and rotate the original grid to create a side. Stretch the object with the Pick tool and align the side with the bottom grid.

5. With the left-hand side in place, Shift-select both grid groups and choose Arrange|Transformation. Click Scale And Mirror, click both the Horizontal and Vertical Mirror buttons, and finally click Apply To Duplicate. Now you have a 3D grid "hallway" that you can twist and distort at will (see Figure 14.6).

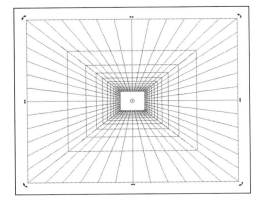

**Figure 14.6**
Duplicating and flipping the left and bottom horizontally and vertically results in the top and right side of a grid tunnel.

6. Select all the grid elements and group them (Ctrl+G). I gave my grid a thin .015-inch magenta outline and no fill. (Remember that these are actually rectangles for which you can also assign a fill attribute, such as a radial fountain fill, for a totally different kind of look (see Figure 14.7,

on the left). Place the grid on a solid black rectangle to suggest the bleakness of space.

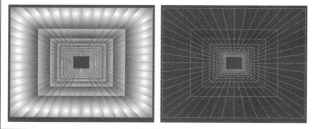

**Figure 14.7**
The grid groups are rectangles and can be given a radial fountain fill for a patterned look (left) or no fill (right) to emphasize the outline-grid look.

7. Because the grid is made up of vector objects, it is the perfect design element to tweak with the Fish Eye lens. Draw a circle, open the Lens docker (Alt+F3), click the Fish Eye option, change the rate to 100%, and then click Apply. This will distort the lines behind the circle to make it look as if the circle were a glass orb (see Figure 14.8).

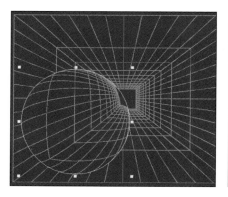

**Figure 14.8**
The Fish Eye lens distorts the lines behind it to make a circle appear to be a solid glass orb.

8. Because a lens does not change any of the objects underneath it (it only changes the way they appear), you can move the circle around to make it look as if it is dancing through the grid tunnel. For a "glass" ball, use the Interactive Transparency sphere illusion from Chapter 7, or just steal the sphere directly from that chapter and use it here. You can move the orb anywhere, and the Fish Eye Lens will redraw each time to create the new illusion (see Figure 14.9).

9. To add even weirder illusions of "bending" space, use the Interactive Envelope tool on your grid group. Select the Interactive Envelope tool from the Interactive Tool flyout, then click Envelope Single Arc Mode on the Property Bar. Now drag the top-center control node of your envelope upwards while holding down the Shift and Ctrl keys. Holding down the Shift and Ctrl keys moves all four center control nodes outwards simultaneously, creating a round distortion envelope (see Figure 14.10).

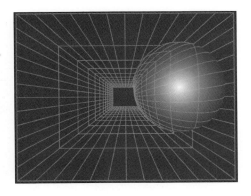

**Figure 14.9**

Moving the "live" lens creates a new illusion wherever the ball is placed.

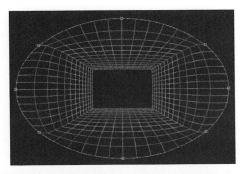

**Figure 14.10**

The Interactive Envelope tool, in Envelope Single Arc Mode, creates a round distortion shape.

That's really all there is to it! Instant grids, automatically redrawing lens effects—heck, what more could you ask for? This file, in various stages of animation, can be seen in the digital color section, in the grids.cdr file found in the \Chapt14\ subdirectory on the companion CD-ROM, and also in an animation, grids.avi, which you'll find there as well. This is a great example of how a good-looking, versatile graphic need not be incredibly difficult to create. Also, because of the nature of lenses, you can move around and resize the orb at will, and CorelDRAW will dutifully re-create the appropriate illusions for you every time.

## PROJECT Black Hole Light Show

I would like to take this opportunity to thank you for buying this book. The money and all that is nice, but if it were not for this book project, I wouldn't have learned so many handy tricks! It was during a moment of experimentation—trying to perfect a look for the black hole section of this chapter—that I discovered the very cool technique I used to create what you see in Figure 14.11. Who says you can't teach an old dog new tricks? Bow wow wow, yippee yo, yippee yay.

This brilliant, colorful design—which is used in the book cover example in the next project (see the color section for the full impact)—is another one of those

**Figure 14.11**

Blend a spiraled set of spokes to a smaller duplicate to result in an impressive light show. Change some of the blend parameters to create colorful black holes.

really fun and easy techniques. It is a simple blend between two shapes, but those two shapes are key to this design. Unlike other blends, this one starts with a distorted spoked curve that, when blended to a reduced duplicate, creates a very unique design. Depending on how tight or loose (lower rotation and fewer steps) you make the blend, you can get a solid mass or a gridlike design. When you offset and reduce the center control curve (in the bottom two examples in Figure 14.11 and in the digital color section), the blend builds as a spiral that is sucking down into the center, which could become a black hole variant.

To create spinning light show blends, follow these steps:

1. First, you need a collection of lines for a "spoked wheel" type shape. This is easy: Draw a straight line with two clicks of the Bezier tool while holding down the Ctrl key. Double-click on the line to reveal the rotation arrows. Grab the corner rotation arrow and drag while pressing the Ctrl key. This will constrain the movement to 15-degree increments. Before you let go of the line, right-click to create a duplicate. Now simply repeat (Ctrl+R) until you get a "spoked wheel" shape.

2. Select all your objects (Ctrl+A) and combine them into a single curve (Ctrl+L).

3. Select the Interactive Distortion tool from the Interactive Tool flyout. On the Property Bar, click the Twister Distortion button, change the Additional Degrees value to 350, and watch the fur fly. Choose Arrange| Convert To Curves to "freeze" the effect (see Figure 14.12).

4. Give this curve a .023-inch yellow outline and duplicate it (+ key). Downsize the duplicate until it is about 30 percent smaller than the original. With the Interactive Blend tool, drag between both objects to create a blend group. On the Property Bar, change the number of steps to 75 and set the Blend Direction to 360 degrees again; then enable one of the rainbow-type effect options (Clockwise Blend or Counterclockwise Blend). Click Apply to watch the show begin (see Figure 14.13).

**Constrain This**

The default Constrain angle value is 15 degrees. You can change this setting to any value that you want, for more or fewer "spokes" in your wheel created in Step 1. In the Options dialog box (Ctrl+J), click Edit. Then, on the Edit page of the Options dialog box, you can change the Constrain angle. You can double the number of spokes in your wheel, or halve the value to 7.5. To decrease the number of spokes, increase the setting to 30 degrees. Click OK to close the dialog box.

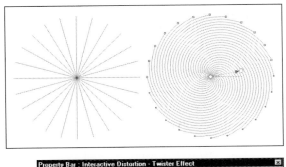

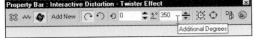

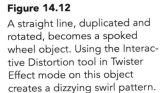

**Figure 14.12**

A straight line, duplicated and rotated, becomes a spoked wheel object. Using the Interactive Distortion tool in Twister Effect mode on this object creates a dizzying swirl pattern.

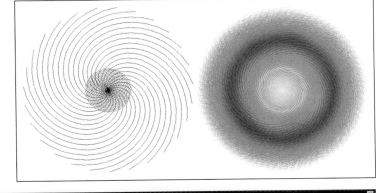

**Figure 14.13**

Blend the two vortex curves (on the left in Wireframe view) to result in a dizzying color show by enabling a rainbow option in the Interactive Blend tool.

5. To get the image used on the book cover, downsize and move the center vortex curve to the right and down from the original. Then select the big curve and change the Outline Color value to cyan. Now increase the number of steps to 125 and reduce the rotation to 180 degrees. With these settings, you will get an image that could be a cornucopia of light, or even a stylized black hole (see Figure 14.14).

"These sure are pretty, but what the heck would I use them for?" you ask. Well, read on!

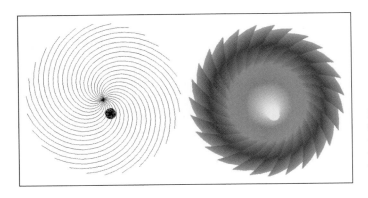

**Figure 14.14**

Change the size and location of the center control curve, increase the number of steps, and reduce the rotation to 180 degrees to produce a different result.

**Figure 14.15**
Combine the grid and light show elements to create a bright and interesting book cover.

## PROJECT Physics

The book cover design in Figure 14.15 uses (surprise, surprise) the light show twirls from the previous project and, yes, the multipurpose, all-season, multilingual, nonstick, available-in-all-colors-and-sizes *grid*.

To suggest depth, we once again turn to the trusty Perspective function, and we also take advantage of the computer medium to almost effortlessly duplicate and mirror the image. The impact of the final image again defies the simplicity of its creation using the power and automation of CorelDRAW. To combine the twirly blends with a grid for an artistic but spacey design, follow these steps:

1. Use the Graph Paper tool to create a grid and again distort it with the Perspective tool. Use the Pick tool to drag the top-center sizing handle to squash the grid vertically.

2. Create (or better yet, just borrow) the light show blend from the previous example. Before you can alter the object with the Perspective tool, however, you must disable the live blend. Choose Arrange|Separate, select Arrange|Ungroup All, and finally use the Group (Ctrl+G) command routine to "freeze" the blend and end up with a group of some 127 objects that you can now distort.

3. With the colorful swirl group selected, choose Effects|Copy|Perspective From and click on the grid shape. This will place the black-hole light show in the same perspective as the grid, making for a more convincing graphic, with all the elements sharing a similar orientation (see Figure 14.16).

**Figure 14.16**
The Perspective tool places a grid in the desired 3D-like orientation; then the same perspective is copied to the black hole swirl object group.

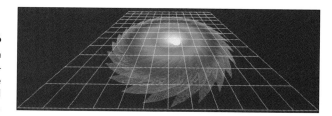

4. Now select both the swirl and the grid, and choose Arrange|Transformation to open the Transformation docker. Click Scale And Mirror to activate that page of options, click the Vertical button down, and then click Apply To Duplicate. Who said design has to be hard?

5. To get the graphic of the white arrow spinning both behind and in front of the objects, use two duplicates of the same curve. Start by drawing an oval with the Ellipse tool; then duplicate it (+ key). Now use the Shape tool to drag the control nodes of the ellipse around (on the out-

side of the ellipse) to create the curve for the area in front of everything. Then use the Shape tool on the other copy to drag the nodes of that ellipse around to create the curve that will be behind everything and that also will match up with the other curve.

6. Choose the Arrange|Order|In Front Of or the Arrange|Order|Behind command to place the lines correctly within the image stack. Select the front arc, open the Outline Pen dialog box, and assign an arrow for the start of the curve (see Figure 14.17).

That's the whole shebang—or in this case, big bang. The image is in the color section in the middle of this book, and you'll find the corresponding file, physics.cdr, in the \Chapt14\ subdirectory on the companion CD.

I love designs like this, which to me seem simple yet visually engaging. When I show other people this artwork, simple never enters their minds; they are just dazzled by the image. That is a good thing—sort of the wizard-behind-the-curtain kind of illusion.

I love book cover designs. I think I will just retire and do nothing but scholastic book covers. Problem is, eventually I couldn't resist the urge to put in hidden graphics or messages for students to find as they while away the hours sitting in class! On second thought, I had better steer clear of those projects.

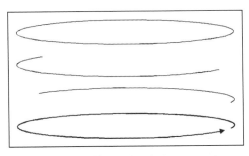

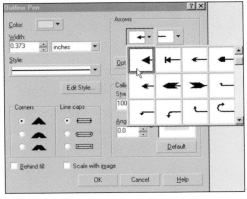

**Figure 14.17**

Use the Shape tool to transform an ellipse into a graceful arc. Repeat the process on a duplicate behind the objects to create the illusion of an arc behind and in front of the grids. Assign an arrowhead end from the Outline Pen dialog box.

**Figure 14.18**

The Interactive Blend tool can create the illusion of space by using lines to represent bending space and light.

## PROJECT Black Holes

I am so thrilled with the image in Figure 14.18. Why, you ask? Well, because it was the eventual solution to my black hole design problem—which involved drawing something that is in essence nothing and yet is so dense that even light cannot escape.

I spent many a moment staring off into space (uh, figuratively, not literally) and trying to come up with an interesting and unique solution (some attempts went into the old circular file…).

This image is a series of lines and circles blended together to create the illusion of bending of space and light that might take place around a black hole. I came up with the idea when I blended two ovals together with the Acceleration option enabled. This created a funnel shape, made from the stacked wireframe circles. As we have seen, grids give you a great way to suggest depth and dimension, especially to objects that don't exude those properties on their own (like the blackness of space or bottomless oceans). With grids on my mind, and the subject being black holes (which occur in the blackness of space), it was a natural to marry the two ideas into one, where a grid suggests both depth and dimension as well as the shape of the black hole. The design also lent itself to bending light, which is associated with black holes. It is a great graphic to illustrate an entity that is very enigmatic from a design perspective—it is literally a black hole. It isn't the only solution to this design problem, but as they say, "I might not know much about art, but I know what I like!" The best part of this design is that the majority of the work is pretty easy, although the project involved some mundane manual labor that I simply could not get around. To blend lines to create a 3D black hole grid, follow these steps:

1. Start with an oval drawn with the Ellipse tool and use the Skew arrows to tilt it up the right-hand side. Now duplicate the oval, move the duplicate down, and reduce it.

2. Drag the Interactive Blend tool between the two objects to create a blend group. On the Property Bar, click Object And Color Acceleration, then drag the Object Acceleration slider to the left to create a black hole funnel (see Figure 14.19).

3. Select the funnel blend and perform the familiar separation dance (choose Arrange|Separate, then select Arrange|Ungroup All). The first blend created the funnel part perfectly, but it also resulted in some gaps with far-apart ovals on the bottom end. With the objects all separated into individual ovals, you can select the oval on each end of a gap and fill them in with the Interactive Blend tool. Be sure to disable acceleration for these in-between blends. Vary the number of steps (sometimes only 1 or 2) to keep the spacing about even for all the objects to create a longneck funnel out of ovals (see Figure 14.20).

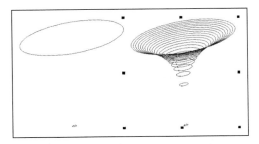

**Figure 14.19**
Use the Interactive Blend tool with the Object Acceleration option to create a funnel-like illusion.

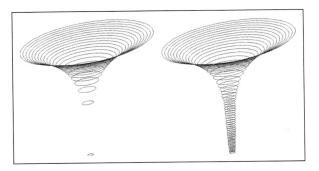

**Figure 14.20**
The original blend pieces are broken up so that the gaps can be filled in with even more blends.

4.  Draw a rectangle to represent the page frame so you can begin to position the funnel object. Choose the Zoom tool, and right-click twice on your page to zoom way out. Select and duplicate the largest funnel oval and enlarge it some 630% by dragging outward on a corner sizing handle. Position this huge circle so that the top is closer to the top of the funnel than the bottom is. Now Shift-select the huge circle and the largest funnel circle and use the Interactive Blend tool again to create 22 duplicates between them. You might need to fiddle with the number of steps on the Property Bar and the Object Acceleration slider to get evenly spaced circular rings. Select all these grid rings, group them, and give them a yellow outline and no fill (see Figure 14.21).

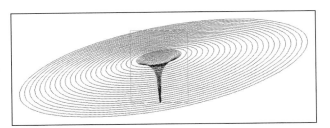

**Figure 14.21**
The Interactive Blend tool creates rings between the funnel and a huge circle enlarged way beyond the page size.

5. With the Bezier tool, draw lines along an imagined X- and Y-axis, tilted at 45 degrees, with the ends sucked into the black hole. Use the Shape tool to simplify the lines and to ensure that each line consists of only three nodes. You don't need more than three nodes for a line like this— one at each end and another about midway down the funnel. You need the same number of nodes in all the lines to ensure that the blends work smoothly in the next step. The top-right and bottom-left lines are magenta, and the other two are cyan. All have a line weight of .013 inches (see Figure 14.22).

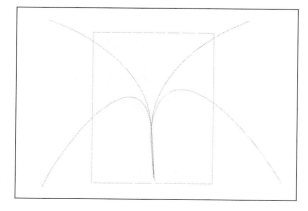

**Figure 14.22**

Draw lines with the Bezier tool criss-crossing the page in an x orientation, with the ends sucked into the black hole.

6. With the Interactive Blend tool, drag from the top-left to the top-right line. Make sure that no acceleration or rainbow effects are enabled on the Property Bar, and change the number of steps to 22. Then select the top-right line and drag the Interactive Blend tool to the lower-right line to create the blend between them. Continue to drag the Interactive Blend tool between the line pairs, until blends connect all the lines. Now our beams of light are being sucked into one spot (see Figure 14.23).

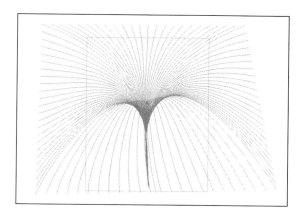

**Figure 14.23**

Blend the lines to create the illusion of light and space being sucked into the black hole.

Houston, we have a problem. (Or should I say Ottawa, since that is where Corel Corporation is located?) If you are particularly detail oriented, you might notice that the illusion begins to break down because the front light beam blend needs part of the lines to go into the vortex and the other half to lie on top. This presents a nasty problem that we've seen before, where an object needs to be both in front of and behind another. Well, as we know, we cannot bend CorelDRAW objects across layers, so we need to fool the eye manually. I won't go into the mostly manual labor process here; I'll just hit on what needs to be done if you decide that you are also a masochist/perfectionist! You need to create three pieces to make the illusion work. From back to front, you need the cyan-magenta light beams being sucked into the vortex, then a half-copy of the vortex itself to place on top of the objects inside it. Finally, you need the light beam blend on top of the grid, bending into the vortex (see Figure 14.24). For an accurate 3D illusion to work, the blend elements need to be broken up so they can be stacked in front of and behind each other to create the illusion of bending light and space. The easiest solution is just to open the blckhole.cdr file in the \Chapt14 subdirectory on the companion CD-ROM and steal the finished image. Feel free to use the artwork on the companion CD any time you want to solve a design problem or take a shortcut.

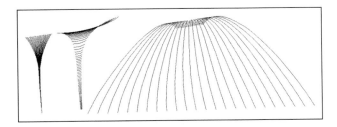

**Figure 14.24**
You need to stack pieces in order to create the light beam that then blends into the vortex.

This image can be seen in the digital color section, with the addition of some text to finish off the book-cover example. If you load the file off the companion CD-ROM to pick apart, you will have to choose PowerClip|Extract Contents to work with the pieces.

# Beyond f/x

Grids and vector-type graphics can work into many design applications. As I said earlier, you can create interesting and fantastical computer screens for video games or graphics where you want to suggest some sort of automated target tracking or something similar. (Remember the weapon systems on the *Millennium Falcon* from *Star Wars*? A grid!) The funnel grid can be used to suggest twisters, or you could work in a drop at the tip of the funnel to represent a digital version of a water droplet hitting a puddle (it has that unique shape of the inverted funnel). Or, with a few changes, the funnel can become a "bowl," which when duplicated, becomes a sphere (see Figure 14.25). If you apply the

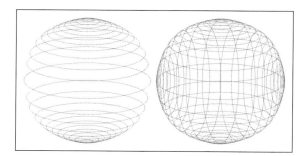

**Figure 14.25**
Blended circle shapes create the illusion of a 3D sphere.

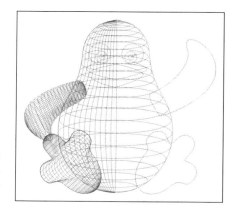

**Figure 14.26**
Any type of shapes can be manipulated and blended to create the illusion of a third dimension.

technique to other shapes—such as the body and limbs of our happy Linux penguin—you can give anything the illusion of three dimensions (see Figure 14.26). The only limit is your imagination!

Grids work out well to organize information for easy consumption, like a hierarchy chart for data. Or you can map out sales territories with a grid over a map. Or create a Web navigation scheme where each page is part of a grid and visited pages go black. Because grids are such a design staple, the uses are endless. Remember the grid design formula if you want to appease a generic, waffling client. Brush script over Eurobold, hovering over a grid. If that doesn't do it, toss in a drop shadow and a few palm trees!

## Moving On

In this chapter, we created a lot of eye-popping artwork using ordinary lines. We used the Graph Paper tool to create simple grids, which we tweaked and twisted into new configurations, and then the Interactive Blend tool was once more called upon to perform its magic. The even spacing that the Blend function affords can create very interesting gridlike elements as well, as we saw in the last project.

Grids and line-based artwork has myriad uses. We saw how flashy color patterns and fancy grid work became book-cover designs, but by no means are they limited to this use. Grids and line art are just too versatile to ignore. If you haven't discovered this already, you will find that many times a simple grid can jazz up a boring logo or page layout, or even aid as an organizational tool. (Whenever you can divide a full-page image into smaller, more easily digested chunks, you will make it more appealing to your audience.)

In Chapter 15, we will continue on the theme of illusions, only this time we'll add the concept of speed and motion. Once again, we will trick the eye into seeing motion that isn't there (unless you happen to fling the book past your face). Fasten your seat belts—we are going to move into the fast lane, hit the gas, and taste some speed!

Chapter 15

# Speedy Things

*This chapter examines techniques to suggest speed and motion, using the Interactive Blend tool and bitmap blurring effects.*

# Using Speed and Motion to Make Images Jump Out at You

These days, with multimedia and the World Wide Web, designs can be much more than simple static images. Animations, jumping and dancing icons, sounds, music, streaming video—you name it—make the modern electronic design experience energetic and interactive. A side effect of this new media avalanche is that it also raises the bar for traditional print applications. No longer is the playing field level, with the flat, two-dimensional page directly competing with all kinds of other media for the reader's attention. Somehow, your printed pages must gain and hold a viewer's attention without the benefit of sound or animation. It's downright unfair!

In this chapter, we level the playing field by looking at a few techniques to make your images pop off the page and look like they are moving and alive. In the first example, three variations of the same theme suggest motion in a racing buggy by using the Interactive Blend tool and a bitmap blur effect. In the second example, a jet fighter is given speed trails with the Interactive Transparency tool to make it speed across the page. Then, a combination of effects is used to create a blurry background for a speeding motorcycle. Finally, we create the unnerving dizziness of an adrenaline rush using the radial fill feature. It's a fast ride guaranteed to blur your vision, but you can handle it!

## PROJECT Bouncing Buggies

The graphic in Figure 15.1 is from a piece I was going to use to illustrate an article I wrote about racing remote-controlled model cars. (Believe it or not, I can write about things other than CorelDRAW!) The magazine I was working for sent me a model to build and review. Well, I ended up smashing the test car into a gazillion little bits when it crashed in an empty swimming pool, which really annoyed my contacts at that magazine and quickly ended my career as a model car journalist.

Getting an image to look like it is moving isn't really that difficult. Using comic-strip-like motion trail images—both straight and strewn along a path to suggest

**Figure 15.1**
Using the Interactive Blend tool, you can suggest movement by blending either just the object outline or the entire image (top and center). With a bitmap of the image, you can exploit the motion blur effects to create some zip and zoom (bottom).

rotation—and blurring a duplicate of the image are universally understood ways of showing motion. In the next sections, we will look at a few tricks to add motion to my bouncing buggy illustration. Each technique suggests a different kind of motion and speed, so you will have to choose the one that is right for your fast designs.

## Green Ghost

One way to suggest motion is to leave a ghostly trail of color behind the speeding object. Like the effect it creates, this trick is also quick and easy. The primary object is blended to a duplicate, which has been placed to the back and behind, and filled with the background color. The blend fades the original into the duplicate, which is the same color as the background, so it appears to fade away altogether. To make a fade-out effect from the buggy to the background, follow these steps:

1. The buggy started as an ink illustration, which I converted into vector artwork using the Corel Trace program on a Windows machine (remember the Linux AutoTrace utility is included on the companion CD-ROM). I imported the CMX trace file into CorelDRAW, where it was easy to color the pieces. This kind of file consists of a lot of smaller objects resting on a big black shape. By selecting the smaller objects and combining some of them (such as all the pieces that make up the main body), you can assign a fountain fill that flows across the entire car body. (I used the same process on the Land Rover in Chapter 9, making it easy to recolor these vehicles.) If you don't select and combine these individual objects first, and then fill them with fountain fills, they will not line up correctly (see Figure 15.2).

**Figure 15.2**

An ink illustration is converted into CorelDRAW objects using Corel Trace. Once imported into CorelDRAW, the pieces can be selected and given outline and fill attributes. Combining several objects that make up one thing (like the car body back, which is separated from the front by a big spring) will make patterns and fills line up.

### Roadmaps for Painters

I have used illustrations such as this buggy to work out color and graphics schemes for real-world applications. You don't need much more than a simple line drawing—a car, motorcycle, jet ski, you name it—to work out really cool paint and graphics schemes.

You can then give this roadmap to the people who actually paint the graphics onto the vehicles for them to use as a reference. Or you can take it one step further and design the graphics to scale and then use the artwork to create the actual masks used when spray-painting the vehicle. Most computerized sign companies will also cut paint masks for you right from your CorelDRAW files, using big sheets of masking tape material instead of vinyl. If paint isn't your style, you can also find places that will print full-color, sun- and weather-proof images on vinyl for stickers of all sizes—again, right from your CorelDRAW files. A dull-looking vehicle is simply unacceptable.

2. Because an image like this one is a bunch of smaller objects on a big black main outline shape, it is easy to select and duplicate this outline shape for the blur effects. Duplicate the black outline pad, give it a solid white outline with no fill, and move it up and to the right. This is the point that your speed blur will fade to solid white. Send this white outline to the back (Shift+PgDn) (see Figure 15.3).

**Figure 15.3**

A bitmap converted to vector artwork consists of many small objects on a big outline curve (shown here in Wireframe view). Select and duplicate the outline shape and move it behind and in back of the original for the blur effect.

3. With the Interactive Blend tool, simply drag between the original and the white outline to create the speed blur effect (typically the default number of steps, 20, is sufficient). For control over the beginning and end colors in the blend, select the black control curve and duplicate it. Now you have the black outline on top of the black control curve. Press the Tab key to select the next "newest" object. (The duplicate is the newest object, with the original behind it being next in line; pressing Tab selects objects in youngest-to-oldest order.) With the control curve selected, click an on-screen color well to change the fill to any color, such as the green that I chose for the color page (see Figure 15.4).

This is a quick and easy way to get your objects moving.

**Figure 15.4**

Blending the black outline curve to a duplicate in white creates a stark motion blur. Duplicating the control curve allows you to change the colors in the blend to soften the speed blur.

## Motion Steps

To offer up a path of travel, you can blend an all-white copy of the buggy along a path. This shows not only motion, but also where the buggy has been and a direction of travel. Follow these steps:

1. Start with a color version of your buggy, drag-select all the pieces in it, and group them. Duplicate the group and give the duplicate a white fill and outline by clicking both the left and right mouse button over the white on-screen color well. This will fill all the objects within the group with white and change the outlines, if any, to white as well. Move the duplicate to where you want the speed blur to fade out entirely and rotate the buggy in an upward angle.

2. Now draw a line with the Bezier tool to show a range of motion. Shift-select both the colored and white-only buggy groups and prepare them for blending by choosing the Arrange|Order|Reverse Order command (we need the colored version in front) (see Figure 15.5).

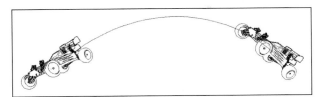

**Figure 15.5**
A colored buggy (left, in Wireframe view) and an all-white copy (right) will be blended along the curve to show a range of motion.

3. Drag the Interactive Blend tool between the two shapes, then use the Property Bar to modify the blend parameters. Click Path Properties, select New Path, and then click on your range-of-motion line drawn in Step 2. Vary the number of steps to as few or as many as you want. Be sure to enable the Blend Along Full Path option by clicking Miscellaneous Blend Options and clicking the appropriate check box. If you like, try the Rotate All Objects option as well (see Figure 15.6).

**Figure 15.6**
Blend the buggies along the path to create a trail of image duplicates.

4. To make all the blended objects more ghostly white, use the Accelerate Fills/Outlines slider on the Interactive Blend tool. Dragging to the left makes the duplicates favor the white end of the blend, so they all become paler (see Figure 15.7).

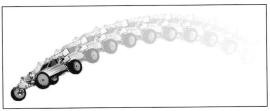

**Figure 15.7**
Use the Accelerate Fills/Outlines slider to change the blend duplicates into a paler set of objects.

That's all it takes to give your objects a trail of motion that indicates rotated movement (as opposed to simple linear movement). Vary the number of steps for many or few ghostly images.

## Transparent and Blurry

This last technique uses a duplicate of the buggy to create a bitmap and, from there, a motion blur. Like the first example, it leaves a ghostly trace where the buggy has been. This time, however, the entire subdued image is in the speed blur. Here's how to get blurry eyed:

1. Select your buggy group again and draw a rectangle around it. Give the rectangle no outline or fill attributes—its function is to provide a transparent background for the bitmap. Shift-select the outline rectangle and the buggy group, and duplicate them. Move the duplicate to the side and use the Bitmaps menu to convert the image to a bitmap. Choose whatever color depth and resolution is appropriate for your project (72 dpi RGB for on-screen, 300 dpi CMYK for print) and make sure the Anti-aliasing and Transparent Background options are enabled before you click OK (see Figure 15.8).

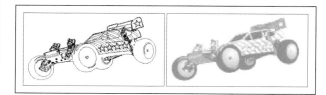

**See Through It All**

When you use the Convert To Bitmap function's Transparent Background option, the transparent background remains that way through all the bitmap effects you apply to the object, so only the image itself shows through. So why is this cool? Because you don't have to worry about only certain colors being see-through, the way you do with the Bitmap color mask.

If you had created a bitmap with a white background and then used a Bitmap color mask to make the background transparent, whoops, the stars and stripes would be transparent as well. While this could be a cool effect, it's generally not what you'll be shooting for.

**Figure 15.8**
Use the Convert To Bitmap option to convert the vector art into a bitmap. The top row (in Wireframe view) shows the no-fill, no-outline rectangle used to assign the area for the transparent background.

2. Select the bitmap, and, from the Bitmaps menu, choose Blur|Motion. Now crank the Distance value up to 50 and change the direction to hit your object head on. Click OK to fuzz the image (see Figure 15.9).

**Figure 15.9**
Use the Motion Blur bitmap filter to add a speed-blur effect to the bitmap.

3. You can repeat the Motion Blur filter as many times as you want to get the image super fuzzy. To soften the image further, choose Effects|Color

Adjustment|Brightness-Contrast-Intensity. Increasing the Brightness value while decreasing the Contrast setting mutes the image (see Figure 15.10).

**Figure 15.10**
Use the Brightness-Contrast-Intensity dialog box to mute the blurred bitmap.

4.  Now place the original buggy objects on top of the bitmap to contrast the light, fuzzy blur with the crisp, high-contrast vector objects. Remember that the bitmap background is transparent, so you can place objects behind the racing buggy—such as this checkerboard—to add depth to the design (see Figure 15.11).

**Figure 15.11**
Stack the bitmap and original artwork on top of other background elements to exploit the transparent background of the bitmaps.

For even more versatility, instead of modifying the brightness/contrast settings on your background blur bitmap, use the Interactive Transparency tool to give it a semi-opaque look. Use the Uniform mode or a fountain fill for different looks (see Figure 15.12).

**Figure 15.12**
Use the Interactive Transparency tool instead of modifying the brightness setting on the bitmap to get a softer background image.

Adding speed or motion to an image might not seem practical, but you'll find many uses for the process. For example, the blending technique is a great way to add both depth and a sense of energy to a logo. (See the image in the digital color section to see how I used this technique on my racing logo to give it a sense of speed.)

That's enough of the bouncing buggies. The race continues in the digital color section and in a file called rccars.cdr, pitting in the \Chapt15\ subdirectory on the companion CD-ROM. Open the file and experiment with the blend steps and the acceleration options for the live blends in the racing logo and bouncing buggies. The logo is especially fun to toy with. A few changes in the acceleration options and you get a totally different set of results!

**Figure 15.13**

Using the Interactive Transparency tool, you can give the jet a sense of speed by leaving clear vapor trails in its path.

## PROJECT Jet Trails

Motion trails are great for adding a sense of speed and motion to an object, as we just saw. The buggy examples, however, did not have a busy background to contend with, which poses some new problems. You will want to create a sense of motion that is appropriate and that is also transparent so that background details still shine through, as in Figure 15.13. This is a great use of the Interactive Transparency tool (the explosion techniques are outlined in Chapter 18).

The same kind of technique can be given more finesse in CorelDRAW using the Interactive Transparency tool to create subtle but convincing vapor trails for a screaming jet, or any other object you want to give motion to. You could use the same technique, for example, on an arrow, showing how to put pieces together in an instruction booklet or installation guide. Motion effects pop up in many design projects. Transparency effects hint at motion without distracting too much from the overall design. To make a jet scream across the sky, follow these steps:

1. Once again, I turned to the versatile art archives of the CorelDRAW clip-art CD. Import a cool plane from the \clipart\aircraft\jets\ subdirectory. To give the entire plane a thick outline, group all the plane objects, duplicate them, and give the duplicate a thick .05-inch black outline. Enable the round corner option in the Outline Pen dialog box (F12), and then send this thick outline group behind the original objects. This is an old line-art illustration trick that I still like to use to isolate images from the background (see Figure 15.14).

**Figure 15.14**

A clip-art jet is given the thick-outline treatment by assigning a heavy outline to a duplicate group of the objects sent behind the originals.

2. Draw a rectangle the size of the desired page and send it to the back. Use a texture fill called Aerial Clouds from the Samples library to fill the rectangle, or choose any other background you want. Guidelines are helpful when mapping out a project such as this, where you need to draw objects (in this case, the motion trails) by hand. To create a guideline, move the mouse pointer over the ruler at the left or top edge of your picture area and drag inwards. A guideline is a nonprinting, non-exporting entity specifically used as an illustration and layout aid. To move a guideline, simply drag it to a new position. To rotate a guideline, double-click it and then drag the pop-up rotation handles. Set up guidelines off the wing tips and other elements to set the stage for drawing the speed blurs (see Figure 15.15).

> **Snap On, Snap Off**
>
> Choose the View|Snap To Guidelines option to add a "magnetic" property to your guidelines. With the Snap To Guidelines option enabled, your objects will attract and align themselves to the guidelines on the page, like magnets to metal. This behavior will aid in page layout. Turn the option on and off as you need it.

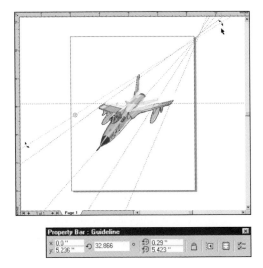

**Figure 15.15**
Guidelines help align objects in a design and are useful to set up vanishing points or help block up art before it is drawn.

3. Use the Bezier tool to draw straight-line shapes for the trailing edges from which you want vapor trails. The Bezier tool is great for this kind of work—you need only click from point to point to draw a straight-lined object. Try to draw the ending line of the curve in the same angle as the edge wing it is paired with (see Figure 15.16).

4. Fill all the vapor trail shapes white and then select the Interactive Transparency tool. Now, one by one, drag the tool along each vapor object to give it a white-to-clear fade. Start at the point where the object butts against the wing, then drag out toward the sky. You will have to experiment with the placement of the clear point on the Interactive Transparency fountain fill control line to make the fade look best for each wing. Straight up or straight across sometimes seems to work better than following the flight path. Experiment to find the angle that looks best (see Figure 15.17).

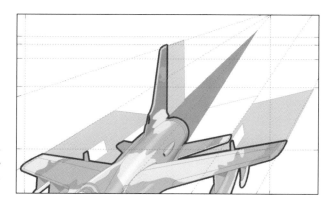

**Figure 15.16**
Use the Bezier tool to draw objects for the vapor trails coming off the wings.

**Figure 15.17**
The Interactive Transparency tool gives the solid objects the white-to-clear fountain fills that create the vapor trail look.

5. More power, Scotty! For an afterburner flame, use a compound blend element. Use the Bezier or Freehand tool to draw a flame object shooting in the correct flight path. Give this object no outline and a cyan fill. Duplicate and downsize the flame shape for a midpoint and give the duplicate a magenta fill. Duplicate and downsize one more time, for the hot spot, and make this smallest duplicate yellow. Use the Interactive Blend tool to drag between the cyan and magenta shapes and create the pink-to-blue color transition. In Simple Wireframe view, drag the Interactive Blend tool between the magenta and the small yellow shape to create the yellow-to-magenta color transition. Flame on! (See Figure 15.18.)

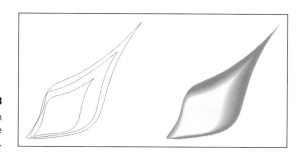

**Figure 15.18**
Blend three flame shapes (left in Wireframe view) to create the afterburner discharge.

The jet screeches across the sky in the color section in the middle of the book and in a file called jetcover.cdr in the \Chapt18\ subdirectory on the companion CD-ROM. If you open the file, you can check out the vapor trails yourself or dissect any of the other artwork pieces. For the aircraft nose art, I used my Slimy Dog tattoo and used the rotation arrows and the sizing and skew handles to put the bitmap in place. It's amazing how much you can get accomplished with just the Pick tool.

The nature of your design will dictate the kind of motion effect you need. For simple motion, try a fade into the background blend, like we did with the buggy earlier. Or you might want more steps to indicate motion and position—if you were making a diagram or instruction book, for example. The transparency tricks add the action more subtly, which might also make things look too fast. It might take a few tries to get what you like. The buggy blend along a path had me staring at the screen for quite a while—I kept changing the number of steps from higher to lower numbers. If you can't make up your mind, it is a good idea to close the file and work on something else for a while. You start to lose perspective when you work on something too long, but if you come back later, things are much clearer.

## PROJECT North Pole Racing

The previous examples deal with using design techniques to suggest motion. This project looks at a technique that mimics the results photographers get when they take pictures of speeding objects, like in Figure 15.19. So in a sense, this might be the most real technique, even though again it is just an optical illusion.

A speed blur is a great way to make Santa's racing team look fast. *Santa's racing team?!* Well, every year I try to come up with an interesting holiday card, and at one time most of my clients were in the motor-sports industry so this card was a big hit.

This image is typical of photos you will see of race vehicles on the move. Photographers, in an attempt to keep the vehicle in focus, will move the camera along with the subject as they shoot the photo. The effect is that the subject stays in focus, but the surrounding images are fuzzy. Replicating the real or natural world in design is a sure-fire way to make an image more believable, even if it is complete fantasy. This technique has many other uses beyond suggesting speed. This is a good design vehicle to isolate and emphasize a person from a crowd or other background noise or to use anywhere else you want to draw attention to a crisp object surrounded by a sea-of-fuzziness crowd (see the last project in this chapter for more on this technique). To take an object and make it appear to move by blurring the background, follow these steps:

1. In typical Shane fashion, this image once again started as an ink drawing. I didn't convert the illustration with the Trace utility; rather, I just

**Figure 15.19**
Creating a background in Corel-DRAW, then converting the image to a bitmap, allows you to add a sense of speed with the motion blur bitmap effect.

**Figure 15.20**

An ink illustration is scanned and then colored by drawing objects beneath it in CorelDRAW. When the black bitmap is laid on top (right), the image appears to be full color.

drew objects underneath the bitmap with the Freehand and Bezier tools to color it, as we have seen before (see Figure 15.20).

2. The next step is to make the rider look like a racer by adding numbers and sponsor logos. Since Santa's race effort is fictitious, I had to invent a bunch of potential companies that would logically stand behind the great bearded one. This was not a problem and made for a very amusing afternoon. Using my formula for logos (serif font over sans serif, or brush over block type, etc.) and the impressive CorelDRAW font collection, it wasn't long before I had a collection of appropriate logos.

3. Group the objects in a logo and use the Pick tool to position, size, and rotate the object. To get the upward curve in a logo, use the Interactive Envelope, in Single-Arc mode (choose the mode on the Property Bar). Use the Interactive Envelope tool on the logo group before you rotate it. It is easier to get a simple arc with your image horizontally oriented than at an angle. Plaster the rider and the motorcycle with the logos and you're off. I'm telling you, you could make a bowl of fruit look racy with the number and logos technique! (See Figure 15.21.)

**Figure 15.21**

Use CorelDRAW's huge font library to invent racing logos, then stick them all over the rider and motorcycle to give them a racy look.

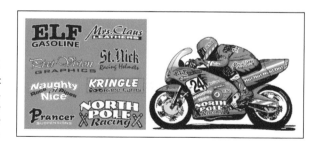

4. Draw a box behind your rider at the desired page limit size (my example is for a 6×4-inch postcard). Then use a texture fill or any pattern to create an abstract background. Pick something that has strong enough light and dark areas to make the blur effect interesting. (I used the Aerial clouds texture fill from the Samples library.) You could, of course, use a photo or scan of an actual landscape if you want.

5. Now select all the motorcycle rider objects, group them, and duplicate them. Move the duplicate on top of the bitmap background. You don't want to forget to make a duplicate of the original Corel-

DRAW motorcycle objects, because once again we will be converting them into a bitmap.

6. Select the motorcycle and background object, and from the Bitmaps menu, choose Convert To Bitmap. (For my project, my goal was a two-color design, black and red.) Two-color projects are inexpensive to print but look so much nicer than just a single color (black) production. For this reason, though, I needed the background to be grayscale. Your project might be different, and you might want a full-color background; it's up to you. From the Convert To Bitmap dialog box, select the desired color depth, enable the Anti-aliasing and Use Color Profile options, and click OK (see Figure 15.22).

**Figure 15.22**
The motorcycle and background are merged into one using the Convert To Bitmap dialog box.

7. From the Bitmaps menu, choose Blur|Motion to open the Motion Blur dialog box. Crank the Distance variable up to around 50 and set the direction of the blur coming at the rider (0 degrees). Click OK. Increase the Distance value if you want to get an exaggerated speed-blur look (see Figure 15.23).

**Figure 15.23**
A high Distance value set in the Motion Blur dialog box creates an exaggerated sense of speed.

8. Drop the original crisp and colored version of the motorcyclist back onto the background, and you are finished.

The race is on in the digital color section and in the santa.cdr file found in the \Chapt15\ subdirectory on the companion CD-ROM. If you open the file, you can see how the motorcycle objects rest on the blurred bitmap. Delete the background bitmap and repeat the steps to come up with your own fuzzy background image. Try a street scene or other bitmap for a unique look for your racing vehicles. Using the transparent background technique from the buggies example, you can also place fuzzy objects in front of the motorcyclist to really get a cool look full of depth and action (see Figure 15.24).

**Figure 15.24**
Use the Transparent background technique to place blurry objects in front of the crisp motorcycle to add depth as well as motion to a scene.

**Figure 15.25**
The Radial Blur effect draws your attention to the center of an image.

## PROJECT Adrenaline Rush

Have you ever had one of those adrenaline-induced tunnel-vision moments, where everything kind of goes into slow motion and takes on a weird, dream-like look? I've been in several semi-nasty motorcycle accidents, where everything took on that surreal appearance, moving in slow motion, with only a small point in focus, very much like the image in Figure 15.25.

While, thank goodness, I haven't been in any more vehicular accidents since those reckless days of youthful idiocy, the adrenaline-rush-induced vision and state of mind still makes the occasional visit to my world—as I am sure it does yours as well (you know, like when you get a bill that is 10 times what you expect, or you come home to a note that says your spouse has run away with an outlaw biker gang). In any case, this technique is a great way to draw attention to a single area, while the rest of the world around it is lost in speed blur chaos. To set the world spinning, follow these steps:

1. In CorelDRAW, import or scan a photo that contains the image you want to emphasize. The focal point does not need to be in the center, but it needs to be pulled away from the edge of the photo.

2. Use the Rectangle tool to draw a perfect square (hold the Ctrl key while dragging). With the Pick tool, move the square around your photo in Wireframe view to align the center of the square with the area in your photo that you want to be the focal point (see Figure 15.26).

3. Now duplicate your bitmap (+ key), choose Effects|PowerClip|Place Inside Container, and click on your positioning square. The reason why we must stuff a copy into a square is that you have no other option for

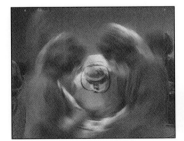

**Figure 15.26**
Use the midpoint of a square to align the focal point of the radial blur effect.

controlling the "focal point" of the radial blur, which defaults to the dead center of a bitmap. The trick of aligning a square dead center over the focal point gives us control of where we want the blur and the focus.

**Note:** If your PowerClip bitmap is not aligned with the original, you first need to disable the Auto-Center New PowerClip Contents feature, located on the Edit page of the Options dialog box (Ctrl+J).

4. With your image stuffed inside a square, remove any outline (right-click on the "x" at the top of the on-screen color palette). Then, choose Bitmaps|Convert To Bitmap to convert the PowerClip into a bitmap that will accept an effects filter in Step 5. In the Convert To Bitmap dialog box, set the Color depth to RGB, Resolution to 300 (or lower for Web apps), enable the Anti-aliasing and Use Color Profile options, and click OK.

5. Now, choose Bitmaps|Blur|Radial Blur. This filter adds a nice sense of vertigo to the photo. Drag the Amount slider to a setting you like; click the Preview button to test the option. When you are satisfactorily dizzy, click OK. (If you can still focus, see Figure 15.27.)

**Figure 15.27**
Use the Radial Blur bitmap filter to create a blurred tunnel-vision effect.

6. To soften the transition between your blurred square duplicate bitmap and the pristine original underneath, use the Interactive Transparency tool (or perhaps you want to emphasize the blurred square, for an interesting variant, in which case I recommend you use the Interactive Drop Shadow tool instead). It is up to you how you want your images to come together. I used the Interactive Transparency tool fading technique to merge the two images, as outlined in Chapter 6.

7. The round, tunnel-vision feel of the blur begs the use of curved text. Draw a perfect circle and align it center to the square bitmap. Give this circle no fill or outline, and switch to Wireframe view. To place text along the top of the circle, simply move the Text tool over the circle, until the cross-hair cursor changes into a bracket. Click the mouse, and voilà! You will type text directly on the curve (see Figure 15.28).

**Figure 15.28**
Moving the Text tool over a curve allows you to type directly onto it.

8. Drag the Text tool to highlight the text, so that you can change the font using the Property Bar.

9. Select the Pick tool, and click on the text to reveal the Text On Curve/Object options in the Property Bar. Here you can change the Vertical Placement value to butt the text up to the top of the curve, instead of on the top. Then change Text Placement to the bottom option. This will move the text to the bottom, but on the inside of the circle, which is no good. To fix this, click Place On Other Side in the Property Bar (see Figure 15.29).

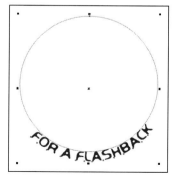

**Figure 15.29**
Use the Property Bar to change the orientation of Text On Curve.

The dizziness can be seen in the color section in the center of this book, and also experienced firsthand in the flashback.cdr file, located in the \Chapt15\ subdirectory on the companion CD-ROM.

# Beyond f/x

As I've mentioned throughout the chapter, you can find all kinds of uses for "speed blur" design techniques. In advertising, a catchphrase or call to action can also be literally active if you use techniques to suggest movement and have the words jump out at you. Guides or instruction books can use multiple subdued images along a path to show how things fit together or come apart. An object can be pulled out of a busy background for emphasis, or a character can be placed in a blurry landscape, with blurry nightmarish characters in front of and behind the subject.

Of course, the obvious uses in motor-sport logos or images also spring to mind. Speed has many connotations that you can exploit, in promotional materials or anywhere. Concepts like "Speeding into the Future" or "The Company That Is on the Move" can work into appropriately speedy graphics. How many times have you heard the words *fast* or *furious* or *high-paced* used in our contemporary world of high-tech business? Now you can create graphics that are synonymous with those concepts! Hurry! Urgent! Get going!

# Moving On

In this chapter, we looked at many ways to get motion in your static designs. Using blurring, duplicating, and transparency techniques, your objects were given life, depth, and the energy to shoot across the page. Better get a paperweight to hold 'em down!

In Chapter 16, we take a mildly dizzying look at patterns and Web tiles. CorelDRAW is a great place to design and build all kinds of repeating images, be they simple geometric shapes or fluid, seamless tiles. Keep the eyedrops handy—the retina punishment continues with the visual bombardment of tessellations, patterns, and tiles!

Chapter 16

# Tessellations, Patterns, and Tiles

*This chapter explores creating repeating images, such as
seamless tiles and geometric patterns, for a variety
of applications.*

# Creating Patterns and Designs with Repeating Shapes and Images

Many applications, from the World Wide Web to textiles, need interesting designs and patterns. Repeating patterns are a visually interesting addition to a design and can do a lot to set the tone of the artwork. You can reinforce a concept or product or even set a mood with a repeating image (for example, a "good" page could have an angel background, a "bad" one could have little devils). With textures, you can create the look of wood, marble, or other traditional building materials to set the stage for the rest of the design. CorelDRAW ships with many premade patterns and tiles, but it is also the perfect medium to create your own unique repeating images.

Many tools within CorelDRAW allow you to create patterns. The Tools|Create| Pattern command lets you create a bitmap pattern by designating an area on screen, which then is available as a tile for use in the Bitmap Pattern Fill dialog box. Or, as we will see later on in this chapter, the tiling option on the Symbols And Special Characters docker also makes great patterns. In addition, with a little creative program tweaking, you can generate all kinds of patterns in CorelDRAW for many applications. Once again, if you can imagine it, you can build it one way or another in CorelDRAW!

In this chapter, we will look at creating interesting background artwork using patterns of repeating images. First, we will create images that repeat endlessly in one direction for such uses as Web page dividers. Next, we will create an "Escheresque" tessellation pattern of tight-fitting objects using "clones" and node editing. Then, using the Tile option on the Symbols docker, we'll create a unique background pattern with repeating star shapes. Finally, we'll create seamless tiles to use as repeating images that extend endlessly in all directions for Web page backgrounds or other patterning applications. Man, I'm getting dizzy already!

**Figure 16.1**

It is easy to plan out "never-ending" designs that repeat forever for horizontal or tubular applications.

## PROJECT Never-Ending Designs

Using graphics as page separators for banners and Web pages is very common. The challenge with the Web is to create as small a tile as possible, fooling the viewer with a bitmap that connects into itself to create a never-ending graphic, such as those in Figure 16.1. This way, one tile can be repeated over and over and connect into a row as long as you want without increasing download time.

The same techniques can be applied to any application where you need a pattern to merge back into itself. Any tubular design project—from embroidered socks to teacups—uses the same kind of never-ending pattern. You can create repeating patterns in several ways, with the results reflecting the amount of work involved (unfortunately, in this case, "more is better").

## Easy

As you might have noticed, you can use a reflection technique to create a seamless row of any image. This is an easy way to make a bitmap that connects into itself indefinitely. The downside is that it is hard to hide the "repeat" because the images are sometimes very obviously mirrored. The upside is that it is "easy." For perfection, you will have to buckle up and head into "hard" territory! To build a never-ending image with the mirroring technique, follow these steps:

1. Start with the image you want to tile. Like I said, the upside is this technique will work with anything, including abstract patterns. If you want to use a texture fill, as I have, you will have to convert it to a bitmap first, using the Bitmaps|Convert To Bitmap command.

2. Duplicate the object and flip it horizontally by dragging the left-center sizing handle to the right while holding down the Ctrl key. Bang! You are done. The two tiles flipped together create a tile that will endlessly repeat end to end (see Figure 16.2).

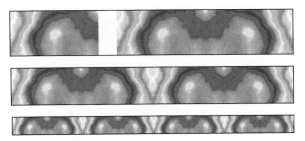

**Figure 16.2**
Any object will connect seamlessly into its reflection. The top left tile is duplicated and flip-flopped horizontally to create the never-ending pattern on the top right. This bitmap will butt into itself endlessly, as shown in the middle and bottom rows.

3. You can take this project one step further and expand the image into a never-ending tile that goes both ways, perfect for a Web page background. Simply take your horizontal tile (consisting of two copies of the original), duplicate it, and then flip it vertically. Now you have a tile that will connect endlessly in both directions for a background image like no other. You can change the proportions in either direction, and the tile will still mesh into itself (see Figure 16.3).

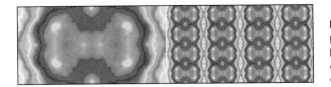

**Figure 16.3**
Duplicating and flipping the horizontal tile vertically (left) creates an image that will repeat endlessly in all directions (right).

Okay, then. So that was *easy*! Now on to *"medium"*...

## Medium

The "easy" tile is quick and dirty, but it's not always a solution. Some graphics—like a string of words, for example—simply cannot be mirrored. With just a little more effort, you can create a never-ending tile. Here's how:

1. Start with a graphic that you want to string along, like my graphic. The chain—described in Chapter 8—uses perfectly symmetrical curves, so it is a great way to start.

2. Draw a box around the area that looks like the "repeat" of the rolling chain segment. With the chain, it is easy to see where this area is—at the bottom of the "swoop." Draw the square at a best guess so that each side slices through the center of a "flat" link (see Figure 16.4).

**Figure 16.4**
A pattern starts with the target image, and a rectangle is drawn around to define the "repeat."

3. Delete all but the pieces necessary for the repeat. Also delete one of the protruding links. It is much easier to start and stop with the same object. Now draw two vertical lines and align them with the left and right ends of the rectangle (see Figure 16.5).

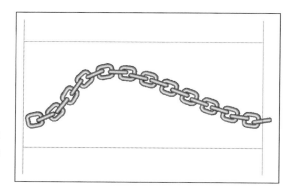

**Figure 16.5**
Vertical lines will serve as guides to align the parts that overlap in the pattern "repeat."

4. Select the right flat link and align it to the vertical center of the right vertical guideline. Duplicate the link and align the duplicate to the left vertical guideline. Basically, that's it! (Okay, maybe this rates as "easy" as well!) Because the links are duplicates of each other, they are already aligned horizontally. Use the guidelines to ensure that they are also in alignment vertically for the patterning, then delete the guidelines.

5. Select all of the chain bits, including the two that hang over, and stuff them into the reference rectangle with the PowerClip function. Remove the outline of the rectangle, and you have a never-ending tile that will

create endless chains to divide your Web pages! Test your tile by duplicating it and aligning the tiles. The links should melt seamlessly into one another, as shown in Figure 16.6. If not, make sure that the Automatically Center PowerClips option is disabled.

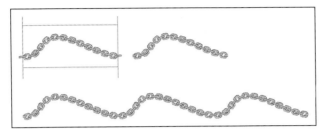

**Figure 16.6**
With the overlapping objects in perfect alignment, the pieces can be stuffed into a rectangle with the PowerClip function to create a seamless tile.

The chain is a "medium" example, as is any artwork that is made up of smaller pieces. The chain, razor wire, rope, and other examples will work well. Making a pattern out of smaller objects that can be aligned to the reference points isn't a big deal. Now on to horizontally tiling objects that are not segmented.

## Hard

Some artwork takes a little more effort to make into a pattern. It isn't really "hard," but it does take some guesswork. To tile other artwork, follow these steps:

1. Start with artwork that isn't made of smaller objects—in this case, two tribal-looking bits made with the Artistic Media tool. You could just create a bitmap "as is" and bump these images together end to end for a page divider, but that wouldn't result in the intermeshing optical illusion we want. So group the original pieces, duplicate, and move them horizontally (while holding down the Ctrl key to guarantee no vertical movement) until you get to the point where you want the pieces to overlap. Duplicate the two again and repeat until you get an idea of the pattern (see Figure 16.7).

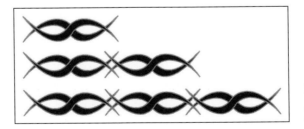

**Figure 16.7**
Arrange the pattern pieces by eye into the desired design.

2. Switch to Wireframe view, zoom in, and draw a rectangle from each point at the overlap for reference. You are defining the area of overlap, so find a recognizable shape, such as the diamond area created by the overlapping points. Draw the rectangle so that it just touches each endpoint on this area (see Figure 16.8).

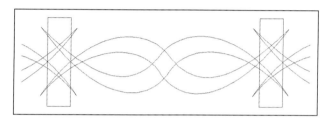

**Figure 16.8**
Draw a rectangle to define the area of overlap.

3. Duplicate the rectangle and move it to the same place over to the right of the target piece. You will find that your "eyeball" pattern was probably way off the mark, with the right set of tribal curves too close or too far away from the group to the left of it. Use the reference rectangle to measure out the position of the right group so it is in the same orientation as the left, using the same reference points as before (see Figure 16.9).

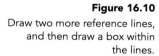

**Figure 16.9**
Use the reference rectangles as guides to position both the left and right art pieces the same distance from the center group.

4. Draw a vertical line and align it to the center of the left reference rectangle; repeat for the right. Delete the reference rectangles. Use the lines as guides to draw another rectangle around the art, starting and stopping at the reference lines. The rectangle should have no fill or outline values (see Figure 16.10).

**Figure 16.10**
Draw two more reference lines, and then draw a box within the lines.

5. Delete the reference lines, select all three of the duplicate pieces, and choose Effects|PowerClip|Place Inside Container to stuff them into the rectangle. The result is a bitmap that will create an endlessly repeating row when butted up end to end (see Figure 16.11).

**Figure 16.11**
The art is stuffed inside the rectangle with the PowerClip command, which creates a tile that will endlessly repeat.

Creating tiled artwork is just one of those little tricks to make your Web page load faster. The CorelDRAW 9 Web site (**www.slimydog.com/corelfx9**) has examples, if you want to take a peek. This technique has many applications; you can design literally in circles. The same process works in both planes to create seamless tiles that work both ways.

## PROJECT Tessellate, Schmessellate

Chalk up this example to children's television. I was babysitting my niece and desperately trying to get her interested in the television so I could go do something else. Well, this brilliant plan backfired—I ended up fascinated with a kids' program on tessellations, which are patterns made from similar geometric objects (I am easily amused; what can I say?). A brick wall, for example, is a very simple tessellation. You probably have built many "tessellations" and just didn't know it! In any case, my niece spent the afternoon playing with the toy cars I got her, while I fiddled with tessellations in CorelDRAW.

Tessellations make for cool patterns on Web sites or any other application where you want a unique, eye-catching pattern. Report covers or ads can benefit from a "themed" tessellation, using an object that relates back to the topic at hand. (The puppies in Figure 16.12 would work well for a dog or cartooning theme.) They are by no means easy to make, and I am not M. C. Escher, so most of this is "theory." (Hey, they made you learn about atomic theory in school, and you have never seen an *atom* either.) The PostScript Texture fills in CorelDRAW (accessed from the fill flyout) contain several tessellations: birds, reptiles, fish scale, patio. These fills output only on PostScript printers, but you can at least see them if you don't have a supported printer by clicking the Preview Fill option in the PostScript Texture dialog box. (For more on the subject, do a keyword search on "tessellation" on the Web. Many sites are dedicated to this topic, some with very concise, step-by-step lessons.)

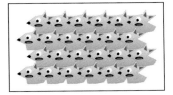

**Figure 16.12**

Using the clone feature of Corel-DRAW, you can design and manipulate an endlessly repeating pattern of similar geometric objects (a tessellation).

The trick behind tessellations and other patterns in CorelDRAW is cloning. Instead of copying an object, you clone it. What this does is create child objects that will reflect any changes you make to the original object, the parent. This technique has some handy uses beyond patterning. Think of a unique headline graphic you use repeatedly for a catalog or menu project. If you use clones instead of duplicates, when your client asks you to change them all from blue to green, you need only change the original parent, and all the clones will automatically follow suit. Please, please, no thanks are necessary. Just another handy tip from your crazy Uncle Shane!

Clones are helpful in tessellation during the building stages. By placing clones around the parent, you can see how a change is reflected in all the objects and how they work to create a pattern. It is a strange way to work—with all the clones changing "magically" when you change the parent—but it is a great visual aid and the only way I can create a tessellation more complex than a brick wall! Here's how to use clones to create a tessellation:

1. Use the Polygon tool to draw a six-sided shape (right-click over the tool to open the Properties dialog box, where you can set the Polygon option and change the number of sides). Press down the Ctrl key as you drag to create a perfect hexagon. With the hexagon selected, choose Clone from the Edit menu. This will create a clone of the original, which will automatically reflect any changes that you make to the parent. Position this clone below and to the right of the original so it fits perfectly like a honeycomb. Now with the clone selected, you can duplicate it with the + key to create another clone. Continue to duplicate and position the clones until they surround the original, for a total of four hexagons (see Figure 16.13).

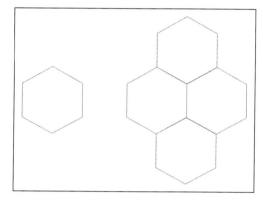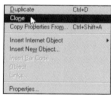

**Figure 16.13**
An original hexagon (left) is surrounded by three clones (right).

2. Select the original hexagon and convert it to curves (Ctrl+Q). Now use the Shape tool to drag the nodes into a shape that works as a tessellation. This is a trial-and-error process with the three clones butted up against the original, however. You have immediate feedback and know whether the shape you are making will work. To make things easier, Shift-select opposing node pairs instead of just one node at a time. By selecting a pair, you are ensured that the opposite side will mate up in true tessellation fashion (see Figure 16.14).

3. When you get a shape that starts to look like something—in this case, an animated puppy head—you can stop the node-editing phase and start coloring. You can delete the three clone shapes, because they will not reflect the addition of objects on top of the parent curve. The clones were only a visual aid to facilitate the creation of the primary shape. Use the Ellipse tool to draw eyes and a mouth, and use the Bezier tool to click in some ear details. The nose is a circle trimmed to the shape of the head with the Arrange|Shaping|Intersection command.

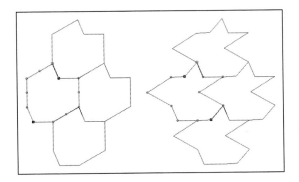

**Figure 16.14**
Selecting and moving node pairs create intermeshing geometric objects.

4.  Select all the objects in your cyber-puppy, and again choose Clone from the Edit menu. Now move and duplicate the clone groups as before to create a pattern of tessellated pooches (see Figure 16.15).

**Figure 16.15**
Simple shapes liven up the image, which is grouped and again cloned to create a pattern.

5.  You can duplicate and move the clones to create as complicated or as simple a pattern as you want. You can even use this type of pattern to create the "seamless" tiles as outlined in the last project of this chapter. The beauty of a pattern made from clones is that all you need to do is change the parent object, and all of the obedient clones will follow. You can select a single object in the parent group by holding down the Ctrl key when you click on it, and then change the fill or outline. Or you can drag and drop new fill attributes onto the objects in the parent group, and all cloned objects will follow suit (see Figure 16.16).

The tessellation is in the digital color section, as well as in the pooches.cdr file in the \Chapt16\ subdirectory on the companion CD-ROM. The clones are still "alive" in the file. If you drag and drop different colors onto the objects in the parent pooch, you can see how this changes things in all of the duplicates. Not sheep, but cloning nonetheless!

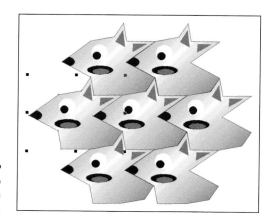

**Figure 16.16**

Changes in the attributes in the parent group will be reflected in any of the corresponding clones.

## PROJECT Symbol Patterns

Yes, my "Velcro-brain" strikes again. While innocently browsing through the CD bins at the local music store, I saw an album cover that really appealed to me. It was very similar to the graphic in Figure 16.17, with a photo covered in a geometric pattern. I, of course, elaborated on the process, adding a Lens effect to the pattern of geometric shapes, to get a chaotic and bright effect. Like I said, I never can leave well enough alone!

**Figure 16.17**

You start with a pattern set up by tiling a symbol; then a star object becomes a pattern used to recolor a photo using a Lens effect.

In addition to being a great source for images and icons, the Symbols And Special Characters docker is also set up for patterning. When you're using the Tile option, any symbol you choose can be instantly set up as a pattern for any project you can imagine. Unlike in the tessellation example, these objects do not interlock, although you can change the density, size, and spacing of the pieces. The patterns by default are spaced in an even grid arrangement of horizontal and vertical rows, which works well for most applications. In this example, however, I decided to break up the grid pattern into a slightly different variant by offsetting every alternative row of symbols. Either way, the Symbols And Special Characters docker makes for easy patterning, so you can move on and concentrate on the design as a whole. To use the Symbols And Special Characters docker to create a pattern, follow these steps:

1. Start a new design (Ctrl+N) and open the Symbols And Special Characters docker (Ctrl+F11). Locate the Stars1 library and a star you like. Change the Symbol Size to .25 inches.

2. Next to the current library name in the docker is a small right arrow. Click it to open a pop-up menu, and then click Tile Symbol/Special Character. Then, open this pop-up menu again and click Tile Options. In the resulting dialog box, you can control how big your pattern grid is. In the Tile Options dialog box, change the grid size to .5 inches Horizontal and .5 inches Vertical, and then click OK. Now drag the star onto your page and watch the pattern emerge (see Figure 16.18).

> **Note:** Getting the density and spacing right with the Tile option in the Symbols And Special Characters docker is a bit of a crapshoot. Experiment with different-sized numbers and grid sizes until you get what you want. Remember that you can always enlarge or decrease the pattern, so just worry about density and spacing in general. You can also delete pieces to perfect your pattern as needed.

**Figure 16.18**
With the Tiling option enabled, many duplicates of a star symbol create a design.

3. A pattern set up in this fashion is really the original parent shape; the rest of the duplicates are clones. Select the top-left star, change the fill to cyan, and give it a .023-inch ice blue outline (see Figure 16.19).

4. The grid pattern is nice, but it's too regimented. To create a staggered pattern, shift the stars in every other row one star length to the right. To select all the stars in each alternate row, hold down the Shift key while dragging around them. In this way, you can easily select all the stars in

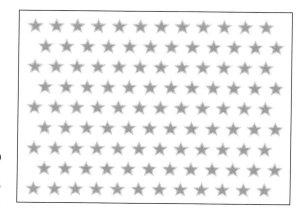

**Figure 16.19**
Selecting and changing attributes of the parent shape will change all the "clone" objects in the pattern grid.

**Figure 16.20**
Create a less-regimented pattern by moving every other row to the right.

every second row and move them slightly to the right. Try to align the stars in the rows you are moving so that the top point of each star is midway between the two stars above it (see Figure 16.20).

5. For an even more striking effect, use the Interactive Contour tool to create a second, slightly larger set of stars behind the original. Choose Arrange|Separate, then Arrange|Ungroup All to break the two curves into separate curves.

6. With the rectangle tool, draw a box around both sets of stars. Now issue the Select All (Ctrl+A) command and combine the three objects into one (Ctrl+L). This will create a solid rectangle shape, with the thick-star cutouts.

7. Import a bitmap (Ctrl+I), such as my reclining woman, and place it behind the cutout star rectangle. Open the Lens docker (Alt+F3) and assign the star cutout shape the Heat Map lens option. Very trippy results (see Figure 16.21). Whoa, dude, I'm having a Chapter 10 flashback....

The star lens is in the digital color section, as well as in the \Chapt16\ subdirectory on the companion CD-ROM (the file is called stargirl.cdr). Combining a pattern with other effects can make for some very cool imagery. And it's easy, too!

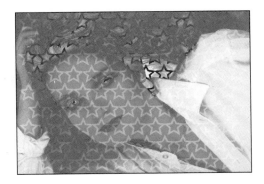

**Figure 16.21**
Combining both star curves to a rectangle creates a solid shape with star cutouts. If this shape is placed over a bitmap and given a Lens effect, the result is a patterned and recolored image.

# PROJECT Tiles: Non-Ceramic

Background patterns are very popular and easy to use, and they can personalize and make a Web page or other art project unique. The challenge with Web pages is to create interesting graphics without using bitmaps that are big and slow to download. This is why background tiles are so popular—you need download only one small image to fill the screen with a unique pattern. We already saw how using the reflection technique will make anything a tile—and even how to create horizontal "never-ending" tiles—so now we just need to work in both directions simultaneously!

The challenge with creating Web tiles is to create an image that is not immediately recognizable as a background tile. If your pattern tile has an awkward or stark transition, the duplicate tiles will not merge together smoothly and thus will look choppy or will create an abstract pattern. Bad tiles also look literally like bad tiles because bitmaps are unavoidably rectangular by nature and

## Patterns and Underwear

At this point, I need to take a moment and thank the powers that be for women's underwear. What the heck am I babbling about? Well, all of my pattern and smooth tiling knowledge comes from a stint in the art department of a major underwear manufacturer. Yes, for many months I was busy arranging flowers and paisleys on sexy negligees and sleepwear. The experience taught me, among other things, about how patterns repeat and the need to "hide the repeat."

A good pattern dissolves seamlessly into itself to create a never-ending series of images. Most everything that has a decorative print—from wallpaper to the aforementioned underwear—is actually just a small pattern area repeating over and over. A relatively small silk-screen press is responsible for repeatedly printing on the fabric, creating the endless roll that eventually becomes the garments. The trick is that the right side of the pattern merges into the left, and the top with the bottom. To get a seamless "repeat" the old-fashioned way, a designer would tape a piece of paper into a tube and then sketch out the image so that the image would go round and round indefinitely. When you untape the paper, you have a left-right seamless tile. The process is repeated for the top and bottom, resulting in a square block that will fit into duplicates of itself to create a smooth, never-ending design.

"Hurrah and hallelujah, underwear boy," you think, "but how does this help me out?" Well, the concept of a seamless tile works great in creating backgrounds for Web pages. If you design a tile that is "seamless" (like our previous chain example, only this time in all directions), it will create a smooth, seemingly endless image that flows together in a way that defies its simple, single-bitmap origin. Create a good seamless tile, and your viewers will wonder how you defied the rules of physics and got such a huge background image to download so quickly!

consequently can become a distracting array of boxes in the background if you are not careful.

## Webs for the Web

Remember, you need to work the background into the whole design scheme of the Web page. Web tiles can very easily make a Web page illegible and defeat the purpose of your efforts. The background tile in Figure 16.22, which assembles into a spider web, was a good way to build both the Web site and also the printed promotional material, but in general I am not a huge advocate of Web page tiles.

**Figure 16.22**
A seamless tile can create an interesting background for a Web page, advertisement, or both.

For use on the Web, you could decrease the contrast to keep the page legible; and for print, keep it as is. To design a seamless Web tile, follow these steps:

1. For patterning, it is a good idea to start with a perfect square. Draw two lines to crisscross through the center of the square. Select them both, then drag inward on a corner sizing handle while holding down the Shift key to get them to fit within the square (see Figure 16.23).

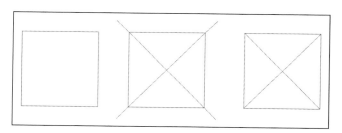

**Figure 16.23**
A perfect square perfectly bisected by two lines is our starting point.

2. Duplicate the x-square and flip it horizontally. Select both of these squares, duplicate, and flip vertically. Now you have a set of squares that already create a seamless tile, with each angled line exiting the square on one side only to reenter on the opposite side. This is the key to this pattern.

3. Now you can use the Shape tool to node-edit the straight lines into the sweeping configuration that is the look of the spider web. You can combine the smaller lines so that they connect at the center into a larger *x*

if you don't change the position of where the lines exit the square. As long as you don't change the exit points, you can change the way the lines curve within the square as much as you want (see Figure 16.24).

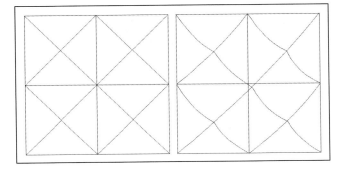

**Figure 16.24**
The array of squares creates the tile layout, and then the straight lines are curved to suggest a spider web.

4. Using the small squares as a guide, draw another square the size of the four smaller squares and in the same location. Fill it with black or another subtle dark fill, and then delete the smaller squares. Give the lines a thick .033-inch dark blue outline. Duplicate the web lines, give the duplicates a smaller .008-inch white outline, and offset them a hair up and to the right. This creates the dark, spooky web graphics (see Figure 16.25).

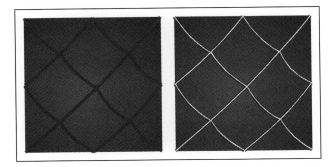

**Figure 16.25**
Dark coloring in the square and lighter shades on the lines create the web.

5. Select all the lines and choose Effects|PowerClip|Place Inside Container to stuff them inside the dark boundary square. The PowerClip step trims away the parts of the line that stick over the edge when you give them heavier line weights. This finishes up the tile, which is ready to spin into a web tile (see Figure 16.26).

**Figure 16.26**

With everything constrained within a square, the image is tile-ready.

**HTML**

To get a background in your Web page, simply add **back-ground="TILENAME.GIF"** to the **<BODY>** area of your Web page programming. Replace **TILENAME.GIF** with the name of your own custom Web tile, as described in Step 6.

6. Select the PowerClip group and open the Export dialog box (Ctrl+E). To create a bitmap of the web for use as a background tile in a Web page, in the Bitmap Export dialog box, change the Color setting to Paletted, enable Anti-aliasing and Use Color Profile, and set Resolution to 72 dpi. Click OK to create a tile you can use in a Web page as a background tile.

You can find this and the next example in the digital color section, or you can load it in a Web browser to see the tile in action. With your Web browser running, open the corelmag.htm file from the \Chapt16\ subdirectory on the companion CD-ROM. The process in Internet Explorer is File|Open, click Browse, and then find the corelmag.htm file in the \Chapt16\ subdirectory on the companion CD-ROM. As of this writing, the Web pages in this chapter are still in development, so the graphics are really too big and unruly to download off the Web, but they work great right off the CD-ROM. The native file is called webtiles.cdr and is in the same directory.

**Figure 16.27**

A graphic group can be made into a seamless tile; then, using the Pattern Fill option in CorelDRAW, it can be used to fill any object.

## PROJECT Lava Lamp Not Included

Similar to working with the chain link for the horizontal tile, constructing a graphic made up of smaller units into a never-ending seamless tile is easy. The freaky background in this psychedelic design is a seamless tile created using a round Deadhead paisley image I had lying around (see Figure 16.27). Yes, you read right: a paisley design using skulls. Some bad things have happened to my brain, and I blame those many hours of making patterns for underwear!

I created this tile in a flat configuration with the intention of using it as a square tile. When I was using the Pattern Fill feature to create the background for the title graphic, I remembered that you can change the horizontal and vertical tile size. Reducing the vertical dimension of the tile makes the circles look like they are floating at an angle, so I left it like that. For the Web tile, just squish the bitmap in Photo-Paint horizontally or vertically to get this effect. To make the floating disks into seamless tile, follow these steps:

1. Start again with a perfect square; then draw and align guidelines to all four sides of the square. Next, import the item that you want to make into a tile—in this case, the "deadhead" paisley. Align the object to the

center of the right vertical reference line. Duplicate the object and align the duplicate to the left vertical line. You are ready to start getting seamless (see Figure 16.28).

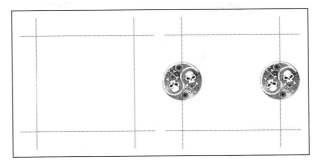

2.  With the square defining the area of the tile, and with the art objects aligned horizontally and exactly at the center of each of the boundary lines, your seamless tile is already at work. Where the paisley exits the rectangle on the left is the exact point that it enters on the right. The distance between the two objects, determined by aligning to the reference lines, is critical. Now you can select the paisley pair and move them around to create a unique arrangement for this pattern. Any of the objects can stick out beyond the boundary box as long as you start with a pair of objects. Align the object pair to opposing reference lines; then you can move them as a pair freely and still maintain the seamless tile orientation in the square boundary box (see Figure 16.29).

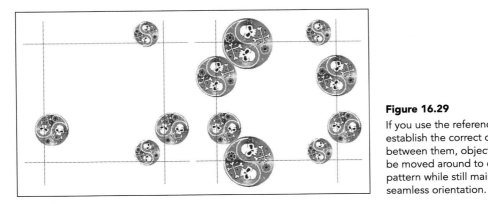

**Figure 16.29**
If you use the reference lines to establish the correct distance between them, object pairs can be moved around to create the pattern while still maintaining a seamless orientation.

3.  After you have placed all of the object pairs around the square, you can take a deep breath and throw some more objects inside the rectangle. Anything within the image tile needs no special attention. Only the ones that hang over need to be properly aligned so that they enter and exit the square in exactly the right orientation.

4. When finished, delete all the guidelines. Then, select all the pattern objects, choose Effects|PowerClip|Place Inside Container, and click on the rectangle boundary box to stuff all the objects into a perfect square. Remove any outline, and you have a seamless tile (see Figure 16.30).

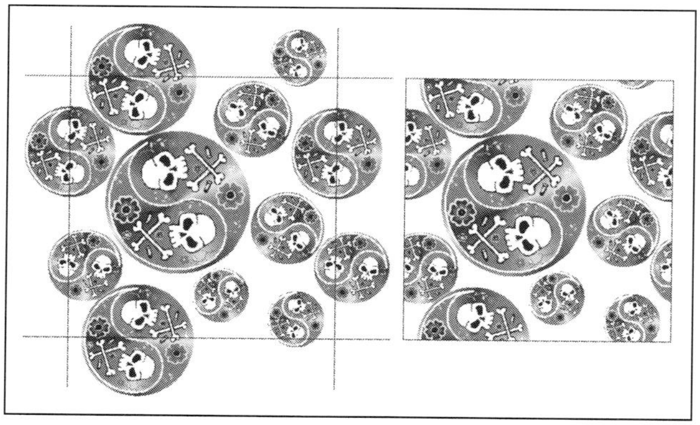

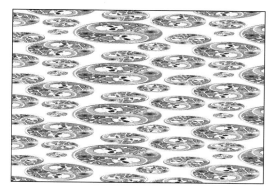

**Figure 16.30**

More objects inside the tile area finish off the pattern, which creates a seamless tile when the objects are stuffed within a rectangle (shown here on the right with an outline for clarity) using the PowerClip function.

5. Select the tile and export it as a bitmap appropriate to your current project. For a Web tile, that is 72 dpi with an RGB color depth for JPEG format, or Paletted (8 bit) for GIF format . For printed applications, you will want a 300-dpi image with a CMYK color scheme. For a Web tile, you can add the code to your HTML file to get the tile to appear (see the HTML tip in the previous project).

6. In CorelDRAW, you can fill any object with the tile using the Bitmap Pattern fill. Open the Pattern Fill from the Fill tool flyout and click Load to find the freshly made tile. You can use the same height and width values or experiment with different values to make the disks flatter or wider (see Figure 16.31).

**Figure 16.31**

The Bitmap Pattern Fill option lets you fill any object with your new seamless tiles.

This mind trip can be seen in the digital color section and in the webtiles.cdr file in the \Chapt16\ subdirectory on the companion CD-ROM. It is also available as a Web page, called slimy.htm, in the same subdirectory. You can see how a single seamless tile fills the background with an apparently solid image. The nice thing is that no matter how big or small you resize your screen or browser, a Web tile will recalculate to fill the whole screen. A clever background tile and a bitmap on top that takes advantage of the transparency options available in the GIF image format can come together to create a pretty cool Web page. Now it's your turn!

# Beyond f/x

Patterns are everywhere; and, with the World Wide Web offering more and more opportunities in design, they are no longer a specialized phenomenon. They can be used to set the mood (a fluffy cloud background sets a much different tone than, say, red-hot lava) or to establish the nature of a Web site (a children's Web page with big fun icons in the background, or perhaps a business Web site with a subdued marble background). Patterns can be used in advertising, playing off the concept with phrases like "We have designs on the future" or "Patterned for success." Holiday theme backgrounds—with little red hearts, candy canes, pumpkins, or whatever—suggest the season at hand and are an easy way to add a timely feel to a monthly newsletter or other periodical.

Entire industries are devoted to the creation of patterns for their products. From high-end silk ties to cheap wrapping paper, you will find patterns everywhere. The textiles industry alone is huge. Think about it. Beyond clothing, there is upholstery, bedding, drapery, even rugs, all of which need patterning skills to create. It's an interesting and rewarding career in itself, if you can handle working with underwear all day. If you're interested, I can even give you a few leads....

# Moving On

In this chapter, we looked at many ways to create patterns for use in a variety of applications. From freaky tessellations to simple backgrounds made with the Symbols And Special Characters docker, many interesting variants are available with CorelDRAW. Once you have artwork finished, you can take it a step further to create seamless tiles for horizontal, vertical, and "all-ways" applications. These patterns are perfect for both Web and print applications as main design elements or secondary background images.

In Chapter 17, we will continue to look at ways to use CorelDRAW for on-screen applications. From interface design as a whole, to multistage button elements in particular, we examine the screen as the interactive medium. Press here, click there, next, back, previous, home, cha-cha-cha.

# Chapter 17

# Buttons and Screens

*This chapter explores interface design ideas, dynamic elements, and unique navigation pieces for on-screen projects such as Web sites or presentations.*

# Using CorelDRAW to Add Life to On-Screen Applications

If by now your artwork has not evolved to include multimedia and Web-page development, it is just a matter of time before it will. Whereas the huge multimedia hype of a few years back hasn't quite panned out as anticipated, the influence of the World Wide Web has. Everyone and his brother-in-law (literally—my brother-in-law has a Web development company) are making Web pages these days, with a level of ability that varies from professional to pathetic. I am no exception, with a long list of obligatory Web sites under my cyber-belt. The nice thing is you already have the tools and ability to explore this medium; you just have to take on the challenge.

The advantages to developing on-screen projects with CorelDRAW are many. For starters, you get all the obvious benefits of endless versatility, countless effects, and color options at your fingertips. CorelDRAW objects, as we have seen in many examples, are ready for animation; and with Photo-Paint in the graphics bundle, you are armed for bear! Basically the whole enchilada—including all the effects in this book—can work their way into your multimedia projects.

Using CorelDRAW for multimedia and Web development offers some incredibly strong advantages, beyond the obvious graphics factor. CorelDRAW images are vector based, which means that graphics designed for a low-res on-screen application, such as a Web site, can migrate directly into other high-res peripheral support material, such as advertising and printed promotion. Not to mention, as vector-based Web technology gains momentum (such as Macromedia's Flash program), you stand ready to create the unique graphics necessary to populate this digital dimension.

With the never-ending versatility of CorelDRAW artwork, your original efforts in the planning stages (hierarchy charts, dummy pages, site plan, storyboards, etc.) become the groundwork for the actual images. Why enter that text twice? A font change, a new fill color, a unique background, and suddenly your comps are fleshed out into the real deal, be it the pieces for the Web site or the postcard to promote it. Recycle, exploit, divide, and conquer!

In this chapter, we will look at creating graphics useful for on-screen applications, such as Web pages, presentations, and multimedia applications. (With the broad variety of Web and multimedia development tools available these days, we will depart from the specific "step-by-step" format at times to discuss broader-reaching production tips and design principles.) The first project deals with creating multiple images for a custom control panel to animate buttons for "at rest," "rollover," and "depressed" states, for use in a Web site or multimedia application. After that, we will take a look at planning and developing an on-screen production using CorelDRAW as both an organizational tool and an asset generator. Then, we will look at some of the Web-specific features of CorelDRAW, such as image mapping and actual HTML publishing. It's a wild on-screen ride, and this chapter has additional support files on the companion CD-ROM, so slap that baby in the drive and let's go!

## PROJECT Sit, Roll Over, Lie Down

These days, buttons are more prolific on the Web than coffeehouses are in Seattle. The whole graphical user interface (GUI) thing thrives on buttons, with your entire workday filled with pointing and clicking. What surprises me is that, for the most part, buttons and user interfaces look like they were added at the last minute with little or no creativity involved in their layout or construction. I am far from your super Webmeister, but I at least try to make interesting button shapes and navigation panels, such as the one in Figure 17.1.

**Figure 17.1**
CorelDRAW objects are perfect for creating multistate buttons. On the left, we have the buttons at rest; in the center, the buttons each light up as the mouse travels over them; and finally, on the right, the buttons flatten out when pressed with a mouse click.

If you plan ahead and know what you need before you even start thinking about graphics, you will be much better off. In this example, I figured out all the buttons I would want on the control panel way ahead of time. Then, I created an interface that had all the buttons, with the primary navigation buttons larger than secondary options. In CorelDRAW, it is easy to create custom button designs based on your exact needs at hand, and the result will be a unique interface that is much more interesting than those rectangles everyone else is using. Once you have the basic interface in place, it is easy to create graphics for multiple button states. Instead of just lying there, your buttons can be very animated. They can change colors when the pointer is moved on top of them (called a *rollover*), when they are clicked on (*mouseDown*), and also when they are released (*mouseUp*). Even if you are not creating images for on-screen applications, faux interfaces and buttons make interesting design elements for print applications. To design and build a custom user interface and create graphics for all the button states, follow these steps:

1. First, establish the number and type of buttons you need in your control panel. I wanted a total of six buttons, with two large arrows for "next" and "back" navigation. I chose an up/down configuration to facilitate a round-center area that I could later fill with an animation or logo design. The oval center mapped out the look of the control panel, although the same basic scheme would work for a left/right orientation of the buttons.

2. Use the Ellipse tool to draw an oval. Then, use the Rectangle tool to draw a perfect square centered to the oval (hold the Ctrl key as you drag). Duplicate the square and enlarge it slightly. Move the pointer over a corner of the selected square to round out the corners on the larger rectangle by dragging the node down (CorelDRAW will automatically switch the Pick or Rectangle tool to the Shape tool when you hover over a node). Select the smaller rectangle and rotate it −45 degrees, like a diamond. These three shapes will generate all the buttons for your custom interface (see Figure 17.2).

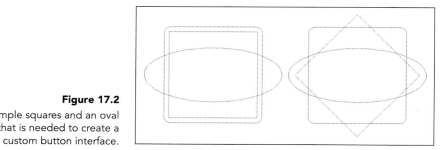

**Figure 17.2**
Two simple squares and an oval are all that is needed to create a custom button interface.

3. Select the oval shape, and then choose Arrange|Shaping|Trim. Enable only the Leave Original Other Objects option, then click Trim and click on the round-corner square. This will cut the oval away from the center of that shape.

4. Now select the diamond, click Trim again, and once more click on the round-corner curve. Select the round-corner curve and create four individual buttons with the Break Apart command (Ctrl+K).

5. Select the oval again, click Trim, and then click on the diamond. This will create the up and down arrows after you use the Break Apart command (Ctrl+K) to separate the shape into two curves. Fill all these buttons with a neutral gray color (see Figure 17.3).

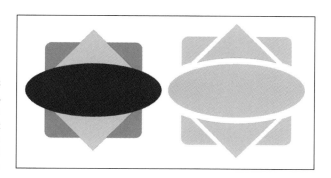

**Figure 17.3**
Use the Trim command on the shapes to create three separate curves (left). Use the Break Apart command on each curve to create the individual buttons (right).

6.  Drag the Interactive Extrude tool on your shapes, using the Bevel and Lighting options on the Property Bar to add depth and dimension. Use the Effects|Copy Effect|Extrude From command and the Copy VP From option (on the Property Bar) to give all the elements the same Extrude values.

7.  Add text elements to label each button. I used a font called BankGothic. When finished, duplicate the entire button group and set it aside.

8.  Now to freeze the bevel groups, use the Arrange|Separate command. Then follow with the Arrange|Ungroup All command so that all the pieces can be individually manipulated. This way, you can give the top pieces of the beveled buttons an interesting custom color blend to look more like shiny metal.

9.  I exported the oval object as an Adobe Illustrator file for use in Corel-Dream. I used the 3D program to create the cells for an animation that plays continuously inside the navigation panel. The center panel oval could also be a great place for a message board that changes to tell you what each button does as you roll over it. My program was so simple I didn't need a pop-up help screen, but you might want to add such a feature to your interface design (see Figure 17.4).

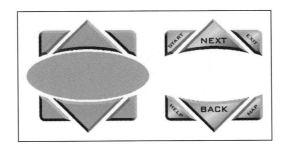

**Figure 17.4**
The button shapes are given depth with an extrude bevel; then the faces are filled with a custom color blend to look shiny.

10. The first of the buttons with the black text were individually selected and exported for the "buttons at rest" graphics.

11. Select and change the black text to red-filled, yellow-outlined text elements. These again were individually selected and exported for the "rollover state" button graphics.

12. Select the duplicate button group with the live bevels from Step 6. Now change the bevel depth from deep to very shallow on each button shape, using the Property Bar. Also change the text to some other color, like blue. These buttons, when individually selected and exported, will become the "down-buttons" graphic (see Figure 17.5).

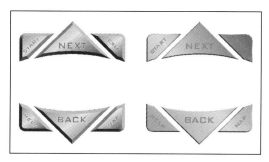

**Figure 17.5**
The buttons are given bright-colored text for the "rollover" group; a duplicate set is given shallow bevels for the pressed-button group.

I imported each button graphic into Macromedia Director as its own cast member. The "at rest" group was laid out on the page, with the animation oval in the center completing the console. The Lingo script swaps out each button graphic depending on the state and location of the mouse. If the mouse rolls over a button, the program swaps the existing graphic with the "rollover" art. If the button is depressed, the art is again swapped out, this time with the "button-down" art. You can also get the same action on a Web site using a little creative coding or with after-market Java programming tools. To use pieces in Flash 5, use the SWF (Shockwave, the Macromedia Flash file format) export filter in CorelDRAW to create objects for use in that program. It is very simple to get multistage buttons to work in your on-screen events. You just need a

## "Instant" Animated Buttons

Instead of creating all the elements for your buttons in CorelDRAW, you can take advantage of a third-party plug-in to speed up the process in Photo-Paint. For example, you can follow the same simple steps used to create the beveled effects for the puzzle pieces in Chapter 7 to create multistage buttons. Simply create "flat" geometric art in Corel-DRAW and export the art as a bitmap to manipulate in Photo-Paint (see the left-hand image in the figure). Then, use the Magic Wand tool to select the color areas of your button art, and use filters such as Alien Skin's Eye Candy collection to transform it instantly into a 3D-looking button (see the right-hand image in the figure). Use the Inner Bevel filter to create the button look. Use the Glow filter for the rollover effect. Finally, the Outer Bevel filter makes an object look "depressed." It's the quickest and easiest way to create very cool multistage button graphics.

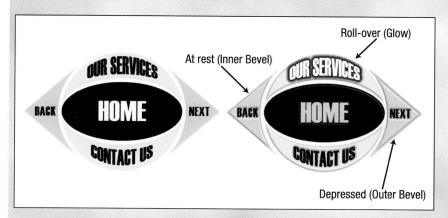

Simple geometric shapes generated in CorelDRAW (left) are quickly transformed into multistage button graphics in Photo-Paint using plug-in filters from Alien Skin (right).

unique graphic for each of the button states, and then computer programming takes over and makes the magic happen.

You can watch the button action work firsthand by starting the doggone.exe program, nestled in the \Chapt17\ subdirectory of the companion CD-ROM. With the program running, click on the spinning globe to initiate the introduction sequence. After the introduction (which you can skip by clicking on the slow-scrolling text), the control panel will appear with the buttons created in this exercise. The buttons will just sit there until you move the mouse over them, and then they spring to life. Click the Next button to move to the next screen and notice how the button changes to the "down" graphic when you do. This is a fairly common example of button action, which you can expand on to create your own cool interface.

You have all kinds of options for getting animated type buttons (see the "'Instant' Animated Buttons" sidebar for more ideas). The potential is really unlimited. The native button pieces are in a file called buttons.cdr, located in the \Chapt17\ subdirectory. This file also contains the custom interface from the next example. The interfaces were made in exactly the same way, starting with simple shapes, creating custom shapes using the Trim function, and, finally, adding depth and shading with the Interactive Extrude tool. Much more interesting than a row of rectangles!

## PROJECT Animated Interface

Where at one time my workload was predominantly for projects destined for paper, that has long since changed. Now the bulk of my responsibilities consists of on-screen projects. Web-page graphics, interface design, multimedia kiosks, and "speaker support" presentation material are the kinds of projects that make up most of my current workload. The image in Figure 17.6 is the main navigation screen for an information kiosk that sits in a cyber-café.

Note: As of press time, Macromedia's Flash and Director programs are not available for the Linux OS, but only for Mac and Windows systems. Macromedia's Generator 2 application, however, is a Linux-specific Web-authoring tool that supports Flash/Shockwave elements. I hope that Flash will one day be a Linux application as well, but in the meantime I have included the Flash and Director tutorials and references in this chapter for those of you who, like me, work in business environments with multiple operating systems, computers, and development tools.

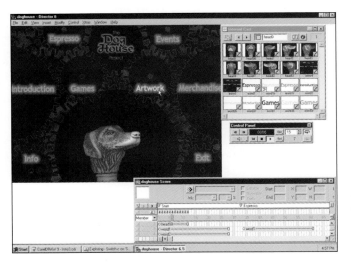

**Figure 17.6**
CorelDRAW is a great program for designing an interface, then producing the graphics you need to bring it to life in Macromedia Director.

## What Is Director?

If you are new to multimedia creation, think of Director as the assembly tool to piece together all the elements—such as graphics and sound—into a new and unique on-screen experience. Director itself isn't a good tool for creating the necessary assets; rather, it's the means to bring them all together as a whole. Director is not an illustration package, bitmap editor, or 3D modeling program but, as the name implies, the overseer of a Hollywood-like production. Director does not create cast members; it only tells them where to be and what to do. You need an outside source for your digital actors. CorelDRAW and Photo-Paint are great places to design and generate the graphics that become "actors" within Director. For this reason, the Corel graphics suite is a perfect companion to Director, making for a powerful alliance with amazing potential.

For this project, I mapped out all the graphics in CorelDRAW first, for final assembly in Macromedia Director (Director has long been the de facto program for creating multimedia applications, on both the PC and Mac platforms). The process of designing the project in CorelDRAW first and then producing the pieces for use in another program has many uses. In addition to multimedia development, you can design Web pages in the same way. While you can publish Web pages directly from CorelDRAW using the Publish To Internet feature (as we will discuss later in this chapter), anyone serious about Web development/management uses other purpose-specific programs.

I use CorelDRAW with Director in essentially the same way I use it to produce a Web site. Because CorelDRAW is object oriented, anything I create on the CorelDRAW workspace is infinitely malleable, as well as recyclable. This is a key feature; I can begin by "storyboarding" in CorelDRAW, gathering up pieces and text to help visualize the screens, then literally use those pieces later on to generate the actual graphics. Images generated within Director, on the other hand, using its simplistic bitmap editor, are just that—bitmaps—which means you cannot enlarge or distort the images without fear of losing resolution. CorelDRAW objects are more flexible, and although you will eventually need bitmaps for all the images you plan to use in Director (or the graphic elements on a Web page), during the planning and layout stages it is nice to be able to design freely, without any limitations. To design an interface in CorelDRAW and bring it to life in Macromedia Director, follow these steps:

1. Start building a site map in CorelDRAW, to help with organization and visualization. The key to a successful project is organization, so a simple flowchart (see Figure 17.7) is the first place to start. Once you know exactly what you need, it makes the design task much simpler. For a main navigation screen (like a home-page graphic), if you can boil down your project to a finite number of pages, you can work that into your design. From the flowchart, I saw that eight destinations are possible. In addition, I noted a strong sense of symmetry, with the four destinations on the left mirrored by four on the right. Planning out the project in advance not only influences the design as a whole, but it also

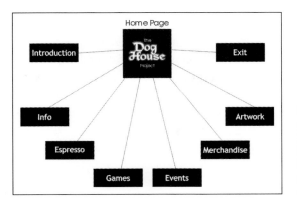

**Figure 17.7**
Outlining the project in Corel-DRAW with a flowchart not only helps in the organization process, but it also begins to create assets (such as the text objects) that you can use later.

gives you a better sense of scope as well. With every area/page mapped out, you'll find it much easier to divide up the workload if you are working in a group. Simply assign certain pages, or specific elements on each page, to certain people. Proper planning is not emphasized enough in design books, and it is really one of the greatest design challenges. Once you know what to do, doing it really isn't that hard.

2. For the easiest transition from CorelDRAW to Director, set up your page at the same size as your Director movie. (To find out how big your movie is, in Director right-click over the movie and open the Movie Properties dialog box.) In CorelDRAW, change your page size to match your Director movie. Double-click the page (or choose Layout|Page Setup) to open the Options dialog box. Change to a Landscape (horizontal) format, change the Paper setting to Custom and the Resolution to 72 dpi, and then key in your movie size (typically 640 pixels wide by 480 pixels high). Finally, click OK to resize your page (see Figure 17.8).

For The Dog House Project, I gave each destination a text description and a unique location on the screen. The concept was to have the 3D dog head ro-

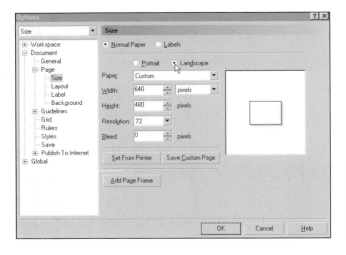

**Figure 17.8**
Set the physical dimensions in CorelDRAW to match those of your target destination for the easiest cross-application compatibility.

## Understand Bandwidth

The complexity of your on-screen design is limited to the available bandwidth, or data-transfer rate. If you are design-ing a Web page, you don't want it to take so long to download that your audience loses patience and moves on. For a multimedia kiosk—which accesses a local hard disk or CD-ROM rather than downloading off the Internet—your design is not limited by bandwidth issues. This kiosk design, for example, is far too complex—with large image files and complicated programming—to make it practical for a Web site, but it runs great on a single computer. So while you can port a Director movie directly to the Web using Macromedia's Shockwave technology, using this approach may not be a good idea unless you can design the program to download quickly and efficiently from the beginning.

tate and "look" at whatever button was selected. Use CorelDRAW to begin to visualize the home page. Copy the flowchart file, and use the text elements as pieces for the main home-page navigation graphics. Use the gear shapes from Chapter 13 as design elements here.

To get the images I wanted for the dog's head looking around, I simply scanned a real-world object with my flat-bed scanner (I have a walking stick with the dog-head). Use the scanned image as a design element in your page layout. Ex-periment and try different things, laying out the elements on the page to achieve a sense of balance and functionality. My first layout idea (see Figure 17.9) had the text elements embedded in the gear pieces, which I later abandoned in favor of a simpler design. With CorelDRAW's flexibility, you don't have to worry about wasting time during the initial layout process—you can always reuse and recycle your pieces later.

### Clear Transformations

If you change your mind about an effect or modification you have made to text, you can usually restore the original version without having to retype it. Choose Arrange| Clear Transformations, and that should return your text to its previous state before you "tweaked" it. If you want to "unwrap" text that is on a path, choose Text|Straighten Text.

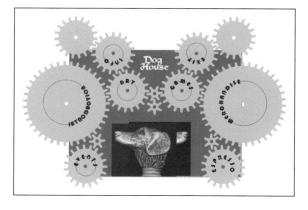

**Figure 17.9**
Using the flexible and object-oriented design tools of CorelDRAW, you can begin to organize and visualize your multi-media or Web project.

Working in CorelDRAW also helps you expand your potential, without adding too much work. While laying out the pieces for my home-page design, I de-cided it wouldn't be much more effort to animate my gear shapes to create a dynamic "live" interface. I positioned the gear shapes in two symmetrical halves, with the right half being the mirror of the left, only with each gear one tooth advanced in the mirror copy. This meant I could use the image for one animation cell and had only to flip it horizontally to create the second anima-tion cell. When these two copies are looped, it looks like the gears are animated.

(This process sounds complicated, but really isn't; I've outlined it step-by-step in the next chapter.)

Lay out all the gear shapes on the page, layering duplicate copies to create a sense of depth. For a background, draw a rectangle and fill it with the Blue Lava texture fill, changing the default colors from blue and white to blue and black for an eerie color scheme. I gave the closest set of gears a purple outline and a blue fill. To make them look strangely translucent, I used the Custom Color Map Lens effect, again changing the default colors to black and blue. This gave the home page a unique, layered look. To make the text "glow," use the Interactive Drop Shadow tool, as outlined in Chapter 3.

Keep working on your graphic in CorelDRAW until you are satisfied with your interface design. Now you need to get the image into Director (or another multimedia development tool). You have several ways to do this:

- Because you set up the page at "actual size," you can use the Copy/Paste shortcuts. Select the element in CorelDRAW and choose Copy (Ctrl+C). Now switch over to Director, find an empty spot in your cast, and paste (Ctrl+V). Set your preferences in the Image Options dialog box, and then click OK. This produces acceptable results, but the images can get "grainy" in the process. For better results, read on.

- Select your single element in CorelDRAW and export it (Ctrl+E). With your object selected, open the Export dialog box (Ctrl+E). Change the Files Of Type option to JPG—JPEG, enable the Selected Only option, and click OK. In the Bitmap Export dialog box, enable the Anti-aliasing and Use Color Profile options, and set Size equals 1 to 1 and Resolution to 72 dpi. Click OK to generate the bitmap. Now in Director, again after locating a free spot in your cast, choose File|Import, then locate the bitmap you generated in CorelDRAW. This will give you the best possible results, with a smooth-looking graphic in Director.

- A third way to get your image out of CorelDRAW is to export the entire page as a single JPG bitmap and import it into Director. This is useful for "whole-screen" graphics, such as a background or even the entire layout. You can then use the Paint option in Director to "cut" individual elements of the page to create different cast members (double-click on the cast member to open the Paint dialog box in Director).

To facilitate button animation in Director, you will need an image for each effect or motion you are after (as in the first project in this chapter). For instance, I wanted my buttons to change color when the mouse rolls over them and to change color when clicked. In Director, you have an amazing amount of control using Macromedia's scripting language—Lingo—to manage all kinds of events. If you have the time, you can program a single button event to do almost anything. But you must plan for each event beforehand—such as in this project, where I needed four graphics for each button: at rest, rollover, depressed, and one to change the position of the dog's head.

With eight buttons in my example—the dog head and the background images—the home page alone required 34 unique graphics! To make things even trickier, for the rollover programming to work seamlessly it is important that each related graphic have the same physical dimensions as the one it is replacing. Again, this sounds intimidating, but it isn't that hard.

It is a bit of busy work, creating all the unique pieces, but when you see them come alive in Director you'll get a big smile on your face.

Once all the pieces are in Director, you can drag them onto the stage or the score to begin programming your movie. If the pieces are not exactly the same size (they should be, but sometimes they can be a pixel or two off), you can resize and tweak them once they are sprites on the Director stage by dragging on the sizing handles, just like you do in CorelDRAW.

Building a movie in Director becomes a function of arranging the assets created in other applications—such as CorelDRAW, CorelDream, or Photo-Paint—on the stage in the order that you want them to appear. This, of course, is a generalization, and Director does have a pretty steep learning curve. However, much of the work is in the planning stages and image preparation, which is similar to any other complex project you might already have undertaken. A print catalog has no fewer steps preparing images and text, and the disadvantage is that you must also keep traditional printing-on-paper problems in mind. On-screen development means you just have to be able to see the image somehow, and like we saw, you can then screen-capture and paste it into your project. So ultimately, multimedia programming could be easier and more profitable than what you are currently doing. Maybe.

## Web Site from Hell

Designing for the World Wide Web is the new challenge for the contemporary artist. CorelDRAW offers many features to help you create a powerful Web experience, and it also offers the flexibility to deal with some of the limitations and challenges unique to the medium. No other design forum has issues like "download speed" or "target audience screen resolution" dictating project parameters—which can make designing for the Web very frustrating! Suddenly demographics also include modem speed, monitor size, and display capacities. It's a barrage of technical concerns enough to make a right-brainer cry.

This section will deviate from the step-by-step formula in order to focus on Web-specific tips and tricks. I used these techniques to create the Web page design in Figure 17.10, which is my "old" CorelDRAW f/x site.

Web design is such a huge topic in itself; volumes have already been written on the subject. Here I will just hit you with a few of my own favorite insights and some CorelDRAW-specific tips and tricks.

**Figure 17.10**
CorelDRAW makes it easy to plan out the whole look of a Web page; you can generate the Web-friendly graphics and any other support graphics you might need directly from the Corel-DRAW file.

## Webbing in CorelDRAW

Designing a Web page layout in CorelDRAW has many advantages. The flexibility and techniques available to you for printed projects are also available (if not more so) for projects that will end up on the Web. The Web even allows you to take your graphics further, with the addition of animation, sound, and interaction. Your CorelDRAW Web-page design can migrate effortlessly to printed materials at the correct resolution for cross-promotion projects. In addition, as you will see in the upcoming example, CorelDRAW allows you to actually publish HTML pages directly from the program. The Publish To Internet features in CorelDRAW 9 offer powerful HTML translation (including tables) to get WYSIWYG (What You See Is What You Get) porting direct from your CorelDRAW files right to the Internet.

CorelDRAW's Web-publishing features are nice and handy as support tools; however, I highly recommend you use a specifically Web-oriented package to build and maintain your Web sites. CorelDRAW should be your primary source of graphics, but by no means your primary Web building and maintenance tool—the power just isn't there. The HTML publishing features in CorelDRAW—with its tables, layers, and styles support—are very impressive, but a page doth not a Web site make! A Web site typically needs more than just pretty text and pictures; it also needs animations, forms for viewer input, email support, maybe even online shopping opportunities and the like that CorelDRAW does not support. In addition, a single change on one page can have an impact on many pages on a site; other purpose-built, Web-site-specific software packages are designed to manage link changes and CorelDRAW simply isn't such a package. With all the links, graphics, and other issues, it is just not the smartest solution anymore to build a Web site page by page using CorelDRAW. Rather, you should compose a site as a whole using Web-specific software. Macromedia's *Generator 2*, Bluefish, WebDesigner, Quanta +, Screem 0.2.1, gnotepad+, WebMaker, and so forth are all much better products for real-world Webbing. Not only do these programs allow for painless Web-page creation, they also offer flexibility and power (such as data entry forms, Java applets, and email options) that you won't find in the focused CorelDRAW graphics suite. CorelDRAW is for graphics creation, and it excels as an asset-builder. As a Web-site builder, however, it lags. So, use CorelDRAW's powerful graphics tools to enhance your Web site, but exploit true Web-building power elsewhere.

That's just my two bits on the topic, and anything is possible. It is perfectly feasible to build a nice site with nothing more than CorelDRAW. Heck, I built most of my first Web site using CorelDRAW for the graphics and nothing more than a text editor to do the HTML coding. If you are looking to throw a few pages together for a personal site, then CorelDRAW will be all you need. If, however, you find your business now includes building and managing complex Web sites, get an additional Web-management program.

## Making Pages

Although you might want to build and manage a site with other software, CorelDRAW is still an invaluable addition to the Web-designing experience. As you saw in the previous project, the advantage of an object-based design application like CorelDRAW is that you can use the same pieces through all stages of the Web-site–building process.

I suggest that, after you create a flowchart, you mock up the entire Web site, page by page, in CorelDRAW. This process helps you work out design problems and other Web-specific issues. Remember that Web design is both horizontally biased (screens are wider than tall, unlike printed pages) and vertically enhanced (you can scroll down indefinitely).

Working with the screen set at the actual resolution and color depth of your target audience also helps you create a more appropriate design (see the "Stay on Target" sidebar).

The advantage to first creating the pages in CorelDRAW as opposed to a Web-builder program is that you can design whole-page artwork instead of slapping in buttons and graphics haphazardly as you go along. The whole-page design can then be broken into smaller pieces and assembled into one solid graphic using an HTML table. Breaking up an otherwise solid graphic like this lets you create animations for specific sections of the page and lets you take advantage of speedy-download tricks. If you use common graphics in more than one page, they need to be downloaded only once, speeding things along.

Figure 17.11 shows how the top of my full-page graphic is broken up into four sections. The right sections change with each page, while the left two pieces are common to all. The left two pieces were also made into animated GIFs to

## Hands Off My Graphics

Theft prevention is another reason to design your site using the full-page approach, where individual graphics are on top of a signature background and they all fit together like a puzzle. The background behind the buttons on the demo site connects to the background in the top graphics, subtly creating a whole-page feel while also keeping them from floating free. Free-floating Web graphics are easier to pilfer and work into other designs; just a few paint strokes are all that the image thief needs to customize them. A background makes this much more difficult to do because, for one thing, it would be impractical to paint it away. The background will look wrong on another site but perfect on the site for which it was designed. This is not a huge issue, but when you invest a lot of time into, say, a unique animation for your Web site, you don't want to have it ripped off! While I highly discourage the practice of using other people's images in your own Web pages (a practice that is unethical and potentially illegal), unfortunately the nature of Web technology is that everything is subject to duplication. If you can see it, you can steal it—and that goes for your code as well as graphics. So keep that in mind and be careful what you put in your pages as far as personal information.

**Figure 17.11**
Breaking up a full-page graphic (shown here in Photo-Paint) lets you add animation to sections of the page. With an HTML table, the pieces fit together seamlessly on a Web site.

add motion to the site; they need to be downloaded only once and are common elements on every page.

Another bandwidth-saving trick is to use a horizontally repeating graphic for page breaks. The chain page-break graphic on my test site is actually just one small bitmap that is tiled four times across the page (see Figure 17.12). Once loaded, the graphic can be used as many times as you like without increasing future download time. (Creating these kinds of repeating graphics was explained at length in Chapter 16, remember?)

**Figure 17.12**
Using a single bitmap (top) that can be tiled across indefinitely (bottom), you increase your design capabilities without increasing download time.

## Stay on Target

Set up your monitor to preview your Web site at actual size. A pitfall for many designers is that they forget to design for their target audience and really miss the mark. Most computer artists have much larger screens and more graphics capability than their target audience, and they design to their own system and not the end user's. To set up your display for the most common screen size and color depth, right-click on the Corel Linux desktop and choose Properties from the pop-up dialog box. This should open the Control Center window. Click on Video Settings so you can change to a more appropriate screen size—640x480 with a color palette of 256 colors is considered the "least common denominator"; however, you should assess your target audience and set your screen accordingly (typically I design screens at 800x600). When you have finished making your changes, click Apply and then restart the system (Ctrl+Alt+BackSpace). Back in CorelDRAW, set your zoom factor to 1:1 and you are on the money!

# Web Graphics

Creating images for the World Wide Web is so much easier than creating them for print applications. For one thing, the graphics needed are at screen resolution, which is a low 72 dpi. The palette typically is also a meager 256 colors, which makes for small files that are easy to create and manipulate. Creating Web graphics is one of the few design tasks where the old WYSIWYG acronym is actually true. The low-resolution nature of Web graphics also ensures that they won't be stolen for paper-publishing purposes (but remember that you shouldn't use 72-dpi Web graphics for this purpose either!).

Once you have your graphics and page for your Web site laid out in Corel-DRAW, you can either select them individually or export them as a whole as bitmaps to use with your Web-builder program to assemble your Web pages. Or you can GIMP screen-capture capabilities to generate the bitmaps. Of course, you can also export the page as HTML code using the Publish To Internet features (see the next project for more on that process); it is up to you and your Web needs.

CorelDRAW gives you plenty of Webbing options. Obviously, you don't have to break up a Web image as I did, but for the Web-site design I had in mind, it was the only way to go. With four separate images instead of just one, I was able to create an animation for the bat and the Shane's World graphic. These images need to load only once; if used on any of the subsequent pages, they won't require any more download time (I used basically the same scheme in the "new" CorelDRAW 9 f/x and design Web site, only with different graphic elements). Use your favorite browser to review the new CorelDRAW f/x and design Web sites to get some ideas for building your own Web pages using CorelDRAW as the asset-generator.

## Audience-Specific Design

The first thing you need to do when you set out to develop a Web site is to determine the technical abilities of the target audience. You should establish the average modem speed, screen size, and color depth, as well as a user profile to make sure your graphics and interface are appropriate. It is a common trap for designers—with our big screens, fancy computers, and fast Internet access—to fall into designing Web pages that are inappropriate for the market. Until very recently, the largest user base was still limited technically to browsers that did not support frames, Java-Script, or even animation. That is not necessarily the case now, but you still need to consider these issues and design with the target market in mind. Try to view your site via different access providers and a variety of modem speeds, and try using different brands of computers, operating systems, and browsers to get a feel for how your page will really look. For example, I had to abandon my original test pages because they did not build correctly in Netscape Navigator on a Linux box, but they looked fine in Microsoft Internet Explorer on a Windows machine (Internet Explorer is not as popular a browser choice for Linux as Netscape seems to be). It's a good thing I checked, or the pages on the CD would have looked awful for anyone using Navigator. Also, while the Flash/Shockwave player is common on the Mac and Windows operating systems, you may need to actively seek out the plug-in for Linux (you can find it here—**http://www.macromedia.com/shockwave/download/alternates/**). A few years from now, universal standards might exist, but for now, you have to do your homework.

The next projects get away from on-screen design "theory" and move on to on-screen design "practice," working specifically with the Publish To Internet features of CorelDRAW. I didn't want to dive directly into CorelDRAW's Publish To Internet features without first exploring the more realistic real-world approaches to on-screen design. The Publish To Internet features are nice, but you are much more likely to exploit the power of CorelDRAW and Photo-Paint to create bits and pieces for use in other on-screen events (PowerPoint presentations, Web pages, multimedia programs, and so forth) than create Web pages directly with the product.

## PROJECT Out-of-Site Map

Color me fickle, but I never seem to be happy with my Web site. After a while, I end up hating what I have and can't rest until it meets my criteria of the moment. Currently I am working on a total redo, calling for the Internet equivalent of a Web site "Mulligan." As my skill set evolves and my tastes change, it seems I am never quite satisfied with my personal Web site. And, in a typical scenario among designers, my own Web site—not being a "paid" project with any kind of deadline—is very low on the list of priorities.

One big problem with Web sites in general is that by nature they are always changing. Where this really becomes a hassle is with pages that have graphical representations of site maps (like the one in Figure 17.13), which are a practical and popular addition to a Web experience but a big pain to implement and a bigger one to maintain.

**Figure 17.13**
Setting up a living document such as a Web site map in Corel-DRAW is an easy way to maintain the graphic as well as to generate the associated image map needed for Web navigation.

With the built-in Web features that CorelDRAW offers, this task is no longer as nightmarish as it once was. Using the Internet Objects toolbar (located under the Windows|Toolbars menu), you can associate an Internet link or Uniform Resource Locator (URL) with every CorelDRAW object right in your design and then generate both the graphic and the image map directly from the .cdr file. With an ever-changing entity like a site map, this is a gift from the cyber-gods! (Many Web-building software packages will autogenerate a traditional site-map for you, with a flow-chart–like structure, making it easy to see and navigate the Web site as a whole. This might not be as "pretty" as your own graphical interpretation of the site-map, but it generally is more practical because Web-building software packages automatically create and update these for you. So you need to balance "beauty" with "practicality.") Let's look at setting up a graphic with URL associations in CorelDRAW.

Again, the nature of your project will dictate how this graphic looks. My site is broken up into four major areas, so the graphic had to reflect that organization visually. The graphic needed to incorporate many text elements, be flexible for adding and deleting objects, and not be too big. My site map is pretty simple, with triangles dividing a big rectangle into the four main sections of the Web site. Each section has the title of a page fit to a set of circular paths that repeat through the graphic and serve as a guide for the text objects. Follow these steps to set up a similar graphic with associated "hot spots."

1. Use the Fit Text To Path option on the Text menu to put the text objects into place. If you want to move them free of the curve and assign the text an individual Internet address, use the Arrange|Separate command (see Figure 17.14).

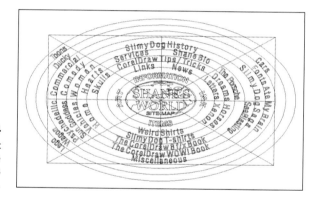

**Figure 17.14**
A graphic with an individual text element for each page on the Web site is laid out using circles as a guide.

2. Select a text element to which you want to assign a URL. Choose Window|Toolbar to open the Options dialog box. Select the Internet Objects option in the Toolbars area, and then click OK to display the Internet Objects toolbar.

3. Now you can enter a link for the selected object in the Internet Address box. The default setting of Use Object Shape To Define Hotspot is fine, so after you enter your URL for the object, press the Enter key.

4. Repeat this process to define a URL for every object in your site map (see Figure 17.15).

5. Once you have assigned a URL to each link object, you are ready to create the bitmap and the HTML file. (Use the Show Internet Objects

**Note:** If you are linking to a local file in the same sub-directory as the site map file, you need only define the target name, such as "index.htm". If you are linking to another site, you will need to include the entire URL, such as "http://www.slimydog.com/corelfx9/index.htm", to make the links work correctly.

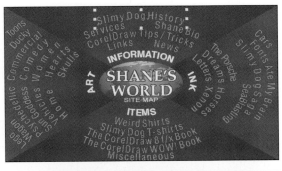

**Figure 17.15**
The Internet Objects toolbar lets you assign a URL to each object in your CorelDRAW file.

button on the Internet Objects toolbar to check that all objects have been assigned a URL.) From the File menu, choose Publish To Internet. Select the target folder where your source code will be generated, then change the HTML layout method to Single Image with Image Map and click Next.

6. In the next window, pick either JPEG or GIF. GIF used to be more universally acceptable and is still the only format that supports multiple frame animations, but it is your choice. GIF images allow you to assign a transparent background, while JPEG images can compress to smaller sizes and allow for more colors. (I use JPEG whenever I can.) Make your choice, and enable all the other options in this Publish To Internet dialog box. Then, click Next.

## GIFs or JPEGs

Creating images for the Web also means choosing between these two file formats for your bitmap images. GIF images are limited to 256 colors (although dithering can simulate colors beyond the 256 palette), while JPEG files can be in the millions of colors. It used to be that you had to address the least common denominator with building a Web site, which is a screen size of 640x480 and a color depth of 256 colors. With technology changing so fast, the bar has been raised a bit to larger screen sizes and bigger palettes, but the old rule remains if you want to guarantee that your site can be viewed by all. The GIF format, although limited in color depth, also supports multicell animation, whereas JPEG images do not. Since I use so many animations—and I don't find the 256 color palette an insurmountable restriction—I use the GIF format almost exclusively.

For nicer images (it really makes a difference with photos, for example), the JPEG format is better and also takes advantage of file-compression technology. When you save a JPEG, you have the option to change the "quality factor." Lower quality means smaller files but also degrades the image. (Keep a copy of the high-quality original before you start experimenting with the quality factor option in case you need to start over!) If you use this format, find a happy medium between small file size and high quality. (The CorelDRAW 9 JPEG Export dialog box lets you preview the results of the compression before you execute the export, which is nice.) If you use the CorelDRAW 9 Publish To Internet Wizard, the default action is to export bitmaps greater than 256 colors in the JPEG rather than the GIF format. Remember that you can mix and match both formats within one Web page; however, as in my example, if you build a big graphic in pieces and then assemble it with a table, you will want to stick to the same file format within that connecting graphic.

7. In the next window, choose the file name of the HTML file you are creating and then click Finish to make it all happen. When CorelDRAW finishes generating the HTML code and the graphic, it will launch your primary browser and open the page so you can see the results, as shown in Figure 17.16. Pretty neat trick, eh?

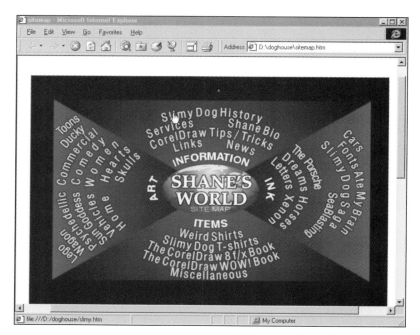

**Figure 17.16**

When CorelDRAW finishes generating the HTML and Web-friendly image, it will launch your browser and open the page so you can see the results immediately.

With the CorelDRAW-generated page open in the browser, you can check that all is well and that the links are working correctly (move the cursor over a "hot spot" and check to see if the link information in the browser status bar is correct). If not, simply toggle back to CorelDRAW from the browser window (Alt+Tab), make any changes, and repeat the Publish To Internet process until everything is perfect.

What the Publish To Internet feature does, using the Single Image with Image Map option enabled, is create two files: the bitmap and an HTML file that has the image map information in it. You can open the file directly with your browser or use a text editor to drop the image map text section into your own

## One Graphic, Many Links

You can also use the CorelDRAW Internet Objects/Image mapping technique to assign multiple hot spots on a single CorelDRAW object, such as a big bitmap. Import your bitmap and then draw shapes over areas you want to connect to links as hot spots, using the Internet Objects toolbar. Assign URL information to these objects as before, only don't give them any outline or fill attributes. Now these are "invisible" areas over the bitmap, but when you create the HTML and bitmap for the Web, they will be live and act as links. Nifty deal. This is just as easy as using one of those image map utilities, but the bonus is that you can also mix and match other CorelDRAW images and Internet associations along with the bitmap to get some really custom results.

HTML file. Text elements make for some very complex coding to define the hot spots—but no matter, it is all automated! (See Figure 17.17.)

You can load the page layout plan for the site map from the sitemap.cdr file in the \Chapt17\ subdirectory on the companion CD-ROM. If you load the CorelDRAW file, open the Internet Objects toolbar so you can click on an object and see the corresponding link. You can practice by adding links to the custom button interface below the site map, which does not have links yet associated with the graphic. The built-in Internet features are a powerful addition to CorelDRAW, and you can accomplish a lot using this power, as you will see in the next project.

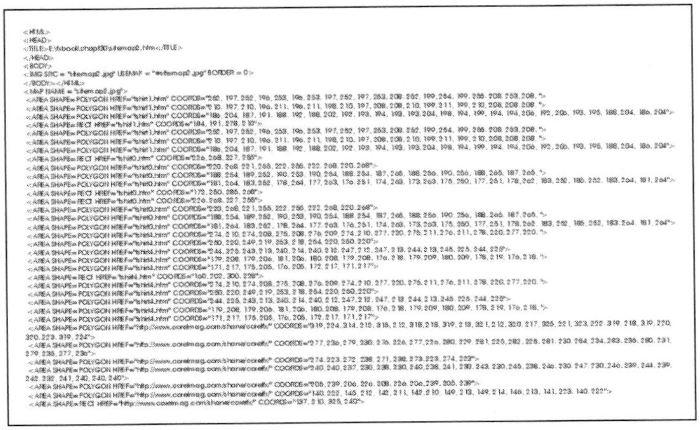

**Figure 17.17**
CorelDRAW creates both the bitmap and the HTML coding defining the image-mapped hot spots. You can use the file as a stand-alone page on your Web site or copy and paste the text into your own HTML code to take advantage of the complex image-mapping programming.

## PROJECT  Making Web Pages

While I continue to suggest that anyone serious about Web publishing use "site-builder" type software, you can publish Web pages directly from CorelDRAW. With a little planning using an organization chart, it is feasible to create as big or complex a Web site as you want, one page at a time, using the Publish To Internet feature.

Since you can design your pages within the flexible and familiar, object-oriented universe of CorelDRAW, the program offers a painless way to create Web pages without a steep learning curve. The image in Figure 17.18 is from a site that I designed and built entirely within CorelDRAW. Once I'd laid out all the pages in CorelDRAW, I converted them to HTML and Web-friendly graphics using the Publish To Internet feature.

This process is a bit tedious, because you must not only organize the site manually but also design and generate each page one by one. But like I always say, anything is possible; once you have your Web pages built in CorelDRAW, it is really not hard to build and maintain a Web site using this process. To build and publish a Web page, follow these steps:

1. Begin by setting up your page size as before to match your target audience's screen. Double-click on the page border to open the Options

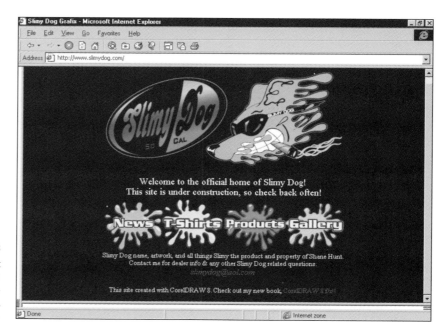

**Figure 17.18**

Using the Publish To Internet feature in CorelDRAW, you can design Web pages and automatically convert them into HTML and Web-specific elements.

**Note:** In CorelDRAW 9, if you click on your page (or start a new document), the Property Bar offers a way to customize your page. You can change the page size, drawing units, and orientation, but not the resolution. So you still need to access the Page Size options from the Options dialog box (Ctrl+J).

dialog box. On the Size page, change the Resolution setting to 72 dpi first, then set Width to 800 and Height to 600 for a typical Web-page size (or smaller or larger, depending on your audience). Click OK to change your page size.

2. Now build a specific page for your Web site. Use your flowchart to organize the page names so you can assign links to objects. For example, this CorelDRAW page is destined to become the newsmenu.htm page. The links on this page will be to three unique Web pages, named news1.htm, news2.htm, and news3.htm. You need to build the pages that these links refer to one by one in CorelDRAW, using the correct HTML file names, or the linking will not work. Most of the work in creating a Web site page by page with CorelDRAW is organizing everything so that the file names and links all work.

3. Select a button or text element to which you want to assign a URL link. Choose Window|Toolbar to open the Options dialog box. Now enable the Internet Objects option in the Toolbars area, and then click OK to display the Internet Objects toolbar.

4. Assign the correct HTML file name to your menu items so that the links will work. For example, the top menu item on the newsmenu.htm page needs to link to news1.htm, so type that into the Internet Address area on the Internet Objects toolbar. Since the layout of the menu is simpler than the rounded text in the previous site-map example, select the Use Bounding Box To Define Hotspot option on the Internet Objects toolbar.

This will simplify the link programming in HTML for faster loading and running pages. If you also select the Show Hotspots option, you can see which elements on your page have active HTML links (see Figure 17.19).

**Figure 17.19**
The Internet Objects toolbar allows you to assign an Internet address to objects, displayed in a mesh grid with the Show Hotspots option enabled.

5. Repeat the process of assigning a link to any "button" or "image map" that you want to include in your Web page.

6. Everything on your page will automatically convert to a Web-friendly graphic format when you go through the Publish To Internet process. To help speed up the download process and make your pages less complex, however, you should modify large blocks of text. If you can prevent text elements from converting to bitmaps and instead remain true text, the pages will load faster. To do this, select a large text block and choose Text|Convert To Paragraph Text (or skip this step if the text is already in Paragraph Text format). Then choose Text|Make Text HTML Compatible. This will keep your text objects as simple as possible for the translation to HTML.

7. When you have all of your graphic elements in place and any large text areas converted to HTML Compatible, it is time to publish your page. Choose File|Publish To Internet to open the Publish To Internet dialog box. Select the destination for your source code, then set the HTML layout method to HTML Table (Most Compatible). Click Next to continue.

8. Set the graphics conversion option to JPEG (which affords better image quality), and select the Export Bitmaps As Distinct Files option, as well

---

### Font Fiasco

The downside to the Make Text HTML Compatible command is that you lose control of the fonts. If your target viewers do not have the same font on their system, text elements will default to a standard font (such as Times Roman or Arial). So you must convert your text into bitmaps on your Web page if you demand control of the font. Large areas of text converted into a bitmap using the Render All Text As Images publishing option, however, take forever to download off the Web, so use the Make Text HTML Compatible feature whenever you can. (The text will convert to whatever bitmap option you choose [JPEG or GIF] in the Publish To Internet dialog box.)

as the Resample Bitmaps To Screen Resolution. This will ensure that all graphics are in the smallest, most Web-friendly format. Make sure that the Render All Text As Images option is *disabled,* so that you can take advantage of the Make Text HTML Compatible process in Step 6. Click Next to display the next dialog box.

9. Now click the file name to change it to the correct page you are publishing (in this case, newsmenu.htm). Enable the Replace Existing Files option if you are updating the page. Also, select View Page In Browser so you can check how the conversion process went. Click Finish to publish your page.

10. Typically, you will see a Publish To Internet warning dialog box, suggesting that your design contains potential conflicts. This usually happens when you have a text element that has not been given the Make Text HTML Compatible treatment. Since there are many times you will want text to convert to a bitmap, you will not want to use the Make Text HTML Compatible feature, so inevitably you will see this error dialog box. Click No to ignore the conflicts and proceed with the publishing-to-the-Internet process.

11. Once CorelDRAW has finished converting your file into HTML, you will need to launch your browser and view it to see how things went. Double-check how the final Web page will look to your audience. If things seem too big or small, simply resize your artwork in CorelDRAW and repeat the publishing process.

Publishing a Web site using CorelDRAW isn't very difficult; it is just a matter of organizing the details to ensure all the pages and menus link together as planned. If any of the pages change, or you want to add or delete pages, you will have to manually update and republish each page. This is why I stress that a "professional" Web-builder application is a better solution; for the occasional or home Web page creator, however, CorelDRAW may be all that's needed. It's up to you!

The paint-ball splat buttons are on the companion CD-ROM, in the \Chapt17\ folder, in a file called splats.cdr. These are bright and fun images I used to create the navigation graphics on the original Slimy Dog Web site. You may want to use the images on a similar fun Web project.

## PROJECT Vector Pieces for Flash

The happiest Web-related marriage is between CorelDRAW and Macromedia's Flash program. (As I said earlier, Flash is not yet available for Linux, but maybe one day....) This is because Flash uses vector-based graphics, the same format that CorelDRAW creates. Vector-based images are relatively small compared to their bitmap brethren, so Flash can use them to save on download and processing time. Flash, however, is lacking in the powerful draw-tools arena, and that is where CorelDRAW steps in.

Creating custom navigation panels such as the one I created for the CorelDRAW f/x and design Web site (see Figure 17.20) uses the same techniques that we saw at the beginning of the chapter, except I exported the pieces using the Shockwave filter rather than converting them to bitmaps. To create objects for use in Flash, follow these steps:

**Figure 17.20**
Use the powerful design tools of CorelDRAW to create pieces to build a Web site in Macromedia's Flash program.

1. First, decide which shape you want for your panel. With Flash, shapes can be unique and not limited to the problems of using bitmaps or image maps to define "hot spots" and button areas. With this in mind, I thought a bending, twisting navigation panel around the Linux penguin might be interesting. So, starting with a silhouette of the penguin (which I made by using the Arrange|Shaping|Weld feature), I used the Interactive Contour tool to create a set of multiple outlines extending beyond my parent object (see Figure 17.21).

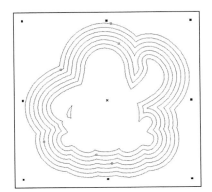

**Figure 17.21**
Use the Interactive Contour tool to create multiple outlines extending outward from your target object.

2. With a handful of outlines to choose from, I then broke everything apart with Arrange|Separate, Arrange|Ungroup All so I could pick and choose between the pieces. Delete all but the most outside, most inside,

and center paths. Then Shift-select the outside and inside paths, and combine them (Ctrl+L) to create a solid object around your center. The remaining center path will be used to align text within the buttons (see Figure 17.22).

**Figure 17.22**
The outer most and inner most of the new paths are combined to create a solid ring (gray). The middle path is retained to align text later.

3. Draw a circle with the Ellipse tool, then drag on the control node with the Shape tool to create a "pizza" slice. Align various copies of the pizza slices to outline the areas that you want to convert into button shapes. You should know how many destinations your Web site will need at this point, so, as I have been stressing throughout this chapter, you need to do a little planning to get your design right. I needed five buttons (see Figure 17.23).

**Figure 17.23**
Use the Shape tool on a circle to create "pizza" slices, designating your button areas.

4. Now use the Arrange|Shaping|Intersect feature to create solid shapes where the pizza slices and the fat outline shape intersect. These are now your specialized, custom-fit buttons! (See Figure 17.24.)

5. With the Text tool hovering over the center-path shape, begin typing your button labels. The letters should follow the contour of the path

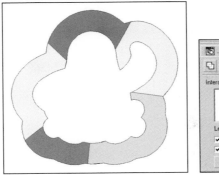

**Figure 17.24**
The Intersect function transforms the pizza slices into the custom button shapes.

below. Use the Shape tool to drag the letters along the path to move the labels over each specific button. Use the Property Bar to control how the letters appear on the path (see Figure 17.25).

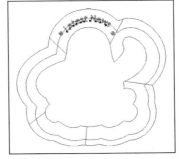

**Figure 17.25**
The commands on the Property Bar allow you to control where your button labels go.

6.  Once your panel is finished, it is just a matter of using the File|Export command to export the pieces for use in Flash. It is a good idea to isolate each element (such as one button) and export the pieces individually, rather than as a whole, for more flexibility later. Select a button group, then choose File|Export. Give the piece a useful name, enable the Selected Only option, and then change the Files Of Type option to SWF—Macromedia Flash. Now, click OK. In the SWF Export Options dialog box, set the bounding box to objects, and that's it! You have created the perfect piece for use in Flash (see Figure 17.26).

7.  Now in Flash, issue the File|Import command to import the pieces and assemble them into your movie. It's a great way to create shapes and artwork for use in your Web site that would otherwise be difficult—if not impossible—to do in Flash alone.

You'll find the bits and pieces, along with the final results, in the color section and on the companion CD-ROM in the \Chapt17\ subdirectory. pengiflash.cdr

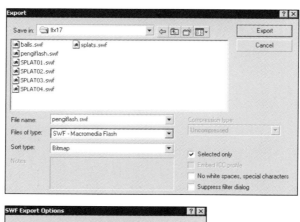

**Figure 17.26**
Use the SWF option in the Export dialog box to create pieces for use in Flash.

is the CorelDRAW file, and pengiflash.fla is the Flash movie. Also be sure to check out **www.slimydog.com/corelfx** to see the Web site in action.

# Beyond f/x

On-screen designs—with their high-tech buttons and navigation panels—can also be used for traditional print projects. You can get a high-tech look by using icons and graphics associated with electronic publishing technology. Many ads use the computer-screen analogy, with pull-down menus and buttons suggesting interaction and motion. The same kind of trick can be used to create a Web-browser look for an ad or brochure—which is also a good way to promote a Web site.

Beyond the literal look of on-screen interfaces in print, more esoteric concepts of worldwide connectivity or electronic communication can benefit from tangible artwork like buttons or screens. Of course, buttons and screen designs work the best for Web applications or multimedia events, where CorelDRAW's design flexibility turns into dynamic interaction. Multiple-graphic objects—such as buttons that change or animations that move—make on-screen experiences much more interesting. Just don't get too crazy and make everything sing and dance, or your interactive audience may just sit there, too dazzled to move!

# Moving On

In this chapter, we looked at how CorelDRAW can help you create on-screen applications. CorelDRAW is a natural for creating images for Web sites and multimedia applications. With the handy, fat Corel clip-art and font libraries at your disposal, your Web sites should be bursting with creative imagery. The versatile nature of CorelDRAW artwork makes Web-site management a snap and also facilitates easy Web promotion, with the artwork migrating painlessly to print applications. Without question, CorelDRAW is an indispensable weapon in the sticky World Wide Web war.

In Chapter 18, we will continue to look at ways to use CorelDRAW for Web enhancement by using the program to create interesting animations. The flexibility that CorelDRAW affords is perfect for designing the multiple images necessary for on-screen animations or movies. With the ability of Photo-Paint to assemble and manipulate movie files, you have powerful animation capabilities right on your desktop. Get ready to make your Web sites sing and dance as we explore the possibilities of computer-aided animation.

# Chapter 18

# Animation Action

*Using CorelDRAW to create unique cells and Photo-Paint to assemble them, you can create animated movies for on-screen applications such as Web pages.*

# Using Animation to Make Your Images Come Alive

Images that create the illusion of movement are becoming very commonplace. With everyone clambering to get on the Web, many designers are being pulled into the electronic design forum by their clients. Multimedia and Web applications are both a blessing and a nightmare. The new opportunities bring along a host of technical difficulties. Suddenly, designers are supposed to be programmers, 3D artists, audio-engineers, and yes, of course, animators!

It does make sense that electronic print designers would take on the tasks of electronic formats. If you have the artwork for other projects in the computer, you are ready to take on the Web or multimedia projects. The art is in place; you just need to find some ways to make it more alive. Fortunately, with a few tricks, even the most animation-challenged artists can bring artwork to life in CorelDRAW.

Animation goes beyond the traditional sense of creating happy, dancing cartoon characters. With contemporary media, elements like advertising banners, buttons, pointers, and even text can all be image stacks that refresh in sequence to create live images.

We have already touched on the theory of adding motion and other effects to bring artwork alive in many examples in this book and on the companion CD-ROM. Now we will walk through the complete process of transforming artwork into a set of *cells*, which can be assembled into an interesting, animated entity for your Web site or other on-screen application.

We will first make a lively graphic out of a still image. Then we will create a word out of jiggling gelatin and alter the background colors to electrify and bring an ad to life. After that, we'll use animated text effects with multiple images as well as lens effects to get the headlines on your Web site noticed. Then, we will create perpetual motion by using frames for intermeshing gears. We will then blow things up with an animated explosion technique, and then we'll use a "working backwards" technique to reassemble something. Finally, we will use the Extrude feature to create an animated spinning text logo. You might think cartoons are for kids, but I guarantee that animations will be a part of your very adult design world if you continue to function as an electronic artist now and in the future!

## PROJECT Biking Madness

**Figure 18.1**
Use a lens to alter the background of an illustration to bring a dynamic sense of motion to a static image.

The problem with animation for many commercial applications is that it is way out of the budget of most projects. I already charge an exorbitant amount for a *single* illustration; imagine the cost of, say, a *dozen* illustrations for a very basic animation. Now take into account the insane amount of work that goes into organizing and orchestrating such an undertaking. To get our hero in Figure 18.1 to ride and leap would require a lengthy photography session to get the necessary reference material, weeks to ink up the illustrations, and then hours of coloring and assembling the images in the computer. It's the kind of project that is just not going to happen with your average client.

With a few simple tricks, however, you can get a dynamic sense of motion without actually moving anything. Your goal is just to create an interesting animated graphic out of a static image to make your Web pages dance and sing like everyone else's. Little tricks like this bridge the gap between expensive animation and low-budget images that bring a Web page to life. Here, you'll learn how to get attention and add interest to an existing graphic by introducing a flashing background color effect.

This project started as—big surprise—one of my hard-edged ink line drawings. It was scanned as a 1-bit bitmap, imported into CorelDRAW, and then colored in the now all-too-familiar process (Chapter 2 for you skip-ahead readers!). I won't bore you with redundant details. The file is called foes.cdr in the \Chapt18\ subdirectory on the companion CD-ROM if you want to see things firsthand. The ink illustration turned out to be the limiting factor in this project. Because I had no intentions of using this illustration for anything but its original purpose (a bold T-shirt design), the image of the cyclist is connected to the black background. Not the kind of graphic that lends itself easily to animation, but I really wanted it on the Web site. Left with few options, I came up with the flashing color scheme, similar to the angels "double-vision" technique from Chapter 9, except that I didn't have the luxury of foreground/ background flexibility. To get some animation zing out of an otherwise limiting image, follow these steps:

1.  To create a different color scheme for the background in each animated cell, you can either simply recolor the background by hand or use another object on top of the background, which changes how it looks with a Lens or Transparency effect. Creating a new "effects object" to modify the look of your image offers more flexibility with less work (which is good!), so that is what I recommend. Draw a yellow rectangle and place it in front of the background coloring elements but behind the rest of the design. The easiest way to do this is to work in Wireframe view, send the rectangle to the back, choose Arrange|Order|In Front Of, and click on the background coloring object. Now it should be in place within the image stack.

2.  Select the Interactive Transparency tool, change the Type setting on the Property Bar to Fountain, and then click the Radial button. Done. The transparent yellow mixes with the existing background colors to create new colors, just like on an artist's palette. In this illustration, the yellows mix with the colors underneath to make oranges and yellowish browns.

3.  Open the Export dialog box (Ctrl+E) to create a Web-friendly, 72-dpi, RGB bitmap in the TIF format. Don't be too concerned about actual size or color depth at this point; just export at 72 dpi and RGB color (24 bit; 16 million colors), and we can tweak the images specifically for the

Web later. When we assemble these images in Photo-Paint as a movie, we will also tweak the size and color palette to exactly what we need. Remember to number the cell—foes1.tif, for example—so that each file is unique for each individual cell. This way, you'll also keep track of the creation order. Be sure to use the same settings for each export, because even a slight variant will be noticeable. (For example, I didn't enable Anti-aliasing for one of the cells in the weenie2.avi animation on the companion CD, and the result is a fuzzy-flash effect.) See Figure 18.2.

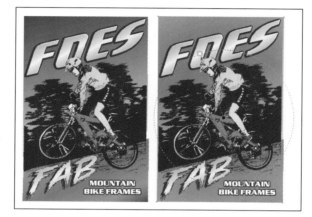

**Figure 18.2**
A yellow rectangle with a radial fountain transparency (right) mixes with the original background colors (left) to create a cell in the color flash animation.

4.  With the transparency rectangle selected, change the fill value from yellow to cyan and repeat the export process for cell number two. Then, fill it with magenta and export for cell number three. Finally, fill it with black and export for cell number four. Save your CorelDRAW file and exit the application.

5.  Start Photo-Paint and then open the first of the cells you just created. Choose Movie|Create From Document to convert from a single-image to a multiframe AVI (movie) format. Don't worry about cropping away anything if your cell has image information you don't want in it yet (such as the white space on the right of the image, created during the Export process from CorelDRAW).

## Capture It

You can use the screen capture feature of another Linux graphics application, GIMP, to copy and paste images for Web animations. However, you will have to work with the entire screen intact through most of the process to ensure that each cell is exactly the same size. This is why the Export feature might be a better option, because CorelDRAW is very good about creating exactly the same size image each time and you can selectively pick parts of a design to export with the Selected Only option. I created the animations in Chapter 17 (in the sample Web sites) using screen captures. The examples in this chapter were all created with cells made with the Export function. To make a screen shot in GIMP, in the toolbox, click Xtns|Screen Shot. To grab the active window, make your choices in the Screen Shot dialog box (i.e., Include Decorations). Then click OK (or Grab). After a few moments, your screen dump will appear in a new window in GIMP, where you can save it out for use in CorelDRAW or Photo-Paint.

## Repetitive Motion Injuries

Public service announcement time. As I used to be in charge of office automation for Southern California's number-one grocery chain, I am also an expert on proper workstation habits (I preach to all my friends; bugs the crap out of them!). Make sure you are in a natural work environment in which you are comfortable and that you are using proper posture. Get a good chair with solid lumbar support and a computer desk that has an adjustable keyboard rest so your keyboard will be in a position that is comfortable for you with as little wrist bend as possible. The new ergonomic mice and keyboards are pretty nifty, too. Position your monitor so you can look either directly at it or slightly down at it (as if you were talking to someone your height or slightly shorter). Make sure no surrounding lights are reflecting back at you in the screen. And on a regular basis, get up and stretch your back and neck, touch your toes, and exercise your eye muscles.

Many problems, like headaches and the inability to focus after working for long periods, are the result of not stretching your eye muscles. When you stare at your computer monitor all day, you end up using a very narrow range of your eye muscles. Take a break now and then, and focus on something really far away, like mountains, planes, or the person walking past your window (or cubicle). Then, focus on something really close, like your finger near your nose, your elbow, your next deadline, and so forth. This will stretch your eye muscles. Repeat this exercise a few times a day, especially before you get into the car. Nothing is more frightening than trying to drive after a day at the computer and everything past the windshield is just a big fuzzy blur! Stretch everything before and after the commute, and you will be in much better shape. Oh, and don't forget to drink plenty of liquids, make backups of your work, defrag your hard drive, and write timely thank-you notes.

6. Time to add some frames. Choose Movie|Insert From File, then click on file number 2, which you exported out of CorelDRAW. In the Insert File dialog box that pops up, choose either Before or After (I usually work sequentially from beginning to end, so I chose After), then click OK. Now you have a two-frame "movie." Since the images are the exact same size, with the pieces in the same place, only the background changes.

7. Repeat the process until you have a movie file that contains all your image cells. Easy! (See Figure 18.3.) Take a moment and save the AVI to disk.

**Note:** To test your "movie," choose Movie|Control|Play Movie. This will loop the current frames. To stop the movie so you can continue editing, choose Movie|Control|Stop Movie.

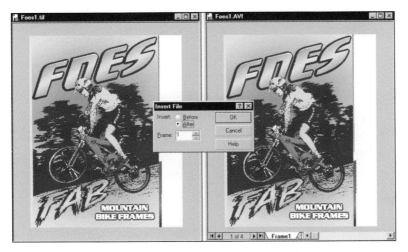

**Figure 18.3**
A single-frame bitmap can be made into a multicell animation in Photo-Paint.

**Figure 18.4**

The Paper Size dialog box lets you change the size of the image area and trim away unwanted material from all cells in a movie.

**Note:** If you want to target your results to a specific audience using a known browser, you can specify this preference in the Palette option. Change Palette to Netscape Navigator or Microsoft Explorer to use color palettes optimized for those products.

8.  With the movie working and all the frames in place for smooth animation, we can start to fine-tune the image. For starters, we need to get rid of all that dead space to the right. From the Image menu, choose Paper Size to open the Paper Size dialog box, where we can trim things down. First, disable the Maintain Aspect Ratio option or any changes we make to the width will also affect the height. Change the Placement setting to Center Left so our changes will affect the right-hand side only. Now decrease the Width value, using the preview window as a guide. Keep downsizing until all the white is trimmed away from the right and click OK. Even though you can view only one cell in the Paper Size preview, the changes affect all cells (see Figure 18.4).

9.  You can repeat the trimming process as many times as necessary to reduce and remove the image down to just the desired material. With the movie working and appearing perfectly, it is time to manipulate it further for your application. From the Image menu, select Resample to open the Resample dialog box. Here we can control the physical size of the movie and its resolution. First of all, change the Resolution value to 72 dpi, which is what on-screen applications call for. Now change the Image Size setting to the exact size that you need and click OK. All cells in the movie will resize in unison.

10. If you want to use the animation as an AVI for multimedia applications or what have you, the RGB format is fine. For an image stack to use in a Web page, you need to convert the graphic to a 256-color palette. No sweat, Photo-Paint is here to serve you! Choose Image|Mode| Paletted (8-bit). This will open the Convert To Paletted Image dialog box, where you have a few options. Change the Palette setting to Adaptive and Dithering to Ordered. Then, click OK to convert your movie.

11. Now to use the "movie" on a Web site, save the animation in the GIF format. Choose File|Save As, change the Files Of Type setting to GIF— GIF Animation, and click Save. In the GIF89 Animation Options dialog box, you can control things further. On the File Settings page, modify such settings as Repetition to your taste. (I always tend to choose Loop Frames and Forever for non-stop animations, but sometimes you will want an animation to play only once or just a few times.) On the Frame Settings page, you can assign a Transparency color. (In this case, the None option is used because we are not using a Transparent background in this example.) This page includes the Frame Delay option, which specifies how short or long you want a frame to display on the screen. You can control each frame individually, so one can display longer than another if you want. Change to one by clicking on it in the left

preview window (or hold down the Shift key to select multiple frames). Click Apply All to make your changes stick, then click OK to save to disk.

Hanna and Barbera should be shakin' in their shoes, because that's all there is to it! You can just stick the GIF file in a Web page to see the animation, or view it with a browser (File|Open). Or use a media player to view the movies. (Just double-click on the files and they should play automatically.) This movie is called foes.avi, and you'll find it in the \Chapt18\ subdirectory of the companion CD-ROM. You'll also find foesa.avi, where I took a cell from the first animation and created a new one from there. I used Photo-Paint's tools to copy the rider, change the background, and then paste him back into place. This made for two frames of moving background, which assemble into another movie. You can animate any stack of bitmaps into a movie or GIF file using Photo-Paint, and you can also take advantage of the program's built-in bitmap editing features. Not only can you assemble a stack of images, you can also trim down the animation to size and change the color depth to customize the animation for its specific assignment. No better or easier way exists for taking an AVI and making it into a GIF for the Web. It is the kind of power that is easy to abuse, as can be seen in the silly dance.avi file, also found in the \Chapt18\ subdirectory of the companion CD. I created this movie from a brochure that I had made many years ago and just happened to stumble across. The movie is a series of still images of me dancing around like an idiot. (I am my own favorite parody victim—I almost never sue myself!)

If you want to work through the tutorial step by step, you'll also find the original bicycle file, foes.cdr, in the \Chapt18\ subdirectory, or better yet, each of the exported, numbered bitmaps (foes1.tif, foes2.tif, etc.). It is an easy enough concept to grasp, and I won't bore you with the step-by-step details of assembling the frames in Photo-Paint for the following examples. Once you know how to do it, you can create an animation out of nearly anything!

When we first got a copy of CorelMove years ago (CorelMove is an application that lets you build a simple animation), my buddy Eddie and I were thrilled to finally have a way to create our own cartoons. Well, after about 12 hours of learning the program, scanning and coloring the illustrations, adding a few

## Trap

It is a very common mistake to build a Web site using a color table that is specific to your machine and not your audience's. A buddy of mine built an entire Web site on his PC to show his client, and it looked awesome. When he went to his client's office, his client was using a Mac, which has a different system palette. They loaded up the site and it looked awful. Not a good way to make an impression! In a situation like this, find out the exact computer and monitor type and associated color table that the big decision maker is using so your presentation will go better. If you have no idea and you want to make your Web site as universally viewable as possible, select the Adaptive color palette from the Convert To Paletted Image dialog box.

## Progress, Progress, Progress

In the passing years, as technology has so rapidly changed, so has the nature of a commercial art studio such as ours (and I am betting yours, too!). At first, our office was essentially a big warehouse filled with tables for paste-up, mechanical-drawing machines, a giant stat-camera, rollers, exacto-knives and waxers, and a pukey little computer for bookkeeping. Over the years, those paste-up tools were all tossed, the pricey mechanical-illustration machines were declared worthless, and even the trusty camera was chucked in favor of a scanner. Soon everything was electronic, and even things like ink illustrations began to fade away in favor of high-tech, computer-generated images. Just when we got really good at making pretty pictures for print (we even moved next to our service bureau to work out Mac versus PC output issues and take care of that hassle), our clients started asking about multimedia and World Wide Web projects, and we had to start the learning process all over again! The challenges just never stop.

sounds, and assembling the frames, we had a movie of about 15 seconds. It was a caricature of our friend Dave inside a television, sticking his tongue out. That's it. No plot, no dialogue, no exciting acrobatics, nothing, and it took us all day. I have had undying respect for animators ever since!

## PROJECT Jay-Eee-Ell-Ell-Oh, You Know?

This animation (jello.avi in the \Chapt18\ directory on the companion CD-ROM) came out of a conversation with the marketing staff at The Coriolis Group. For those of you unfamiliar with the world of publishing, the marketing people start promoting the title long before it is even finished. They were picking my brain at the beginning of the project for features they could promote; in the course of the conversation, somehow jiggling Jell-O got thrown into the mix. They loved the idea, and I hung up the phone, thinking, "Well, now I have to figure out how the heck to do that!" Nothing like agreeing to the unknown!

The solution to creating cells for jiggling text came from the Brian the BrainBot example (from Chapter 13). If a blend could build and rebuild the robot arms automatically, then why not the jiggling gelatin? The attraction of using a blend like the robot arm example is that you can select and move one of the control curves and the image will rebuild automatically. That's the kind of automation I am after! The same kind of trick works here to rebuild the Jell-O after each move. Here's how you can make text jiggle on top with a rigid base:

1. Start with text that is at an angle and use the Perspective function to alter it. Fill it with a dark red and duplicate it. Move the duplicate above the original and fill it with pink. Now drag the Interactive Blend tool between both objects and create a 200-step blend. (Use the Property Bar to increase the number of steps.) See Figure 18.5.

**Figure 18.5**
Create a solid gelatin text object by blending two objects together.

### Speaking in Tongues

To add to my frequently random and comedic life, the book you are holding in your hands is being translated into various and sundry foreign languages (Russian, Chinese, Italian, etc.). This fact alone slays me, especially when I think of someone across the planet opening files such as dance.avi on the CD and getting a good laugh. What is more annoying than funny, however, is that I tend to scatter "Americanisms" throughout my text, and these don't always translate well. For example, many countries don't have push-button phones, let alone the "dial 411" information service, so if I type "here's the 411 on that," only North America gets the joke! The reason I bring this up here is that Jell-O gelatin is pretty much unknown to much of the world. This has resulted in many strange discussions with confused translators across the globe, and me pulling my hair out! Hmm, maybe that should be my next animation example....

2. Select the top control object and duplicate it. Next, from the Fountain Fill dialog box (F11), use the Cylinder 22 preset to give the top of the gelatin a nice set of reflections. (You don't want the whole blend to have this fill, just the top, so that is why you duplicate the control object first.)

3. Now you have the live Jell-O word ready to get a jigglin'! Select the top copy with the custom color blend and then press the Tab key. This will toggle and select the control curve right below it. Hold down the Shift key and select the very top piece again. Now you have both top pieces (which you cannot group together because of the live blend, so you have to do this little Tab-Shift-Select cha-cha each time).

4. With both the top coloring object and the control object beneath it selected, you can move them around anywhere, and the blend will rebuild to create a new jiggle. You can move, resize, twist, slant, whatever, for mild-to-wild gelatin activity! (See Figure 18.6.)

**Figure 18.6**
Moving the top coloring and blend control objects will create cells for a jiggling animation.

5. Set your gelatin text in any stage setting you choose. My set was a campy '50s-looking ad, with the text centered in a white burst made with the Polygon tool. The text is arched along a circular path at the top, and the font is called Beatsville, which looked sufficiently corny for this application.

6. With the stage set, you can set out to generate each animation cell. I wanted to use this as a Web animation, so that usually means trying to milk the most animation out of the fewest cells. The minimum number of cells to get the gelatin word to jiggle back and forth is four, with cell two repeated twice to create an endless loop. It goes like this: left-center-right-center. This animation will repeat endlessly as left-center-right-center-left-center-right-center-left-center-right-center, and so on. So basically you need to generate three cells: left, center, and right.

7. Working out the logic for this animation also revealed an interesting possibility for a flashing background effect. If you notice, every other cell is in the center, so if you change the background on that cell to another color, it will cause the graphic to flash. So that is what I did!

Export each cell, moving the top pieces as shown to create a stack of images that will assemble into a jiggling gelatin text object. Change the background color of every other image for a flashing effect. The movie is called jello.avi, and you'll find it in the \Chapt18\ subdirectory on the companion CD-ROM. The parent file is also there; it's called jello2.cdr. If you load the CorelDRAW file, you can see how selecting the top two pieces of the Jell-O and moving them causes the blend to rebuild the rest of the object in the new orientation. Blends make for quick and easy animations, and the color flash technique makes for eye-catching icons on a Web site.

While you are perusing the CD-ROM, take a look at the splasha.avi animation. This animation also uses a live blend. In this example, a white circle is blended to a black one; for each cell of the animation, however, I changed the colors of these control circles. I lightened the dark circle by 10 percent each time, and darkened the white by 10 percent as well. So in the span of 10 frames, the blend logic is reversed; what was once black becomes white, and vice versa. The "live" blend automatically generated the in-between shapes each time, making the process simple.

## PROJECT Text That Lives!

You can find oh-so-many ways to animate text to grab attention on a Web site. You can create multiple copies of a headline (like in the world.cdr file from Chapter 9) and create cells where each duplicate is moved slightly. (Check the animation called jitters.avi in the \Chapt18\ subdirectory, for example.) You can create spinning logos with the Interactive Extrude tool (as outlined in the last project in this chapter, and also seen there in the fxspin.avi file). Even complex still images can get a new level of interest by just exporting two cells with slightly different backgrounds and using different Anti-aliasing settings for each cell. (Check out weenie2.avi in the \Chapt18\ subdirectory to see what I mean.) If you can think of it, you can animate it.

Some effects, however, are so cool that they defy their easy CorelDRAW origins. The text-through-a-keyhole effect (fisheye.avi in the \Chapt18\ subdirectory) is a perfect addition to a Web site. It is the result of the simple task of moving a lens over some type. Another great payoff with just a little investment! To create the fisheye text, follow these steps:

1. Start by using the Artistic Text tool to type the phrase you want to appear in the keyhole. I used a font called AmerType, which looks like it was typed on an old-fashioned typewriter. Color this text white (or any color).

2. Rest your text on a black (or any color) background object. Now draw another box on top of the text and the open the Lens docker (Alt+F3). Give this object the Fish Eye lens at a rate of 150%. This will bug out the text beneath it (see Figure 18.7).

### Don't Go Gray

Colors: 256=256. It's interesting to note that a file created with a 256-color palette is often the same size as one created with 256 shades of gray. You might not save any file size by creating black-and-white images for animated Web GIFs. Since you can't save a GIF in the 1-bit black-and-white color depth to take advantage of a smaller file size, you have to use the 256-shades-of-gray option. That could create a file that is the same size as one that uses 256 colors! So go for the color option, and see if it isn't much bigger than black and white.

**Figure 18.7**
A text object (in Wireframe view above) is distorted by a rectangle with the Fish Eye lens.

3.  Start with the lens over the left side of the text; then, with the lens object selected, open the Export dialog box (Ctrl+E). If you use the Selected Only option, only the rectangle will export, but because it is also a lens, it will export the distorted text below. This makes lens effects ideal for creating animation cells. Each cell is the exact same size as the lens object, so you don't have to trim down the image with other tricks (like the PowerClip feature, for example) before each export.

4.  Repeat the export process many times, each time moving the lens object a little to the right before the export. The bigger the move, the fewer the cells in the animation. You can get away with just a few connecting images for a Web graphic; if you use too few, however, it will be hard to read the text. I created 23 cells for a smoother, easier-to-read, fisheye animation.

Lens effects lend themselves to all kinds of animations. If you place a Heat Map lens over an object, for example, and then change the Palette Rotation value for a stack of animation cells, you can get a very freaky effect. Or use a Transparency lens over an object, varying the opacity in each cell to fade to or from black. Or keep things simple, and just change the fill value of the object. Check out the dogban1.avi file on the companion CD-ROM, where I just changed the fountain fill in the Web banner a little for each animation cell. The variety of animations you can generate in CorelDRAW is limited only by your energy and imagination!

## PROJECT  Perpetual Gears

As we saw in Chapter 17, you can use animated gears as navigation buttons. These gears look complicated, but they are a great example of something that looks hard to create but isn't. It is also a perfect example of *closure* (see the sidebar, "Closure"). The animation is only two frames, yet it repeats endlessly to look like turning gears.

To get the machine moving, follow these steps:

1.  Start with a set of gears as outlined in Chapter 13. Arrange them inside a boundary box, which will again guarantee that both bitmap cells have the same physical dimensions.

## Closure

*Closure* is more than ending an experience in your life; it is also your eye's natural tendency to fill in the blanks to make things whole even when they are not. When you watch a movie or cartoon, it is really a series of static images, but you see it as a solid stream of motion. Another example is water flowing out of a faucet or hose. It looks to be a solid stream but it actually consists of bursts of water one after another. (If you blink your eyes really fast, sometimes you can catch the droplets in the stream. If not, high-speed cameras will convince you!)

Your computer monitor is actually a single row of pixels refreshing from top to bottom. This row refreshes so fast that you think it is a solid image. To prove to yourself that this is actually happening, stand in front of your monitor, stick out your tongue, and make an obscene raspberry noise. This will vibrate your head and eyes and break up the closure phenomenon enough to see the scan lines in the screen. Vary the pitch and frequency of your tongue vibration, and you can see the screen begin to flash, wiggle, and wave. (This trick works best on monitors with a slow refresh rate.) Now wipe the spit off the screen, and try to explain to the other people in the office what the heck you are doing. (It might be easier just to say you were critiquing some software!) For more proof (or to avoid spitting on your expensive computer equipment), take a picture of your television screen with a high shutter speed, and you will see the scan lines.

2. Position the gears as you desire and combine them into one group. Duplicate this gear shape and boundary box, and move off to the side. Select and duplicate the gear shape in the first group one more time.

3. Break apart this duplicate into the individual gears again so you can manipulate each one individually. Select each free gear and rotate until the gear teeth are exactly in between those below it. Repeat this for all the gears.

4. With the top gears in the rotated orientation, select them all and combine them into one curve again. Now delete the reference curve for this set, and you should have two gear groups (see Figure 18.8).

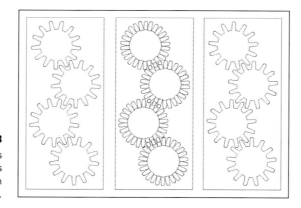

**Figure 18.8**
An original set of gears is duplicated and each object is rotated to create the in-between gear orientation.

5. Shift-select both of the gear curves and fill them with an appropriate color. I used the Gold Plated fountain fill preset to give the objects a metallic look.

6. Use the Interactive Extrude tool to drag on your objects and create an active extrude group. Use the Property Bar to modify the extrude group,

to create the beveled, dimensional look just like we did before with the gear shapes in Chapter 13. Be sure that the vanishing point for the extrude is set to VP Locked To Object and not To Page. This feature makes the gears look amazing!

7. Select the non-extruded gears and choose Effects|Copy Effect|Extrude From, then click on the other completed gear extrude group. Sometimes the vanishing point goes perquacky during this process, making the duplicate look wrong. If this is the case, also use the Copy VP From option from the Vanishing Point Properties pull-down on the Property Bar to copy the identical vanishing point values to both of the extrude groups (see Figure 18.9).

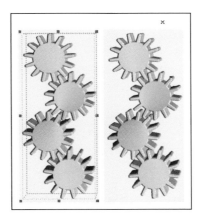

**Figure 18.9**
Add depth and shading with the Interactive Extrude tool on a gear curve, and then copy the values to the second gear group.

There you have it! You have the two frames needed to create the perpetual motion gear animation. You can watch the gears twirl in the gears.avi file on the CD in the \Chapt18\ subdirectory. Even though only two frames are there, you could swear the gears are counter-rotating like a fancy piece of machinery. Aren't optical illusions fun? You could use more dramatic gears, moving robotic arms in a printed piece, to suggest movement. Any string of images that can be animated in an on-screen movie can also be used in a print project to add a sense of motion and energy (see Figure 18.10).

## PROJECT Explosions

What's fun about CorelDRAW is exploring the unknown. From solving a specific design problem to just open-ended experimentation, CorelDRAW gives you a powerful universe to explore. I was trying to get an explosion effect without investing too much effort when I discovered this technique (see Figure 18.11). It thrills me to get big payoffs with little creative effort. Here's how to blow things up:

1. Use the Ellipse tool to draw a circle. Duplicate this circle (use the + key on the numeric keypad) and then move the duplicate over and down

**Figure 18.10**
Animation techniques can add a sense of motion to a static image, such as this flyer, where animation cells are placed in a movie-like film strip border element.

**Figure 18.11**

Blending multiple sets of circles using the Acceleration feature results in a nice explosion.

**Figure 18.12**

Start with a single circle and duplicate it with the + key on the numeric keypad. Keep duplicating and moving until you have a blob of circles.

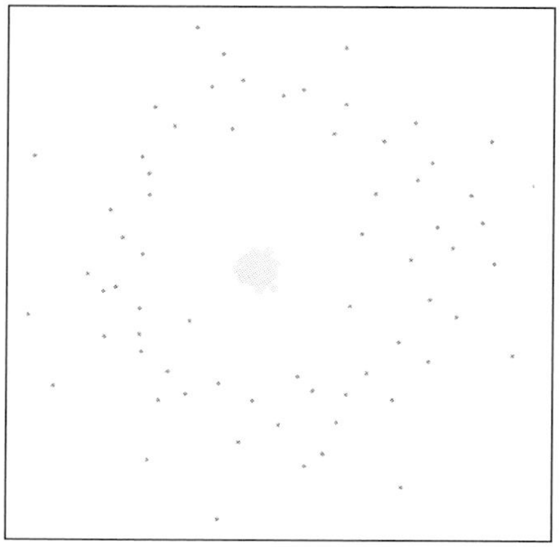

slightly. Now drag-select both circles and repeat the duplication process until you have a blob of some 60 or so circles. Group them (Ctrl+G) and then fill them solid yellow by left-clicking the yellow swatch (to the right of the screen). Remove any outline by right-clicking the "no fill" color well (it looks like an *x*). Figure 18.12 shows what you will end up with.

2. Duplicate this group and color the duplicate magenta. Now ungroup the circle objects (Ctrl+U) and deselect them (click on a blank space to deselect or press the Esc key). One by one, select and drag each of the magenta circles away from the center to form a scattered circle around the yellow cluster. When you've finished scattering, drag-select all the pieces, or choose Select All (Ctrl+A). During this process, you will also select the original yellow cluster. Hold down the Shift key and click on the yellow cluster to deselect it, leaving only the desired outside circles. Now, group these objects (Ctrl+G). See Figure 18.13 for the result.

**Figure 18.13**

The original set of circles is duplicated, and the duplicates are scattered around one by one.

3. Now Shift-select both object groups and then select the Interactive Blend tool (it is on the same flyout as the Interactive Drop Shadow). Drag from the center group to an outside circle to start the blend, which will also display the Blend options on the Property Bar. On the Property Bar, change the Number Of Steps setting from 20 to 50 and click Apply (see Figure 18.14). Pow! That was easy!

4. Click on the Object And Color Acceleration button on the Property Bar to open that dialog box. Now drag the top Object Acceleration slider almost all the way to the left and the Accelerate Fills/Outlines slider just

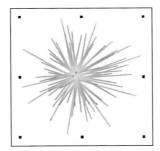
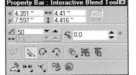

**Figure 18.14**
Blending the scattered objects to the inner cluster results in a convincing explosion.

a tad to the left (you might need to disable the Link Accelerations option first). The Object Acceleration setting will cluster the blend closer to the center, while the Fills/Outlines setting will result in the blend objects staying yellow longer. After applying the acceleration settings, it looks more like fragments are being thrown violently away from the hot center (see Figure 18.15).

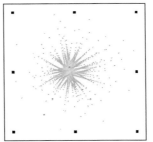

**Figure 18.15**
Changing the acceleration parameters clusters the blend objects more in the center while delaying the blend from the inner to the outer color.

5. I duplicated the explosion blend group to create vapor trails. Change the fill color of the outer control group objects to 40% black and the inner control group to white. When working with complex blends, it is a good idea to switch to Simple Wireframe from the View menu. In this mode, only the control objects in a blend are shown, hiding the dizzying array of in-between objects. Now switch back to Normal view, click

## Mouse Tricks

To speed up zooming and panning in CorelDRAW, install a Microsoft Intellimouse (or compatible product). "Wheel" mice add a small dial between the left and right buttons, for easy-access control. Spinning the wheel forward and backward zooms in and out. Holding the wheel down activates a panning feature. It is by far the easiest way to navigate in CorelDRAW, and it's a great way to boost your productivity. The mice are not expensive (especially the non-Microsoft "clones") and well worth the investment!

If you don't have a wheel mouse, you can still take advantage of many shortcuts using the right-mouse button. Right-clicking reveals a pop-up menu to speed up many tasks. Copying and pasting, for example, is simplified with this menu. Changing the Order (To Front, To Back, etc.) is also here, for quick rearranging.

In addition to "shortcuts," the right-mouse menu is where you set the Overprint value for your printing job on or off. (See the sidebar "Overprinting" for more information.)

**Figure 18.16**
Reversing the acceleration settings creates vapor trails of the exploding objects.

on the blend group, and use the Property Bar to modify the blend. This time, slide the Accelerate sliders to the right (see Figure 18.16).

6.  Arrange the second vapor trails blend behind the first. (Shift+PgDn is a shortcut to Send To Back, or right-click over the object and use the Order flyout shortcuts.) Now your exploded pieces seem to leave a trail of smoke as they blast through the cosmos. Look at Figure 18.17 to see the effect.

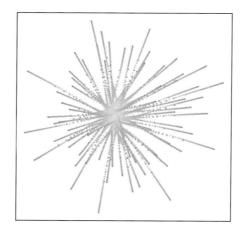

**Figure 18.17**
The vapor-trails blend behind the scattering-pieces blend creates the explosion. Bang!

## Overprinting

Overprinting is a feature that professional desktop publishers use to help control problems in the printing process, which is helpful when sending files to an imagesetter to create film. For example, if you have a large body of black text over, say, a screened back blue photograph, you will want to enable the Overprint Fill option. This will print the black text on top of the photo without first knocking out the image below. The reason you want to do this is that, without Overprinting the black text, the computer first clears away the photo underneath, to create a white area for the text. The black text will fit perfectly and print in this white area, but what happens is that if the printing press is slightly out of registration, you will see this white "shadow" around the text. This is bad. With Overprinting, the black text is printed *over* the photo, without first knocking out a white area. This will eliminate print-registration problems. Use this feature to help eliminate registration problems or to achieve special effects. Enabling Overprint Fill on a yellow object, on top of a magenta photo, will create orange where the two objects are printed over one another.

7. For a glowing center, I placed my explosion on top of a perfect circle with a white-to-dark radial fountain fill. Hold down the Ctrl key as you drag the Ellipse tool to create a perfect circle. Next, drag the Interactive Fill tool across the circle to start the fountain fill process, then click the Radial option on the Property Bar. Drag colors off the on-screen palette to change the beginning and end colors in the fill. Also, you can drag the two color points themselves, as well as the slider between the color chips, to change how the radial fountain fill looks and how the colors mix (see Figure 18.18).

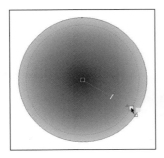
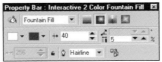

**Figure 18.18**
Draw circles with the Ellipse tool, then use the Interactive Fill tool to create and control fountain fills.

It is easy to duplicate the explosion; simply select the control groups and re-color them for a sky full of unique bursts. The great thing about this effect is that an explosion group will reblend itself at any size, so, like a real explosion, it is small and compact and expands as you enlarge it. Because of this fact, it is easy to export animation cells to create an explosion animation. Simply start with the blend group as "small," then enlarge a little for each animation cell. This is how I created the explode.avi and volcano.avi animations on the CD in the \Chapt18\ subdirectory. To manipulate the explosions for yourself, open the boom.cdr file from the \Chapt18\ subdirectory and you will appreciate the "live" nature of a blend. Enlarge or reduce the whole blend group or just the control groups to see how CorelDRAW recalculates your blend each time. All of the design elements needed to create the image in the digital color section are also on the CD, in a file called jetcover.cdr.

## Work Backwards

The easiest way to create objects exploding apart or a logo slowly building itself is to work "backwards." What I mean by this is to start with the end image intact, then duplicate it to create the *preceding* animation cell. In the duplicate, move or delete some pieces, then repeat the process to create yet another *preceding* cell. The end result will be a series of images that you can turn into an animation (see Figure 18.19).

This technique is a snap, and you can use it to create some very engaging movies. To create a logo build from a complete piece of art, follow these steps:

344 Chapter 18

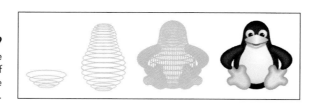

**Figure 18.19**
You'll start with a complete graphic (on right). Duplicates of the original are deleted to create a logo-build animation.

1. Start with your completed character, such as my penguin, or use a clip-art image. I wanted to create the look of a 3D wireframe coming to life. First, I used the techniques outlined in Chapter 14 to create the illusion of a 3D model of my penguin character (really just multiple blends of outline shapes). It's always easy to create "fake" computer renderings of objects, and these in turn make for cool animation effects.

2. Draw a box around the character with the Rectangle tool to define the bounding area. This will ensure that each animation cell has the same dimensions. Remove any outline or fill from this box (see Figure 18.20).

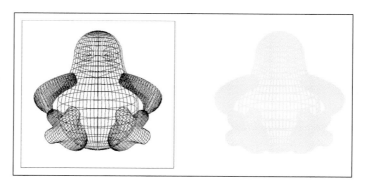

**Figure 18.20**
A complete graphic (shown in Preview view on right) is surrounded by an "invisible" bounding box (shown in Wireframe view on left) to ensure each cell will have like dimensions.

3. Now select the box and everything in it, and drag to the left. Before you release the mouse, tap Spacebar to create a duplicate.

4. Once you have a duplicate of your cell, begin to think backwards and delete pieces to create the "build" illusion. I wanted a rather complex animation, so I deleted just a few pieces for each cell. After you have deleted some pieces, select the current cell, and again drag to the left, doing the tap-Spacebar dance to create yet another cell. Each time, you will duplicate the current cell with fewer pieces, creating a series of cells in reverse for your logo build (see Figure 18.21).

5. Continue this process until you have a series of duplicates corresponding to each cell you want in your animation. I ended up with 25 unique cells for my animation.

6. Now, one at a time, starting either at the beginning or the end of your animation, select and export each cell group as its own unique file. For

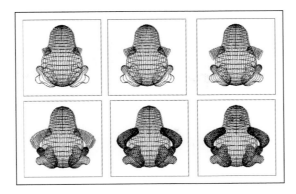

**Figure 18.21**

Each cell has some items deleted, then is duplicated to create the starting point for the previous cell, resulting in ever fewer pieces.

example, select the first cell group, then choose File|Export. In the Export dialog box, make sure you have the Selected Only option enabled, then name your file "cell01". Specify the Files Of Type setting that corresponds to your current project. (I chose the Shockwave Flash filter because my pieces were destined to be assembled in Flash, but you could export each cell as a bitmap to assemble in Photo-Paint, as in the previous projects.)

That's it! Now you have a series of cells that you can assemble into an animation. To see the movie firsthand, open the pengi.exe file on the CD in the \Chapt18\ subdirectory. Also, you'll find the "pengiani.cdr" file, which has all of the cells of the animation in one place. The Flash file is also there, along with each exported cell, if you want to fiddle with those pieces. It can be a bit tedious to do complicated multiframe animations this way, but the upside is you don't have to be overly creative to get cool results.

## PROJECT Twirling Stones

An Extrude Group created with the Interactive Extrude tool is a "live" entity within CorelDRAW. This means that at any time you can change the parameters for a new result, or even remove the extrude entirely. The result is an amazing amount of flexibility, as you can always change the texture and orientation of your objects while still maintaining the advantages of vector artwork (as opposed to a 3D modeling package such as TrueSpace, where you can output images only as bitmaps, which are big and clumsy to work with). This flexibility adds power and potential to your design cycle and can even lend itself to animation projects.

This example will show you how you can indefinitely alter an extrude group for the life of your design, either to add built-in flexibility (for a corporate logo that your client wants to see at different angles, for example) or in this case for animation applications (see Figure 18.22). I did assemble this series of twirling objects into an animation (the fxspin.avi file in the \Chapt18\ directory on the companion CD-ROM and on the CorelDRAW f/x Web site at

**Automated Spins**

This Extrude docker rotation process is a bit heavy on the manual-labor side of the equation to be used for creating low-res on-screen animations such as animated GIFs for the World Wide Web. Other programs (CorelDream 3D, or Vecta 3D for Flash images, for instance) can create such animation files with significantly less effort. Also, be sure to research the Web for CorelDRAW scripts that help animate this process. I would have included them on the CD, but I could not secure the rights. But they are on the Web, so go for it!

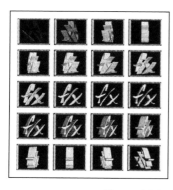

**Figure 18.22**
When you increment the 3D Rotation values, the extrude object will appear to spin around.

www.slimydog.com/corelfx9), but just because I am a masochist doesn't mean you have to be! To twirl stone objects in 3D space, follow these steps:

1. To make this process as simple as possible, I wanted to limit the shapes to a single curve. The font is called Tiger Rag. From the Fill flyout, choose the Pattern fill option. In the resulting dialog box, choose the Bitmap option, then select a texture that suits your project. I like these fill options the best because they give the most "realistic" results.

2. With the Interactive Extrude tool, drag on your object to start your own new extrude, modifying the parameters on the Property Bar to get the look you are after. For a quick shortcut, open the fxalone.cdr file in the \Chapt18\ subdirectory on the companion CD-ROM (see Figure 18.23).

**Figure 18.23**
For an animation, a single extrude group is easier to manipulate, necessitating only one change per frame export.

3. With the extrude group selected, click the Extrude Rotation button on the Property Bar (if you linger the pointer over a button, a pop-up box will tell you what it is). In this dialog box, you can key in the rotation values manually. In this example, I increased the second value ("y") by

## Interactive Extrude

CorelDRAW 9 has "total control" of your extrude groups with "live" interactive object manipulation tools. (See figure.) Drag the on-screen "x" to change the vanishing point. Drag the slider back and forth on the line pointing toward the vanishing point to adjust the Depth value. Double-click your extrude group to reveal a set of 3D rotation arrows. If you drag up or down in the center of your object with the 3D rotate arrow tool, it will spin horizontally or vertically. To rotate the object clockwise or counterclockwise, move the cursor over the perimeter dotted-line circle, then drag. These interactive tools offer quick ways to create and modify an extrude group; for precision and control, however, use the options on the Property Bar.

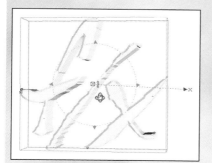

The Interactive Extrude tool allows realtime manipulation of your object, letting you twist, turn, and tweak to your heart's content.

15 each step to create the spinning logo illusion. I also added a second, less intense light source on the left so that my shading would not be solid black; that way, the object can be seen against the dark background. Key in your new values, and your object will spin accordingly (see Figure 18.24).

**Rounded Corners**

If you drag a node on a rectangle with the Shape tool, it will change the corners from harsh 90-degree angles to soft corners.

**Figure 18.24**
Incrementing the Rotation values on the Extrude docker will spin your object in space.

4. Continue to create frames by incrementing the rotation value and then exporting the image (Ctrl+E) as a bitmap for assembly into an animation later (as described in detail earlier in this chapter). You can continue to spin the object around, even until it is backward, with the "y" rotation value at the maximum of 100 (see Figure 18.25).

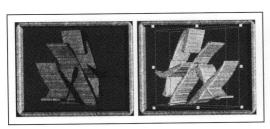

**Figure 18.25**
The max "y" value of 100 will spin your object completely around.

5. With increments from 0 to 100, your object will spin completely around. To spin it back around toward the front continuing in the same rotation axis, you need to increment from –100 back to 0, using only negative numbers (see Figure 18.26).

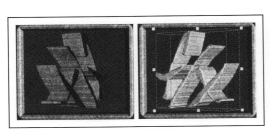

**Figure 18.26**
To rotate the object from back to front in the same axis of rotation, you must use the negative number range, from –100 back to 0.

6. To simplify the process, you might even want to start at –100 and work toward zero. Decide how many cells you want in your animation and divide by 200 (the total number of available rotation steps) to get your increment value. For example, for a 20-cell animation, you start at –100 and add 10 each time (200/20=10) to the rotation value. This will generate a smoothly rotating animation.

The file fxspin.cdr in the \Chapt18\ subdirectory of the companion CD-ROM contains all of the rotated objects used to generate the image in the color section. Also in that directory is the fxspin.avi file, where you can see the logo moving in the assembled animation. You can also load the fxalone.cdr file and practice changing the axis of rotation to get a feel for the process before you start an animation sequence of your own. In this example, we changed only the horizontal rotation value, but you could get some wild results by also incrementing the other two rotation values. Again, this is only one example of what you can do with this tool and not the most practical. But hey, you might be as nuts as I am and want to create animations like this too!

# Beyond f/x

With more traditional designers being pulled into new media markets, animation is becoming a very common task. You can use animations to add interest and gain attention in many applications, the most obvious being Web pages. Things ranging from information kiosks to automatic teller machines make use of the kind of animation you can produce right this very minute with the hardware and software sitting in front of you. Even print media can benefit from animation; for example, you can use a set of cells as a border element to suggest motion, as we showed in Figure 18.10. Animated buttons or those annoying ad banners that show up everywhere on the Web are just a few of the things you could be creating with multiframe images in CorelDRAW, and you would be fattening up your bank account in the process. So get cracking—or perhaps I should say get *stacking*!

# Conclusion

In this chapter, we looked at many examples of how to assemble images created in CorelDRAW into animations. You can use these animations in many applications, including Web pages and multimedia programs. Virtually any stack of images can be made into a playable movie using the animation power of Photo-Paint or a companion product such as Flash. It's a simple process, with only your time and patience limiting the complexities of your animations.

And as they say in Hollywood, "That's a wrap!" I hope you have found this book to be a worthwhile purchase and an entertaining read. I have tried to squeeze as much as I could get away with into this monster. Anyway, I had a great time putting this beast together and discovered many great techniques along the way. I always look forward to experimenting and trying new things, and I hope you do too.

Why are you still reading? Fire up CorelDRAW and get busy!

# Index

# If you like this book, you'll love these...

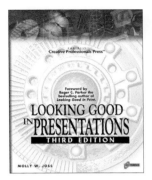

## LOOKING GOOD IN PRESENTATIONS

**Molly Joss**
**ISBN: 1-56604-854-0**
**384 pages • $29.99 U.S. • $43.99 CANADA**

Learn all you need to know about how to create and deliver professional presentations–the ins and outs of good design, how to make an audience sit up and take notice, and how to keep to your deadlines. This book does more than tell you how to create and deliver a presentation, it teaches you what not to do and how to choose the best presentation medium.

## ILLUSTRATOR® 9 F/X AND DESIGN

**Sherry London**
**ISBN: 1-57610-750-7**
**560 pages with CD-ROM • $49.99 U.S. • $74.99 CANADA**

Features new information and projects on styles and effects, how to integrate with Adobe® Web products such as LiveMotion™ and GoLive™, as well as other enhanced features. With real-world projects, readers learn firsthand how to create intricate illustrations and compositing techniques. Readers also learn how to work seamlessly between Illustrator® and Photoshop®.

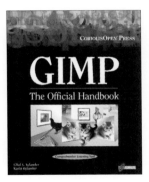

## GIMP: THE OFFICIAL HANDBOOK

**Olof S. Kylander and Karin Kylander**
**ISBN: 1-57610-520-2**
**960 pages • $49.99 U.S. • $73.99 CANADA**

Teaches all aspects ranging from installing, to scripting, to working faster and more efficiently through shortcuts. Thoroughly covers the most powerful aspects of GIMP–filters, including how to create images invoking Cubism, Van Gogh, embossing, warping, rippling, glass tile, and fractals.

## 3D STUDIO MAX® R3 IN DEPTH

**Rob Polevoi**
**ISBN: 1-57610-432-X**
**700 pages with CD-ROM • $49.99 U.S. • $73.99 CANADA**

Build your special effect skills while becoming familiar with the many features of 3D Studio MAX®. By following along with the book's visual examples, you will receive quick answers to common MAX questions in an easy-to-use and easy-to-understand manner.

**The Coriolis Group, LLC**    Telephone: 480.483.0192 • Toll-free: 800.410.0192 • www.coriolis.com
Coriolis books are also available at bookstores and computer stores nationwide.

# What's on the CD-ROM

The **CorelDRAW Linux f/x & design** companion CD-ROM contains elements specifically selected to enhance the usefulness of this book, including:

- All of the tutorial files in either native CorelDRAW or Photo-Paint formats, to load and learn
- Sample animation files
- Button and interface design examples
- Sample web pages and vector-based web bits, pieces, and demos
- Clip-art images from Time Tunnel
- Linux graphics utilities and plug-ins
- Plug-ins and utilities (see the PLUGINS and SCAN|SANE directories) from *GIMP: The Official Handbook,* by Olof S. and Karin Kylander. (Scottsdale, AZ: The Coriolis Group, 1999.) ISBN: 1-57610-520-2. Used with permission of the publisher.

## System Requirements

### Software:

- Corel Linux or Linux Kernal Release 2.2 or higher/X Window System
- Glibc libraries 2.0, 2.1, or compatible
- Package management software for installing Red Hat or Debian Packages
- CorelDRAW for Linux (includes Photo-Paint)
- Web browser with Flash plug-in to view Shockwave examples

### Hardware:

- An Intel (or equivalent) Pentium 200MHz (or faster) processor
- 64MB of RAM (128 MB recommended)
- 255MB of disk storage space
- CD-ROM drive
- Wide-eyed curiosity (recommended)
- Adventurous spirit (helpful)